Ms. Beatrice Falkenburg
247 Empire Ave.
Dyersburg, TN 38024-5268

D0386021

INVENTING
AL GORE

INVENTING AL GORE

A Biography

BILL TURQUE

HOUGHTON MIFFLIN COMPANY

BOSTON · NEW YORK

2000

For information about permission to reproduce selections
from this book, write to Permissions, Houghton Mifflin Company,
215 Park Avenue South, New York, New York 10003.

Library of Congress Cataloging-in-Publication Data
Turque, Bill.
Inventing Al Gore : a biography / Bill Turque.
p.   cm.
Includes bibliographical references (p.   ) and index.
ISBN 0-395-88323-7
1. Gore, Albert, 1948–   2. Vice-Presidents — United States —
Biography.   3. Presidential candidates — United States —
Biography.   I. Title.
E840.8.G65 T87   2000
973.929′092—dc21   99-058523

Printed in the United States of America

Book design by Robert Overholtzer

QUM 10 9 8 7 6 5 4 3 2 1

To Melinda,
who showed me the way

Contents

Introduction

"I T's A NEW DAY," declared Al Gore. He looked like a man who needed one as he stood in the parking lot of his transplanted campaign headquarters near downtown Nashville on the morning of October 6, 1999. Less than four months before the first primary ballots would be cast, the presidential candidacy he had planned for nearly a decade was close to a shambles. This had been Gore's race to lose, and he was proving every bit up to the task. Seldom, if ever, had a front-runner for his party's nomination squandered his advantages with such breathtaking speed. The early months of the Gore 2000 campaign had been a blooper reel of muddled messages, botched events, backstage intrigue, profligate spending, and plain bad luck. His missteps, and the unexpectedly broad appeal of his sole opponent, former basketball star and New Jersey senator Bill Bradley, had transformed virtually assured victory into a bona fide race.

Looking for ways to deflect attention from the eroding poll numbers and months of bad press, he challenged Bradley, whom he had foolishly ignored, to a series of debates, and he promoted an African American woman, his political director Donna Brazile, to campaign manager. But his most dramatic decision was to pull the entire Gore 2000 operation out of Washington and move it to the state he had represented in the House and Senate for sixteen years, setting up shop hard by the railroad tracks a couple of miles from downtown, in a drab, one-story building that once housed a physical rehabilitation center. The resettlement was expected to winnow the organization's top-heavy payroll of those not interested in packing up their lives and making the 560-mile trek. But it was symbolism, not cost-efficiency, that propelled the change of address.

It was Gore's way of saying that he was free: from the ways of Washington and, most importantly, from the shadow of the president whose scandal-pocked image was undermining his candidacy. A new look on the road reinforced the message of metamorphosis. He shed his dark blue business suits for earth tones, khaki, and cowboy boots and traded in his lectern with the vice presidential seal for stools and wireless microphones. Autobiography replaced worthy ten-point policy proposals in a retooled stump speech as he spoke in more detail than ever before about the legacy of his politician-parents and his own winding path to public service. Finally, his advisers proclaimed, the "real" Al Gore had come to the party. "Prometheus unbound!" exulted one young aide. In recent days Gore had even taken to quoting from the old Janis Joplin tune: "Freedom's just another word for nothing left to lose."

But far from a new day, the retreat to Nashville was part of an old story for Al Gore. Once more he was trying to convince the world, and perhaps himself, that he was his own man — not a senator's son packing off to the army or a vice president dutifully defending his disgraced benefactor. Gore is an unusually thoughtful politician who has been an important, even prophetic voice on issues like global warming, arms control, and the changes wrought by the Information Age. But his life and career have also been punctuated by separations never quite achieved, and by bold strokes never quite converted into personal or political liberation.

I began work on this book in early 1997 with two questions in mind: Who is Al Gore, and what forces shaped the man who may be the first American president to take office in the twenty-first century? The vice president was an intriguing subject, because so much of his story seemed to be unexplored. After twenty years in public life, he still existed largely in the broad sketch lines of caricature, known mostly for his wooden public style and fervent environmentalism.

No one is a caricature, and the fuller portrait that emerged was complex and conflicted. Al Gore is at home with ideas but deeply wary of people, religious but possessed of an equally abiding faith in the blessings of science and technology, protective of his family's privacy yet willing to exploit personal tragedies for political gain. His carefully tended Dudley Do-Right image obscures a keen, and sometimes ruthlessly competitive nature. As an elected official, his record reflects the impulses of caution and daring that compete within — with caution usually prevailing. And there is, of course, the disconnect between his so-called stiff public presence and the warmer, more spontaneous personality known to family, friends, and journalists working off the record.

The schism is real — a vestige of the old senatorial formality embodied by the father he revered and feared — and to contemporary audiences he can come off as contrived and phony, even when he's not. But the problem has been exaggerated, given a life of its own after years of being picked over by the press, pundits, and even his own handlers. It is also, in the end, a distraction from the real paradox of Al Gore, a man who at critical moments has proclaimed independence and then retreated from it, stood on principle and deferred it to political ambition.

Gore learned early how to make others' agendas his own. He is both beneficiary and prisoner of an extraordinary political education, provided by parents who yearned to see their son follow them into public life, and perhaps reach the presidency. The great expectations weighed heavily on the young Gore and turned him into what one friend called "the secular equivalent of the preacher's son," intent on modeling perfect behavior and avoiding any action that might reflect poorly on his father.

Confronted with his first adult decision of conscience, he made it not as his own man but as a political agent of his father. He hated the Vietnam War as a Harvard undergraduate and scorned the country's obsessive anticommunism, calling it a "national madness" in a letter to the senator. As graduation neared in 1969, he found himself torn between misgivings about the draft and concern for his father's political career, imperiled in 1970 by his own outspoken opposition to the war. Al Gore maintains that his motivation was ethical — to prevent some less-connected boy registered with his Tennessee draft board from having to go in his place. But some of his Harvard friends clearly sensed that Gore was discharging a family duty, protecting not the kid down the road but a political franchise. Had his father been a bank president or insurance executive, he would have contrived to avoid service, as most of his classmates did. Instead, he marched off to a war he believed was wrong.

After the senator's bitter 1970 defeat and a short Vietnam tour, Gore returned home to Tennessee with another vow to forge his own path. He announced that he would have nothing to do with politics and instead threw himself into religious studies and a promising newspaper career in Nashville. To the dismay of Albert and mother Pauline, he talked about a life of painting and writing, or perhaps parlaying journalism and law into a career. But it didn't take much to draw him back into his parents' design for his life. His father sold him a farm just across the Caney Fork River from the family home, one that also happened to be in the congressional district that Albert Gore had represented. When the seat opened up in 1976, the younger Gore immediately jumped into the race. He delighted the old senator by running but crushed him by asking that he not play any public role in the campaign. It had been only six years since Tennesseans turned Albert Gore out of office, and he remained a divisive figure in some parts of the state, including his old home district. Gore didn't want the political baggage, but more important, he wanted to be seen as standing on his own. His father complied, although he and Pauline played a critical behind-the-scenes role, marshaling old friends and supporters — including businessman Armand Hammer — to underwrite their boy's first victory. At twenty-eight, Gore was on his way to Washington.

When his father first pushed the idea of a run for the presidency in 1988, Gore resisted, believing that it was not his time. After a clique of big Democratic contributors offered to back him, he changed his mind and, at thirty-nine, became the youngest major party candidate since William Jennings Bryan. He announced that his principal issues were the future of U.S.-Soviet relations and the environment, but when his message didn't connect with voters or opinion leaders, he reinvented himself as a more traditional corporate-bashing populist, sticking up for "working families" (a mantra that has resurfaced in his 2000 campaign) and "people over profits." As he struggled to win a critical Super Tuesday primary in North Carolina, the self-proclaimed environmentalist cozied up to a notorious corporate polluter for support.

The collapse of his campaign, followed a year later by the near-death of his son in a car accident, triggered a midlife reassessment and a new resolve to change course. He renounced the poll-driven cynicism of modern politics and promised a bolder approach. "I have become very impatient with my own tendency to put a finger to the political winds and proceed cautiously," he wrote in his 1992 eco-manifesto, *Earth in the Balance.* He also said he understood why so many voters had come to hold politicians in contempt. "Put simply, most people are just fed up with the artificiality of most political communication today," Gore wrote. He would, he said, talk about what mattered most to him: the rescue of the environment, which he regarded as "the new central organizing principle of civilization."

But the fiery evangelism of *Earth in the Balance* dimmed later that same year when Gore accepted Bill Clinton's offer to become his vice presidential running mate. After resolving to speak with a new political voice, Gore pursued a job that, by definition, demanded not boldness but deference and discretion. He went on to become perhaps the most influential vice president in history, having an impact on broad areas of administration policy — but at a price. Faced with political extinction after the 1994 Republican landslide, Gore eagerly built an alliance with Clinton strategist Dick Morris, the personification of the finger-to-the-wind expedience he had denounced two years earlier. Together, Clinton, Morris, and Gore outmaneuvered the Gingrich Congress in the battle over a balanced budget, but they also moved the center line of the Democratic Party closer to Republican values on their way to reelection in 1996.

Gore leapt at the vice presidency as his stepping-stone to the Oval Office, but by 1998 his partnership with Bill Clinton looked like a Faustian bargain. At a time when he needed to begin to look less like an understudy and more like a prospective chief executive, Clinton's descent into the Lewinsky scandal and impeachment placed Gore in a nasty double bind. Defending Clinton too vigorously would make him look like First Apologist, but stepping too far away would be seen as crass opportunism. He mounted carefully couched defenses, endorsing Clinton's record but not his conduct. While most Americans didn't blame Gore for the sexual predations of his boss, his ties to the president still diminished his stature. He dug an even deeper hole for himself on December 19, 1998, when he told a rally on the South Lawn that Clinton, who just a couple of hours earlier had been impeached by the House of Representatives, would emerge as "one of our greatest presidents."

When his father passed away in late 1998, one great drama of separation ended just as another was beginning. Like the old senator, Bill

Clinton desperately wanted Gore to win the presidency. Their reasons were different but driven by similar brands of narcissism: one wanted a Gore in the White House to bring glory to the family name, the other to validate a legacy. Once again, as he had in 1976, Gore struggled to distance himself from a larger-than-life mentor who had exhausted the patience and goodwill of many voters.

His formal announcement speech on the steps of the Smith County courthouse took dead aim at Clinton's womanizing. "With your help, I will take my own values of faith and family to the White House," Gore said. That same night on ABC's *20/20*, he declared Clinton's conduct "inexcusable" and acknowledged to Diane Sawyer that he never quite bought Clinton's months of denials that he had been involved with Monica Lewinsky. But when the heavy-handed tut-tutting angered Clinton and went nowhere in the polls, Gore backed away and resumed the search for yet another defining moment.

He proclaimed one in early October as he overhauled his campaign and decamped to Nashville. A few days before he opened his new headquarters, he told *U.S. News & World Report*'s Roger Simon to "stay tuned" for signs of the new Al Gore. "I think I have to give up taking a lot of polls and listening to consultants," he said. "I think I have to give up some of the traditional techniques of modern campaigning and just go without a net and walk out there on my own and sink or swim. . . . And by God, that's what I intend to do." The new Gore sounded suspiciously like the old new Gores. The question voters would have to answer was whether this was just another election-year invention or the emergence of a man who was finally comfortable with who he was.

INVENTING
AL GORE

Prologue

Nashville, November 3, 1970

A LBERT GORE JR. knew what was expected of him, and then
as always, he tried not to disappoint. He stood in the oak-
paneled ballroom of the Hermitage Hotel in downtown Nashville and listened stoically as the senior senator from Tennessee, his
father, Albert Gore, delivered a concession speech. The campaign for a
fourth term had been a vicious one, filled with Republican distortions
and smears, but the senator had been through other dogfights, and for
a time it looked as if he might pull through again. But in the last days
it had become painfully clear that the race was over.

At age twenty-two, Albert Gore Jr. watched helplessly as the world
in which he had grown up slipped away. He cherished his Tennessee
ties, but he was a son of Washington, an insider from birth who had
bounced on Richard Nixon's lap and floated his toy submarine in the
Senate pool. Bill Clinton, the smooth-talking Boys Nation senator
from Hot Springs, Arkansas, may have grabbed a brief, electrifying
handshake from John Kennedy in the Rose Garden, but it was Gore
who had listened in on the phone from his family's Embassy Row hotel suite one night in 1962 after the president called his father to curse a
recalcitrant steel executive. Downstairs he could raid the kitchen of
the Jockey Club, Washington's first elegant restaurant and a New
Frontier hot spot where, *Esquire* quipped in November 1962, only
Bobby could get in without a reservation. For his Harvard senior
thesis examining television's impact on the presidency, his interview
subjects had included Arthur Schlesinger Jr., James Reston, and Bill
Moyers. At the 1968 Democratic National Convention, he drafted portions of the speech that his father delivered. Politics was the family
business, and witnessing Albert Gore's removal from the Senate, an

institution he cherished, was like watching him being buried alive.

He had done everything he could to keep this night from ever happening. Like his father, he loathed the Vietnam War. But while most of his Harvard friends slid through the porous draft regulations after graduation in 1969, Gore's only real dilemma was where and how to serve. He marched into the army that summer to avoid complicating the senator's 1970 reelection prospects, which had been weakened by his strong antiwar stance. Once in the army he volunteered — as a newlywed — for the war zone, sending the message that despite his dove's wings, the senator was a patriot who didn't pull strings for his son. Before shipping out, Private Gore came home on weekend passes to campaign with his father, standing straight and true at rallies, an early version of his dutiful vigils at Clinton's elbow two decades later. He filmed ads with the senator, one on horseback, another in uniform, in which his father reached out, touched his hand, and said, "Son, always love your country."

In truth, it was far more than the war that was driving his father from office. Albert Gore's maverick liberalism had grown dangerously out of step with an increasingly conservative South. An accumulation of unpopular positions and far-flung interests — moderation on civil rights, rejection of Richard Nixon's two southern nominees to the Supreme Court, a growing preoccupation with foreign affairs — had left him vulnerable, as had the perception that he preferred Georgetown dinner parties to Tennessee town meetings.

The Nixon White House, seeking to nurture the emerging Republican majority in the South, targeted Gore as a leader of the Senate's "RadicLib" faction and "southern regional chairman of the eastern liberal establishment," as Vice President Spiro Agnew described him. The GOP candidate, Representative William Brock of Chattanooga, ran a campaign laced with personal invective ("I started running against Albert Gore the first time I met him," he told one crowd) and baseless charges — among them that Gore had somehow routed Interstate 40 across land he owned. Republicans played to racial and economic grievances with billboard lines like "Bill Brock Believes" (later expanded to "Bill Brock Believes the Things We Believe In") crafted to appeal to the disaffected whites who gave George Wallace 34 percent of the state's presidential vote in 1968.

The smell of incipient defeat kept most of the big names and old pros elsewhere on election night. It was a loser's crowd at the Hermitage, a collection of family, friends, and scruffy volunteers organized by a friend of Gore's daughter, Nancy, a young Nashville attorney named Jim Sasser. The evening came to a mercifully early end — by nine o'clock the weight of the numbers had crushed any lingering hopes of a real contest. Brock had built an overwhelming lead in the state's heavily Republican eastern third. Thirty minutes later the Gore family came downstairs to say good-bye.

Albert Gore's concession was unrepentant. He was furious about the campaign Brock had run, and in no mood to go quietly. "We knew from the beginning that the odds were terrifically against us, but we almost made it," he said. "We had to make this fight because the issues were so important and the stakes were so high. I told the truth as I saw it." Turning the old Confederate rallying cry on its head, Gore vowed, "The causes for which we fought are not dead. The truth shall rise again!"

Later that night, in private, Al Gore wept, one of the few times Pauline had ever seen her son in tears. He despaired at the sinister turn the country had taken. The Kennedys were dead, King had been murdered in Memphis, and good men like his father had been brought down by what he called, fresh from his study of modern media at Harvard, the "subliminal smut" of Nixon and his agents. He told friends that any interest he had had in politics as a career was gone. Gore would look elsewhere to find meaning and make a difference.

He came back, of course. The pull of the family business, and his own ambition, were too strong in the end to resist. But his father's demise that night at the Hermitage remained in his memory as if etched in stone, a cautionary tale about marching too far ahead of those one represents. The next Gore in politics would pick his fights more carefully and spend his political capital more judiciously. That was fine with Albert and Pauline. They had taught him about the honor in public service, but also about what it took to win. Although their last campaign was behind them, they had their eye on one more, one a lifetime in the making.

1

"Well, Mr. Gore, Here *He* Is"

NO SON of Albert Gore's was going to enter the world quietly. Humility had never come easily to Gore, and underneath his hill country populism lay a touch of the aristocrat. The male heir he had longed for, all nine pounds and two ounces, arrived at Columbia Hospital for Women in Washington on March 31, 1948. The Gores had ten-year-old Nancy, but waiting a decade for a second child had been difficult for the couple, especially Pauline. Having little Albert Arnold, when she was thirty-six, "has always been kind of a miracle to us," she said. And miracles, Albert Gore believed, merited more than passing mention.

Gore had noticed several months earlier that when a daughter was born to Representative Estes Kefauver, his principal rival in Tennessee politics, the story appeared on the inside pages of the *Nashville Tennessean.* He set to work and eventually extracted a promise from the paper's editors. With their help, he would both hail the arrival of his son and one-up Kefauver, who was on his way to the Senate seat that Gore coveted. "If I have a boy baby, I don't want the news buried inside the paper," said the five-term congressman. "I want it on page 1 where it belongs." The *Tennessean* complied with a one-column headline in its April 1 editions, wedged in the left-hand corner between civil war in Costa Rica and a Japanese train wreck. "Well, Mr. Gore, Here HE Is — On Page 1." Before he was home from the hospital, Al Gore had won a news cycle for his father.

The only known postpartum complication was what Pauline called the "battle royal" over their son's name. She favored the traditional "Junior" added onto "Albert Gore," but her husband thought it would be a burden to the young man. "He was adamant about it," Pauline said. So, like congressional conferees, they cut a deal: he would be Albert (called "Little Al" as a child) but could decide for himself later whether he was comfortable with "Jr." When the time came, Gore struggled with the choice. He was Junior and then he wasn't; he adopted it as a teenager, then in 1987, as a thirty-nine-year-old presidential candidate anxious to deflect attention from his youth, jettisoned juniorhood for good.

Survivors of punishing climbs from poverty, Albert and Pauline Gore endowed their son with a granite self-confidence about what was possible, and expected, in life. As full political partners decades before Bill and Hillary Clinton came to Washington, they made politics the family business. The single-minded drive that propelled Al Gore to the House of Representatives at twenty-eight and the Senate at thirty-six — and the hubris that made him a presidential candidate before he was forty — is their bequest. From Albert came a crusader's passion for public service, a globalist's view of issues, and a moralist's disdain for opposing points of view. Just as visible is Pauline's pragmatism, caution, and steely competitive edge. "I think the biggest influence you have on your child is the life you live day after day," she said. Any understanding of Al Gore begins with Albert and Pauline.

Allen Gore, Albert's father, was descended from the Scots-Irish who came to Virginia in the early seventeenth century and moved to Tennessee after the Revolutionary War, where they farmed the rugged slopes of the Cumberland River Valley. Albert, the third of five children he had with Maggie Denney Gore, was born near Granville, Tennessee, the day after Christmas 1907. When his son was two, Allen packed the family in a buggy and two wagons and moved to a 186-acre farm in Possum Hollow, a Smith County community where the poverty and desolation was echoed in the names that surrounded it on the map — Difficult, Defeated, Nameless. They were poor but well fed, producing their own chickens, eggs, and milk and selling the surplus for cash. "We lived apart from the world," Albert Gore wrote in his 1970 memoir, "relatively isolated and therefore dependent entirely on one another."

The unforgiving environment fostered a hard-edged independence and wariness of outsiders among those who coaxed a living from the land, and it left young Albert with firm, often inflexible, beliefs about right and wrong. His father's discipline was absolute and his authority unquestioned. He rose at 4:00 A.M. every day of the year and tasked Albert to get up with him and build a fire. Despite the heavy workload, Allen Gore kept up with the world outside Possum Hollow and encouraged his children to set their sights on it. In the evenings he read the newspaper with a kerosene lamp and talked about the politicians he admired, including William Jennings Bryan, "the Great Commoner" whose populism and anti-imperialism made a lasting impression on Albert, and Cordell Hull, a boyhood friend who served in the House and Senate and as Franklin Roosevelt's secretary of State. Later, as a young aspiring politician, Albert spent Sunday afternoons listening to Hull talk about Washington as he sat in the shade with the whittlers on the courthouse square in Carthage. He became a mentor for Gore, who adopted Hull's advocacy of free trade and progressive taxation as cornerstones of his own politics when he was elected to the House.

Albert's political ambitions were sparked as a grade-schooler, when he saw the picture of a cousin, running for the state legislature, tacked to utility poles and roadside trees. "In my childish imagination I was fascinated by the prospect of seeing my own picture there someday," he wrote. As a teenager, Gore was a good enough fiddler to sit in at square dances and briefly flirted with a musical career, but he soon targeted law school as his platform into public life. It was a struggle to get there. He scraped his way through the University of Tennessee and Murfreesboro Teachers College, never able to afford more than a semester at a time. To put together funds he drove a truck, waited tables, and taught in a one-room schoolhouse in the Cumberland Mountain community of High Land, known more widely as "Booze" for its robust moonshine commerce.

At eighteen, Gore was handsome in a stalwart, square-jawed way, with waves of curly brown hair and a reputation as one of the area's most enthusiastic bachelors. "Listen," said one former Smith County schoolteacher, "every girl in this county dated Albert Gore before he went to law school." Gore also discovered early that he enjoyed being the center of attention. A classmate at Murfreesboro recalled his performance as a young lieutenant in a student production of the war drama *Journey's End*, a play that required him to die in the final scene. "Albert died beautifully," his friend recalled. "But as the curtain started closing, he reached out from his deathbed, held back the curtain, and died a little more. Albert always did like the limelight."

It took him seven years to work through college. After graduating in 1932, he moved to Carthage, the Smith County seat, where he made his first try for public office as superintendent of schools a year later. He lost both the election and his teaching job and returned to his father's farm at the age of twenty-six. Not long before, in the late 1920s, Allen Gore had grown uneasy about the soundness of the banks and spread his life savings of $8,000 among several institutions. Within a few days, the banks had failed. When Albert came home, his family was still better off than many of their neighbors — at least the mortgage was paid — but the Depression's devastation left an indelible mark on him. At market, as he saw "men with wives and children whom they could neither feed nor clothe well and whose farms were not paid for, I recognized the face of poverty: grown men who were so desperate the tears streamed down their cheeks as they stood with me at the window to receive their meager checks for a full year's work."

His fortunes turned when his victorious election opponent, Edward Lee Huffines, fell gravely ill several months after taking office and before his death recommended to the county court that Gore succeed him. The unexpected tribute from a competitor was a signal event for Gore. Over the next four decades, he never made a personal attack on an opponent. Now with the means to finance a legal education, he enrolled in night law school at the Nashville YMCA, working as superintendent by day and driving one hundred miles round-trip from Carthage three evenings a week for three years. Before the long, late evening trip home, Gore would stop for coffee at the Andrew Jackson Hotel, where one of the waitresses was a twenty-one-year-old divorcée named Pauline LaFon.

In the 1930 *Tatler*, Jackson High School's yearbook, she listed her life's ambition as "to keep her husband happy." Whether that statement was playful sarcasm or an attempt to supply a socially acceptable answer, it never reflected her real aspirations. For Pauline, the future wasn't a question of staying at home or going to work; it was how far she could get in the world of work. "I didn't want to be a nurse, I didn't want to be a teacher. I didn't want to be most of the things women were," she said many years later.

It seemed she would have no choice. Walter and Maude LaFon were

Arkansans who opened a general store on a crossroads near Palmersville, just below the Kentucky line in northwest Tennessee. Pauline was twelve when an infection froze Walter's right elbow and left him unable to work. The family's political connections in Weakley County helped Walter land a job with the state highway department in Jackson, the Madison County seat fifty-five miles to the south. The LaFons and their six children moved into a modest house on Poplar Street that they opened to boarders for extra cash. Pauline spent much of her adolescence cooking, cleaning, and looking after her sister Thelma, who was blind from birth. As her parents struggled to piece together a living, Pauline's siblings looked to her for inspiration. "She was the heart of the family," said Whit LaFon, a younger brother and now a retired Madison County circuit court judge. "She just always had a burning desire to better herself. She probably had more guts than anyone I'd ever seen. I don't know where it came from."

Her first marriage, as a teenager, was primarily an attempt to escape from poverty; it lasted less than year. Pauline took Thelma with her to Union College, a small Baptist school in Jackson, where for two years she kept her sister's notes and read assignments to her while doing her own course work. To pay the tuition, she waited tables at a tearoom on the courthouse square. Pauline said in a 1997 interview that her inspiration to study the law came from watching helplessly as her mother lost some land in a dispute with her own family in Arkansas. But Whit LaFon said Pauline's recollection was simply "an old folks' tale" and that she chose the law because it was the quickest and surest way out of Jackson. She borrowed $200 from the Rotary Club and headed for Nashville, where she took a room at the YWCA and entered Vanderbilt Law School, riding the trolley to morning classes and dashing back in time for the dinner shift at the Andrew Jackson. The lone woman in the graduating class of 1936, she is remembered by fellow students for her luminous blue eyes and no-nonsense demeanor. Henry Cohen, a classmate who competed against her in moot court, said she reminded him of a young Margaret Thatcher. "She wanted results," said Cohen. "She wasn't satisfied leaving anything halfway."

Pauline found her late-night customer charming, if a bit too conscientious — even by her rigorous standards. "He was serious even then," said Pauline. "I couldn't tempt him to leave any serious work, no matter how fancy a party we were invited to. That was what bothered me the most at that age." After graduation they took the bar together and for a time went their separate ways, Pauline to a Texarkana, Arkansas, law firm, one of the few that would take a woman in 1936, and Albert to the next level of state politics. Gordon Browning, a reform-minded Democrat Gore had worked for in an unsuccessful Senate campaign, was elected governor that year and made his former aide the state's first labor commissioner.

Pauline spent less than a year in Texarkana, a period she describes as "a disaster." She was hired by Bert Larey, another Vanderbilt alum, and, perhaps because of her own experience, began to take divorce cases for their new two-person firm. After seven months, however, she abruptly returned to Nashville. She said that she planned to wed Albert and help him with his political career. But there was another reason, one she did not discuss publicly for many years: Larey sexually harassed her. (He died in 1984. His son, Lance, an Oklahoma attorney, said such behavior would have been unlike his father.)

Perhaps because her family couldn't afford anything more, or because she was a divorcée and he a member of the governor's cabinet, her wedding to Albert Gore was modest and out of the way, conducted in a judge's chambers just across the state line in Tompkinsville, Kentucky, on May 15, 1937. The "not published" notation on their license meant that news of the marriage was kept out of the local paper. Their first child, Nancy LaFon Gore, arrived eight months later.

Pauline Gore insisted that she had not abandoned personal ambition but had traded her own career for the prospect of bigger rewards by supporting her husband's climb to power. "I was not only ambitious for him but for myself too," she said. The first opportunity for advancement emerged in early 1938 when J. Ridley Mitchell, the Fourth District's incumbent congressman, decided to run for the Senate.

Gore quit Browning's cabinet and assembled several thousand dollars, part of it by mortgaging a small farm he owned. He was not the clear front-runner. Five other candidates crowded the Democratic primary field, and Gore was partial to eye-glazing disquisitions on reciprocal trade. On a stifling July evening at the Fentress County courthouse, Gore was in the middle of just such a talk when he spotted a man headed down the center aisle carrying a fiddle, and two others behind him with a guitar and a banjo. "Here, Albert," said the first man, who clearly preferred Gore the teenage square dance prodigy to Gore the candidate, "play us a tune." Pauline, sitting in front, gestured an emphatic no — she regarded such theatrics as unbecoming of a congressional candidate. Gore was conflicted as well, but he recognized what was at stake. He told the audience that the race meant everything to him, that he'd even mortgaged his home. He offered them a deal: he'd play "Turkey in the Straw" if they voted for him. The crowd, eager for something more lyrical than the balance of trade, agreed.

Gore kept the fiddle with him over Pauline's objections, mixing politics and music for the rest of campaign. He won the primary, and in Tennessee, where Republicans were still all but unheard of, that was as good as winning the general election. In January 1939, at the age of thirty-one, he was on his way to the House of Representatives. Still, while Gore was reconciled to the theatrical requirements of politics, he remained ambivalent, at times almost disdainful. "I have been able to fall into the mode of the southern politician," he said twenty years later. "I can tell good stories, play the fiddle, and rollick with the crowd." But that mode never reflected how Albert Gore saw himself — as a statesman and a thinker who resided on a level above coarse politics.

He quickly gained a reputation in Washington as a New Dealer with a wide independent streak. As a freshman, he threw in with Republicans to scuttle Franklin Roosevelt's $800 million public housing program, and he quashed a New York congressman's attempt to secure $1 million for the New York World's Fair by demanding $5,000 for each county fair in his district. "Why shouldn't my Lebanon, Tennessee, Mule Day be entitled to a little slice?" he asked.

With his eyes on a Senate seat, Gore tended carefully to popular statewide interests, championing funding for big government programs like the Tennessee Valley Authority. When Tennesseans went to war, Gore tried to go with them. A son of the same Tennessee hills that had produced Alvin York, he waived his congressional immunity to the draft in 1943 and was inducted into the army. Roosevelt prevailed on him to stay in the House, but he later served for several months in 1945 as a military prosecutor in France.

Gore was ready to make his move in 1948, but the popular Estes Kefauver jumped into the race ahead of him. So he aimed for the next available target, the ancient Kenneth McKellar, who was up for reelection in 1952. The Senate's "Old Formidable" was nearing eighty and had been expected to retire that year after six terms, but later changed his mind. It would not be easy — challenging McKellar meant taking on his powerful patron, Memphis political boss Edward Crump. Although Kefauver's 1948 victory had weakened the state's dominant political machine, Crump still posed a significant threat and was capable of running up big margins in Memphis and surrounding Shelby County while challengers split the rest of the state. But Gore, tired of the House, had decided it was up or out.

With one-year-old Little Al in tow, the Gores packed their Arlington, Virginia, apartment and returned to Carthage, settling back into their white clapboard house on Fisher Avenue for the duration of the campaign. McKellar's refusal to step aside made his advanced age the real issue in the race, and Gore's backers urged him to exploit it, but he was reluctant. "My present plan is to refrain from any criticism," he wrote to Bernard Baruch, "but instead to refer to him in complimentary terms, always referring to his record and service in the past tense."

McKellar brandished his seniority, and the bonanza in roads, dams, offices, and power plants that he had helped bring home as chairman of the Senate Appropriations Committee. "Thinking Feller Vote for McKellar," said his placard, distributed throughout the state. It was a strong selling point, and Pauline pushed for a memorable response. "Mrs. Gore and I came home one Saturday night after a hard day of campaigning, and she cleaned off the kitchen table and made a pot of coffee and said, 'Well, Albert, sit down here,'" Gore recalled. "So we wrote doggerels and rhymes and riddles and finally came to one that we thought would work." He credits her with the rejoinder, tacked alongside every McKellar poster they could find: "Think Some More and Vote for Gore." He beat McKellar by ninety thousand votes in the Democratic primary.

Gore believed in government as the guarantor of economic justice, plugging tax loopholes for the privileged and spending generously to help those in need up the ladder. "Nothing cures poverty like money," he said. Tired of the poor roads that farmers had to endure to get their crops to market, and remembering his travels on the German autobahn during his army stint, he became Senate cosponsor of the 1956 legislation that created the interstate highway system. Eight years later he helped shepherd the first Medicare proposal through the Senate.

The most enduring image of Albert Gore is his early and outspoken opposition to the Vietnam War. But he walked a cautious, moderate line in the other great political struggle of his day, civil rights. He was a dangerous progressive by Dixie standards, a target of segregationists' scorn, but he never placed himself in the forefront of the movement. Years later, in much the same way that his son would express remorse about trimming back his commitment to the environment as a first-time presidential candidate, Albert Gore would regret his tentativeness on civil rights. "There may have been some political 'heroes' in this cause, but few, if any, were to be found among white Southern politicians. I know I cannot include myself," he wrote after his retirement. As a first-time Senate candidate in 1952, he concentrated on economic issues "and let the sleeping dogs of racism lie as best I could."

Gore hadn't lacked for vivid personal encounters with segregation. On the family's car trips between Tennessee and Washington, the Gores were routinely denied accommodations because they traveled with Nancy and Al's black nanny, Ocie Bell. Gore eventually found a hotel owner near the trip's halfway point willing to put them up if they arrived after dark. And he clearly signaled his belief that the South needed to change: in 1956 he refused (along with his nationally ambitious Tennessee colleague Estes Kefauver) to sign Strom Thurmond's so-called Southern Manifesto, which encouraged southern states to defy federal court orders mandating desegregation. "Hell, no," Gore said, loud enough for reporters in the press gallery to hear, when Thurmond presented the document to him on the Senate floor.

But he sent mixed messages to voters about major civil rights developments. In 1954, when the Supreme Court's *Brown v. Board of Education* decision overturned the doctrine of "separate but equal" in public segregation, he wrote to one constituent: "I do not mean to imply that I am in agreement with the reasoning upon which the Court based its decision. . . . I think all of us must recognize, however, that the decision of the Court is, after all, a decision by the highest Court of our land and that it cannot be completely ignored."

He voted for civil rights legislation in 1957, which sought to expand the attorney general's power to pursue voting rights cases, but only after working to secure an amendment that diluted its impact. He also entered into some questionable alliances. In 1958 he endorsed old-line segregationist Buford Ellington for Tennessee governor in exchange for support in the event that he ran for president or vice president in 1960. As a reelection campaign neared, he opposed the landmark 1964 Civil Rights Act because he believed it vested too much enforcement power in the federal government. "Though I know gradualism is now denounced by many, it is my firm conviction that tolerance, time, patience and education are necessary ingredients to the ultimate solutions," he wrote to Lawrence Jones, Fisk University's dean of chapel. Toward the end of his career, however, he acknowledged that economic advancement and education alone were not enough. In 1965 and 1968 he supported antidiscrimination bills that guaranteed voting rights and open housing.

Though Al Gore would strive to create his own political identity when he entered Congress, his father's influence remained broad and deep. *Earth in the Balance,* his 1992 book on the environment, clearly echoes the elder Gore's concern with the planet's ecological health. "I had the feeling that a basic problem of the world is restoration and conservation of the fertility of the soil," he wrote after a 1951 tour of the Middle East. "Over-grazing, over-cropping, soil mining for centuries have brought millions of people to the very brink of starvation."

Like his son, Albert Gore was a pedagogue and a techno-geek. Where Al Gore has championed the economic and cultural promise of the Information Age, his father's imagination was captured by the ascendant technology of his day — nuclear energy. He helped handle secret appropriations for the Oak Ridge, Tennessee, laboratories that created the first atomic bomb, and several of his ideas in the 1950s about nuclear warfare sometimes took an ominously crackpot turn. In 1951 he proposed to Harry Truman that a strip of the Korean Peninsula be turned into an atomic death belt, seeded with radioactive material "that would mean certain death or slow deformity" to North Korean and Chinese troops.

But Albert Gore also understood the catastrophic potential of the nuclear arms race, and as chairman of the Arms Control Subcommittee of the Senate Foreign Relations Committee, he led the fight to negotiate and ratify the Anti-Ballistic Missile Treaty. He decried the "race to the top of the nuclear volcano," warning that the new generation of multiple-warhead MIRVs (multiple independently targetable reentry vehicles) represented "a uniquely dangerous type of escalation." In the early 1980s his son picked up that mantle by promoting development of the single-warhead Midgetman missile to supplant the MIRVs.

The Gores also shared a considerable frustration with the Democratic Party's northern and urban tilt in presidential politics. The elder complained to Baruch in 1952 that under Truman the party was pandering to blacks and white ethnics, "to Harlems and Hamtramyks" [*sic*] [a heavily Polish American suburb of Detroit]," as he put it. As it was, he wrote, "only those who would cater to extremist elements in the East and North could get the nomination." The party's devotion to liberals like Walter Mondale in 1984 drove young Gore to become a founding member of the centrist Democratic Leadership Council.

Albert Gore also passed on to his son the reserved public style now known in journalistic shorthand as "stiffness." At home in Tennessee, the elder Gore pulled a mean bow at campaign rallies and could deliver a rousing Fourth of July speech. But in Washington, especially as he established himself in the Senate, his style tended toward the solemn and Ciceronian. William S. White, writing in 1956, could easily have been discussing the next generation's Senator Gore when he likened Albert Gore to "that small boy remembered from grammar school who was the brightest and best behaved in the room — and who invariably suffered for this among his classmates. He had a great deal of ability along with his earnestness but is rather short of that instinctively casual touch with his associates that is so helpful in his trade." In the clubby world of the Senate, the elder Gore was an aloof figure whose "divinity student blue" suits and abstemious habits (no cigarettes, little alcohol, and a daily swim in the Senate pool) created the aura "of a man just come from a powerful hell-and-brimstone sermon." "Albert Gore was a fellow who was a little bit hard to know," said George Smathers, the Florida Democrat. "A very attractive guy and a very smart guy, but he was just not friendly."

Gore was shunned by the southern caucus in the 1950s after his civil rights votes, but even his natural allies found him prickly and high-maintenance, a man with a quixotic attraction to demonstrations of principle. Hubert Humphrey offered this warning to Sargent Shriver when he was trying to muster legislative support for the Peace Corps (which counted Nancy Gore among its earliest Washington staff):

Albert's a loner. Albert's a maverick. So he'll need a little loving. I want all of you at the Peace Corps to love Albert. Go to his office. Sit down dutifully. Take notes on what he is saying. As soon as you get back to your office, call him and thank him for the points he made — A, B and C. . . . I don't care if his darling daughter does work at the Peace Corps. Albert's very independent and this is what you'll have to do to make sure of his vote.

His independence irritated John Kennedy, one of his few friends in the Senate ("What does Albert Gore think he is up to?" he railed when Gore opposed his tax cut in 1963), and he exasperated Lyndon Johnson, the ultimate deal-maker. Long before they split on the war, the two had spent years kicking each other in the shins. As Senate majority leader, Johnson initially passed Gore over for the Finance Committee seat he wanted. Gore led an abortive attempt by Senate liberals in 1960 to trim back Johnson's powers as majority leader and loudly protested his bid to preside over the Senate Democratic caucus as vice president in early 1961.

Gore longed for higher office in the 1950s but often found himself eclipsed by two more dynamic Tennessee rivals, Governor Frank Clement and his Senate colleague, Kefauver. All three were in the vanguard of a new generation of southern moderates, and each nursed national ambitions. Gore was an accomplished speaker, but not in a league with Clement, the "Boy Orator of the Cumberland." He also lacked Kefauver's knack for self-promotion as well as his rapport with voters. "The difference between the two," said former *Tennessean* reporter and editor Wayne Whitt, who covered both men,

> was that an old farmer would come up to Kefauver and ask what he thought about admitting Red China to the UN and Kefauver would say, "I don't know, what do you think?" The farmer would ask Albert Gore the same question and get a thirty-minute lecture. The farmer would go home and tell his wife, "That Estes Kefauver may be the smartest man I've ever met. Why, he asked me what I thought about letting Red China into the UN."

While Kefauver made himself a household name with his televised hearings on organized crime, which positioned him as a leading contender for the 1952 Democratic presidential nomination, Gore pursued critical but often politically low-yield issues like trade and taxation. "If he does have national ambitions, he's his own worst enemy," said Eric Sevareid of CBS. "He has no publicity sense or machinery."

Gore believed that it simply wasn't in the cards for a southerner to win the presidential nomination, but in 1956 he coveted the vice presidency. After he met with Adlai Stevenson in his Chicago hotel suite, word quickly leaked that he was Stevenson's choice. But when Stevenson threw the selection open to the convention, Gore scrambled for support. George Reedy, a former Johnson aide, remembered seeing the senator in such a frenzy that at first he didn't recognize him. "A man came running up to us. . . . His eyes were glittering. He was mumbling something that sounded like 'Where is Lyndon? Where is Lyndon? Adlai's thrown this open, and I think I've got a chance for it if I can only get Texas. . . .' I have never seen before or since such a complete, total example of a man so completely and absolutely wild with ambition. It had literally changed his features."

Gore found himself in contention with Kefauver and Jack Kennedy, trailing them both after the first ballot. Although Kefauver enjoyed the support of the *Nashville Tennessean,* the state's dominant Democratic newspaper, Gore stubbornly persisted. Gore claims in his memoirs that he threw his support to his fellow Tennessean Kefauver as a statesmanlike gesture to keep Kennedy from winning. But Charles Fontenay, a former *Tennessean* reporter and a Kefauver biographer, said Gore was under enormous pressure from publisher Silliman Evans Jr. to fold. "Evans told him that the *Tennessean* wouldn't support him for dog catcher if he didn't get out of the race," said Fontenay. Gore headed to the floor and released his delegates to Kefauver.

Like his son, Albert Gore enjoyed a "Boy Scout" reputation for ethical conduct. But also as in his son's case, the label obscures less flattering parts of the picture. His long, profitable relationship with the businessman Armand Hammer broke no laws in its day but did raise serious questions about his judgment. The oil executive, art collector, and philanthropist, who financed cancer research and promoted peaceful relations between the United States and the Soviet Union, has been exposed in recent years as a fraud. FBI files and other documents, brought to light most recently in Edward Jay Epstein's 1996 book *Dossier,* show that Hammer, the first Westerner to do business in the Soviet Union (he ran a pencil factory), was in fact far more than that: he was a Soviet agent in the 1920s, designated by Lenin as the Communist Party's official "path" to the resources of American capitalism. Hammer served as a Soviet courier, laundered funds, and helped recruit Soviet spies.

How much of this Albert Gore knew is not clear. But for at least twenty years he was one of several lawmakers (Representatives Emanuel Celler and James Roosevelt of New York and Senator Styles Bridges of New Hampshire among them) who opened doors in Washington for Hammer. Their collective influence probably helped him evade serious trouble in the anti-Communist investigations of the period. The two met in the early 1950s at a Tennessee cattle auction and quickly hit it off. Both raised and sold purebred Black Angus, and they formed a business partnership that would last through the late 1960s.

Gore had been a cattleman in Smith County since 1940, and his growing stature as a congressman and senator had been good for business. Auctions at Gore Farms became major social events, sometimes drawing buyers who had little interest in livestock but a significant interest in ingratiating themselves with an influential U.S. senator. At a sale on September 13, 1958, Cecil Wolfson, a New York businessman active in construction and shipbuilding, bought ten head for $10,975. Another guest that day was Virginia businessman V. H. Monette, whose food brokerage business sold millions of dollars' worth of products to the military for dozens of major food companies. Monette brought along former New York Yankees star Joe DiMaggio, whom he'd hired, according to Wolfson, "to try to open doors to the military establishment." It's not clear how much cattle Monette bought, but even as a ten-year-old Little Al was a beneficiary of the high-level interest in his father's livestock: he sold Monette a cow his father had given him to raise for $751. Jamie Gore, a cousin who made several childhood visits to the farm, said that Gore accumulated several thousand dollars by raising and selling livestock on his summer vacations, and that he put the money in trust for his college education.

Albert Gore's joint venture with Hammer was modest. The net proceeds were usually small — $8,425 split between them, according to the 1964 year-end statement. The partnership closed out four years later with a mere $907.96 to divide after expenses. The real benefits for both men, however, were less direct. Hammer's presence attracted other customers who fattened the profits of Gore's overall cattle operation.

After a 1963 sale grossed $85,675, Gore wrote to Hammer thanking him: "You helped a great deal by making other people pay for the good ones."

For Hammer, of course, the advantage was the continued goodwill of a U.S. senator. There were limits to what Gore would do on behalf of his friend, but as the cattle business thrived, he performed a string of favors for Hammer and his company, Occidental Petroleum. Some were small courtesies, like acquiring rare books through the Library of Congress. Other services were more substantive, like helping cut through Justice Department opposition to make an FBI agent available to testify in a civil suit involving Occidental. "Evidently your persuasive powers were better than those of our attorneys," Hammer said in an appreciative note.

The Gore family's ties to Hammer did not end when he lost his Senate seat in 1970. Two years later Albert Gore, populist foe of big business, went to work as chairman of Hammer's coal subsidiary, Island Creek, at a six-figure salary. And in 1976, a year after he pled guilty to illegal campaign contributions to Richard Nixon in the Watergate scandal, Hammer, his family, and employees helped underwrite Al Gore's political career, beginning with his first congressional race. While his son inveighed against environmental degradation in Congress, Island Creek ran up numerous regulatory violations, several involving strip mining, on the elder Gore's watch. Albert Gore made no apologies for what some regarded as selling out. "Since I had been turned out to pasture," he said, "I decided to go graze the tall grass."

Those put off by the remote Albert often found a more soothing presence in Pauline. "He didn't understand people like she did," said Nancy Fleming, a Vanderbilt roommate of Nancy Gore's who went on to become a close family friend. "If it had been left up to him, Albert would lose touch with reality. To me, he was head-in-the-clouds. Smart, but not that much horse sense." Pauline oversaw the day-to-day details of congressional politics — who needed to be massaged on the next trip home, the name of the supporter's daughter who just graduated from college, how differences could be smoothed and corners cut. To soften the edges of Albert's reputation, she cultivated her own relationships with Washington reporters, such as Betty Beale, the *Washington Star*'s society columnist. "Pauline Gore was the most po-

litically astute member of the Gore family, more so than her husband," said Ted Brown, an Atlanta attorney who worked on Gore's
Senate staff.

She was discreet in wielding her influence, careful to play the role
of traditional political wife with seamless white-glove femininity.
But beyond public view, friends say that many of Gore's decisions,
both large and small, bore her imprint. In early 1965 Gilbert "Buddy"
Merritt, a politically connected twenty-eight-year-old Nashville lawyer
who briefly dated Nancy in college, was interested in an appointment as Nashville's U.S. attorney, but Gore wrote him off as too
young. "Buddy, I'm looking for someone with a little gray in their
hair," he said.

That evening at the dinner table Gore mentioned that he had
turned Merritt down and looked over at Pauline for affirmation. Instead, she asked, "Do you remember what you were doing when you
were twenty-eight years old?" Gore replied that he was Smith County
superintendent of schools. "I think he knows a lot more about being
U.S. attorney than you knew about being superintendent of schools,"
she said. The next day Gore told Merritt, now a federal judge, that he
would recommend him for the job.

She enjoyed social Washington more than Albert did and occasionally lamented her husband's antisocial ways. "I left at 2:00 A.M. and
things were still going strong," she wrote to Nancy after a 1958 party.
"Fortunately Dad was in Tennessee or the 11:00 curfew would have
held good." She also became restless if she stayed out of the Washington mix for too long. Even summers on the farm, a time to unwind
during congressional recess, turned into periods of frenetic activity, as
she wrote to her friend Katie Louchheim, vice chairman of the Democratic National Committee:

> I've entertained the Middle Tennessee Angus Breeders Association at
> our farm and had to have lunch for 300 — my neighbor across the
> street had a baby the day before yesterday, the one next door had an
> operation, I've visited and sent meals. . . . I would probably be bored
> if it were permanent but the way it is for me, I love it. I have really
> relaxed.

As with Albert, growing up poor had left indelible marks on Pauline. She enjoyed living well, but she always maintained pockets of fru-

gality: she made many of her own clothes to augment the ones she shopped for in New York once a year, and she put Al in cousin Jamie's hand-me-downs. In the winter of 1960 she left Washington to supervise personally the construction of a new house on the family farm. The ultramodern, six-bedroom split-level, built into a bluff overlooking the Caney Fork River, was grandly out of place in Smith County — more Frank Lloyd Wright than down-home Tennessee. But the Gores saw it as a tribute to their home state: the exterior marble came from a Knoxville quarry, and the paneling inside was lumbered from native woods — butternut, chestnut, and worm-eaten spruce.

Albert dreamed of his son one day becoming president, but it was Pauline who strove to ensure that nothing threatened that vision. When Gore ran his first congressional race in 1976, Pauline was a critical behind-the-scenes player, working her own intricate network of contacts and acquaintances to jump-start her son's candidacy. Historian James Gardner, then a Vanderbilt graduate student, remembers a day early in the campaign that he spent at the farm, interviewing Albert Gore for an oral history project. The senator was thrilled by his son's candidacy, but it was Pauline who provided the substantive advice. "She told him who he needed to talk to in whatever community he was interested," Gardner said. Friends say that while she loved and admired Albert, she found his hidebound ways frustrating and encouraged her son to practice a more supple, pragmatic, and, when necessary, combative politics. Just before a candidates' forum in Iowa early in the 1988 presidential campaign, she passed a note to him with just three words: "Smile, Relax, Attack." Watching his career progress, she possessed the pride of a coach bringing along a blue-chip prospect. "I trained them both," she liked to say of the two politicians in her life, "and I did a better job on my son than I did on my husband."

She was also a woman of strong instinctive opinions about whom Al Gore could trust in politics and who should be avoided. Falling squarely into the latter category, years before her son became his vice president, was Bill Clinton. "She thought he had bad moral character," said James Fleming, a Nashville physician and longtime family friend. He remembers standing in the senior Gores' living room one day in the mid-1980s with Gore Jr. and his brother-in-law Frank Hunger, discussing the Arkansas governor, who had just finished a visit to Nashville. Perhaps she had been talking to family members in Arkansas, or maybe her own experience in the workplace had left her with a gut sense about men who were trouble. Whatever the reason, Fleming said, "she looked at [her son] and said, 'Bill Clinton is not a nice person. Don't associate too closely with him.'"

Though slowed by strokes and heart trouble, she remains a zealous guardian, never hesitating to dress down anyone she regards as hostile to the cause. "Stop calling my boy wooden!" she admonished comedian Mark Russell when she saw him at a dinner several years ago. "Don't you know the difference between good manners and other behavior?"

What Al Gore ever knew about his mother's difficult early years, her failed marriage, her sexual harassment as a young lawyer, and how the pain of those experiences shaped his own emotional makeup, is difficult to determine with certainty. In a Senate speech during the debate on Clarence Thomas's Supreme Court nomination, he spoke with conspicuous sympathy for Anita Hill's decision to remain silent for years about her grievances against Thomas, her former boss at the Equal Employment Opportunity Commission: "Why is it so surprising that a woman would push back to the very recesses of memory such unpleasantness? Why is it so surprising that a woman stayed silent rather than move to destroy her still-forming career by taking on a much more powerful and intimidating foe? . . . Why do victims of other kinds of abuse stay silent for so long?"

Gore's answer was that some memories are simply too painful and are exposed only when there is no choice. "There is, quite simply," he said, "a public and a personal truth."

The public truth of Al Gore's childhood was that he lived in a world of privilege and material advantage, created by two striving children of the Depression who endowed him with an immense self-assurance and sense of mission. The personal truth is that those same parental gifts exacted a steep emotional cost.

2

Never an Unhappy Noise

C NN's Wolf Blitzer was trying to coax a little political news out of the vice president, but he wasn't playing. Not in March 1999, nearly twenty months from election day. Sitting in his West Wing office, eighteen paces down the blue-carpeted hallway from the one he wanted, Al Gore carefully deflected all the usual early-campaign questions about emerging from Bill Clinton's shadow and deciding what his "message" would be. Then Blitzer turned the discussion to Bill Bradley, Gore's sole competitor for the Democratic presidential nomination.

"Why should Democrats . . . support you instead of Bill Bradley?" Blitzer asked. Gore put him off with another non-answer, but then, as a way of beginning to talk about his credentials, he said, "During my service in the United States Congress, I took the initiative in creating the Internet."

Which, as most of the world now knows, isn't quite true. The Internet's genesis dates back to the creation in 1969 of a computer network for the Defense Department's Advanced Research Projects Agency (DARPA). Gore was a Harvard undergraduate government major at the time. Blitzer let the howler sail by, but over the next several days Gore was pelted with ridicule for the generous chunk of history he had claimed for himself. Even Dan Quayle, no doubt thrilled to see another vice president pilloried for a change, piled on, suggesting that if Gore created the Internet, "then I created spellcheck."

But the moment was more than a silly gaffe. It was the kind of small, but self-aggrandizing and easy-to-spot untruth that Gore has told throughout his career, from his suggestion that he and his wife Tipper were the inspiration for Erich Segal's *Love Story* to the inflated boasts about his work as a newspaper reporter. For years, Gore described to friends how he'd helped add stirring rhetoric to Hubert Humphrey's acceptance speech at the 1968 Democratic National Convention. In fact, he made no such contribution. These distortions capture something fundamental about who Al Gore is and the way he sees himself. Strands of fact run through all of his claims, but they are broadly exaggerated — and grandiose. What is puzzling is that in most cases the real story would have been equally as impressive. Gore did help write a speech during that tumultuous week in Chicago — his father's. Where the Gores come from, in middle Tennessee, it is a habit known as "lying when the truth would sound better."

The truth is that long before most political leaders, Gore grasped the possibilities and challenges posed by new technologies that move vast amounts of data around the world at split-second speed. He believes that government has a central role to play in the development of "the information superhighway" (a phrase he helped to popularize), not as underwriter and builder but as catalyst. Thirty years later Gore introduced a measure that financed critical improvements to the nation's computer networking infrastructure, paving the way for the Internet. As Clinton told a Silicon Valley audience in 1993, Al Gore is "the only person ever to hold national office in America who knew what the gestalt of a gigabit is."

So why the invention when the truth should have been good enough? In part, because it is how his mother and father would have cast the story. Albert and Pauline Gore made choices for their son with an eye to how each one would fit into a compelling pre-presidential narrative, and important aspects of Gore's early years were routinely embroidered for public consumption. It was possible to do so in part because of the culture of 1950s and 1960s Washington, where private lives were safely off-limits to the press and public figures could frame their images more or less as they wanted. Getting the story just right was especially important in the Gore family, and the vice president had vivid early lessons in how to adjust reality if it didn't play properly.

The 1957 magazine profile of the Gores at home in Washington brimmed with images of familial warmth. Mornings in their apartment at the Fairfax Hotel were a special time, Pauline Gore said, a chance for nine-year-old Little Al and his father to horseplay and banter as they dressed, followed by a leisurely breakfast before 7:55 A.M.,

when the car from St. Albans National Cathedral School for Boys arrived. In the evenings they might take a stroll up Massachusetts Avenue, past the elegant embassies. Pauline made it clear that no matter
what social obligations she and Albert had, she always cooked Little
Al's dinner and sat with him while he ate. "There is nothing lonelier,"
she said, "than a meal eaten alone."

In reality, Al Gore's nurture fell short of Pauline's idealized version.
In both Washington and Tennessee, his care was often delegated to a
network of baby-sitters, extended family, and friends. Although his
childhood was adorned with the privileges and creature comforts of a
senator's son, it was also lonely. As a high school senior, he boarded at
school, even though the St. Albans campus was just up Massachusetts
Avenue from the Fairfax. His cousin Jamie Gore, who lived in a townhouse next door with his brother Mark, sister Celeste, and parents
James and Jill, said that Al "ate dinner with us several nights a week"
and came along on numerous family outings. "Pauline and Albert
were never there," said a longtime family friend who often joined Al
and Nancy at the Fairfax for dinner so that they would not have to
eat alone. "Pauline had a maid who would fix the dinner and leave
it on the table or leave it in the refrigerator. The table would be all
pretty."

The Gores employed two Carthage women, Mattie Lucie Payne and
Ocie Bell, who came to Washington for periodic stays. When Al was in
second grade, the family hired what amounted to a male au pair, Abe
Gainor, who had also worked for the Gores in Carthage. In the mornings he walked Al, Jamie, and Mark to Sheridan, their private elementary school, and met them after finishing his own classes at the public
Francis Junior High. The arrangement filled the Gores' child-care
needs, and with a touch of liberal noblesse oblige. Albert and Pauline
regarded Abe (who stayed not at the Fairfax but with a hotel employee
who lived nearby) as "a very nice, bright young man who showed a lot
of promise for the future," said Jamie Gore. They brought him to
Washington as "an accommodation to Abe's parents, so Abe could be
exposed to urban life." Over summer breaks in Tennessee, Al was often
looked after by Alota Thompson, a Carthage nurse and the wife of a
tenant on the family farm.

Pauline Gore was one of Washington's busiest political wives in the
1950s and 1960s, and even with the help her schedule still produced

periodic child-care crises. She served as president of the Congressional Wives Forum, running a training program designed to familiarize spouses with important issues and campaign techniques, and she was also a mainstay of the Women's Speakers Bureau of the Democratic National Committee (DNC). During congressional recesses, she often traveled through Tennessee with Albert. In September 1956, with Albert on the road until election day, the DNC asked her to take a nine-day speaking tour through Illinois, Florida, and Tennessee. She was interested but had no one to care for her son, and as the *Washington Star* put it in a story on its "Women's World" page, "the problem of little Albert was still up in the air" until the last minute, when she was able to enlist a friend to stay and care for him.

Pauline Gore's usual graciousness cools when she is asked about her absences. She has acknowledged to others her remorse about spending so much time on the road. ("Albert and I were away so much," she told one close Washington friend.) But in the living room of her Tennessee home in February 1997, she angrily disputed the notion. Those who helped care for her son have exaggerated their own importance, she said. She scarcely disguised her scorn for Alota Thompson, who looked after Little Al in the late 1950s and early 1960s. When she read a magazine description of Thompson as like a second mother to Al Gore, Pauline said, "I cried my eyes out. I said, 'Here I have been, all of my motherhood, trying to keep from being a smother mother, and then have this confront me.'" She never, she said, "stayed away from him for more than two weeks at a time."

In the Gore family canon, their boy is a Tennessean — "as Tennessee as a bluetick hound," as former Governor Ned McWherter once said. But Gore did most of his growing up in Washington. The center of his world was the Fairfax, a quiet residential hotel less than two miles down Massachusetts Avenue from his vice presidential home, where elders of the city like Senators John McClellan and Prescott Bush and Admiral Chester Nimitz kept apartments. Although it became a Ritz Carlton in the early 1980s (it is now part of the Westin chain), the Fairfax was a bit more modest in Gore's day, and a convenient location for members of Congress and diplomats to quarter. Billed as "Washington's Family Hotel" the bare linoleum floors and thick steel doors suggested transience and utility rather than family friendliness. Until he graduated from high school in 1965, Al Gore's home was apartment 809, a smallish, two-bedroom suite overlooking Embassy Row and Rock Creek Park.

The Fairfax was a testament to the enterprise of the other members of the Gore family in Washington. Albert's cousin Grady Gore, the son of Allen's brother, was from nearby Wilson County. Another Tennessee kid who thrived after scuffling early, he married his childhood sweetheart, Jamie Shorter, and moved to New York when he was twenty-five to sell mortgages for New York Life. When the Depression hit, he went to Washington and entered the collapsed real estate market, buying up apartment houses around Adams Morgan and Dupont Circle. One of them, in 1937, was the Fairfax. While Albert made his name in Congress, Grady got rich. In 1943 he bought Marwood, a magnificent 125-acre Maryland estate (modeled after Malmaison near Paris), which overlooked the Potomac. Asked about its thirty rooms, twelve baths, pool, and one-hundred-seat movie theater, Grady Gore called it "just a nice comfortable home with a lot of ground around it."

As his wealth grew, so did his disenchantment with the Democrats. He supported Dewey in 1948 and tried to launch his own political career four years later with an unsuccessful run for the Maryland Republican senatorial nomination. The Republican branch of the Gore family contributed several dubious footnotes to political history. One of Grady Gore's two daughters (he also had two sons), Louise, was a Republican national committeewoman and unsuccessful Maryland gubernatorial candidate who opened the Jockey Club at the Fairfax in 1961. But her most fateful moment in politics was an introduction she made at a 1967 party. "I think you two ought to get to know each other," she is reported to have said as she brought together Maryland Governor Spiro Agnew and then-former vice president Richard Nixon. A granddaughter of Grady's, Deborah Gore Dean, was convicted of funneling federal money to Republican insiders while serving as chief of staff to Reagan-era HUD Secretary Samuel Pierce. Before her official misconduct was exposed, her cousin Al had endorsed her 1987 nomination for an assistant secretary's post.

Albert occasionally groused about Grady's children — especially the daughters, whom he regarded as spoiled — but Grady remained an important benefactor, contributing to his campaigns and making the Fairfax apartment available at what one family member called a "generous" reduced rent. Grady also opened Marwood to his Tennessee kin. Little Al swam and roamed the grounds, and Albert and Pauline used it for elaborate entertaining, like their July 1957 poolside "Filibuster Party" for senators stuck in town while that year's civil rights bill was under debate.

The air was ripe with politics at the Fairfax. On warm summer nights the Gores congregated with other Capitol couples on the roof garden to catch the breezes and the latest gossip. Little Al could wander into his living room and encounter Clark Clifford meeting with his father to discuss John Kennedy's 1960 presidential campaign strategy. Or he could answer the phone, as he did early on the evening of April 10, 1962, and hear the White House operator with an urgent message for the senator to call President Kennedy. His parents were out — attending a reception held by the Tennessee State Society of Washington — but Gore got a message through to them and they rushed home. Later that night the fourteen-year-old Gore listened in on an extension as a livid JFK ("mad as hops," Albert Gore recalled) explained that U.S. Steel Chairman Roger Blough had decided to raise prices. The administration, trying to enforce a wage and price stabilization program, had secured an agreement from steelworkers to refrain from demanding a pay increase. "And now this ——— undertakes on his own to undo it all," Kennedy fumed. "Can you get some opposition going in the Senate?" he asked. Gore said he would try. After they hung up, Al Gore told his father, "I didn't think presidents talked like that."

As a presidential candidate in 1988, Gore endured the "Prince Albert" caricature hilariously rendered by cartoonist Garry Trudeau in *Doonesbury.* He wasn't royalty, but his early years were filled with the trappings of his elite status. If Marwood or the Senate pool weren't available for swimming, there was always the Army Navy Country Club, where he had a junior membership. He also presided over a proliferating inventory of toys. "Al now weighs 90 pounds, has a pony, a dog, a bicycle, and more trinkets, junk, space ships, etc., than we can house," the senator wrote to his friend Ali Heravi at the Iranian Foreign Ministry in early 1958, shortly before his son's tenth birthday. To prepare for his eventual participation in the cotillion circuit, the Gores enrolled him in twice-monthly Saturday afternoon dance classes offered by Mrs. Lloyd Parker Shippen, whose studio on upper Wisconsin

Avenue introduced several generations of up-and-coming young Washingtonians to the waltz and the intricacies of good social deportment.

And all along the Gores never hesitated to promote their son in the Tennessee press as a prodigy whose political ascendance was inevitable. The baby hailed on page 1 of the *Nashville Tennessean* was the object of continued tribute in print. One 1954 item, fed to the *Knoxville News-Sentinel*, describes how Gore "out-talked" his father, convincing him to buy a 98¢ bow-and-arrow set instead of the 49¢ version Albert preferred. "He's a Budding Politician," said the three-column headline. "There may be another Gore on the way to the political pinnacle," began the article, accompanied by a photo of the senator helping to pull the bow back for Little Al, who was wearing a feathered headband that said "Little Beaver." "He's just six years old now. But with his experiences to date, who knows what may happen?"

Even with the frequent absences, the Gores enforced a rigorous family code for their son, built on expectation, obligation, and accomplishment.

"My father was the greatest man I ever knew," Al Gore said in his emotional 1998 eulogy to the senator. What Gore would never say is that he was also probably the most difficult. A grandiose and demanding patriarch, Albert constantly set the bar on the highest rung — starting with the fifty push-ups he required of his twelve-year-old son every morning.

Little Al's mission was to exceed the task at hand, to demonstrate that he was worthy not just because he was a senator's son, but because he was willing to pull more than his own weight. When kids at 4-H camp in Crossville, Tennessee, taunted the boy from Washington as a big shot, he tried to win them over by volunteering for kitchen duty. The staff usually reserved those jobs for older, stronger campers, but they let Gore, then twelve, serve meals on the cafeteria line. He mounted special efforts to appear worthy in public forums with Albert, like the 1962 United Nations debate (his father was a member of the U.S. delegation): the fourteen-year-old high school sophomore listened to the entire proceeding in French, despite having barely broken a C average in two years of studying the language. "I am not sure whether he understood it or whether he was giving a demonstration for my benefit," Albert wrote to Armand Hammer. "I enjoyed it."

The senator was by his own admission a taskmaster — part parent, part Marine drill instructor, and part professor — with a penchant for the kind of windy digressions and explanations that his son's own children would one day endure at the dinner table. "His dad was always explaining stuff to him," said Gordon Thompson, Alota Thompson's son and a Tennessee boyhood pal. "If Al asked a question, his dad would go into real detail. Where I would like an answer of about seven or eight words, he'd go on for fifteen minutes." Gore expected the world of his son, but no success was too small for a celebration. One classmate remembers the day Little Al came home from school with an unanticipated A: he watched the senator break into a triumphal dance around the apartment, report card in hand.

Gore never resisted the dynastic harness placed on him at such an early age. He was fiercely protective of his father's image and tried hard to avoid any foolishness that might blot the family name. While his peers tested the forbearance of the adult world, Gore instinctively looked for ways to comply with its requirements. He epitomized the "easy child": pleasant, eager to please, reluctant to complain. "It was, 'I'm fine, Mom, I'm fine.' That was his whole thing," said his Tennessee girlfriend Donna Armistead. "He never wanted to worry anyone."

Pauline was content not to dig too deeply under the placidly agreeable surface for problems. "He grew up in a very happy atmosphere — it was a good time then — and I think that always made him reluctant to raise other feelings. . . . He never wanted to be the person to make an unhappy noise," she said. As he marched through his cameos at dinner parties and other Washington social gatherings, he was less a kid than a miniature grownup, working the room on his parents' behalf. "He told me one time that his way of getting attention was by being very polite," said his Vietnam buddy Mike O'Hara. "He said, 'I was a real little politician.'"

Only when he was away from adult authority did resentment occasionally bubble to the surface, as when he brooded over the senator's unsolicited advice about his high school track team specialty. "What the hell does *he* know about throwing the discus?" he complained to Geoff Kuhn, his senior-year roommate at St. Albans. "His father was ragging on him," said Kuhn.

Even as Gore made his own name, his father remained a source of both pride and prickly defensiveness. Old Nashville friends say they learned to avoid seemingly innocuous comments like, "Your father must be proud of you," for fear of drawing a fiery glare. "Al has a way of looking at you like his eyes are kind of burning," said former *Nashville Tennessean* reporter John Warnecke. "You would get that when you mentioned his dad." Asked in a 1987 interview about relations between father and son, Tipper Gore said: "You remember Oedipus?" She quickly added that she was kidding, sort of. "You had a very powerful father — a hero to many people — and a son coming to maturity and learning to find his own dignity."

Unlike her brother, Nancy LaFon Gore never hesitated to make an unhappy noise. Al Gore's older sister was the anti-Al: rambunctious, defiant, far more of a challenge to Albert and Pauline than their congenitally compliant son. Al tried to find out what you wanted and would do it, Pauline liked to say. Nancy found out so she could do exactly the opposite. "That girl is putting me through the tortures of the damned," she complained to a friend in the early 1960s.

She was a dazzling presence to Little Al, a slender, green-eyed beauty ten years his senior who attracted a procession of suitors. She was also a caregiver who loomed large in his boyhood, a functional parent ready to step in when Albert and Pauline were out politicking. At the Peace Corps, where she worked as an administrator (the "resident Scarlett O'Hara and female political sage," said her colleague Coates Redmon), she was a familiar sight sweeping down the hall in midafternoon with her coat on. "She'd say, 'I have to go,' and I'd ask why," said Charles Peters, a coworker and close friend. "She'd say, 'St. Albans has a basketball game.'" It was more than a matter of simply turning out to watch Gore play, said Peters, now publisher of the *Washington Monthly*. "She loved Al, and it was clear to me that she was filling a role."

While Little Al may have been the "real little politician" in the family, Nancy possessed more of Pauline's instinct for the game. After college she worked for the Democratic National Committee and helped run Albert's 1964 reelection campaign. She had a deft personal touch and a knack for strategy, but there wasn't much future in Tennessee politics then for a young woman, and Little Al was destined to carry the family banner. While he scrimmaged with future masters of the universe on the playing fields of St. Albans, Nancy attended Holton Arms, then a cradle for debutantes and society wives-in-waiting.

But that wasn't really Nancy's world either. Her years as a senator's daughter had left her comfortable in the world of older, powerful men. At straitlaced Vanderbilt, she ignored the dominant sorority scene to chain-smoke and drink bourbon with the law school guys. "She was the most spectacular young woman at Vanderbilt," said former *Nashville Tennessean* and *New York Times* reporter Fred Graham, one of her law school drinking buddies, "a young woman with a very bold look, not at all intimidated by anything in the world."

She could also be spoiled and mercurial, a Washington princess who loved to be fussed over. "I went to the Mercedes-Benz factory and played the rich bitch," she wrote home from Stuttgart in 1958, the year she spent working as a guide at the Brussels World's Fair. "Told them I wanted to buy a 190 SL. I had three men talking to me for an hour and then a 190 and a driver for the morning." When her job in Brussels ended, she traveled the world alone for two months, from Warsaw to Tokyo.

But the sassy style obscured a basic insecurity and lack of focus. She bit her nails to the quick and worried that men were interested in her only because of her father. She never seemed to find her niche, in Washington or in Tennessee. Pauline tried to steer Nancy toward law school or a career in finance, but she never followed through.

To numb the uncertainties and disappointments, she drank. "Nancy was an alcoholic who was never treated," said James Fleming, a close friend and Nashville plastic surgeon who met her at Vanderbilt when he was dating one of her roommates (Nancy Skelton, who later became his first wife). "It was progressive but well controlled. She didn't drink in the morning or much at lunch. She was a nighttime drinker." She partied heavily with her Peace Corps crowd in the early sixties. One evening at a Georgetown apartment, friends wanted to take her home, but she pleaded to spend the night on the couch, saying that she couldn't go home drunk. Wary of her father's disapproval, she asked her hosts, "Can I spend the night? I can't go home and face 'the Baptist.'" Fleming, who has been in recovery for more than a decade and now runs an alcohol treatment center in Nashville, said that as far as he knows no one in the Gore family tried to intervene or help. "Like with most alcoholics, these were things you didn't talk about," he said. "It was like the elephant in the living room."

When she married in 1966, friends were delighted, if a bit puzzled, by her choice of a quiet country lawyer and former Air Force pilot from Winona, Mississippi, named Frank Hunger. They had met through a mutual friend at Vanderbilt and become reacquainted later when he was stationed at Andrews Air Force Base near Washington. The August wedding was one more disappointment for Pauline: she wanted a big affair for her only daughter; Nancy wanted something more modest, insisting on a small ceremony at the farmhouse, which was decorated with marigolds and zinnias from the countryside. She did accede to one of her mother's wishes: she wore a white dress.

While many of Little Al's classmates were packed off to summer camp when school let out, he headed for the family's eight-hundred-acre tobacco and cattle farm about two and a half miles east of Carthage, Tennessee. The trips were less vacations than character-building boot camps designed by Albert Gore to give his privilege-softened son a taste of his own struggles in Possum Hollow. Ironically, Al Gore's Republican antagonists have seized on his recollections of the hard work he did on the farm as another bogus tale about his life. In fact, Gore was up at dawn tending to livestock and hosing out hog parlors. But also underlying the summer regimen his father enforced was a calculatedly political objective: planting roots to help his son's chances of one day winning office in Tennessee.

For parts of virtually every summer through high school, Gore worked with the farmhands and was often assigned an extra project devised by his father. One year he tended to a few acres of tobacco by himself, an experience that often prompted him to boast in numbing detail (as he did for a group of reporters held captive for an hour on a small plane in the 1988 campaign) about "the thirty-two steps" to growing and harvesting a tobacco crop. A Tennessee friend who requested anonymity said that Gore also cleared a hillside of dense brush with small hand tools, a two-day task for a bulldozer that turned into a season-long endeavor. Book work was not allowed to slide: for at least two summers, according to his St. Albans transcript, his schedule included classes in biology, Spanish, and typing at Castle Heights Military Academy in Lebanon. Even the local kids, who might have enjoyed watching a city slicker sweat some, were appalled at how Gore was worked. "It was horrendous," said one woman who knew him well as a teenager. Friends and family members who visited Little

Al from Washington and got put to work thought twice about returning. "Al's father would just work the dickens out of him," said Mark
Gore, one of Cousin Grady's grandsons from Embassy Row. "Up at
dawn, very serious work for a kid. I went down there a couple of times
and I said, 'Uh-uh.'"

Even Pauline thought Albert's regime was unduly harsh, although
not necessarily because of the burdens placed on her son. "I was always up [at dawn], cooking his breakfast, when he worked on the
farm," she said. "I told my husband he wasn't punishing Al, he was
punishing me. I was up getting his breakfast." She tried to draw the
line when her son was assigned to plow a dangerously steep hillside.
When Albert insisted, she shot back sarcastically: "Yes, a boy could
never be president if he couldn't plow with that damned hillside
plow." And that's what he did.

Because of their extended absences, Albert and Pauline often left
the tenant farmers responsible for their son's care and the progress of
his work assignments. "It was, 'Make sure Al does this and Al does
that,'" said Gordon "Goat" Thompson, who moved onto the Gore
farm with his parents William and Alota in 1955. He was three years
older than Little Al, but glad for a new friend. For Gore, the Thompsons evolved into another branch of extended family. He stayed with
them for three or four weeks at a time in the summers and one entire
winter in the late 1950s, sharing a bed with Goat in a drafty tenant
house that had no indoor plumbing and only a small coal-burning
stove for heat. After a day's work in July or August, they swam at the
Carthage city pool or, more often, just plunged into the cow trough, a
murky brew that had, as Thompson put it, "a little bit of everything in
it." On warm summer nights the two boys ran an electrical cord into
the yard and set up a pup tent, where they stayed up late playing cards
or checkers.

William Thompson was a spare, soft-spoken man who didn't always follow Albert's prescriptions for his son to the letter and carried
him to bed after he fell asleep in his clothes at the end of a long day on
the farm, easing him under the covers next to Goat. He took them
coon hunting in the hills after dark, teaching Little Al to listen for the
change in the dog's bark as he treed a raccoon. Gore grew especially
close to Alota Thompson, who worked as a nurse in Carthage. "She
thought as much of Al as she did of me," said her son. Despite its rig-

ors, the Tennessee summers gave Gore the chance to be more of a kid, and he sometimes seized the opportunity. As a teenager, he was driving his father's new Chevy back from Castle Heights one morning when he ran off Highway 70 North onto a steep shoulder, rolling the vehicle several times. He was not seriously injured, but the impact knocked his shoes off. "I don't know how many times he rolled, but he totaled it," said Goat Thompson.

Late one afternoon in the summer of 1962, Gore was walking out of the Petty-Green Clinic, the hospital in downtown Carthage where Alota Thompson worked as a nurse, and noticed Donna Armistead parked in front, listening to Ray Charles on the radio. He had seen her around; her mother was also a nurse at Petty-Green, and her younger brother, Steve, worked from time to time at the Gore farm. She lived in Elmwood, a tiny community just east of Carthage, and although her parents were alive, she usually stayed in an apartment with her grandparents in back of their general store on Highway 70 North.

At sixteen, she was two years older than Gore, a tomboyish redhead with a delicate, freckled face and a sweet manner that won her the title "Jolliest Junior" at Carthage High School in 1962. The age difference didn't daunt Gore, who decided that this was the moment to make his move. Armistead remembers a polite, self-assured boy who walked up to the car and struck up a short conversation that ended with a modest proposal. "He said, 'Well, you know, let's go to the movies, or let's do something.'" Gore disclosed up front that at age fourteen, his license prohibited nighttime driving. Donna replied that they might be able to double up with her older brother Roy, who was going to the Cookeville Drive-In that evening.

Armistead doesn't remember the movie, only that they sat in the backseat and talked about sports for two hours. They were both basketball players, Gore at St. Albans and Armistead for the Owlettes, the girls' team at Carthage High. She was struck by his nice manners and by how carefully he listened. When Roy and Donna drove him home, he insisted that she come in and meet his mother. The next day he asked her to go steady.

For three years Donna Armistead was Al Gore's girl, the only real romantic relationship in his life before he met Mary Elizabeth "Tipper" Aitcheson, the woman he married. Armistead was an emotional safe harbor for the guarded and often lonely young Gore, and he opened up to her as he has to few people in his life. During the school year the relationship was conducted exclusively in letters — hundreds of them, often written twice a day by Gore. In the summers, when they had time off from the farm and the classroom, they water-skied on nearby Center Hill Lake and ate cheeseburgers with banana shakes at the B&B Diner in Elmwood.

But the hangout of choice was the palatial Gore home, where the entire basement was "Al's apartment," as Donna called it, outfitted with a ping-pong table, a stereo, and a small kitchen. For a girl living in back of a general store, it was not merely swank, but a link to a wider, wondrous world. He introduced Donna to the art of presidential eavesdropping, although this time it wasn't clear that the senator knew his son was on the other extension. "He comes over and says, 'We have to get back home in a hurry. Kennedy's calling Dad tonight,'" she said.

Armistead is bewildered by descriptions of the adult Gore as wooden and aloof. The Gore she dated was certainly serious and plenty ambitious (he had targeted Harvard as a destination by his early teens) but also had a great belly laugh, an impish sense of humor, and what she called "a northern mind and a southern heart." He would "sit and listen to you, and show you all kinds of respect, even to the point of letting you inside his soul, until you prove you don't deserve that."

As for sex, she said it was "between Al, God, and myself," but a close friend of the young couple said Armistead reported that they always stopped short of consummating the relationship. Years later Gore liked to describe the two of them as "the Barbie and Ken of Elmwood," a reflection of their all-American wholesomeness and implied chastity. Both had received parental lectures on the perils of teen passion. At least once, according to a neighbor, Pauline came downstairs to her son's bachelor pad, pulled the two apart, and ordered him to take a cold shower. One clear summer night in 1962, they were sitting in a car at the end of a dirt road, doing nothing more, said Donna, than putting their feet up and looking at the moon, when a set of headlights suddenly appeared in the near-distance. A panicked Gore recognized them as his father's, and in the scramble each put on the other's shoes. As he jumped out of the car, Gore was bathed in his father's high beams, modeling his girlfriend's Weejuns. "What do you think you're doing?" Albert Gore asked. "Don't you think it's time we were getting on home?"

But with the Gores' schedule, they weren't always there to oversee the young couple, and although there were other adults around, Donna Armistead's recollection is that Al spent a great deal of time alone on the farm. By 1962 the Thompsons had moved off to a house in a neighboring town. Although Gore remained close to Goat and his parents, his relationship with Donna brought the Armistead clan into his life as his newest surrogate family. He soon became like another sibling to Donna's four brothers and sisters, often eating lunch with them after his morning classes at Castle Heights, then returning after a searing afternoon on the farm for dinner. Steve Armistead came closest to being the older brother that Gore never had, a garrulous "good ole boy" who called him "punk" and loved to let the air out of any pretensions his friend might have imported from Washington at the beginning of the summer. Armistead's mouth could occasionally land him in trouble, and once Gore stood by and watched his friend scuffle with some other local kids. Later he confessed to Donna his guilt that he hadn't come to Steve's aid: "Do you think I'm chicken if I don't fight?" he asked her.

Gore was especially close to the matriarch of the family. Edna Armistead, Donna's grandmother, was a righteous, auburn-haired church woman who studied scripture and political developments in the Nashville newspapers with equal zeal. "God, family, and the Democrats" was her summation of life's priorities. The general store she ran with Floyd became another second home for Gore, who loved to sit with Edna and talk religion and politics. "They could spend three hours together, just the two of them, him questioning and her answering," said Donna.

Edna Armistead played an important role in Gore's early religious education, deepening his involvement in New Salem Missionary Baptist Church, where his paternal grandparents, Allen and Maggie Gore, had taken him when he was younger. New Salem was a thriving conservative spiritual community — "real hellfire and damnation," said one former member who attended services with Donna and Al. Gore didn't go every day but did go to the steamy weekend revivals and Sunday school. It was here that he acquired some of his extensive knowledge of scripture.

In her years as Al Gore's girlfriend, Donna Armistead never visited him in Washington. She never had the money for the trip, she said. The more likely reason, however, was Gore's instinct, or perhaps that of his parents, that Carthage and Washington were two worlds best kept separate. The relationship frayed and finally ended by Gore's freshman year in college. Within a year Nancy married a Carthage High School classmate and burned all but one of the hundreds of letters she had received from Gore. She also kept a tiny silver ring he gave her one Christmas, now pounded into a squarish shape from years of wearing it while dribbling a basketball. Gore remains in close touch with Steve Armistead — he slipped into Nashville several years ago for Armistead's fiftieth birthday party — but has not spoken to Donna in nearly two decades. Divorced and living in a Nashville suburb, where she works as a nurse, she believes that her family, Elmwood, and New Salem still remain in his memory as a zone of safety, a rare place where he could be himself. "That we could be so happy, and not have much, was one of the things that kind of amazed Al," she said. "The only thing he had better was a pretty house, and a pretty house sometimes does not make a home, you know?"

◆ 3 ◆

Al Gorf

FROM HIS earliest days at St. Albans, Al Gore won the plaudits of teachers, if not always the affection of his classmates. "Al is a careful and precise worker," his fourth-grade teacher, Mr. Smith, wrote in a 1957 evaluation. "He never rushes through his work, which is always excellent — an enjoyable boy with a fine sense of humor." But even at age nine, recalled the headmaster of the lower school, Alfred True, "his classmates found him a bit stuffy, because he wasn't interested in pranks."

For Albert and Pauline, St. Albans was the ideal school, one that offered their son the head start they never had and reinforced their essential message to him — that he was born to lead. Founded in the late nineteenth century for the choirboys at Washington National Cathedral, St. Albans promoted itself as an American facsimile of the British boarding school, offering an education that emphasized stern moral guidance, spiritual growth, and social obligation. Canon Charles Martin, the irrepressible headmaster, made his rounds through the campus of gray Gothic stone accompanied by a bulldog named Mark Antony and liked to greet students from behind with a viselike grip on the back of the neck. He preached "the hard right over the easy wrong," and his lunchtime lectures in the Cafritz Refectory, over slabs of meatloaf and apple brown Betty, covered everything from how to buy a new pair of shoes (not too shiny, so as not to call attention to yourself) to vivid examples of intellectual and athletic achievement. One day in early 1965 he called the boys' attention to a *New Yorker* article about a remarkable Princeton basketball player named Bill Bradley. He instructed the school's parents as well, writing to them regularly to dispense advice on subjects like discipline: "Love — not

the kind that is sentimental and soft, but real love with the iron of justice and right in it — is the basis of all good relationships."

The school's larger cultural role in Washington was as an incubator
for sons of the city's ruling class. Franklin Roosevelt, Dean Acheson,
Robert and Ted Kennedy, Phil Graham, James Reston, and George
Bush, among many others, sent sons to St. Albans. Even the school
hymn celebrated the boys' preparation for a life not merely of Christian virtue but of secular power and influence:

> Men of the future stand, and watch each fleeting hour
> To make your lives what God has planned, to spread abroad
>   His power
> In work, in game or play, suppress all fear and hate
> Show forth a spirit generous, true — for God and for the State.

Martin liked to caution that "St. Albans exists not to get boys into
the Kingdom of Harvard, but to get them into the Kingdom of
Heaven." But the real message, said David Bartlett, one of Gore's classmates, was less high-minded. "Everybody understood that the idea
was to go out and be a success and lead as much of the world as
you could get your hands on, and that the Kingdom of Heaven would
take care of itself." Matthew Simchak, another schoolmate and son
of a prominent politician — his father was mayor of Chicago in the
1930s — said the school had three kinds of boys: "those whose self-
confidence and soul had been broken by their parents' fame, those
who sought to emulate it, and those unaffected one way or another."
Al Gore, he said, was the second kind.

He left behind no single mark of distinction at St. Albans. He was
an able student, but not an outstanding one, ranking twenty-fifth of
fifty-one boys, according to his transcript, by the time he graduated
in 1965. He would fill out enough in his teens to play the offensive line
on the football team and was named captain in his senior year, but
he often found himself beaten by blitzing defenders who nailed his
quarterback, friend, and future Harvard roommate, Bart Day, to the
turf. Other classmates commanded more respect as leaders, like Dan
Woodruff, the strapping all-prep running back and track star who also
served as student council president. He and Gore were among the ten
seniors elected prefects by the student body to enforce codes of conduct and dress. But that elite group named Woodruff, not Gore, senior
prefect, a post Gore coveted.

Classmates remember him as a supremely serious and compulsively competitive kid whose outsized ambition drove him to master virtually everything he took on. He won school awards with his artwork and headed the liberal party in government class, the Thursday evening debating society where sons of the establishment deliberated the great Cold War issues that their fathers addressed during business hours. He made himself a formidable senior lounge pool player. "Frighteningly competent in everything," said his football teammate George Hillow.

Yet for all of his achievements, Gore's earnestness and painfully upright manner left him somewhat isolated as a high school student at St. Albans, where adolescent rebellion and sneering prep school arrogance were in full flower. "We were all Holden Caulfields to a large degree," said Geoff Kuhn, his senior-year roommate. "Cynicism ended up being a problem. We were all tragically hip. Not that Al was square, but he was somewhat different, and different wasn't appreciated." Cliques formed and calcified, separating the hip from the clueless, the jocks from the brains, and the new divisions fractured some friendships Gore had enjoyed since fourth grade. Although he maintained ties in each camp, classmates don't place him with a specific group. "No close enemies, no close friends," said John Siscoe, a member of the government class.

Editors of the 1965 *Albanian* yearbook paid a not entirely friendly tribute to Gore's versatility. The caption selected for his portrait was, "People who have no weaknesses are terrible." Attributed to Anatole France, the caption was accompanied by a drawing of Gore as a statue on a pedestal (similar to one of George Washington that stands on campus) with a football, basketball, and discus stuffed under his arm. "Popular and respected, he would seem to be the epitome of the All-American Young Man," the editors wrote. "It probably won't be long before Al reaches the top. When he does, all of his classmates will remark to themselves, 'I knew that guy was going somewhere in life.'" Gore was occasionally capable of taking the edge off his deadly seriousness. His self-adopted nickname, in the space under his yearbook picture, was "Al Gorf."

There was a kind of endearing excess in some of Gore's competitive zeal, best illustrated by his determination to be the boy who could sleep the latest and still make it on time to morning chapel. Like his rivals, he used a clip-on tie, but Gore prevailed by going a step further: he cut the back out of a white dress shirt and donned it like a surgeon's gown, saving him the crucial seconds it would have taken to fasten the buttons. "He took his jacket off in lineup and showed us his bare back," said Hillow. "And this is at a school where you'd get demerits for wearing no socks." He squeezed every possible minute out of late afternoon naps as well, sometimes showing up for dinner with imprints from the cotton ridges of his dormitory bedspread lining his face, a condition that came to be known among classmates as "Gore's Disease."

In the Gore era at St. Albans, acts of social defiance were comically benign given the historic turbulence just over the horizon. Challenging authority meant sneaking off to the lobby of the McLean Gardens apartments on Wisconsin Avenue, where a clique that called itself "the Horde" went to smoke cigarettes. But the clubby atmosphere also included pockets of racism and anti-Semitism, imported from dinner tables at home. Jim Gray, the second black student to attend the school, joined the class of 1965 in the ninth grade and suffered from hives for most of his first year from the stress. "It was a lot of Jewish jokes and black stuff," said Siscoe. "You drank it with your bourbon. It was in the social mix."

Donna Armistead remembers a joylessness that suffused Gore's letters, which chronicled the pressure to comport himself as a prefect, athlete, and senator's son. "I think they were lonely times for him," she said. Most St. Albans students lived at home, but Gore, whose Fairfax apartment was only a few blocks away, boarded at least part of the time because of his parents' schedules. He called Armistead every Saturday evening, often from a school pay phone, where she could hear the jangling of the quarters and dimes he fed as the operator broke in every few minutes. He joined a handful of other boys, some of them the sons of American diplomats posted overseas, in the school's austere dormitory at Lane Johnson Hall. As an underclassman, he slept in an open cubicle called a "coop," before getting a room in his senior year. While underclassmen had a 10:00 P.M. lights-out, seniors' experiments with life on three hours' sleep were under way, with guitars, beer, and bull sessions. But Gore was usually in bed before midnight.

Gore was not above basic dormitory mischief. After he and an accomplice snipped the front of Mead Miller's hair as he slept, Miller broke into Gore's desk and lifted a collection of letters from Donna Armistead. Gore avenged the theft by hauling him outside and punching him in the nose. Things didn't always go smoothly when he tried to be just one of the guys. Kuhn remembers Gore telling him about the night shortly after graduation when he was out again with the family car, chucking cherry bombs out the window when one bounced off the driver's side door frame and ended up back in his lap. He recovered in time to pitch it out, but if he hadn't, he told Kuhn in a falsetto voice, "I'd be talking like this." Such displays were quickly overtaken by his usual sense of caution and discretion. Simchak said he imagined young Gore tethered to a huge, parentally regulated rubber band. "You had the sense that when he broke out and did something silly, it wouldn't be long before it snapped back."

Students were required to play team sports — the core of the "muscular Christianity" that Martin extolled. Gore was a mainstay of the athletic program but played on some of the worst teams the school ever fielded. He captained a football squad that, *The Albanian* noted, was "humiliated by less talented but scrappier teams" on its way to a 1–7 record in 1964. He was also a talented perimeter shooter for a basketball team that lost twenty-three of twenty-six games in his senior year.

He found a more satisfying refuge in painting. Dean Stambaugh held his art classes in a basement studio with flowering hibiscus, caged canaries, finches, and, four days a week, classical music. (Students' choice, within reason, prevailed on Fridays.) A lean and dapper man who had taught at the school since 1942, Stambaugh could tease art out of the unlikeliest boys. He usually discouraged abstracts but allowed Gore to pursue them on a looseleaf-sized tablet. "You'd think his paintings would be very representational," said Alfred True, "but he painted very delicate little things." Hillow, now a college theater professor, likened them to "Georgia O'Keeffe abstract realism, with vivid color and swirling patterns. I remember them being bold." It was the only high school course that Gore consistently aced, and his passion for painting stayed with him. As an army private stationed in Alabama, he called it "my great emotional catharsis."

Music was his other welcome release. Gore loved collecting records; as a young adult, he made an entire closet in his Tennessee farmhouse a walk-in shrine to 1960s and 1970s rock and R&B, wall-to-wall with LPs and eight-tracks. On February 11, 1964, he joined a classmate named Reed Hundt and others at Washington Coliseum for the Beatles' first U.S. concert. That same winter Gore saw that James Brown, another of his favorites, was appearing at the Howard Theater. The old house at Seventh and T Streets was a regular stop for Motown and Stax artists, and a walk-on-the-wild-side thrill for white Washington kids in the 1960s. He asked Jerome Powell, a young black doorman at the Fairfax, to take him to Brown's show. Powell, who sang in his church choir and idolized Jackie Wilson, was four years older than Gore, the son of a nurse and cook who had started working part-time at the hotel while attending D.C.'s Coolidge High. The two had become friendly and would slip down to the alley in back of the hotel on weekends to toss a football and talk music.

Powell, who went on to a successful career singing in nightclubs (as well as at gigs like Gore's fund-raisers and his daughter Karenna's 1997 wedding), remembers his amazement that Albert and Pauline signed off on the outing. Gore clearly had "never been in a black atmosphere before," but he reveled in Brown's high-energy show. "He was into it," said Powell.

The concerts were high points for the St. Albans boys, whose social scene would have made *Happy Days* reruns look edgy. They dated girls from other Washington private schools, and the weekend action generally ran from debutante dances to more informal gatherings in someone's finished basement. They would "listen to Johnny Mathis, dance real slow, drink two beers, and make out," as Gore's classmate Mead Miller described the protocol. Although Donna Armistead remained Gore's girlfriend, he pursued other women during the school year, including the daughter of his father's Tennessee rival.

For St. Albans guys, Diane Kefauver was the prize. Tall, redheaded, and beautiful, she boarded at Madeira during the week, but on weekends the basement of her family's Spring Valley home was a favorite site for get-togethers. She was a gracious hostess with a worldliness that only increased the mystique. When she came back from a trip to Britain in 1963, she introduced friends to their first Beatles forty-fives. "Everyone was smitten with Diane," said Geoff Kuhn. That included Al Gore. Kuhn and others saw them as a natural item, children of the Senate and a Tennessee political dynasty in the making. Like Gore, Kefauver had reacted to life in a political family by developing "a self-conscious and persistent desire to please," observed Matt Simchak.

They dated a few times as sophomores, but the relationship quickly devolved into a friendship. It isn't clear who backed away, although Kefauver would tell Kuhn years later that Gore had "an ego as big as a house." She ultimately chose Gore's football teammate Bart Day, whom she dated steadily into their college years. Gore's friendships were often tinged with competition, and in Day, the blond quarterback with the choirboy looks — who was, in fact, a Washington National Cathedral choirboy — Gore had both a friend and a competitor. However serious he was about Donna Armistead, Gore didn't like being elbowed aside. The friendship survived, according to classmates, but was strained for a time.

Gore's choice of college was settled early in his senior year. Vanderbilt or the University of Tennessee might have been the more politic destinations in the short term, but Albert and Pauline knew that an Ivy League education would give their son credentials and contacts that could sustain him for a lifetime, especially one in pursuit of high office. According to his St. Albans transcript, he applied only to Harvard. John Davis, who ran the school's college placement program, said that the overall strength of Gore's record made him competitive for admission regardless of his status as a senator's son. His credentials were good, if not quite stellar: B average, cumulative SAT score of 1355 (625 verbal, 730 math), National Merit Scholarship semifinalist, and a slew of extracurricular activities. Davis added that St. Albans' long relationship with Ivy League schools, and the success of its alumni at Harvard, also weighed in Gore's favor.

He graduated under the vaulted ceilings of the Washington National Cathedral on Saturday, June 5, 1965. The commencement speaker, former headmaster Rev. Albert Hawley Lucas, admonished departing seniors to attend church regularly, limit their excursions to women's colleges to one weekend a month, stay virgins until marriage, and remember that no gentleman ever takes more than two drinks. Lucas's counsel was a last hurrah for a way of life. Signs of the impending storm had been visible for months, from the streets to the pop charts to the political landscape. On March 24, the first Vietnam teach-in was held in Ann Arbor, Michigan. The Saturday before Easter, twelve thousand antiwar protesters marched in Washington. By summer's end President Lyndon Johnson would double the monthly draft call to thirty-five thousand and among the top songs on AM radio, until then the province of the Beach Boys, the Beatles, and Elvis, was Barry McGuire's "Eve of Destruction."

Gore's relations with his St. Albans classmates followed a telling arc as the years passed. When he made it to Congress in 1977, old envy and resentments continued to smolder. Reed Hundt tried to put together a combination class reunion and fund-raiser at a Georgetown rowhouse for Gore's 1984 Senate race, sending out scores of invitations. But "hardly anybody from St. Albans showed up," he said. Still, Gore tried to help at least a couple of school chums get their careers back on track at midlife; for instance, he wrote a letter of recommendation for Mead Miller's unsuccessful application to law school at the University of Alabama-Tuscaloosa. As Gore's celebrity grew, feelings among his old classmates began to thaw. A 1995 reunion dinner at his official Naval Observatory residence was extremely well attended. Suddenly, said Kuhn, Gore found himself with a number of new "old friends."

Gore's most lasting bond from St. Albans was forged in his last hours there, at the graduation dance. Mary Elizabeth Aitcheson was already a familiar face at class parties, having dated several of Gore's classmates. The sixteen-year-old junior from St. Agnes, an Episcopal girls' school in Alexandria, was difficult to forget: she was a willowy beauty with long blond hair, an angelic face, and a charming nickname, Tipper, taken by her mother from a Spanish song that also became a popular 1938 big-band number, "Ti-Pi-Tin," about a young girl who holds off her boyfriend's advances for a respectable period:

> He said he was glad he met her
> And soon he would come and get her
> But she said, "No, no, I cannot go
> Until I know you better."
> Ti-pi-ti-pi-tin
> Ti-pi-tin
> Ti-pi-ti-pi-tan
> Ti-pi-ta.

There may have been more sexually venturesome girls on the school's dating scene ("The thing about Tipper was you didn't go out with her to get some action," said Geoff Kuhn), but few were as enjoyable to be with. She was smart, funny, and loved rock and roll —

"Rolling Stones forever," she wrote, in French, to her pre-Al boyfriend Gordon Beall on a forty-five of "Get Off of My Cloud" — and she even played the drums in an all-girl garage band. Perhaps most alluring, she drove a snappy blue Mustang. Her life plan was to find the right guy and settle down. "Have all the fun you want, Meedie Tweedie," she wrote in the yearbook of Mead Miller, another St. Albans beau, "but someday I'm going to marry you."

At home, however, there was a darkness she struggled to keep at bay. Her mother, Margaret Carlson, was a World War II widow in 1947 when she married Jack Aitcheson, an Alexandria plumbing and heating supply dealer. The family firm, J&H Aitcheson, had been in business since the turn of the century. The marriage collapsed when Tipper was just fourteen months old, and in the 1949 divorce papers she filed, Margaret Carlson Aitcheson accused her husband of beating her. Jack Aitcheson's cross-complaint denied the charges and declared her "lacking in normal maternal instincts," as evidenced by her failure to get out of bed in the morning to feed or clothe her infant daughter. She was, he said, "of a nervous, volatile, flighty and erratic temperament, a person who would seize upon some idea or trend with fanatic fervor, to the exclusion of a common sense participation in everyday life."

Margaret Carlson was mentally ill, suffering from serious bouts of depression for which she would be hospitalized twice. When the marriage broke up, she retreated with Tipper to her parents' Tudor-style house in the Aurora Hills section of Arlington. Margaret's mother, Verda, did most of the cooking and filled the gaps in Tipper's care. Divorce was scandalous enough in 1950s suburban Virginia — Tipper endured the taunts of school kids for having no father — but a psychiatric disorder in the family was beyond mention in polite company. Carlson suffered in silence for years, enlisting her only child to cover up the problem and hiding it even from doctors treating her for other illnesses. Her mother's ordeal eventually inspired Tipper's interest in mental health issues — she has a master's in psychology from Peabody College in Nashville — including her campaign to improve health insurance benefits for those suffering from emotional disorders. And it may well have left her vulnerable to her own struggles with depression.

Tipper was Gordon Beall's date when Gore first spoke to her at the graduation dance. She described the moment years later as "pure animal magnetism," and although they didn't ditch their companions for the evening, Gore called Tipper the next day to invite her to another postgraduation party. "I'll never forget it," she wrote in 1996. "We put on a record and danced and danced. It was just like everyone else melted away. And that was it. We've been together ever since."

It actually took a bit longer than that for others to melt away. Donna Armistead said that she and Gore didn't mutually agree to part until the middle of Gore's freshman year at Harvard, and that Gore spent time with other Tennessee women well into his sophomore year, after Tipper had joined him in Boston. While she was honeymooning in a cabin on the Cumberland River near Carthage in December 1966, Armistead says she saw Gore with a local girl in a neighboring cabin for two nights running.

Tipper continued to see Gordon Beall during the summer of 1965, although she made it clear that she was Al Gore's girl. She even asked Beall to re-create her favorite date with Gore — dinner and an evening at the theater. "Tipper told me Al did this, and wouldn't it be nice if I did it too," recalled Beall, now a professional photographer. "So like the stupid schmuck that I was, I took her to this French restaurant on Pennsylvania Avenue where we had chateaubriand for two and then on to the theater."

Someone else less than thrilled by Al's new love was Pauline Gore. She wanted to protect her son from the dangers of becoming too serious too soon — at least with respect to romance. And she strongly implied to friends that he could do better than the cute but uncredentialed girl from across the river. "Pauline thought Little Albert should spread his wings and go up there to Harvard and go out with all those sophisticated women, check out what they're like up there," said Fred Graham. His mother's opposition landed Gore "in crisis" with her, according to another close family friend.

But for once Al Gore decided to depart from the script crafted by his parents. Tipper was his one extravagance, his break from the cautious mold of a senator's son. The daughter of a family broken by divorce and the son of one frayed by political ambition saw that there was a future they could make together. He was the rock she had lacked, and she was his link to a wider emotional world he found difficult to inhabit. "With Tipper, you feel held emotionally," said

Lance Laurence, a University of Tennessee clinical psychologist who got to know the couple when he worked with them on family policy issues in the 1980s. "I am absolutely certain that's what some of the substance of their connection is. For Al, I think it was important for him to find someone he could feel held with." He would go to Harvard, but Mary Elizabeth Aitcheson would come to Boston too.

◆ 4 ◆

"Gore, Albert A."

JOHN TYSON wasn't sure what to make of the clunky white kid with the sturdy handshake and the strange accent standing in the doorway to his room at Harvard's Lionel Hall. A heavily re-cruited high school football star from Montclair, New Jersey, Tyson was the son of a West Indian immigrant father and an African Ameri-can mother who had grown up wary of white southerners while watching the civil rights movement unfold on television. When he heard the slight southern accent, he assumed it belonged to someone dumb, evil, or both. Gore explained that he was from Mower B, the residence hall next door to Lionel in the northwest corner of Harvard Yard, and that he was running for a seat on the freshman council. Whatever issues animated freshman politics in September 1965, Tyson, now an international business consultant in Washington, has long since forgotten them. What he does remember is the imposing polish of Gore's brief talk — like a rookie pitcher unexpectedly popping the catcher's mitt with his fastball on the first day of spring training. When he left, Tyson's roommate, Glenn Price, also a candidate for the council, was ready to concede. "This is not fair," Tyson remembers Price complaining. "How am I going to beat this guy?" He didn't, and Tyson found himself surprisingly intrigued by the precocious student campaigner. Within weeks they were good friends and, the following year, roommates.

From the first, Tyson had little doubt about where Gore was headed in life, and Harvard only reinforced that sense of destiny. With its powerful alumni and faculty perpetually shuttling between classroom and cabinet room, the school radiated a sense of grand and inevitable succession. "Yale might make its little contribution to the foreign service; Princeton, to Wall Street and the oak-paneled law firms. But Harvard governed the country," wrote Roger Rosenblatt, a resident tutor at Dunster House when Gore lived there as an upperclassman. Gore made critical connections in Cambridge — cultivating mentors whose advice still sustains him, and gaining his first serious exposure to the issues that have shaped his identity as a politician: arms control and global warming.

Like other campuses in the late sixties, Harvard was unraveled by student protest, but Gore was invisible in these politics of upheaval. "He always wanted to blend in as one of the guys in a wild period but was never quite all the way there," said Jeff Howard, a friend of Tyson's who headed the school's Association of African and Afro-American Students and who got to know Gore. "Sort of not all the way in with the sixties. There was something else going on with Al." He was not among the protesters who occupied University Hall in the spring of 1969, demanding, among other things, abolition of the ROTC program. Nor was Gore one of the undergraduate council members who drafted a letter to Lyndon Johnson decrying the war or who later met with Secretary of State Dean Rusk.

In a world where the establishment was held in escalating scorn, Gore readied himself to join it, taking quiet and methodical steps toward following his father into public office. The government major spent part of the break between his junior and senior years in 1968 steeping himself in the background of the state he intended to one day represent, studying Tennessee history at Memphis State University. That same summer at the Democratic National Convention in Chicago, while demonstrators and police battled in Grant Park, Gore was inside the hall with his father, helping him draft a speech. On April 4, 1969, one week before the taking of University Hall, Gore borrowed $45,224 from the Cookeville Production Credit Association, a Tennessee farm cooperative. He used the money to buy twenty acres of pastureland his father owned along Highway 25 just outside of Carthage. It's not clear what collateral — aside from his last name — a twenty-one-year-old college senior could offer to qualify for a loan of that size. But its purpose would become plain later — to lay down business roots as a precursor to a political career.

Though Gore kept his distance from the political turbulence on campus, it didn't stop him from seeking out a mentor who was immersed in it. His first semester included a seminar taught by one of the school's most charismatic and influential left-wing dissidents. Martin Peretz's classes were becoming a popular way station for ambitious undergraduates bound for careers in journalism, politics, or law. "Selected Problems of an Advanced Industrial Society" was a loosely structured mix of sociology, political science, and psychology, with readings that ran from Tocqueville to Marx and Freud. Enrollment required an interview with Peretz, who was surprised, and impressed, when Gore appeared at his Kirkland House office wearing a jacket and tie, a formality rapidly disappearing on campus. There was a dignity in Gore's appearance, he thought, the manner of a gentleman at a time when there weren't many around. He asked Gore whether he was related to the senator from Tennessee. Gore smiled, a bit sheepishly, but gave him no encouragement to talk about it.

The class was packed with rhetorically flashy freshmen, but Gore, perhaps reluctant to say anything that might undermine or damage his father, usually avoided staking out provocative positions. Peretz saw in Gore some of the same aversion to dogma and doctrine that would lead to his own estrangement from the left before the end of the antiwar movement. "He wasn't psychologically prepared for reckless politics," Peretz said. "The overheated politics of ideological debate was just alien to his experience." In Peretz, Gore also found a mentor with money. His 1967 marriage to Anne Labouisse Farnsworth, an heiress to the Singer sewing machine fortune, helped him buy *The New Republic* from Gilbert Harrison in 1974. Peretz re-created the magazine, a venerable voice of the liberal consensus, in the image of his own evolving politics, sending it on a mission to puncture old left-wing hypocrisies and pieties. Gore's cerebral liberal centrism won him constant plaudits from his teacher, who endorsed his 1988 presidential candidacy on the cover. Throughout Gore's vice presidency, Peretz has remained an enthusiastic, even slavish, supporter with little tolerance for unflattering commentary about his former student.

Socially, Gore's college years were considerably less stifling than his St. Albans period. Free for the first time from the confines of the Washington-Carthage corridor that had shaped his life, he stretched, if only a bit. He drove a motorcycle he had bought from his cousin Jamie back to Cambridge in a driving rain after freshman Christmas break, and he enjoyed offering unsuspecting dorm mates white-knuckled late-night rides along Memorial Drive. He forged close relationships with a collection of diverse and forceful personalities chasing vastly different ambitions. Tommy Lee Jones, a self-consciously theatrical West Texan ("always on," said Tyson), landed in Gore's three-man Mower B suite (St. Albans friend Bart Day was the third) on a football scholarship, but by the end of freshman year he was appearing in stage productions at the Loeb Drama Center. Mike Kapetan was a 6 foot 7 inch kid from blue-collar suburban Detroit who wanted to sculpt, and by 1993 he was sculptor-in-residence at Washington National Cathedral. Tyson, an All-Ivy defensive back with a passion for African culture, quit football as a senior because he didn't want to be "a hired gladiator" for his Harvard masters and emigrated to Kenya after graduation to develop several successful businesses. Bob Somerby, a basketball player from Winchester, Massachusetts, had a razor wit and timing to match that he put to use as both a teacher and later a stand-up comic. Gore also bonded with J. G. Landau, a brassy, kinetic baseball player from Long Island who beat him regularly at pool, ping-pong, and poker.

Not that lack of success ever stanched Gore's competitive drive, which, if anything, only deepened at Harvard. He made the freshman basketball team and rarely played but worked on his game incessantly. Tyson remembered Gore's habit of challenging him "out of the blue" to push-ups, a vestige of the boyhood regimen imposed by Albert. He "wanted to challenge you or himself, intellectually or physically. He was always, 'I bet I can beat you at the last thing you did.'" That included chugging beer, over which Tyson held dominion among freshmen on the Yard. Late one night, alone in front of Mower B, the two faced off with sixteen-ounce cans. The outcome has always been in dispute. "We both came down [with our cans] pretty much at the same time," Tyson said.

By the end of freshman year, Gore, Tyson, and their circle decided to apply for space together in one of Harvard's nine "houses" for upperclassmen. They ended up in Dunster, the most isolated of the school's houses, sitting at the fringe of campus on the Charles River just below the Weeks Memorial Bridge. "Turn left at Leverett [House] and don't give up hope," went the frequently cited directions on how to reach the remote Dunster.

Today Gore depicts his Harvard years as filled with anxiety over the Vietnam War and the draft. "A dark mood of uncertainty from that

tragic conflict clouded every single day we were there," he told graduates in a 1994 Commencement Day speech. But for at least his first two
years in Cambridge, the clouds seemed few. He went to class and hung
out with friends in Dunster's basement rec room, where he discovered
Star Trek, the space saga that became one of his favorite TV shows.
Gore was naturally drawn to the twenty-third-century Trek universe,
where technology had turned Earth into a utopia and propelled the
human race to the far reaches of the galaxy. He was transfixed by another popular science fiction work of the period, Stanley Kubrick's
2001: A Space Odyssey. "It was epic grandeur. God, science, technology, HAL," said Mike Kapetan, who saw it with him during the 1968
spring break in Washington. For weeks afterward "he'd say, 'Remember that opening sequence with all those sunrises? There were seven
of them!'"

In the fall of 1966, the beginning of his sophomore year, Tipper
Aitcheson settled in at Garland Junior College, a short ride on the
subway from Harvard Square. Her framed photo sat on Gore's desk
throughout his freshman year as she finished at St. Agnes, and despite
Pauline's misgivings, he remained resolute about keeping her in his
life. Gore had brought her to the farm for the first time over his freshman Christmas break, and Tipper went all out to impress Gore's parents. "She was dressed fit to kill," Albert said of the evening she arrived. "I was even more struck by her beauty the next morning. She
came to breakfast with every eyelash in place. She was dressed for an
evening ball." The debut must not have been an easy one for Tipper,
still just seventeen and under the collective scrutiny of the formidable
matriarchs in Gore's life — Pauline, Nancy, Edna Armistead. Donna
still lurked in the background as well, at church and parties. Some of
the Elmwood crowd remember Tipper as nervous and quite shy. "She
was a mouse," said one Gore friend, who recalled that she had to be
coaxed out of the car when he brought her to the store to meet Edna.
But the couple continued to make their own plans. Tipper came to
Boston — with her grandmother Verda as chaperone — over Harvard's
Spring Weekend in April 1966, staying at the Copley Plaza while Gore
took her to see the Temptations and to check out schools for the following year. That summer there was no toiling in the fields back on
the farm. Gore got his own apartment in Arlington, closer to Tipper
and the offices of a tour guide service where he worked.

Gore was ecstatic when she arrived (the top-forty hit "Please Come

to Boston" later became a sentimental favorite), and they became inseparable. Dunster mates were likely to find them throwing a Frisbee
along the Charles or on double dates with Somerby and his girlfriend,
often to the art cinemas in Boston. Parietals were still in force — no
women were allowed in rooms after 11:00 P.M., a rule honored more
in the breach, even by the hypercautious Gore, who encountered
Rosenblatt as he escorted Tipper out of Dunster early one morning. "I
saw the terror in his Boy Scout eyes, which might have read: 'There
goes the presidency,'" wrote Rosenblatt, who let the infraction slide.

There were occasions when his Dunster crew pried him away. In
October 1966 Gore was featured in a country music and comedy act
that they took on the road to a Wellesley coffeehouse. The first and
last public appearance of Tommy Lee Jones and the Ben Hill County
Boys had Somerby on the autoharp and Jones and Roger Mannell, another Dunster friend, on vocals. Gore was featured as an Ivy League
Minnie Pearl, doing what Kapetan called "this rube shtick, telling
stories about friends and acquaintances in Carthage." He bought an
oversized, three-piece tweed suit from a secondhand store and transformed himself into Dr. Albert A. Gore, an old-style elixir salesman
who, according to a handbill composed by Somerby, was "the highly
respected professor of animal husbandry and the curative sciences."
Gore told the same corny Tennessee stories he liked to tell offstage —
about the best way to hypnotize chickens or his father's prize bull that
fathered a thousand calves but never had sex. His delivery endeared
him to his friends, said Tyson, especially the infectious cackle. "He'd
start laughing and everybody would start laughing. So you're laughing
at him, and he's still trying to get out the rest of the story."

One place where Gore's attention lagged was the classroom. According
to his Harvard College transcript, he was an unfocused and mediocre
student in his first two years, never earning more than a B-plus (in the
required freshman composition course) and getting mostly Cs. When
he received a D in a natural sciences survey course called "Man's Place
in Nature," Somerby said he concluded that having flunked evolution,
his friend was clearly headed for a big career in Tennessee politics.

Politics was in his blood, but like many students beginning their
college careers, Gore experimented. He told friends he was interested
in a writing career and would major in English to prepare himself, but

his interest waned quickly. In a freshman survey of great books, he found himself flummoxed by Chaucer, and after sophomore courses in Russian literature and American poets, Gore began looking for another academic specialty.

Meanwhile, he used his father's contacts in 1967 to land a summer job as a copy boy at the *New York Times*. He shared a West Side apartment with friends and went to work at the paper's West Forty-third Street offices. But there was no writing or news gathering involved. The official job title in the union contract was actually "office boy." He spent his days retrieving the ten-part "books" (special paper comprising nine carbons and an original) from reporters at their typewriters and hustling them up to the metropolitan desk, where he broke the copies up and routed them to the appropriate editors. "He looked like a tree even then," said reporter John Kifner, who was asked by a friend in New York Democratic politics to look out for the husky, stolid kid from Harvard. Gore enjoyed his summer in New York, and when Tipper visited, they stepped out for their favorite evening — dinner followed by theater. One night he took her to the Spindletop, a popular theater district steakhouse, and then the musical *The Fantasticks*.

When Gore returned to Cambridge in the fall of 1967 as a junior, his moribund academic career suddenly gained new energy and direction, much of it owing to Richard Neustadt's course on the American presidency. Neustadt was a Washington insider as well as an academic, an adviser to Truman and Kennedy who filled his classes with vivid case studies of modern presidential decisionmaking — Truman and MacArthur, Eisenhower and Little Rock. His groundbreaking book *Presidential Power* challenged scholars to revise the way they studied occupants of the Oval Office. Instead of viewing a president as a commander, and those around him as pure instruments of the orders he issued, Neustadt regarded the chief executive as a persuader and educator, using the power of personal prestige and reputation to govern.

His twice-weekly lectures in Government 154 required some patience. A chain-smoker, Neustadt punctuated his talks with long, theatrical pauses to light up, exhaling, *The Crimson Confidential Guide* noted, "apparently with smoke still stored from the last lecture." On the days he brought his pipe, he stopped as many as forty times. But those who tolerated the exasperating technique usually felt rewarded. Even to a senator's son, the material seemed fresh and challenging. He soon switched his major to government. Gore was also inspired by his section instructor for 154, Graham Allison, who organized role-playing exercises around decisionmaking in the Cuban Missile Crisis. His father had long been preoccupied with national security issues, and he was likewise "very interested in nuclear questions," said Allison, who would go on to become dean of the John F. Kennedy School of Government at Harvard and serve as an assistant secretary of defense in the Clinton administration. Gore "retained a vivid sense of nuclear danger," added Allison, who also discerned "a clear thread" from the classroom to Gore's work on arms control in the early 1980s to his efforts as vice president to secure the former Soviet Union's arsenal.

The English student who plodded through Chaucer and pulled a string of Cs started getting As and Bs, and his academic program began to look more like a preparation for public life. The next semester he aced a course in how to prepare and deliver a speech. Neustadt, who was "always looking for people worth nudging along toward elective politics," saw one in what he called the "keen and serious" young man who asked sharp questions in class. And Gore found another mentor, friend, and family surrogate. He became a regular guest at the carriage house on Traill Street where Neustadt and his wife Bertha served in loco parentis for many students over the years, feeding them dinner followed by an evening of the official Neustadt family entertainment, charades. Gore also struck up a friendship with their son Rick, another member of the class of 1969, who lived at Leverett House. Gore's visits included two Thanksgiving dinners, and if he was disheartened about being separated from his family on the holiday, it wasn't apparent to Neustadt. He was struck by the sense of fun he saw in Gore on those two holiday afternoons — playful, joyful, full of courtly charm for his wife, and surprisingly versatile at charades. It was a side he had never seen before — and hasn't seen since.

Under Neustadt's tutelage, Gore wrote a senior thesis that married his renewed fascination with politics to his interest in journalism. The resulting ninety-nine-page work, "The Impact of Television on the Conduct of the Presidency, 1947–1969," reflects early stirrings of his interest in new technology and its social consequences. Gore concluded that the president's ability to dominate television news coverage gave him a powerful new tool of communication and policymaking but left the less visible legislative branch at a serious disadvantage. As a young member of the House a decade later, he became a leader in the effort to open congressional proceedings to radio and television coverage.

The thesis is also a strangely prescient work, one that at least tacitly anticipates his own troubles with television. Using the evolution of the presidential press conference as a case study, Gore explores the medium's hunger for informality, and its unforgiving nature toward those unable to master its demands. He writes with some sympathy about Lyndon Johnson, who suffered in comparison to the charismatic John Kennedy. Like Gore, Johnson was widely derided by opinion-makers as stiff and artificial. "Johnson seemed unmistakably reluctant to face the cameras," Gore said. "They seemed to intimidate him from being himself." An unnamed Johnson aide told Gore that LBJ's problem might have been a fear of comparison with Kennedy's witty and relaxed performances at press conferences. Johnson tried to find other ways to communicate with reporters, but Gore said it was too late. "Unfortunately," he wrote, "the process had gone too far to be stopped."

Gore's access to A-list Washington sources bolstered his research appreciably. In addition to Bill Moyers, his interviewees included Johnson aide Jack Valenti, *New York Times* columnist James Reston, historian Arthur Schlesinger Jr., and several top network news executives. Neustadt admired the thesis but as Gore's adviser had no hand in grading it. His colleagues evidently didn't share his enthusiasm. Gore graduated a couple of levels below top honors in June 1969, earning a cum laude with his bachelor's degree. Senator Gore, however, was so taken with his son's work that he sent a copy of the thesis to Richard Nixon's White House communications director, Herb Klein.

At a graduation party hosted by Neustadt, Albert and Pauline Gore thanked him for "turning on" their son — reorienting him toward a political career. "They were very appreciative. I take it they never believed in Chaucer," Neustadt said, although he remains somewhat skeptical of his actual influence. "I think 'turning on' was coming to terms with his father's profession, a required coming to terms, getting over something, growing out of something," Neustadt said.

It was a pattern Gore repeated over the years, distancing himself from the call of his father's legacy, then returning. At Harvard he was, as he acknowledged later in *Earth in the Balance,* "at that awkward stage of life when the challenge of discovering and defining one's 'identity' is the primary task." The search stimulated a long-term interest in psychology, and he took a course taught by Erik Erikson that explored the dynamics of life's critical stages. Those around him sensed the struggle to find his own way. "I think he might have had a somewhat more complicated time distancing himself from the father figure," said Mike Kapetan. Another who observed Gore's search for identity was Erich Segal, an Oxford classics professor and Guggenheim Fellow who was spending his 1968 sabbatical at Dunster House. Segal was best known at the time for writing the screenplay for the Beatles' *Yellow Submarine* animated feature, and Gore, a huge Beatles fan, struck up a friendship with him. Segal began working on another script while in residence at Dunster, one that eventually became *Love Story,* and he saw in Gore some of the elements for Oliver Barrett IV, the blue-blooded Harvard hockey player who falls for Jennifer Cavilleri, the smart-aleck Radcliffe musician.

Segal sketched Barrett as an amalgam of Tommy Lee Jones — the tough guy with the poet's soul, who performed Shakespeare when he wasn't playing football — and Gore, who, Segal recalled, was "always under pressure to follow in his father's footsteps and that was the conflict, to keep up the family tradition." Gore never explicitly presented his father in this light, Segal said, but made it "inferentially clear" that he carried the weight of great expectations. "He was nervous. He was sensitive to being Albert Gore Jr."

The literary footnote became an embarrassment to Gore three decades later when he suggested to reporters traveling with him on Air Force Two that he and his wife were models for the young lovers. Once again, as with the Internet, an interesting story wasn't sufficient. Being merely part of the inspiration for Oliver wasn't enough; he needed to be all of it. Segal was forced several days later to concede that Gore was only half right about Oliver and completely wrong about Jenny. "I did not draw a thing from Tipper," he said. "I knew her only as Al's date."

Segal may have immortalized Gore in a best-seller — sort of — but other scholars made more significant contributions to the shape and direction of his political future. Roger Revelle was a scientist of sprawling intellect and presence — 6 feet 4 inches with size 15 feet that sometimes caused him to trip over himself. But he moved gracefully between the worlds of science and public policy and impressed on Gore the importance of a close working relationship between those who push back the boundaries of knowledge and those who make the laws. Gore sees himself today as a voice for scientific reason in the political world, and one early inspiration was Revelle. Neither scientists nor politicians are held in high regard by society, Revelle said, "yet between them they hold in their hands the future of mankind."

As a young scientist at the Scripps Oceanographic Institution in the early 1930s, he studied mud samples collected from the sea floor, work that sparked a lifelong curiosity about the carbon dioxide content of the oceans and a hunch that the earth might be growing warmer. In 1957 Revelle and another researcher, Charles David Keeling, began annual measurements of atmospheric carbon dioxide from the top of the Mauna Loa volcano in Hawaii. By the second year the data showed the beginnings of the greenhouse effect: escalating levels of carbon dioxide trapping the sun's heat, thereby raising planetary temperatures. By 1975 Revelle and Keeling's numbers suggested that atmospheric carbon dioxide had increased by 5 percent in twenty years, one-third of it probably caused by the clearing of forests (a major consumer of carbon dioxide) for timber and agriculture.

Revelle, founding director of Harvard's Center for Population Studies, discussed the first eight years of his data in a course Gore took as a senior. It was the genesis of what has become Gore's signature issue as a public figure. Revelle's work, he wrote later, "taught me that nature is not immune to our presence, and that we could actually change the makeup of the entire earth's atmosphere in a fundamental way." Twelve years later Revelle was the lead witness at one of the first congressional hearings on global warming, chaired by Gore.

As Gore began his junior year in the fall of 1967, the war's shadow lengthened. The Johnson administration announced an end to most graduate school deferments effective the following spring, a seismic event for thousands of young men who had counted on three or four years in the snug harbor of a Ph.D. program to help them wait out the end of their draft eligibility at age twenty-six. Prior to that fall, students at Harvard and other elite schools decried the inequities of a draft that claimed the poor and disadvantaged and spared the well-off. When the rules changed, the spirit of solidarity ebbed.

"In September the new climate was obvious," wrote Steven Kelman, a Harvard antiwar activist in the Gore era. "A peaceful campus, only marginally concerned with Vietnam, suddenly became desperate. We felt boxed in. We were like the man about to go into the gas chamber, with no way out and walls slowly but inexorably closing around us." Kelman, now a professor at the John F. Kennedy School of Government, said the fear led to a "new Cotton Matherhood of burning frenzy" aimed at anyone supporting the war. Students for a Democratic Society (SDS) and other activist groups suddenly had an opportunity to broaden their base with an infusion of students newly radicalized by the change in their draft prospects.

Exit strategies for the draft started to dominate dining hall conversations. Exempted academic programs like divinity school and protected professions such as teaching enjoyed unprecedented surges in popularity. Sometimes stretching the rules meant stretching bodies. *Harvard Crimson* editor James Fallows, a year ahead of Gore, starved himself below the 120-pound cutoff and told an army physician that he had contemplated suicide. Medical students helped undergrads search for disqualifying conditions that happened to have been overlooked during years of robust health, like migraine headaches and mildly dislocated shoulders.

The war at home began to escalate as protests grew in number and vehemence. In October hundreds of young men burned their draft cards or turned them in to the Justice Department, prompting Selective Service director, Lewis Hershey, to retaliate by directing that local draft boards immediately reclassify to 1-A anyone who destroyed or returned a card. Thousands of demonstrators marched on the Pentagon, and 119 were arrested for blocking entrance to the Oakland Army Induction Center. At Harvard SDS-organized protesters confined a recruiter for Dow, the manufacturer of napalm, at Mallinckrodt Hall for five hours, an action that eventually landed 70 students on probation.

A few months earlier, in the summer of 1967, just before the antiwar movement at Harvard intensified, military service was a part of Al Gore's plans. Jamie Gore recalls a series of conversations with his cousin, including one during his stint as a *Times* copy boy just before his junior year, in which it sounded like a sure thing. "Never, ever did he indicate to me that he wasn't going to go in," Gore said. "I think Al always wanted to go into the army. Not as a career, but for a brief interlude." Gore had no great passion for soldiering, but neither was it in his nature to buck the system. There were also family and regional traditions in place. Albert Gore had waived his congressional immunity to join the army during World War II, turning down an officer's commission to serve as a private, like most of his fellow Tennesseans. In a place called the Volunteer State, it was simply expected.

But as Gore neared graduation, he found himself caught between two nearly irresistible forces: the newly charged moral and political climate at Harvard and a deep sense of obligation to protect his father, whose antiwar position was imperiling his political future in Tennessee. Each wrenched at his conscience. In 1968 he became chairman of Tennessee Youth for McCarthy — Martin Peretz was a major contributor to the antiwar insurgent who helped push Lyndon Johnson into retirement — although Democrats in the state don't remember much about what he actually did. Still, he was in many respects the paradigmatic youthful McCarthy worker, as described in a campaign memoir by speechwriter Jeremy Larner: "Politically they were inclined to some romanticization of the NLF, Ché Guevara and Malcolm X. But whether they came with beard to shave or not, these were kids who reacted against the violent anti-Americanism of the New Left, whom they far outnumbered. Though they hated the war and the draft, they still believed that America could be beautiful — if it would live up to its own principles. American optimists at heart, immune in the long run to ideology, they were terribly grateful to have the chance to do something real."

On election night 1968, Gore stayed up until dawn with Bob Somerby watching the returns, and, in Somerby's words, "praying for Hubert Humphrey," even though he'd been discredited by his refusal to break with Johnson on the war. More ominous than Humphrey's overall total were his numbers in Tennessee, where he drew just 28 percent of the vote, running behind George Wallace and Richard Nixon. Gore's liberal father would clearly be an endangered species in his 1970 reelection campaign. A son taking a slide from the draft could only weaken his chances. As Gore wrestled with his dilemma, some old acquaintances on campus, accustomed to a more arrogant, cocksure Gore, were actually encouraged by the signs of indecision. "He was a little adrift," said Phil Rosenbaum, a St. Albans classmate who lived in Leverett House. "I liked that."

Gore claimed to be repelled by the dogma of New Left groups like SDS, but some of his letters home seemed influenced by their polemics. "We do have inveterate antipathy for communism — or paranoia, as I like to put it," he wrote to his father. "My own belief is that this form of psychological ailment — in this case a national madness — leads the victim to actually create the thing which is feared most. It strikes me that this is precisely what the U.S. has been doing. Creating — and if not creating, energetically supporting — fascist, totalitarian regimes in the name of fighting totalitarianism. Greece, South Vietnam, a good deal of Latin America. For me, the best example of all is the U.S. Army."

Gore's draft story is a complicated piece of family business, with cross-currents of competing and conflicting explanations offered by Gore and others as the tale has been told and retold over the years. He has said that his motivation for enlistment was ethical: that evading or manipulating the draft by pulling strings available to him as a senator's son was inherently unfair to less-connected friends in Tennessee. "I came from a small town where I knew most of my contemporaries," Gore explained in 1986, stretching his summers and holidays on the farm to cover his entire youth. "I knew how the quota system worked, and I realized that if I decided not to go and figured out some way to get out of it, that would mean somebody else from my hometown would go instead of me. I thought about that a lot. I felt that would outweigh my own personal calculation of the rights and wrongs about the country's policy." His father's predicament, he said, was secondary, a matter he sometimes expressed in coldly clinical terms. "It was not the causative factor in my decision," he said, "but it made it easier to analyze the matter and reach the correct decision."

But solicitude for his "hometown" friends, while laudable, didn't necessarily reflect reality. At least a couple of his closest pals were finding their own exits from the draft. Goat Thompson, who joined the Tennessee National Guard, even allowed that few of Gore's friends and neighbors would have blamed him for trying to sidestep service. "I wouldn't think they would have thought that harshly against him," he said. Even in the patriotic Cumberland Hills, deep misgivings about the war were in plain view by 1969. A July 31 editorial in the *Carthage Courier* mourned a local boy, Shannon Wills, a nineteen-year-old Marine killed by shrapnel two weeks earlier in Quang Nam Province. "His death could be accepted with more grace if our country were fighting for its life, or if we were threatened with invasion, or if we were threatened with extinction as we were in World War Two," the *Courier* wrote. "The question all of us ask, and for which we have found no answer is, why?"

His Harvard friends remember Gore's ethical concerns, but they also recall a series of explicit signals from his parents about what needed to be done. "I wouldn't say it was necessarily pressure," said Tyson, "but they certainly wanted him to know that his father was running for reelection. That's all they had to say." Privately, others recall Gore acknowledging that family politics gave him no choice in the matter. "I recall very specifically a conversation in April 1969 when we were having a discussion about how the decision was reached," said a close Harvard friend. "It's fair to say that he said if he had my parents, he would have made a different decision. He was committed to his father's situation."

Albert and Pauline Gore always maintained that they were prepared to accept whatever decision their son made and insisted that he leave politics out of the equation. "We bore down on it over and over and over that he must not let that have any effect on what he did," said Pauline. Again, the evidence is not black and white, but shades of gray. While Albert Gore delighted in the idea of his son one day becoming president, it was Pauline who strove to ensure that nothing placed that vision at risk. Had Al Gore elected to avoid service, his father would probably have accepted the decision, despite its political consequences for him — even admired it as a matter of conscience. "Those who know the senator suspect that he would not have minded at all running a campaign with a son who refused to go to Vietnam," David Halberstam wrote after the 1970 campaign. Charles Fontenay remembers Pauline telling him that the senator even offered to pull the strings that would have eased their boy out of the draft. "A man will do things for his son," said Fontenay. Pauline Gore may not have been so supportive of a choice to opt out. It was Pauline, not Albert, who oversaw the family political network — such as it was — and who kept her ear to the ground for rumblings of trouble. One sounding she certainly picked up was the anxiety among Gore operatives in Tennessee about the possibility that young Al might try to evade service. "There was a lot of concern," said Ted Brown, a former legislative and campaign aide to the elder Gore. She also wanted nothing to jeopardize the entry of a second Gore generation into politics. Although it has been widely reported over the years that Pauline Gore offered to pack off to Canada with her son if he chose to flee the country, an old Harvard friend rolled his eyes at the notion. The family's political circumstances dictated only one option. He said the message Gore got from his mother was, in essence, a rhetorical "Guess what you're going to do?"

Other influential voices in Gore's life, also trying to safeguard what they saw as a promising future in politics, told him that a shaky draft record would put him at a serious disadvantage in Tennessee. "Somewhere down the line, you'll be in politics yourself," Steve Armistead told him. "You don't have much choice." Neustadt, speaking for the "Private Ryan" generation, agreed that doing what the boys in Tennessee were asked to do was the right thing. He also told Gore that "if he ever wanted to go into politics, [military service] would stand him in very good stead, both because of what he would learn about people and because of the legitimacy it would convey."

By the spring of 1969, Gore's decision appeared locked in place, anchored by conviction, self-sacrificial loyalty, and political calculation. It was a painfully isolating choice, nevertheless, as friends at Harvard, and some in Tennessee, opted out. Perhaps galling as well, for a young man eager to strut into the world on his own terms. Faced with his first critical adult decision of conscience, Gore found himself making it not wholly as his own man, but as a senator's son.

The remaining piece of unfinished business was deciding how he would serve. He was back in Washington on spring break, mulling his future at Max's, a bar near the Key Bridge in Georgetown. Tipper was with him, and they were joined by a man a few years Gore's senior, distantly related to his mother, from an old, socially prominent Washington family. He was also an army veteran, and Gore had grown friendly with him in the last few years. In time he would also become a financial benefactor, contributing a large sum of money to the Democratic Party and the 1996 Clinton-Gore campaign. For the moment, though, he was another in young Al Gore's burgeoning network of mentors and advisers.

Gore said he was going to be in town for the next couple of days and needed to talk. "I have a decision to make," he said, according to his drinking companion. Let's talk now, his friend replied. But Gore insisted on doing it later, at the man's Northwest Washington home, as if the matter were too sensitive for discussion in a public place.

The question on the table that night, and in a series of conversations over the next several weeks, concerned the senator. Joining the military, in Gore's estimation, was not enough to protect his father. He wanted to ensure that the kind of service he chose did not inadvertently expose him to political harm. Should he enlist, or wait for the draft to come his way after graduation? Would officer candidates' school carry too heavy a whiff of elitism for Tennessee voters?

His friend pointed out that enlistment would decrease his chances of seeing combat. "I can survive anything," Gore said, reiterating his principal concern. "How do I do this without hurting my dad? I don't want to be the issue." His friend, who knew something of military culture, was less concerned about Albert's well-being than that of his son. Military commanders harbored considerable hostility toward the congressional doves, and he worried that Gore might be vulnerable to bureaucratic harassment or other forms of "ratfucking." He said he wanted to discuss Gore's options with someone he knew socially, someone knowledgeable about the possibilities and pitfalls of military service for a VIP's son. Gore consented, although he never asked who his adviser planned to consult. He was ready to set aside, for the moment, his distaste for using his privileged position to smooth his way in the world.

His friend's contact was General William Westmoreland, the U.S. Army chief of staff. He met twice that spring with the former commander of U.S. forces in South Vietnam, the first time on the porch of his home in Fort Myers, Virginia. Westmoreland knew Albert and Pauline Gore from his days as a commander at Fort Campbell, Kentucky, near the Tennessee border. But Gore's friend trod lightly in the first session, asking the general what would happen to the hypothetical son of an antiwar senator who joined the army. Technically nothing, Westmoreland replied. Realistically, he said, there could be problems.

Realizing that the object of this discussion could be only one of a tiny handful of young men, Westmoreland pressed his visitor for a name. Gore's friend begged off, saying he first had to check with the person in question. "I'm dealing with someone, and I have to use your name," he told Gore over the phone. Gore, who didn't learn until several months later that the person involved was Westmoreland, was leery of anything that smacked of political influence. He wanted no favors, he insisted. His friend assured him that none were being sought.

At the second meeting with Westmoreland, Gore's ally finally named names and expressed concern about his vulnerability to hazing or other mistreatment. Westmoreland asked what Gore wanted to do if he joined. His friend said that he was interested in journalism, and that he would most likely apply for that occupational specialty. Westmoreland made no promises and guaranteed no special treatment. But he left Gore's friend with one vague assurance: "I believe he will be watched," he said. "He will be cared for."

Westmoreland, now eighty-five and living in Charleston, South Carolina, said he has only sketchy memories of a discussion with someone who represented Gore's interests. "I do recall some sort of meeting and giving some advice," he said. But he insisted that he was "not a party" to Gore's assignment as an army journalist. As for Gore's parents, their son's friend said they were aware of his discussions with Westmoreland but never took an active part. Pauline, though, was "keenly interested in how it would go."

On June 17, 1969, five days after he graduated from Harvard, Tennessee Draft Board 87 in Carthage stripped Gore of his II-S student deferment and reclassified him 1-A.

Albert and Pauline Gore describe their son as still undecided after graduation, although the evidence suggests that the only real question was whether to enlist or to wait for the draft to take its course. By their account, the three of them sat in the living room of their Tennessee farm home shortly after graduation and discussed, inconclusively, what other young men were doing to avoid the draft and what legal obligations Gore faced. The talk continued later that day on a long father-and-son walk beside the Caney Fork. Albert Gore said he made no effort to steer his son's decision but only tried "to assist him as best I could in analyzing the situation." Gore took another walk by himself after dinner. When he returned, Pauline recalled, he said: "I'll go. I won't wait for the draft. I'll volunteer tomorrow." Then he paused for a second, she said, and added, "But I may be the only one from Harvard who will."

It was actually several weeks before Gore volunteered. Before enlisting, he embarked on a kind of farewell tour. The itinerary included Tyson, Landau, and Peretz, and he took the occasion to explain that his decision had a moral, not political basis. "He wanted to touch base with all his soulmates before he went ahead," said Tyson. "He really wanted us to know where he was coming from, that this was about him, and not what the scenario suggested." He and Tipper stayed with the Peretzes at Truro on Cape Cod over the weekend of July 19. "He was looking for diversion," his teacher said. There was no shortage: he swam, rode horses with Anne Peretz, and was riveted to television coverage of the first manned moon landing. At a Sunday evening dinner party hosted by the Peretzes, Gore and Tipper joined Irving Howe, Lionel Trilling, and the wives of Kennedy advisers Richard Goodwin and Arthur Schlesinger Jr. in a lively discussion of events on Chappaquiddick Island near Martha's Vineyard, where a young woman had drowned in a car driven by Ted Kennedy after it rolled off a wooden bridge.

He ended up at Tyson's Montclair home in early August. His old roommate, headed to Harvard Divinity School and then on to a business career in Kenya, remembers Gore as peaceful and resigned. Although registered with the draft board in Carthage, he decided to enlist down the road from Tyson in Newark. Gore says that the unlikely point of entry into the military gave him "a better chance of getting treated as myself there" and not as part of his father's story. But there may have been a bit more to it. His friend the army veteran counseled that his chances of landing a reporter's job would be enhanced by enlisting at a station close to a major training installation (Fort Dix was nearby), where there was a wider selection of jobs. Army historians say there is nothing in military records to support such a claim.

But it may well have been part of his thinking when he reported to the Armed Forces Entrance and Examination Station in downtown Newark on August 8, 1969. Several days later, after tests and interviews, he took the oath of enlistment. An official army photo shows him freshly crew-cut, with a dazed, saddened look in his eyes, holding up a small black placard that said "Gore, Albert A."

Men on Horseback

W HEN Al Gore became Private E-1 Gore, he set aside his misgivings about becoming a soldier and approached the army as he has every other big step in his life — with caution, meticulous attention to appearances, and a plan. Instead of the usual three-year enlistment, he opted for a two-year commitment, the same as if he had been drafted. That choice, in addition to getting him in and out of active duty more quickly, looked better on paper: three-year volunteers had the option of selecting their army jobs, but two-year enlistees were dropped into the same manpower pool as those coming through the draft. Gore would legitimately be able to say that he had put himself at risk of receiving a combat assignment. "You don't get to choose the job you have," he said as a presidential candidate in 1987. "The young lieutenant at the end of the testing procedure looked at my tests and said, 'We think you'd make a good reporter.' And I said, 'Yes, sir.'"

As a practical matter, Gore had his pick of military specialties and his chances of seeing combat were vanishingly small. Even at the war's height, 88 percent of all servicemen were assigned to noncombat occupational specialties. Although technically eligible for the infantry, Vietnam-era enlistees with above-average aptitude or skills were routinely plucked from the personnel pool and assigned specialized jobs, often far from the fighting. The opportunity to avoid combat by volunteering rather than waiting for the draft was even part of the army's sales pitch: "Make your choice now. Join, or we'll make the choice for you," said one ad of the period.

And despite General William Westmoreland's suggestion that it probably took "some political maneuvering" to secure his assignment as an army journalist, there is no hard evidence that Gore's father, other government officials, or top commanders intervened on his be-half. Dess Stokes, staff sergeant at the Newark Armed Forces Entrance and Examination Station on the day he walked in, doesn't remember any communication from superiors about Gore. A kid with Gore's background (a 134 IQ and a Harvard degree), he said, didn't need to be a senator's son with high-level contacts to get the military job he wanted: "You pretty much got your choice of assignments." Still, to ensure that he landed the "information specialist" post he wanted, Gore stretched his summer copy boy's job at the *New York Times* into a slightly loftier civilian credential. According to his army person-nel file, Gore described his *Times* position as a "newspaper trainee," clearly suggesting that he'd worked as a reporter when he had not. Penciled into the section for hobbies, as if to bolster his case, was "writes poetry."

Private Gore was not destined to fight, but he still had to endure ba-sic training, and Fort Dix, New Jersey, fifty-five miles to the south, was his first stop in the army. His eight weeks in C Company, Second Battalion, Second Training Brigade were a string of 5:00 A.M. reveilles and twelve-hour days immersed in the bleak arts of war, from cam-ouflage to hand-to-hand combat. Gore was not gung-ho about sol-diering, but he became a pretty good shot. Perhaps as a legacy of the summer evenings spent coon hunting with the Thompsons, he even-tually won citation as an M-16 rifle "expert." In early October he was assigned to the public affairs office (PAO) at Fort Rucker in southeast-ern Alabama. He had two weeks of leave before he was due, so he headed back to Cambridge, where Tipper was beginning her senior year at Boston University.

The brief homecoming was a sobering one. Dick Neustadt was stunned by his prize student's transformation. The chunky kid who had sat in Government 154 was crew-cut and "spare as a rail" after two months at Dix. He was also, by Cambridge standards, now part of the problem, not the solution. This was the autumn of the mammoth peace rallies. On October 15, Moratorium Day, millions of Americans stayed away from jobs or classes to protest the war. A month later more than 500,000 journeyed to Washington for a second demonstra-tion and a massive "March Against Death." The undergrad who only a few months earlier had basked in the reflected glory of his father's an-tiwar advocacy was treated like a pariah as he walked through his old campus in uniform, scorned by students who knew nothing of the circumstances that had driven his decision. He wanted to save his father, not undermine him. The arrogant presumption of those who shouted epithets enraged him.

Fort Rucker, in southeast Alabama's wiregrass country, was on a full war footing when Gore arrived in October 1969. The home of the army's aviation school was turning out new classes of helicopter crews every two weeks. As the thumping of chopper blades filled the air, lawyers from the judge advocate general's office conducted back-to-back meetings with young pilots and door gunners ready to ship out, helping them draw up wills and settle their affairs. Returnees, some hollow-eyed and edgy, told harrowing stories about what they had seen and done.

Gore's PAO post was an amiable backwater far from the flight line that cranked out news releases about medal ceremonies and published the base newspaper, the *Army Flyer*. His office mates shared his grave doubts about the war and had no illusions about their task — putting a good public relations face on a troubled army. "We all recognized that what we were doing was a kind of parody," said PAO photographer Bob Delabar, one of Gore's closest friends from his military days.

When a real piece of the war occasionally found its way to the PAO in box, it only reinforced their cynicism. In late 1969 Delabar and Gore were assigned to cover a medal ceremony whose honorees were to include the U.S. Army helicopter pilot Hugh Thompson, who was decorated with the Distinguished Flying Cross for rescuing South Vietnamese civilians from a village in Quang Ngai Province called My Lai. The official line was that Thompson flew in and extracted the villagers under heavy enemy fire on March 16, 1968. But when Delabar and Gore tried to find the war hero for an interview after the ceremony, they discovered that he had left abruptly. A few months later, along with the rest of the world, they learned that the civilians had actually been fleeing from Lieutenant William Calley and his troops, who had murdered at least five hundred other civilians. Thompson had set his chopper down between the villagers and the marauding infantrymen, ordering his crew to open fire if the soldiers harmed anyone else. Were it not for him, even more lives would have been lost in one of American military history's darkest moments.

When Thompson's actual role was revealed, Delabar developed a twenty-by-thirty-inch print of his appearance at Rucker and hung it on the office wall. It would be nearly thirty years before the army officially acknowledged what Thompson, who testified against Calley at his court-martial, did that day at My Lai, but to the PAO crew at Rucker he was the hero of an American mission that had gone horrifically wrong.

Life at Rucker was also a last taste of bachelorhood for Gore, who had proposed to Tipper on the banks of the Charles River in Cambridge before graduating and would marry her the following spring. He joined several office and barracks mates in renting a weekend beach house on the Florida panhandle near Panama City. Over steaks, cigars, and a cheap wine called "Tickle Me Pink," they listened to Led Zeppelin on their eight-track stereo and swapped stories. Gore talked mostly about Carthage and the family farm, rarely mentioning Harvard or Washington. He also organized the athletic events. "Al introduced us to football on the beach," said Richard Abalos, a housemate and lawyer in the judge advocate general's office. "We had read about the Kennedys doing it."

Women were available, but by all accounts Gore remained strictly spoken for, even when another PAO staffer who was dating a New Orleans flight attendant arranged for Gore and Delabar to join him, his girlfriend, and her two roommates for several weekends in a row. Gore did manage, however, in his own way, to let *les bon temps* roll. One weekend in January 1970, during Delabar's last big fling before leaving for South Vietnam, he and Gore devoted a long evening of drinking to the uncertainties that lay ahead. Around 2:00 A.M., still feeling the effects of the evening's revels, Gore got up and made his way to the shoulder of a freeway near the apartment where they were staying and spent two hours scrounging on hands and knees for "the perfect four-leaf clover" to give Delabar for good luck. He never found it, but did attract the attention of the Louisiana state police, who encouraged him to look elsewhere.

Still, as a rule, Gore remained exceedingly careful about his comportment, down to the razor-sharp crease in his khakis. The Rucker brass named him post soldier of the month in May 1970, an honor that came with a $50 savings bond, a letter of commendation for his military bearing and leadership qualities, and a hearty handshake from the base commander, General Delk Oden.

He occasionally sounded like a sixties dropout, telling one beach-house friend, Marnie Hendrick, that he wanted to go back to Tennessee, live on a commune, and grow his own vegetables. But no one was persuaded. Gore's surpassing seriousness and Washington bloodlines always marked him as someone on a different track. In the barracks day room, where the traditional chain-of-command photos hung, from President Nixon down through General Oden, someone made room for a picture of Private Al Gore.

Something else distanced Gore from his friends at Rucker, although only a few knew at the time. He had volunteered to go to Vietnam. Why did Gore want to wade deeper into a war he claimed to loathe? The family business had already been taken care of. Putting on the uniform should have been cover fire enough for his embattled father. As with his original decision to enlist, Gore's motivations were a mix of personal ambition and familial obligation, and shipping out was a last full measure of devotion to the senator's cause.

Those around him at the time felt that volunteering for Vietnam was also a way of holding the door open for his own political aspirations. Gore surely knew that a stint in a combat zone was a valuable credential to bring to a political career. "I figure it had something to do with politics, something that would look good on a résumé," said Gus Stanisic, a PAO colleague who had already done a Vietnam tour. "He's pretty smart. He can usually figure things out. He was good at calculating probabilities. My impression was he had decided that the probability of something happening to him [in South Vietnam] was low in public affairs."

Once again, Westmoreland hovered in the background. At the end of a visit to Rucker, the army chief of staff was shaking hands with General Oden when he spied Gore, covering the departure for the *Army Flyer*. Delabar, who was shooting the story for the paper, said it was as if Westmoreland had spotted an old friend. "He said, 'Oh, Al,'" Delabar recalled. As Oden and his staff cooled their heels, Westmoreland walked the young private over to the edge of the tarmac for a conversation that lasted at least ten minutes.

Delabar said that Gore never discussed the details of his talk with Westmoreland, but he's always had the strong impression that the general influenced his decision to go to Vietnam. Over the years Gore has left others with the same idea. Michael Zibart, a Nashville friend, said Gore told him that Westmoreland "thought it was important for him to be on the front lines," and that he "would be making a grave error if he didn't serve in Vietnam."

But after he had made the decision to go, Gore's orders took months to come through. He has suggested, but never been able to prove, that election-year politics kept them bottled up in the military bureaucracy. Having a young Al Gore in harm's way diluted the White House message in Tennessee — that Albert Gore was a sneering, unpatriotic elitist, or so the scenario went. He didn't embark until shortly after Christmas 1970, nearly two months after his father's defeat. Gore alleged in a 1986 interview that his orders were "mysteriously canceled" earlier that year. This accounts, he said, for his unusually short tour of duty in South Vietnam — less than five months. "That just infuriates me," Gore said when he reiterated his suspicions in 1988. "I wanted to go. . . . All I know is, I was not allowed to go until the first departure date after the November election."

Former Nixon administration officials, including Defense Secretary Melvin Laird, Army Secretary Stanley Resor, and White House congressional liaison William Timmons, say there's no basis for the charge. "Just not true," said Laird. And yet a close friend of the Gore family — the same one who discussed Gore's military options with Westmoreland in 1969 — says that a few months after Gore enlisted, he learned from a secretary in Westmoreland's office that Gore's personnel file had been pulled by the White House and had remained there, in the custody of persons unknown, for several weeks. Westmoreland said he "vaguely" remembered such a situation, but that it did not surprise him. "I'm sure the White House got involved," he said.

Seven months before Al Gore shipped out, he and Mary Elizabeth Aitcheson said their vows before Canon Charles Martin at the high altar of the National Cathedral, next door to St. Albans. There was no wild bachelor party the night before, just an uneventful pub crawl through Georgetown after a rehearsal dinner at the Capitol. The ceremony, early on the muggy evening of May 19, 1970, was a royal Washington affair, if a little dusty: the Cathedral was still under construction, and ushers had to escort guests across a wooden catwalk flanked by huge plastic drapes that covered the scaffolding. Gore was ribbed mercilessly when he returned to Rucker after a Hawaiian honeymoon for having worn dress blues at his wedding, not standard issue for an army private. The groom's party, in tails, was a convergence of his Washington, Cambridge, and Carthage worlds. J. G. Landau, sporting a top hat, was best man; cousins Jamie and Mark Gore ushered, along with Tommy Lee Jones, Bob Somerby, Mike Kapetan, and Steve Armistead. Warren Steele, a friend from Dunster House, played the organ, including a Beatles recessional, "All You Need Is Love."

Tipper Gore thought she was prepared to be a soldier's wife, but the transition from storybook Washington wedding to a trailer park in Daleville, Alabama, was more of a lurch than even she could have anticipated. She cried when she opened the refrigerator door at one prospective residence and found that the interior seemed to be painted black, until the roaches began to disperse. Home eventually became trailer number 10 (the ten-foot "Expando model") at the Horsley Trailer Park, a couple of miles from the base. Tipper did what she could to decorate the modest digs, and on paydays Gore's buddies would gather for poker games and a special meal — either Tipper's beef stroganoff or Tex-Mex courtesy of Abalos.

If Al Gore had any worries about his father's reelection that spring of 1970, he never revealed them to friends at Fort Rucker. "He was extremely confident," said Abalos. "I got the impression he thought his father was going to win." Gore kept his faith despite some serious red flags. Two weeks before the wedding, Texas Democrat Ralph Yarborough, another liberal antiwar senator, lost his primary to Lloyd Bentsen, a wealthy moderate who went on to beat Republican George Bush in the November general election. Bentsen ran ads assailing Yarborough's war opposition, his liberal views on racial integration, and his apparent sympathy for student demonstrators at the 1968 Democratic convention in Chicago — all parts of Albert Gore's own increasingly vulnerable portfolio. The senator's primary opponent, Hudley Crockett, press secretary to Governor Buford Ellington, was sounding many of the same themes as Bentsen.

The larger picture was even more ominous for Gore and his New Deal liberalism. White flight from the Democratic Party, fueled by racial and economic resentments, had been eroding its dominance in the South for several years. In 1966 Howard Baker became the first Republican since Reconstruction to win a Senate seat from Tennessee. Two years later George Wallace took 34 percent of the state's presidential vote.

Although his son may not have grasped the level of jeopardy, the senator did. He made a rare concession to the age of television-driven politics and hired Democratic filmmaker Charles Guggenheim to produce a series of ads that would reconnect him to Tennessee voters. The spots had a stylized, cinema verité feel, showing the candidate in what were supposed to be unscripted encounters with his constituents: playing checkers with the codgers at the Smith County courthouse ("If you beat me two straight games, I'll cut off your Medicare," he tells one, with his characteristically edgy humor), talking with hard-hat construction workers — symbols of blue-collar enmity toward the antiwar movement — and visiting an organization of young businessmen. Two of the most memorable ads were father-son scenes. One emerged from a long, unrehearsed conversation that Guggenheim filmed in the family's farmhouse living room. At the end, the senator reached out and touched the hand of the uniformed Gore and said, "Son, always love your country."

The famous "horseback" spot evolved, said Guggenheim, "out of a totally spontaneous moment" one Sunday in June at the end of a weekend shoot on the Gore farm. Spotting some horses in a barn, Guggenheim thought some footage of his candidate galloping through the countryside might be a prescriptive for the polls revealing that voters regarded him as a Washington aristocrat. As the two generations ride into the shot, the senator on a white Tennessee walker, his son on a bay mare, there is only the muted sound of horse hooves and a reverential narrator: "The pace and direction a man sets for his life can tell you a lot about his inner spirit," the voice intones. For a brief moment, young Gore's face fills the screen. "Those closest to him value his integrity and his judgment and his determination to take the right path as he sees it. . . . The people of Tennessee have learned to gauge his measure by the battles he's fought for them along the way . . . for TVA, tax reform, Medicare, interstate highways." The ad ends with the two horsemen moving off into the distance as the narrator says, "Albert Gore, the Senator."

Al Gore enjoyed his bit parts in political show business and recounted the making of the ads in detail for his army pals. "He'd talk about riding into the sunset on his horse and then having to turn left," said Abalos. "He'd get the biggest kick telling us about that." But the horseback spot backfired, its message inappropriately magisterial for a moment in which Albert Gore needed to look like a man of the people. Dressed in black and atop a white horse, he looked like something from the pages of an antebellum novel. Guggenheim said he can't remember whose idea it was to have his son ride along like a young prince. But his presence evoked a sense of dynasty that also seemed out of place. Albert Gore won the primary but drew an alarmingly weak 51 percent of the vote against Crockett.

The Nixon White House threw money and muscle behind the GOP nominee, Representative Bill Brock, the thirty-nine-year-old heir to a Chattanooga candy manufacturing fortune. Two former Nixon operatives, Harry Treleaven and Kenneth Reitz, were imported to run the effort. They painted Gore as an elitist whose pacifism, opposition to two Supreme Court nominees from the South, Harold Carswell and Clement Haynsworth, and chummy relations with the Kennedys had left him out of touch with Tennesseans. The Kennedy connection was especially damaging when memories of Mary Jo Kopechne's drowning in a pond on Chappaquiddick Island a year earlier were still raw, as was Gore's maladroit defense of Teddy: "We all have an eye for a pretty face, but if that is meant to imply immoral conduct I have not heard it and I do not believe it," he said. Kennedy threw a big fund-raiser for Gore at his McLean, Virginia, home, and pictures of the two made their way into the Tennessee papers, prompting Republicans to dub him "the third senator from Massachusetts." Nixon chief of staff H. R. Haldeman told aide Harry Dent in a memo that Gore's "cocktail party liberalism offers a chance to rebut his folksy image" and urged that the Brock camp research the society pages of the Washington newspapers to develop a list of fancy dinner parties attended by Gore, including the menus. "The Frenchier the better," Haldeman wrote.

Brock held Gore responsible for a hair-raising litany of societal ills. "Our college campuses are infested with drug peddlers," he said in a typical stump speech. "Our courts are disrupted. Buildings bombed and schools threatened. Our law officers are threatened, beaten and murdered. Pornography pollutes our mailboxes. Criminal syndicates infiltrate legitimate businesses. Rapists, robbers, and burglars make our streets and homes unsafe."

It was grist for a vicious, sneering campaign, one that wrote the playbook for a generation of Republican victories over liberal Democrats. Brock had nothing to say to the state's black voters, and his rhetoric was laced with indirect appeals to the racial and cultural resentments of the white middle class. "Bill Brock Believes in the Things We Believe In," said the billboards and television ads, crafted to appeal to disaffected Wallace Democrats. "Believes is the codeword for Nigger," wrote David Halberstam, a Gore family friend since his days as a reporter for the *Nashville Tennessean* in the 1950s. In a 1971 retrospective, he called Brock's campaign "the most disreputable and scurrilous" he'd ever seen in Tennessee. "It is not the old, sweaty, gallus snapping racism," he said, "rather, it is cool and modern."

Brock's cause also benefited from a stream of illegal money raised by Nixon operatives. He received more than $200,000 in contributions from "Operation Townhouse," a secret 1970 campaign fund that steered nearly $3 million into GOP House and Senate races from deep-pocketed conservatives like Walter Annenberg, W. Clement Stone, DeWitt Wallace, and Richard Mellon Scaife, the Pittsburgh tycoon who two decades later would spend millions subsidizing the right-wing assault on Bill Clinton. It helped Brock keep Gore off-balance throughout the summer and fall with a barrage of distortions and outright smears. Brock even charged that Gore's antiwar statements were responsible for helping the North Vietnamese brainwash American POWs.

One of the South's last liberal lions tried to stave off winter for another season. Friends had long warned him that he needed to spend more time in the state. When he had returned in recent years, what many saw instead of a fire-breathing populist was an effete character in a red jacket and snappy Tyrolean hat, presiding over another celebrity-studded cattle auction at the farm. But as his political predicament deepened, he began dashing back constantly — full-time during recesses and weekends when the Senate was in session — leaving his Methodist Building apartment on Capitol Hill every Friday evening in time for the 9:00 P.M. flight to Nashville. Albert Gore was as Tennessee as turnip greens and hog jowls, he assured the crowds. After years on the shelf, his fiddle reappeared.

The last campaign was a solitary, even lonely, enterprise. Gore had never built a statewide organization of any substance, and the mount-

ing odds against him had driven his few friends in the state's Democratic establishment underground. With little outside support, the
family dug in for a last stand. Their bunker was a slightly down-at-
the-heels seventh-floor suite at the Hermitage Hotel, overlooking the
state capitol in Nashville, where they would gather after sixteen-hour
days to return phone calls, change clothes, and grab a few hours of
sleep. While Senator Gore carried the main load, the wives — Pauline,
Nancy, and now Tipper — hit the road too, blanketing the women's
coffee circuit and serving as the candidate's backup. In the familial
pecking order, as described by Nancy, Pauline filled in when Albert
had to cancel, and Nancy then stepped up for her mother. The novice
Tipper, who called herself "the caboose," took up the rest of the slack.

Their son was there on weekend passes, occasionally in uniform,
standing by his father at rallies. His presence afforded the senator at
least some protection against questions about his patriotism, but not
everyone in the Gore camp thought that the strapping young GI was
an asset. Ted Brown, a Senate staffer and campaign aide, said that even
in uniform there was "some anxiety about giving him too high a
profile" because of his connections to Harvard and the 1968 presidential campaign of Eugene McCarthy, for which he had done some work
in Tennessee as a student coordinator.

Political pros in the state had left Gore for dead, but in October the
race tightened. Two weeks out, some analysts had him even with
Brock or even slightly ahead. But the resurgence owed more to Republican overreach than to Gore's tenacity. Brock's shrill attacks, and his
high-profile White House support, triggered a backlash. His issues began to lose their edge. The war wasn't the hot button it had been even
a few months earlier. Nixon had proposed a ceasefire; at twenty-four,
American combat deaths during the last week of October were the
lowest since 1965. Carswell, one of the Nixon Supreme Court nominees Gore had rejected, lost a Senate race in Florida, suggesting to Tennesseans that if his own state didn't want him for high office, Gore
might have had legitimate reason to oppose his elevation to the Supreme Court. As voters took a second look, he tried to gloss over the
deepening cracks in the New Deal coalition of blacks and low-income
whites: "If you scratch a Wallace voter, you find a populist," he told an
interviewer. "We disagree on civil rights bills, I tell them, but I represent their economic interests."

In the end, however, Gore still fell short. Brock hurled a final-week spitball of misleading charges, alleging that Gore was against prayer in schools and legislation to curb busing. The unusually stringent antibusing measure was, in fact, opposed by some Republicans, including Howard Baker. And Gore opposed only compulsory, not voluntary, prayer. But badly outspent by the GOP, his campaign never managed to garner the same attention for his rebuttals as was given to Brock's original attacks.

Gore faced deficits he simply couldn't overcome. The New Deal Democratic coalition, which tolerated his views on civil rights and foreign policy because he had helped raise living standards, had been pulled apart by race and class tensions. Wallace Democrats turned on the news and hated what they saw — college students trashing their campuses, blacks rioting and collecting welfare, hippies smoking dope. They knew Albert Gore wasn't responsible for it all, but it seemed to them that he was too indulgent of those who wanted to tear the country down. "I have a kid at Memphis State University who has grown hair down to his shoulders and gave me the peace sign the other day when I told him to get it cut," one Tennessean told Kelly Leiter of *The Nation*. "He keeps telling me how great Gore is, and if that's what Gore is for, then I'm not."

During thirty-two years in office, one can lose old friends and collect new enemies; Albert Gore had simply done too much of both. After nearly eighteen years in the Senate, his aloof, often sanctimonious style had finally worn thin. "Albert seemed to have a disdain for the people," said Phil Sullivan, a former reporter and editorial writer for the *Tennessean* who covered Gore's first Senate race in 1952. "He wanted to fight for the little guy, but he didn't want him in his presence." The mystery, said Bill Allen, his longtime administrative assistant, is not why he lost, "but how he survived as long as he did."

The Gores voted in Carthage and returned to the Hermitage Hotel to wait for the returns. Tennessee's unique political geography, the "Grand Divisions" that separated the traditionally Republican eastern counties, the Democratic middle, and the battleground west, brought an early end to the evening. Gore told advisers that to survive he had to hold Brock's margin in the east to sixty thousand, win big in the middle, and run even in Memphis and the rest of the west. But Brock took the east by more than eighty thousand, making it impossible to make up the losses elsewhere.

At 9:40 P.M., the family came downstairs to the Hermitage ballroom. Albert Gore was ready for the moment, quoting a line from an Edwin Markham poem: "Defeat may serve as well as victory to shake the soul and let the glory out." Never mentioning Brock by name, he added: "We do not have a perfect system of government, but it is the best devised. It has been a very long and very hard fight. We knew from the beginning that the odds were terrifically against us, but we almost made it. We had to make the fight because the issues were so important and the stakes were so high. I told the truth as I saw it. . . . The causes for which we fought are not dead. The truth shall rise again!" As his son ascended in national politics, Gore's words that night came to be understood among friends and supporters as a prophecy. Journalists loved the generational angle — fallen patriarch passes the mantle of southern progressivism to his son — and the Gores, who knew a good story when they saw it, encouraged the theme. Yet those who knew Albert Gore best understood that nothing could have been further from the truth. Eager as he was to see his son follow him, and surpass him, in politics, he was not a man given to sharing the spotlight, especially his last moments in it.

The Gores said their good-byes and staggered back upstairs. Defeat had always loomed as a possibility, but as the reality settled in, it began to shake the family to its foundations. Marnie Hendrick had driven up from Fort Rucker for what he thought would be an election night of beer drinking. He arrived in the middle of the concession speech and knew instantly there would be no celebration. Al Gore begged off, saying he needed to be with his family. "I think they were stunned," said Hendrick. The senator at first refused to put in the traditional phone call to Brock, unable to bring himself to congratulate a man who had run such a race, preying on people's fears and insecurities the way he did. A damnation, he called it, Baptist preacher to the last.

The family seemed poised at the edge of an emotional abyss. Al Gore would embark for South Vietnam in less than sixty days, bitterly disillusioned about a political system that could drive a man like his father from office. Pauline and Tipper feared for his safety and worried about how the senator would absorb defeat. Some old Senate friends, like Oklahoma's Mike Monroney, were never well after they lost. When he returned to Washington to finish out his term, Albert Gore cut a bleak, disconsolate figure on the Senate floor. "Albert Gore, who loved the Senate in every manifestation, sits staring straight ahead, wan and wistful," wrote one Washington commentator. "For some of the others, the last hours make the Senate easier to leave. For him, nothing helps."

Pauline grieved as well, but with the loss came a sense of release — from the coffees, the handshakes, and the phony congeniality toward people who wished her family ill. The morning after on the farm, an old antagonist called to complain one last time about her husband's opposition to the war. She cut him off and snapped: "I have listened to the likes of you for thirty-two years, and I don't want to hear it this morning!"

That same day Al Gore canoed on the Caney Fork with his despairing father. It was the moment, he recalled years later, when he felt that their roles had for the first time been reversed. The dutiful son had become a parent, fielding a difficult question from a father devastated by defeat. "What would you do if you had thirty-two years of service to the people, given to the highest of your ability, always doing what you thought was right, and had then been unceremoniously turned out of office? What would you do?" the senator asked. Al Gore knew the answer, both for the senator and himself. "I'd take the thirty-two years, Dad."

◆ 6 ◆

Saving Private Gore

AL GORE reported to the 20th Engineer Brigade at the sprawling U.S. military complex in Bien Hoa, South Vietnam, on January 8, 1971, with the intention of serving out his remaining seven months in the service as just one of the troops. But like the war itself, very little went according to plan. Even before he arrived, there was grumbling around brigade headquarters about the VIP handling some felt he was certain to receive as a senator's son. "A lot of guys made up their minds that they weren't going to be too happy about someone who was getting the lobster treatment when everyone else was getting the fishbones," said Alan Leo, a photographer in the brigade press office where Gore worked as a reporter. Leo, a specialist E-5, was a wiry, intense man who had begun his army career as a demolitions expert in 1969. He was the most experienced hand in the press operation and enjoyed the freedom that came with the job, especially the priority travel pass that allowed him to hop on a helicopter and fly virtually anywhere in pursuit of heroic stories about the engineers. Leo also had a reputation for picking spots where enemy activity was hot — where the engineers clearing rain forest or paving roads were taking fire. "He lived on the edge," said Bob Hinchliffe, another photographer in the unit. "He kind of got off on it. He had that look in his eyes."

Leo didn't give the newcomer much thought until he was summoned by the 20th's commander, Brigadier General K. B. Cooper. Leo liked Ken Cooper, and thought he was a gentleman, more engineer than warrior, but he wasn't prepared for the mission Cooper had in mind. Albert Gore's son was coming into the unit, Cooper said, and he had "a great amount of respect for the senator." He asked the gung-ho

Leo to make sure that nothing happened to the young Harvard graduate. Reporters and photographers from the public affairs office were
frequently paired as teams on assignments in the field. "He requested
that Gore not get into situations that were dangerous," said Leo. That
meant, Leo understood Cooper to say, that Gore should cover only
military operations where security was good.

Leo asked Cooper if he could go off the record. He said he wasn't
happy about the prospect of standing down from his more challenging assignments. But Cooper was adamant. "He just quietly said, 'Do
your best. Can I count on you?'" Leo said he did what he could to
carry out Cooper's directive. He described his half-dozen or so trips
into the field with Gore as situations where "I could have worn a tux-
edo." Leo added that he never disclosed to Gore his conversation with
Cooper, regarding it as "confidential." Nor does he believe that Gore
was ever aware of the arrangement. Although Gore "wanted to see a
little more excitement," Leo said, he doesn't recall Gore making an issue of it.

Cooper, now retired and working in Washington as a consultant to
the Institute for Defense Analyses, acknowledged that he knew Senator Albert Gore "casually" from a previous posting as executive assistant to Army Secretary Stanley Resor. But he said that he has no recollection of even meeting Leo, much less discussing Gore's safety with
him. "I'm not saying it didn't happen, but I don't remember it," he
said. However, Wayne Pelter, a stenographer at brigade headquarters
when Gore was assigned to the 20th, said the young Harvard grad's
protected status was widely discussed. "He didn't have to go out on
real dangerous missions," said Pelter, a specialist E-5 who retired from
the army a few years ago as a master sergeant. Pelter added that it was
"not Gore's decision," but one that had clearly been imposed by senior
commanders.

Gore's colleagues acknowledge that, the army being the army, an attempt by the brass to shield Gore was certainly possible. No commanding officer wanted a VIP's son harmed on his watch, especially in
the waning days of a lost war. Hinchliffe says his buddy Leo never told
him about the conversation with Cooper, but he distinctly remembers
that Leo's assignments became tamer after Gore arrived.

The evidence indicates that if there was an official effort to guarantee Gore's safety, it was uneven at best. His clippings from the *Castle*

Courier, the newspaper of the U.S. Army Engineering Command, and other publications suggest that he pulled his weight, which in his case meant choppering around to report features about the good works of the 20th Engineers, who were tasked with paving roads, building bridges, and clearing jungle to support combat operations. William Smith, another reporter attached to the 20th, recalls the morning in early 1971 when a sergeant asked him to go to Khe Sanh, fifteen miles south of the Demilitarized Zone, to cover the engineers' role in re-opening an abandoned airstrip. When Smith said he was scheduled to leave for R&R in Hawaii, the sergeant called for volunteers. Gore stepped up and spent a cold night in a foxhole. "Al did what everybody else did," said Mike O'Hara, the photographer who shot the Khe Sanh assignment. Although the fire at the airstrip was nearly all outgoing, Gore took no chances, reinforcing the tarmac covering the foxhole with metal sheets. "He seemed a little concerned," recalled O'Hara, who had several more months' experience on the ground. "I told him, 'Al, relax, nothing's going to happen.' He seemed very intent on forti-fying our position."

Gore seldom spoke about politics while in Vietnam, and usually only when he was drawn out. The sting of his father's defeat was still fresh. His pain was visible one evening when a GI launched a lengthy, drunken harangue about Albert Gore's position on school prayer, one informed mainly by Bill Brock's misrepresentations. Gore just sat and listened. "It was one of those ten-minute soliloquies that could have taken a minute," O'Hara said. When the soldier left, Gore said quietly, "They crucified him for it."

Writing for military publications, Gore had little choice but to reit-erate dutifully the official line on a war that he opposed and that his father had decried in the Senate. He reported triumphally on the re-opening of the abandoned Marine base and airstrip at Khe Sanh ("The forklift operators had their hands full — or rather, their forks full . . ."), an operation that was actually part of an unsuccessful at-tempt by U.S. warplanes and South Vietnamese ground forces to cut off the flow of enemy supplies from the Ho Chi Minh Trail in eastern Laos. The operation, called Lam Son 719, not only failed to cut the trail but exposed serious deficiencies in the South Vietnamese troops.

Some of Gore's Vietnam writing foreshadowed the pedagogic style that readers of *Earth in the Balance* came to know well: his keen inter-est in explaining highly technical material, often at eye-glazing length.

One dispatch from Soc Trang in the Mekong Delta detailed a process called clay-lime stabilization, an army engineering technique for building roads in areas with little indigenous rock. "Calcium ions, which carry a positive charge, attach themselves to the minute clay particles in the soil, which carry a negative charge. As the moisture begins to evaporate in the sun, the mixture hardens into a highly stable molecular lattice-work."

In a 1988 presidential campaign brochure, Gore included a picture that showed him toting an M-16 rifle through the countryside. Although the weapon was standard issue, and the leaflet never explicitly called him an infantryman, the image leaves a misleading impression. Gore has added to it over the years by telling interviewers that he faced direct enemy fire when he did not. The closest Gore got to combat was through after-action interviews with GIs. One of his journalistic staples was reconstructing battles in dramatic prose. "Through the darkness, a band of shadowy figures moved silently toward the U.S. firebase," one piece began.

His most ambitious story was an account of a Vietcong attack on a fire support base manned by Company C, Thirty-first Engineer Battalion, near the Cambodian border on the night of February 22, 1971. There were no American fatalities, but Gore's copy evokes the terror and chaos of a close-quarters engagement:

> "Overrun" is a fairly explicit military term, but its full meaning is known only to those who live through it. It describes the most nitty-gritty conflict that a soldier ever sees. For that soldier, all the elaborate plans and maneuvers of the opposing armies fade momentarily into abstraction as the real nature of war is crystallized in a battle for his life. . . . The explosions kept up. And they all seemed to be hits. The eight-inch [gun] was already gone, one of the dusters [twin 40mm guns mounted on tracked vehicles] was now in flames, the sandbag bunker beside it was flattened, an entire row of hootches was destroyed. Either they were damned accurate shots or . . . "VC in the compound! VC in the compound!" Suddenly everyone was yelling it. And the dogs were barking.

Gore and Leo had pieced together the story with several hours of interviews at the firebase the day after the attack. Sylvester Thompson, a medic for the Thirty-first, remembers Gore the army reporter as thorough, professional, and quick. "They got right back on the helicopter before dark," he said. "When it was dark, they were out of there."

Gore's mission had little to do with what was actually happening in South Vietnam in early 1971. The American effort to disengage from the war was in its final, excruciating throes. Two years of withdrawals had left American troop strength at 280,000, down from more than half a million at the end of 1968. The forces that remained behind were disintegrating, their morale ravaged by waning public support for the war. Nixon's "Vietnamization" policy, designed to hold the line against the enemy until fighting could be turned over to the South Vietnamese, unraveled discipline in the field. Men who knew they were marking time in a lost cause killed officers who tried to order them into combat. The U.S. command estimated that by 1970, 65,000 GIs were using drugs, mostly marijuana and heroin. Racial tensions were spiking.

Gore has rarely spoken publicly in any detail about his Vietnam experience, although he suggests that despite his noncombat assignment and quick exit, what little he saw upset him immensely. On Veterans Day 1992, as vice president-elect, he stood in a driving rain at the Vietnam Veterans Memorial and confessed that more than two decades later it was still difficult to talk about the war. "It's been hard for me to find the words with which I can come to terms with what Vietnam and the Vietnam War was all about," he told the crowd. "I bet there were — I bet there are — a lot of people in this audience, at this gathering here, who came home and just didn't want to talk about it at all."

His Harvard roommate Mike Kapetan remembers hearing haunting descriptions of the wretchedness in the faces of the orphans and prostitutes whom Gore said he encountered on long walks through the streets of Saigon. "These were things he'd never seen before," said Kapetan. "They were upsetting, off-putting." Richard Abalos said that Gore's letters back to the States were shrouded in despair. "He sounded freaked out about the killing. It seemed like he was despondent," said Abalos. One letter to Gus Stanisic, which Abalos remembers Stanisic reading out loud, contained a promise: "He told Gus that when and if he got back from Vietnam he would go to divinity school to atone for his sins."

For a young man who continually wondered whether he was in the right, becoming part of such a morally ambiguous mission — even to protect his father — may have come to seem sinful. It was surely dispiriting and deeply confusing. Those who later tried to discuss it with him, like Lloyd Armour, his boss on the *Nashville Tennessean* editorial page when he returned home, found themselves cut off. "Mostly he'd give a defensive answer or try to fend it off," said Armour. "He seemed to be saying, 'I went, so they can't blame that on my father.'"

Some of those who served with Gore say his experience was closer in spirit to *Good Morning, Vietnam* than *Platoon*. Most evenings, after a shower and a hot meal, Gore and the other "information specialists" kicked back on lawn chairs in front of their hootches, where Budweiser and marijuana were always available. "We mostly just vegetated," said O'Hara. (As a first-time presidential candidate sixteen years later, Gore would say that he smoked "once or twice" while off-duty in Bien Hoa.) To fill some of the downtime, Gore piled into a three-quarter-ton truck with teammates on the brigade basketball team to play other units in the area, or hitched twenty miles to Saigon, where his Fort Rucker buddy Bob Delabar was stationed. The beach at Vung Tau was also an easy day trip, and there was Hong Kong, where Gore and Delabar spent a week of R&R. "I think if you were to ask him, I think he'd say he had a lot of fun in Vietnam," said Delabar.

What is clear is that his tour of duty caused him to moderate his conventional Harvard Yard take on the conflict. The prospect of watching a country fall to a Communist insurgency was no longer a seminar abstraction. Vietnam, he said in 1988,

> certainly matured me in a hurry. It also gave me a tolerance for complexity that I don't think I had before. I didn't change my conclusions about the war being a terrible mistake, but it struck me that opponents to the war, including myself, really did not take into account the fact that there were an awful lot of South Vietnamese who desperately wanted to hang on to what they called freedom. Coming face to face with those sentiments expressed by people who did the laundry and ran the restaurants and worked in the fields was something I was naively unprepared for.

His war experience, combined with the political penalty his father paid for opposing American involvement, left him wary of the reflexive anti-interventionism — the so-called Vietnam Syndrome — that characterized Democratic attitudes toward foreign policy in the 1970s and 1980s. Gore often compared the party's stance to the Mark Twain story about the cat that, once burned by a hot stove, never again

touched any stove. As vice president, he was a strong and early propo-
nent of military action in Bosnia. In Congress he supported intervention in the Persian Gulf and Grenada and, in some instances, aid to the
Nicaraguan contras. "We've overlearned the lessons of Vietnam," he
said as a Senate candidate in 1984. "Central America is a different part
of the world. We have a much stronger national interest in Central
America than we did in Vietnam. We have a natural land bridge. We
have the threat of refugees like we've never seen. The stakes are much
higher."

The war may have exacted a much steeper emotional toll from Gore's
wife. Married less than a year and now separated from her husband,
she was, as one friend remembers her, a frightened and troubled
young woman. "Tipper was freaked out about Al being over there. It
was extremely hard on her," said former *Tennessean* reporter John
Warnecke, who, along with his wife Nancy, a photographer at the paper, became friends with the Gores during the 1970 campaign. She was
uncomfortable alone at the farm with Albert and Pauline while Gore
was overseas, and she became a frequent guest at the Warneckes' small
red brick and frame house on Belvedere Drive near downtown Nashville. While Tipper Gore says that she first experienced depression after her son was hit and nearly killed by a car in 1989, Warnecke, who
has also battled the disease, suspects that she may have been ill while
Gore was in Vietnam. He vividly recalls entire days she spent in bed,
and that he once stayed up with her all night, "holding her like a father," as she wept. "It was very scary, very sad," he said.

Warnecke doesn't recall her seeking medical attention, nor is he
sure how much Gore knew about her condition while he was gone.
When he returned, the worst of the symptoms subsided, and Warnecke said it was never discussed among the two couples. "He didn't
talk about it," said Warnecke. "It was, 'Al's back, so everything's going
to be fine.'"

Gore's contacts in Tennessee helped ease him back into civilian life.
Tennessean editor John Seigenthaler, a longtime family friend, had
seen his big piece on the overrun firebase and reprinted it. Gore didn't
make anyone forget Ernie Pyle, Seigenthaler said, but he showed some
genuine writing and reporting talent. There would be a job for him if
he wanted it. In April 1971 Gore was granted an "early out," or dis-

charge, from the army. He had less than three months left on his two-year hitch. Regulations allowed for early release of personnel to teach or attend school if their services were deemed "not essential to the mission," and Gore certainly qualified. The war continued to wind down, and by fall the 20th Engineers would be sent home and deactivated. He spent another month at U.S. Army Engineer Command in Long Binh before leaving Vietnam on May 22.

Gore's world had shifted on its axis in the one year, nine months, and seventeen days he was in uniform. He had a wife waiting anxiously for him in Tennessee. His father had been driven from the U.S. Senate. His Vietnam experience had left him looking for a deeper understanding of who he was and what he was meant to do. As he had promised in the letters home, Gore made final plans to attend Vanderbilt Divinity School. He was accepted through a Rockefeller Foundation program designed to attract promising young people into divinity studies. Although recipients of the one-year grant were encouraged to pursue careers in the ministry, it was not strictly for those who had heard the call. Tom McGee, another 20th Engineers friend, saw an element of rebellion in the choice, a message that Gore was not prepared to jump immediately into the dynastic script written for him by his family. Said McGee: "He wasn't going to be pushed or rushed into anything when he left."

❖ 7 ❖

"I Must Become My Own Man"

H E HAD been in South Vietnam for barely five months, and in the army for less than two years, but Al Gore struggled with the transition back to civilian life. On warm, sleepless summer nights he got up and took long walks around the family farm, where he and Tipper were staying. The Elmwood gang he ran with during his teenage summers saw dismaying changes in their old friend. The Gore they knew had always been naturally ponderous, but when he felt safe his carefully guarded goofy side emerged and he would tell dumb jokes or sing off-key rock and roll songs. The soldier who came home in the spring of 1971 seemed to have grown a new outer shell of joylessness. "He was scarred," said Steve Armistead. "He kind of withdrew."

As recounted by Gore, his years as a young adult in Tennessee were a personal journey from estrangement to rediscovery. Shaken by Vietnam, and angry about the brutish Nixon attack machine that had bloodied his father, he says that he renounced the political destiny his parents created for him and sought a new direction in life. It led to a soul-searching year of religious study at Vanderbilt University and the start of a promising journalism career at the *Nashville Tennessean*. "There was a time when I felt politics was the absolute last thing I would ever do," he said in 1992. Later, when he uncovered local government corruption as a reporter, his indignation rekindled a passion for public service. "I began to get a sense that I had something to contribute," he said. This realization, he contends, brought him back to the family business.

The truth is more complicated, rooted less in his five years as a newspaper man than in a larger struggle to find his own place in his family and the world. Gore never abandoned the prospect of a life in politics. He was indeed searching when he got home — but not for an alternative to a political career. Rather, he wanted a way to begin one on terms he could legitimately claim as his own, and that meant first developing a life apart from his family's calling. The nighttime walks into the woods were more than the restless wanderings of a veteran trying to readjust. They were the first tentative steps out of the long shadows cast by his parents.

Gore savored his Nashville days, not as the beginning of a new life, but as the final unencumbered moments before the inevitable beginning of the public one. "He was free to float," said Andrew Schlesinger, son of historian Arthur Schlesinger Jr., who became friends with Gore while covering the 1970 campaign for the *Tennessean*. "He was unanchored, and he appreciated the unanchoredness. He must have also sensed that it was going to be short-lived."

Donna Armistead harbored the same suspicion, a feeling that was reinforced in late 1971 when Gore paid a last visit to her grandmother Edna, who would die within a few weeks from pancreatic cancer. He spent nearly three hours alone with the Armistead matriarch who preached "God, family, and the Democrats," and while Edna never explicitly said so, she indicated to her granddaughter that Gore had revealed his plans. "He told her he was going to run for office and was asking for her advice," she said.

Albert and Pauline Gore were worried about their son but remained hopeful that he would emerge from his confusion and begin a political career sooner rather than later. If Al needed to find himself, they believed, he should do it while attending law school, the educational path they had both taken. A law degree provided a more sensible, and remunerative, cushion to fall back on than journalism, they argued. They were also ambivalent at best about their son working at the *Tennessean,* the paper that had forced Senator Gore out of the race for the vice presidential nomination in 1956. On at least one occasion they enlisted a family friend to promote their views; the Gores asked former *Tennessean* reporter Bill Kovach, then at the *New York Times,* to talk to their son. Kovach told Gore that he could be a reporter any time, but that the opportunity to attend law school might be more limited. "He was smart enough to ignore my advice and do both," Kovach said.

Gore did follow through on one parentally inspired project, the home-building business his father set up for him. While Gore was in basic training at Fort Dix, he had been officially installed as president of Tanglewood Home Builders, Inc., formed to develop a residential subdivision on the several hundred acres along Highway 25 outside of Carthage that he had purchased from his father before graduating from Harvard. When he left the army, it was strictly a weekend venture for Gore, who would give a once-over to building plans and chat with prospective buyers. His partners were his father and Walter King Robinson, a longtime family friend who oversaw the enterprise, which built and sold eighteen modest ranch homes priced in the midtwenties over a three-year period. The venture was lucrative enough to retire Gore's bank note and put some money in his pocket, according to Robinson. But his real interests were fifty miles away in Nashville.

Vanderbilt's divinity school was a liberal enclave tucked into a staunchly conservative campus. The university was controlled by a powerful board that included some of the city's most reactionary political figures, such as *Nashville Banner* publisher James Stahlman. It flashed to prominence in 1960 when James Lawson, a divinity student and the Nashville organizer for Martin Luther King's Southern Christian Leadership Conference (SCLC), was expelled for leading sit-ins to integrate the city's restaurants. Lawson's removal, which was supported by Vanderbilt's student newspaper, triggered a massive faculty protest that eventually forced his reinstatement.

Like many young people, Gore was drawn to religious study not as a path to the ministry but as a means of answering ethical and existential questions. "The Vietnam experience left him wondering about a lot of things. It left him wondering about what counted in life," said Jack Forstman, then chairman of the graduate department of religion, who called students like Gore "searchers." Like his classmates and teachers at Harvard, the Vanderbilt faculty saw a young man struggling to sharpen his sense of himself. "Al Gore had always been a role," said Eugene TeSelle, who taught a course in theology and natural science that Gore took. "The question was: Who was he? And what did he want to do?"

Gore's early religious life reflected the dual influences of his family's roots in Washington and Tennessee: the cool Episcopalianism of

St. Albans and the rigorous, individual soul-searching and Bible-based Sunday school lessons of his summers at New Salem Missionary Baptist. The Southern Baptist Convention was still under the sway of moderates and liberals during his "searcher" period in the early 1970s, and the denomination, with its history of support for civil rights and opposition to the Vietnam War, was in tune with Gore's inner voice. The convention's politics then were "very Clinton-Gore," said Nancy Ammerman, professor at the Hartford Seminary and author of *Baptist Battles.*

While he claimed to have washed his hands of a political future, there was little doubt among the faculty that he was preparing himself to lead. "I assumed where he ought to go was public life," said Yale divinity school professor Tom Ogletree, who taught at Vanderbilt when Gore attended. Although he didn't formally enroll in the class, he frequently attended Dean Walter Harrelson's lectures on the Old Testament prophets Amos, Isaiah, Hosea, and Micah, who raged against Israel's corrupt ruling class — the brutal kings, venal judges, moneyed capitalists, and avaricious priests. The prophets' message, to "let justice flow like water, and integrity like an unfailing stream" (Amos 5:24), was that to love God was to make an unwavering commitment to fairness and equality. "What he got from Amos was an understanding of the demands of God to see to the needs of the people," said Harrelson, "and to avoid taking advantage." In TeSelle's class Gore was exposed to dire predictions about the future of the global environment, themes that would become the core of *Earth in the Balance.* His reading included *The Limits to Growth* by the Club of Rome, an examination of the threats posed by uncontrolled industrialization and population growth.

Gore also pursued more esoteric areas of study, including mysticism as a psycho-religious phenomenon and supernatural influence in primitive religions. His teachers say that while Gore never intended to get a degree or to enter the ministry, he didn't come across as a dabbler. "I remember him as a serious student with enormous spontaneous intellectual interest," said Edward Farley, Gore's professor in a Ph.D.-level course on embodiment — philosophical problems in the dualism of mind and body. Gore's interests apparently didn't include satisfying his course requirements. Of the eight classes he took over three semesters, according to his Vanderbilt transcript, five ended in

Fs or incompletes that lapsed into Fs, including his grade in Farley's class. But Harrelson said that didn't matter. "He came to get from those courses what he wanted. The question of credentials was not important. He learned what he felt he needed to know."

When he returned to Washington to join the House of Representatives, he and Tipper began attending Mount Vernon Baptist Church in Arlington, where they were "born again" in the late 1970s. He was also, at least through his first vice presidential term, part of a small weekly prayer group, and friends say that religious faith is a cornerstone of his life. "I believe in serving God and trying to understand and obey God's will for our lives," Gore told Harvard seniors at his 1994 commencement speech. "Cynics may wave the idea away, saying God is a myth, useful in providing comfort to the ignorant and in keeping them obedient. I know in my heart — beyond all arguing and beyond any doubt — the cynics are wrong." The Baptist influence still echoes in some of his public speaking, which takes on an uncharacteristic energy in black churches. His two convention speeches about family tragedies, the death of his sister and the near-death of his son, while they served strategic political purposes, also had the flavor of Baptist testimony about suffering and redemption. "In my tradition, we believe the world has been transformed by the willingness of Jesus Christ to suffer on the cross," he said from the pulpit at Ebenezer Baptist Church in Atlanta on Martin Luther King Day in 1998. "Suffering binds us together and enables us to see what we have in common and what we are called upon to do."

But Gore found himself outside the institutional Baptist mainstream as the convention shifted to the right in the 1980s and 1990s. His support for abortion and gay rights earned him an F as a vice presidential candidate in 1992 from the Southern Baptists' Christian Life Commission. Nor is the Southern Baptist Convention especially active in the movement close to Gore's heart — mobilizing the spiritual community in defense of the environment.

Although he remains under the Southern Baptist umbrella, he emphasizes those aspects of Baptist doctrine that are more in harmony with his other personal beliefs, forming a view that seems to be an amalgam of Baptist tradition, New Age spiritualism, and a "call" to save the environment. "I have come to believe in the value of a kind of inner ecology that relies on the same principles of balance and holism that characterize a healthy environment," he wrote in the final pages of *Earth in the Balance.*

> If it is possible to steer one's own course — and I do believe it is — then I am convinced that the place to start is with faith, which for me is akin to a kind of spiritual gyroscope that spins in its own circumference in a stabilizing harmony with what is inside and out. Of course, faith is just a word unless it is invested with personal meaning; my own faith is rooted in an unshakeable belief in God as creator and sustainer, a deeply personal interpretation of a relationship with Christ, and an awareness of a constant and holy spiritual presence in all people, all life, and all things.

After listening to Gore answer questions from religion writers at a White House meeting in the spring of 1999, *New York Times* columnist Peter Steinfels wrote, "What one sensed . . . was a Christianity that is ethical and intellectual but not especially doctrinal." Most of his references were to the general virtues of compassion and kindness and to thinkers whose writings often focused on spirituality in an age of science and politics: political moralist Reinhold Niebuhr, Jesuit paleontologist Pierre Teilhard de Chardin, phenomenologist Edmund Husserl, and existentialist Maurice Merleau-Ponty.

Others who know Gore wonder whether a mind with such a technical and scientific bent could ever make a truly surrendering decision to believe. "I think he is someone who would like to have an irrevocable faith, but he's found it very hard," said Eve Zibart, a friend from the Nashville days who worked as a reporter at the *Tennessean.* "It appeals to him that there is a place where one's failings are forgiven."

If Al Gore had truly shunned politics, then he might have looked someplace other than the *Nashville Tennessean* for his first civilian job as a reporter. As a well-connected Harvard graduate, he could have started a journalism career at any number of newspapers, yet he chose the one that had played a pivotal role in his father's success. Silliman Evans, a Texas airline and insurance executive, purchased the paper out of receivership in 1937 and transformed it over the next generation into a dominant force in state politics. He placed its editorial power behind the growth of the Tennessee Valley Authority, the repeal of the poll tax, and the election to the Senate, in 1948 and 1952, respectively, of Estes Kefauver and Albert Gore, breaking the Democratic machine headed by Edward Crump of Memphis. A stalwart Democratic voice, Evans's *Tennessean* was one of only four major U.S. dailies to support Harry Truman in 1948, and he spent liberally to fulfill what he regarded as the paper's mission: to express "the ideals, and the moral, economic, social and political aspirations of the people." Anyone not in step with that mission, as Evans or his son Silliman Jr. saw it, could feel the paper's strong arm, as Albert Gore did in 1956. The *Tennessean* championed the civil rights movement (although it did support James Lawson's expulsion from Vanderbilt), and its generally progressive politics made it a magnet for first-rate young journalists on their way to the top, such as David Halberstam, Fred Graham, and Bill Kovach.

One of the paper's toughest, most streetwise reporters was John Seigenthaler, whose coverage of Teamsters Union violence in Tennessee attracted the attention of Bobby Kennedy. He left the paper to work in the 1960 presidential campaign and later as Kennedy's assistant at the Justice Department, where in the summer of 1961 he was beaten unconscious trying to rescue two Freedom Riders from a Montgomery, Alabama, mob. Returning to become the *Tennessean's* editor in 1962, he led its coverage of a voting fraud scandal in the city's Second Ward, where a Democratic Party hack named Gene "Little Evil" Jacobs tried to steal a congressional election for his candidate by filling out absentee ballots with the names of people residing in the local cemetery. "Second Ward Dead Men Vote" was the headline that eventually sent Jacobs to the state penitentiary and consolidated Seigenthaler's position as the man to see in Nashville politics. Frank Ritter, a former reporter and editor and now the paper's ombudsman, remembers days when city government job seekers waited outside his office, hoping for a brief audience and a favorable recommendation.

Fresh from the front lines of the New Frontier, Seigenthaler filled the *Tennessean* newsroom with the energy, ambition, and optimism of the Kennedy years. He sent reporters undercover to expose the inner workings of the Ku Klux Klan or troubled local institutions like the state mental hospital. He threw the paper behind the next generation of civil rights battles, including the push for congressional reapportionment and the creation of metropolitan government, uniting the city with surrounding Davidson County to prevent white flight from eroding the urban tax base. The *Tennessean* competed ferociously with the *Banner,* whose flag-waving publisher Stahlman "believed 'separate but equal' was a God-given directive," wrote former *Tennessean* reporter James Squires.

Seigenthaler also created a system of celebrity nepotism that brought the sons of influential Kennedy-era figures to Nashville for a taste of newspapering. Those offspring included Andrew Schlesinger and David Kennedy, Bobby's son (killed by a drug overdose in 1984). Not everyone at the paper admired the importation of celebrity bylines; some regarded it as the editor's way of staying in the good graces of his powerful Washington friends.

When Gore arrived in the *Tennessean* newsroom in the fall of 1971, it was assumed that he was simply another of Seigenthaler's A-list ingenues. But it was soon clear that his bloodlines made him more than that. Some sensed from the first that the man to see in Nashville was nurturing not just another young reporter, but a future candidate. "Seigenthaler saw him as someone going into politics," said former reporter Phil Sullivan. "He was not the journalist type. It didn't seem that that was what he was setting out to do."

It was certainly not the typical cub reporter's life — religious studies by day, police shorts, obituaries, and spot news in the evenings. But Gore plunged into it, at first making the same one-hundred-mile round trip from Carthage that his father had made to attend night law school. He had one unusual request of his new employers, one designed to distance him even further from the family business while he made his own name: no political assignments. He was concerned that certain stories would require him to deal with figures from his father's last bitter race. "There were people who played pivotal roles in that election I would have had to interview, on both sides, for and against my father," he explained in 1998. "And I didn't want to try to perfect the craft of reporting while simultaneously trying to navigate in such turbulent waters."

The *Tennessean* editors obliged and started Gore out at the bottom of the assignment-sheet food chain, covering night cops and hardy perennial features like the Hillbilly Day celebration in Madison, Tennessee. "Hillbilly Day had it all," Gore declared in his first byline story on October 3, 1971: "'Goofo' and his circus calliope, the 'Moonshine Peddler' and his sidekick 'Fuzz,' the gold and green oriental band, Uncle Remus and even Mrs. O'Leary's cow."

His rookie earnestness made him the natural target for a time-honored newsroom prank, the bogus story tip. It had become a specialty of Jerry Thompson, who penetrated the Klan for the *Tennessean*. He relished this considerably less risky pursuit, closeting himself in an office off the city room and phoning his target. One evening on the obit desk, Gore took a call from a funeral home announcing the death of Dr. Trebla Erog, a Swedish gynecologist in Carthage. In a string of messages over the next couple of hours, Thompson transformed the item into a dramatic spot news story that had Erog's distraught wife taken to a hospital and killed in a car wreck en route. A credulous young Gore could hardly contain himself. "He was so excited about it," said Thompson. "He would yell up to the editor, 'This thing is getting better all the time! You better get me some space on page 1 'cause this is a hell of a story!'"

After numerous updates, Gore delivered his final version to city editor Ritter. As most of the newsroom watched, Ritter quietly pointed out to Gore how strange it was that the deceased doctor's name seemed to be "Albert Gore" spelled backward. After a few seconds, Gore "turned about as red as red can be," said Thompson.

He was no overnight success as a reporter. Gore's copy was often late and poorly written, and while his stories never lacked for facts, he kept accumulating information as deadline came up, an operating style all too familiar to sleep-deprived aides who have worked with him on major speeches. "His newspaper colleagues were sometimes frustrated by Gore's approach: he wanted to know every minute detail about a situation before he was ready to write, a difficult attitude under deadline pressure," political reporter Larry Daughtrey wrote in a 1984 reminiscence. In the days of manual typewriters and carbon paper, Gore's copy "resembled nothing so much as hen scratching" covered with penciled-in corrections and additions, Ritter recalled. Other times Gore returned to the office with the story well in hand but cogitated over just the right lead until time began to run out. "It seemed like he couldn't really get motivated to write until deadline got really pressured," said Thompson.

Like most newsrooms, the *Tennessean's* was no hotbed of fashion, but Gore brought a countercultural flavor to the usual journalistic dishevelment. His thick, shoulder-length hair was parted in the middle, and he often wore sandals with a pair of jeans or the lone poplin suit he had acquired to get through the steamy Nashville summers. He enjoyed the night police beat, especially taking his car out with a police scanner crackling under the dashboard, cruising the evening streets like some Aquarian Age Joe Friday. He was fascinated by police work and even told Gus Stanisic that he was thinking about becoming a cop. "He seemed about 80 percent serious," said Stanisic. "He said he thought he could be a good cop and not a typical corrupt cop, that he would care about people."

Because Gore's deadlines often kept him in town well after midnight, he eventually rented a small efficiency on West End Avenue, a few blocks from the paper. It was little more than a refrigerator, a hot plate, and a bed, but it saved him the long, late-night drive back to Carthage. The new quarters also made it easier for late-night poker and drinking, which he often did at Do's Grill (pronounced Due's), an after-hours speakeasy in the Printers Alley section of downtown Nashville. His new reporter's life was gradually lifting him from his post-army funk. He enjoyed the freedom, the fellowship, and the challenge of pursuing information and explaining its meaning in a compelling way. Like the old senator, Gore enjoyed nothing better than holding forth on something interesting that he had just learned. Now he had a chance to do it in print, for tens of thousands of people at a time.

He and Tipper also enjoyed a lively social life in Nashville, running with a group of young journalists, lawyers, and businesspeople, some of them the well-connected sons and daughters of his father's friends. One fall they found themselves house-sitting the Tyne mansion, a glorious French chateau–style home complete with servants, owned by one of the founding families of National Life Insurance, a Nashville institution. While in residence, they hosted a raucous Halloween party whose highlights included the arrival of the state Democratic Party chairman, Will Cheek, in a hearse and coffin. The Halloween tradition continues for the Gores, in a tamer form, with annual celebrations at the vice presidential mansion.

They spent a lot of time with two young newspaper couples, the Warneckes and reporter Frank Sutherland and Natalie Dunning, the paper's rock music critic. Sutherland, a Vanderbilt philosophy graduate who once had himself committed to Central State Hospital, a psychiatric institution, for one of Seigenthaler's investigative projects, said that "God, time, and space" dominated their off-hours discussions. "We'd talk about the what-ifs of the world," said Sutherland, now vice president and editor of the *Tennessean*. Their biggest ongoing debate was over how one made a difference. Sutherland believed journalists were doing their job when they illuminated the dimensions of a problem. Gore's approach was at once more activist and pragmatic, said Sutherland. "He would attack problems he thought he could fix. He wanted to go after things he could change for the better."

The Gores and the Warneckes had become especially close in the wake of Tipper's troubled wartime visits at their house. In 1972 the Gores rented the place while the Warneckes moved to another a block away. Like Al Gore, John Warnecke had to negotiate the burdens of a famous and formidable father. John Carl Warnecke was an award-winning architect and friend of JFK's who redesigned Lafayette Square across the street from the White House and, in 1963, created the plan for Kennedy's gravesite. He also became Jacqueline Kennedy's lover after the assassination. The younger Warnecke grew up in San Francisco where his friends included guitarist Bob Weir, a relationship that led to work as a roadie for the Grateful Dead. He later organized students for Bobby Kennedy's 1968 California campaign, managed by Seigenthaler, who eventually brought him back to Nashville. Along the way he married a high school friend, Nancy Chickering, the daughter of a prominent California Republican family.

He was a charming man, possessed, one friend remembered, with an infectious laugh and "the brightest twinkling blue eyes you could imagine." He was also plagued by drug and alcohol problems that would eventually wreck his first marriage. As Warnecke tells it, he and Gore — often joined by Nancy and Tipper — would gather to talk politics late into the night, fueled by Dead albums, cognac, and the high-grade opium-laced marijuana Warnecke imported from the West Coast. They picked apart everything from civil rights to funding for the B-1 bomber to, not surprisingly, the liberalization of drug laws. Dope smoking, said Warnecke, stimulated Gore's "imagination and belief in what was possible. We'd get stoned and talk about what we'd do if we were president. It would allow him to get into the fantasy world of being an elected official." It was clear to Warnecke that despite the professions of disdain for politics, political ambition coursed inside his friend like an underground river. "More than anybody I've ever met, Al was always preparing himself to run for Congress," he said. But Gore needed the distance from his family that journalism and graduate study provided. According to Warnecke, "it was very important to him that he establish himself independently."

Gore insisted as a presidential candidate in 1987 that his dope smoking was "infrequent and rare." He said he smoked marijuana occasionally at Harvard, "once or twice in the army," and "once or twice as a graduate student" before quitting altogether in 1972. But Warnecke and another close friend from Gore's Nashville period, who declined to be named, say that he remained an enthusiastic recreational user through the 1970s, during his newspaper career and up until his first congressional campaign in 1976. They remember him smoking dope as often as three or four times a week: after-hours at Warnecke's house; on weekends at the Gore farm, where they sometimes lit up and canoed the Caney Fork; on an impulsive road trip to Memphis for barbecue; and even once, according to the anonymous friend, in his car cruising the police beat for the *Tennessean*. "He smoked as much as anybody I knew down there, and loved it," said Warnecke.

Al Gore stoned was a mix of expansiveness and paranoia, friends recall. He could be ironically humorous and self-aware about his lot as heir apparent in a political family. But he was also worried about his bright future literally going up in smoke. "He'd go around the room and close all the curtains and turn the lights out so no one could see," said Warnecke. "He was paranoid about getting busted."

Other friends from Gore's youth are extremely guarded on the subject of his drug use. "I think this is one of these areas that could be damaging for Al, so I think I'm going to have to keep my comments private," said Eve Zibart. His Harvard roommate Bob Somerby said that dope smoking was "one area no friend of Al would ever discuss, because it's so inflammatory."

For the most part, Gore kept his off-duty explorations and newspaper work tidily partitioned. Most newsroom colleagues heard little about his religious studies and saw no evidence of his drug use. The one convergence of these worlds came in a long, front-page feature he wrote about a commune of Haight-Ashbury expatriates in Summertown, two hours south of Nashville. Their charismatic leader was a former San Francisco State teaching assistant named Stephen Gaskin, who had won a small but devoted following in the Bay Area with a Monday night class he described as a meditation on "religion, God, love, death, dope, Vietnam, and violence." Weary of the political and cultural turbulence in California, Gaskin led a caravan of buses to rural Tennessee, where he and three hundred followers founded a community based on what another original member, Albert Bates, called "the hippie genre of spirituality" — a mix of Christianity and Eastern religion augmented by marijuana and hallucinogenic mushrooms. Gaskin, the author of a book called *Cannabis Spirituality*, believed that marijuana could help achieve higher realms of meaning and claimed to be able to communicate telepathically with his followers. Their 1971 arrival in Summertown had inspired wild stories and fears of a Manson-esque cult of drug-crazed hippies. In fact, "the Farm" was a benign collection of seekers, dreamers, and dropouts.

When Gore heard that Gaskin and his followers were meeting in a series of spiritual summits with the local clergy, he was intrigued. He drove to Summertown for one of the sessions in the commune's drafty, open-ended barn, decorated with Oriental rugs and warmed by a small woodstove. The gatherings began as an attempt by the churchmen to challenge Gaskin's legitimacy as a religious leader and to "save" his followers. But as Gore chronicled the encounter for the *Tennessean*, it ended in the discovery of surprising common ground around Judeo-Christian principles and a slowly emerging mutual understanding. "The people of Summertown are learning to live with the strange people who have all of a sudden become their neighbors," he wrote.

Gore seemed to find in the Farm an entire community looking for some of the answers he sought. His page 1 story, which got above-the-fold play on March 13, 1972, was a respectful, even enthusiastic treatment, several cuts above the hippie caricatures that had animated other coverage. "Unlike many communes," Gore wrote, "the Gaskin group is committed to leading a religious life." Farm members sensed that he was a kindred spirit. "He was our friend from the beginning," said Gaskin, who recalled his astonishment at the question with which he began his interview, not the usual inquiry from a newspaper reporter: "He said, 'I assume you people are trying to discover the pure state,'" using a phrase borrowed from his religious study.

Gore made several lasting contacts on the Farm, where the collective economy has been transformed since the seventies into a coop that sells mail-order gourmet mushrooms and soy dairy products. He kept up an e-mail correspondence with Bates, an attorney and environmental activist who shared his early interest in global warming. Bates wrote a 1990 book, *Climate in Crisis,* that Gore used as source material for *Earth in the Balance.*

By late 1972 Gore was done with divinity school and fully engaged at the *Tennessean,* which had bigger things in mind for him than the police beat. That fall Seigenthaler packed him off to Columbia University in New York for a two-week seminar on investigative reporting. Gore lifted his personal moratorium on political coverage enough to accept promotion to the metro beat, where he covered Nashville's courts and combined city-county government. He was an ideal beat reporter — dogged, prolific, and energized by the gritty details of local governance. "As the Metro Council struggles with the grueling question of how to finance Nashville's water and sewer program, the lawmakers might find comfort in remembering that the problem is not new," Gore wrote in a typical 1973 dispatch. He produced a stack of front-page stories on problems in the state's property tax appraisal system, which then relied on private companies to map and assess real estate.

Gore's work was solid and enterprising, but his famous byline clearly magnified the impact of his work. Few twenty-five-year-old city hall reporters are invited to discuss their findings with the U.S. Senate, but on May 3, 1973, Gore testified before the Government Operations Subcommittee on Intergovernmental Relations, which was considering a bill to require federal certification of mass appraisal companies. As he addressed the panel chaired by Senator Edmund Muskie (and on which his family's archnemesis, Bill Brock, also sat), Gore sounded more like the chairman of an oversight hearing than a cub reporter from Nashville: "I believe that conflict-of-interest situations are found most frequently in areas where the government is not paying enough attention," he said. "When elected officials do not perform their duties in a careful and conscientious manner, situations like this are allowed to continue and get worse." Gore even offered an amendment to the bill.

His life was accelerating in multiple directions. Tipper was pregnant, and after a round of Lamaze classes, the Gores brought their first daughter, Karenna, into the world on August 6, 1973. True to form, he had read a stack of books in preparation, including one that said newborns were capable of absorbing large amounts of sensory stimulation. At the hospital he held his brand-new daughter up to the roses he had brought Tipper, trying to determine whether she could smell them.

Early motherhood was both a delight and a trial for Tipper. While Gore was working long hours at the paper, Karenna was "overly demanding and had me wrapped around her finger at two years of age," she wrote. She stayed pretty busy herself outside the home, pursuing a master's in psychology from George Peabody College in Nashville, a degree that she received in 1975. Nancy Warnecke taught her the basics of photography in her basement darkroom, and with Nancy's encouragement, Tipper enrolled in a course at Nashville Technical College taught by *Tennessean* photo editor Jack Corn. Tipper impressed him with her discerning eye, easy way with people, and eagerness to learn. One class assignment was to produce a photograph showing that the subject clearly loved her. The result was a sweetly intimate portrait of her bare-chested young husband as he shaved, his face bathed in shadow and lather. Corn offered her a job at the *Tennessean* as a three-day-a-week lab technician.

It was grunt work — making coffee, developing film, mixing smelly darkroom chemicals — but Corn also gave her small features to shoot on her days off, and she continued to improve. He liked Tipper's habit of trying to exceed the assignment. Send her out to do a basic head shot, he said, and she would come back with something a little better. And she began to love photography's power to provoke and inspire. It was exciting when people called to help after the paper ran her photo of an evicted woman sitting in the rain. She thought she had found a career. Her long-term plan had been to become a child therapist, perhaps as a way of easing youngsters through some of the darkness she had experienced herself. But now she was hooked on photography and wanted to go full-time at the *Tennessean*. Corn was ready to give her the next staff opening.

Albert and Pauline Gore were still not thrilled about their son's — and now their daughter-in-law's — deepening involvement with the paper. Memories of the senator's humiliation at the 1956 convention were still fresh for Pauline, who said she once tried to interest the *Washington Post*'s Katharine Graham in buying the *Tennessean*. "Tragedy it didn't work," she said. Albert complained about the "slightly above slave wages" his reporter-son was paid. He wanted to help the young family but was usually rebuffed by his son, who was intent on proving his independence. Gore especially hated anything that smacked of parental pampering. When his parents presented him with a brand-new Chevrolet one year as a birthday surprise, hiding it on the side of the house in Carthage, "he was really upset," said a friend who was there. "It was a show of luxury." Still, he was willing to take other less conspicuous forms of parental largesse, like the 1969 land deal with his father that had positioned him to make money with the Tanglewood subdivision.

Gore also benefited from his father's friendship with Armand Hammer. Hammer liked making money for his friends, and he considered the senator a valuable one. When zinc was discovered in Smith County in the 1960s, the Gore family once again found Hammer eager to help. His company, Occidental, offered Gore and some of his neighbors a more lucrative deal for mineral rights to their land than other mining firms did — $7.50 an acre (per quarter) in advance — in addition to the usual 4 percent production royalty once the zinc was mined.

One critical, mineral-rich piece of land, the McDonald farm just across the Caney Fork River from the Gores, remained beyond the company's grasp. In 1969, while the elder Gore was still in the Senate, he had joined Hammer in calling on Belle McDonald to see whether they could strike a deal. Hammer offered $20,000 a year to lease the mineral rights, double the best price she had received, but McDonald refused. After her death in 1972, Occidental bought the land outright from Cumberland Presbyterian Church (to which she had left her estate) for $160,000, overpaying in a bidding war with another company. Hammer had no interest in a farm, only the minerals beneath the surface, and asked Albert Gore to take it off his hands. Gore said he would if Hammer gave him the unusually lucrative mineral lease terms he had offered Belle McDonald. On August 27, 1973, Occidental sold him the land for $80,000, and in a separate transaction on the same day, Gore bought the mineral rights to it, also for $80,000.

Senator Gore didn't want the McDonald farm either; he had someone else in mind for it. For young Al Gore, the purchase was a bit of a gamble. He would be paying more for it than land in the area was worth, but the zinc lease was potentially lucrative, and the spread gave him something else as well: a residence in the congressional district his father once represented. On September 22, father, son, and Occidental completed the three-way deal. Senator Gore leased the subsurface rights back to Occidental, the terms calling for $20,000 in the first year, $10,000 annually for the next three years, and $20,000 for each year after that. And Al Gore bought the farm from the senator for $140,000, paying $80,000 for the land and $60,000 for the subsurface lease. (His father kept the first $20,000 lease payment.) To close the deal, Gore made a $40,000 down payment out of profits from his other real estate venture and borrowed the rest. The 88 acres of pastureland and 2,100-square-foot ranch-style brick home, visible from his parents' deck across the river, remains his legal residence.

The zinc lease, courtesy of Hammer, did indeed prove valuable. Gore was paid nearly $200,000 over the next eleven years by Occidental, which did some exploratory drilling but no actual mining. It certainly provided a boost to his reporter's salary and eventually helped him buy another home, in Nashville's leafy Bellemeade neighborhood, for $76,000. Occidental sold the lease in 1985 to another firm, Union Zinc, which began mining in the late 1980s. Gore's total revenue from the contract through the early 1990s exceeded $300,000, making it his most important source of income after his congressional salary.

At the paper, Gore's investigative targets were getting bigger. For months he had picked up rumors about bribery in zoning cases coming before the Metro Council. A practice called "councilmanic privilege" gave members virtual veto power over applications to rezone land in their districts. Gore kept hearing of property owners and developers shaken down for cash to have their zoning cases placed on the council's legislative calendar. He spent several weeks buried in public records, and one day in late 1973 he marched into Seigenthaler's office with a forbidding armful of documents, ready to lay out his theory. Seigenthaler adored his young protégé but wasn't interested in an hour-long Goreian seminar on land use. But Gore insisted and walked Seigenthaler through the evidence: in numerous cases council members were using their privilege to introduce, withdraw, and reintroduce rezoning applications for no apparent reason. It remained mostly circumstance and surmise, but Gore strongly suspected extortion. Seigenthaler, now tantalized, gave him dispensation to drop everything else and go after the story.

Gore's inquiry was no secret on the Metro Council, and it frayed his already tense relations with some members. Gore didn't invest a lot of effort in journalistic bedside manner; he was largely indifferent to the schmoozing informality some of the older reporters in town employed with elected officials. His youth, his powerful connections at the *Tennessean,* and their smoldering resentment of his father (Albert Gore's vote against the 1964 Civil Rights Act hadn't been forgotten by some black members) only deepened the council members' suspicions. "Here he was, a snooping reporter, from a political family. . . . We just sort of resented Al Gore Jr. being in a position to snoop on people," said Joe Crockett, a councilman from that era. "He was sharp, and people were scared of him because he knew what he was doing. . . . A lot of people were nervous. A lot of people had done things." Crockett also grumbled about Gore's appearance, which he described as "that laid-back hippie look."

The tensions broke into open warfare in November 1973, when the council voted itself a brazen junket, sending thirty-three members and staff to San Juan for the National League of Cities annual meeting. Gore followed along and had a great ride with the story, including one hilarious account of the hotel reservations snafu that erased the council's luxury beachfront bookings, landing them in a rusting inland firetrap. Nearly all of the irate delegation snubbed a breakfast at which the mayor of San Juan showed up bearing a case of champagne to make amends. "Pouting Metro Junketeers Get a City's Apology," read the front-page headline.

Neither Gore's investigative work nor his San Juan stories sat well with Councilman Robert "Dude" Reasoner. When the council-bashing reporter also began helping himself to food and drink from a hospitality suite that Reasoner was sponsoring, he unleashed a wallpaper-peeling tirade that included a threat to throw Gore out of a window. "I don't even have language like that in my repertoire now to phrase things the way he phrased it," said one council member who witnessed the outburst. "He just went wacko, and Gore stood there and took it." The run-in left Gore shaken and concerned enough about his ability to continue covering the beat that he asked the council's attorney, Milton Sitton, to help mediate the hard feelings. "He was concerned that he created a big problem for himself," Sitton said.

But he also kept digging, and shortly after Christmas he found what he was looking for. Real estate developer Gilbert Cohen, serving a term as foreman of the Davidson County grand jury, complained to Gore one day about his difficulty in securing council approval of an alley closure required for construction of an office tower near the Vanderbilt campus. The ordinance had been placed on the calendar for a first reading in October but was pulled before its second required consideration on November 20. The project was in the Twentieth District, represented by Morris Haddox, a popular, up-and-coming young politician who owned a pharmacy on Charlotte Street not far from the site. Cohen thought he was merely prodding Gore into a story on councilmanic inefficiency. Gore told him he was on to something bigger.

But instead of pursuing the story in the traditional way, the *Tennessean* elected to become partners with local law enforcement, setting up what amounted to a joint sting operation run by Democratic District Attorney Tom Shriver, a former *Tennessean* copy boy who enjoyed a long, friendly relationship with Seigenthaler. Cohen agreed to be wired for sound and met Haddox at his pharmacy on the morning of January 19. Gore parked just out of view, crouched in his yellow Volkswagen. Tennessee Bureau of Investigation agents listened nearby in unmarked cars. Haddox first asked for Cohen's help in working out a real estate deal, then questioned him about the furniture business. Finally, he said: "Your biggest commodity is money." Cohen replied, "My biggest commodity is money, that's right."

Cohen asked what it would take to pass the alley closure. "It'll take a grand to get it done," said Haddox. Cohen called him later and told him he would be at the corner of Seventh and Union downtown at noon with a $300 down payment (cash supplied by the *Tennessean*). It was not an arbitrary location: three *Tennessean* photographers had a perfect view from the offices of the paper's legal counsel, directly across the street. Haddox swung by in his Lincoln Continental as Cohen, still wearing a wire, handed him an envelope.

The *Tennessean* had a councilman cold, on audiotape and film, taking a bribe. Yet it held the story for three weeks to let the criminal investigation ripen. Gore continued to play junior G-man, transcribing the tapes and going over them with the DA's office. It must have been an unbearable interval for him. Worried that his notes and records might fall into the hands of the *Banner* or another competitor, he stashed them at John Warnecke's house. On February 5, Haddox reintroduced Cohen's alley closure, which passed unanimously. Gore and the *Tennessean* photographers testified the following afternoon before a grand jury, which indicted Haddox for bribery the same day. He was arrested that evening in the Metro Council chamber — taken into custody while attending a session of the council's ethics committee.

Gore began the kind of hot streak that most reporters only dream about. On February 7, the Haddox story was stripped across the top of the front page, with a sequence of pictures showing Cohen making the payoff. Just the day before, another investigative project Gore was pursuing had made it to print. He reported that Metro Councilman Jack Clariday owned $20,000 worth of stock in a campground he helped make possible by sponsoring the rezoning of the land it occupied. Clariday was also eventually indicted for bribery. Gore rode the zoning scandal throughout that spring, producing a flurry of page 1 follow-ups and Sunday "explainers."

Haddox, who is black, and his supporters cried entrapment. They charged that the paper's close collaboration with the district attorney, with whom Haddox had clashed in the past, made the indictment suspicious. James Mock, chairman of Concerned Citizens for a Safer Nashville, called the case the result of a political "scenario" written by Seigenthaler and Gore. He accused them of "character assassination" and "attacking the whole political structure of our black community." The charge was untrue, but not quite a paranoid fantasy. Haddox was planning to run for the state senate against incumbent Avon Williams, a favorite of the *Tennessean* and personally close to Seigenthaler. "Haddox was in a different group," said courthouse reporter Ken Jost, who covered the trial. "Williams was the recognized leader of Nashville's black community, and Morris Haddox was up and coming."

Another strange twist to the story makes the purge scenario even more unlikely. As Gore closed in on Haddox, Seigenthaler facilitated an eleventh-hour attempt to warn the councilman that he was at risk. On Sunday, January 13, six days before Cohen wore the wire, Seigenthaler was at home watching the Miami-Minnesota Super Bowl with Mansfield Douglas, another black Metro Council member. He received a call from one of his closest friends, attorney Gilbert Merritt, who said he was aware that Haddox was seeking money from Cohen and his partner. Merritt later testified that he asked Seigenthaler to intercede and get Haddox to back off, but that Seigenthaler said he had an obligation to Gore to stay out of it. But inexplicably, he handed the phone to Douglas, who heard the same plea from Merritt and agreed to speak to Haddox. Douglas testified that when they spoke Haddox denied that he had made any attempt to solicit a bribe.

What looked to be a slam dunk ended as a bitter defeat for Gore and his paper when the Haddox case went to trial. The tapes were virtually inaudible, ruined by the rustling of Cohen's clothing against the hidden microphone, and the trial judge refused a state motion to provide jurors with transcripts. Haddox claimed that he took the money only to turn it over to the authorities. Defense attorney William Wilson played the race card, charging that the case against Haddox was "a prearranged plan . . . born in the office of the *Nashville Tennessean*" to ruin his career. "Thank God the day has arrived when a black man can hold his head high and be elected to public office in this community. Thank God the day has arrived when the word 'Nigger' has disappeared from this language," Wilson said, looking directly at one of the four black jurors.

It ended in a mistrial, the jury deadlocked 8–3 in favor of conviction, with one member undecided. Three black jurors held out for acquittal, which Haddox won in the retrial a month later. Gore, who testified in both proceedings, sat stunned on a bench outside the courtroom, his head in his hands.

Like his father's defeat, the case was more painful evidence that righteousness did not guarantee victory. Others saw also in Gore's anguish a streak of white liberal guilt. The denunciations from the black community stung a young man who grew up believing that he and his family were on the side of the angels in civil rights and race relations. "Gore was very tense when it was over," said former metro reporter and managing editor Wayne Whitt. "I think it bothered him that the one he caught was black. He was troubled by that."

Despite his disappointment over the Haddox case, the previous three years had afforded Gore a new emotional and intellectual autonomy. He was still Albert Gore's son, but he had stretched his horizons beyond politics, distinguishing himself as a journalist and studying life's critical questions in divinity school. Public office was now more of a personal choice, not simply the fulfillment of a familial obligation. He took a leave of absence from the *Tennessean* and on August 28, 1974, entered Vanderbilt Law School, the move his parents had been urging for years. He said later that his experience with the Haddox trials compelled him to learn more about the power of the law. He also spoke of combining journalism with a legal background, as had been accomplished by his sister's friend Fred Graham, whom he called "a role model."

But neither his Nashville friends nor his professors believed he would ever make a career of the law. It was clear to those around him that the school was a final staging area for his entry into politics. "It was my sense that he had very carefully thought through his desire to be politically active," said Donald Hall, Gore's professor in a second-year legislative drafting seminar, in which he wrote a hypothetical speedy trial statute for the state of Tennessee.

His grades were once again average to mediocre, mostly Bs and Cs. He joined a study group with two other students that met at 7:30 A.M. and again in the evenings. Steve Cobb, later elected to the state legislature, said Gore was "a little embarrassed to talk about" his academic standing, but that when his time came to stand up in class and recite cases, "he did as well as anyone else."

Despite intentions that were now in plain view, he still actively discouraged any discussion of his political plans. In August 1975, when Representative Richard Fulton's election as mayor opened up Nashville's congressional seat, Gore's name surfaced in speculation about the race. But Gore went out of his way to douse the talk. "He always said he was going to finish law school, and nobody believed him," said Eve Zibart.

Even before he left the paper for law school, Thompson, Sutherland, and other newsroom friends considered his future such a fait accompli that one evening over post-deadline beers they mapped it out through the millennium, election by election. "We planned his ascendancy to the presidency," said Sutherland. "He went to Congress ahead of schedule, and he went to the Senate ahead of schedule." (The vice presidency was one way station no one factored into the scenario.)

Gore wasn't quite through with newspapering. In 1975 he returned to the *Tennessean* as an editorial writer. Seigenthaler signed off on an arrangement where he would take most of his law classes in the morning, then spend the afternoon and evenings at the paper. It was like one more graduate course, this one immersing him in national policy and, in the words of his fellow editorialist Phil Sullivan, giving him "a feel for how newspapers select and support candidates." He also had a series of conversations about the future with Seigenthaler, who was encouraging him to make the leap into politics. He thought Gore would have made a first-rate journalist, but he also had larger concerns about the pool of talent within the state's Democratic Party. "He felt we needed some young blood, young Democratic blood," said editorial page editor Lloyd Armour. Others say that someone with an even more powerful influence, his sister Nancy, was telling him that this was his time. "Nancy, more than anyone, was really encouraging him," said his cousin Mark Gore.

Ultimately, Gore didn't need much convincing, just the right opportunity. On Friday morning, February 27, 1976, he was at home, between law school classes and his shift at the paper, when Seigenthaler called with the news. Fourth District Representative Joe Evins was going to announce his retirement over the weekend, opening up the Carthage congressional seat. The story would be in Monday's *Tennessean*. Seigenthaler didn't need to say anything else. "You know what I think," he told Gore.

The call is another cherished episode from the Gore canon, told and retold unvaryingly over the years. It was a moment of epiphany and impulse, the Gores contend, rather than careful planning and calculation, that resulted in a life-changing decision. In recounting this scene, Gore has claimed complete surprise at Seigenthaler's message. "I hung up the phone and told Tipper, 'I think I'm going to run for Congress.' She said, 'What? 'You're kidding.'" Then, perhaps trying to cope with the stress of finally committing himself to the destiny his parents had envisioned, he dropped to the floor and began doing push-ups.

There was probably a little more of a plan at work than Gore let on. The February 23 *Banner* had run a story all but predicting Evins's retirement. The fifth-ranking Democrat on the House Appropriations Committee, Evins was a master pork-barreler who had steered hundreds of millions of dollars in dams, roads, and other lucre to the Fourth District. But with the post-Watergate class of young House liberals shaking up the Democratic Caucus, purging old southern bulls of leadership positions, his days were clearly numbered. After surviving one coup attempt and a heart attack a few years earlier, Evins had clearly decided to leave before he was forced out.

Gore made scores of calls to friends over the next three frenetic days, ostensibly seeking their advice on whether to make the race, but few people he spoke to thought there was any doubt about his plans. *Tennessean* political writer Larry Daughtrey, whose wife, Martha Craig Daughtrey, was one of Gore's Vanderbilt law professors (and is currently a federal judge), saw Gore in the newsroom after Seigenthaler's call and asked him whether he was interested in Evins's seat.

"When are you going to make up your mind?" Daughtrey asked.

"I already have," said Gore.

He finished off his last editorial assignment and left it in Lloyd Armour's box. It never ran, but Armour remembers the lead: "Education in Tennessee is a disgrace."

Gore wished the timing had been different; it bothered him to leave law school after less than two years. Not that he had any great fondness for it: he told friends later that a year was all anyone really needed. But it was a credential that his parents wanted him to have, and one that future opponents were likely to possess. Even after reaching Congress, he made inquiries about finishing his degree in Washington. Some of his teachers encouraged him to stay with it while he ran, but Gore knew he needed to throw all his energies into the campaign. Seats like Evins's opened up once a generation in Tennessee; there would be no better chance to get a toehold in politics. "He said, 'If I'm going to do it, I should do it right,'" said James Blumstein, his municipal law professor.

There was a far more sensitive piece of business for Gore to deal with: telling his parents. They were at the University of California at Davis, where the senator was lecturing, when Gore reached them with a post-midnight phone call. At first they worried that there had been an accident. But then their son told them of Evins's retirement and his decision. "Well, son," said a thrilled Albert Gore, "I'll vote for you."

But then Gore delivered the crushing addendum. He wanted his father to play no public role in the campaign. Pauline Gore remembers the moment: "What he said to his father was, 'I must be my own man. I must become my own man. I must not be your candidate.'" As a political matter, the issue was a wash. The name on the ballot, Albert Gore Jr., left no mystery about whose son he was. Those who still hated his father were not going to vote for him, and those who admired him were likely to — whether the senator went into hiding or not. Albert was deeply hurt by his son's decision, although he later said he understood. "I realized he was right," the senator told Larry King in 1993. "I had seen — and I should have remembered it — I had seen a number of congressmen and senators whose sons and daughters had run, and they would get out and help and they'd get beat."

Albert and Pauline flew back immediately to help behind the scenes, and Gore summoned a circle of family and friends to his farm that weekend for the first strategy session. On Sunday, the same day that news of Evins's retirement broke, Gore's small band of supporters fanned out across the Fourth District with a letter to key Democrats, announcing that he would make his candidacy official the next day. To the last he played coy, even with his own paper. When a *Tennessean* reporter putting together a story on potential successors to Evins called to ask about his plans, Gore stonewalled. "I have no statement on that," he said.

Gore had barred his parents from any visible role, but they remained active offstage, especially the indomitable Pauline. As Gore finished each draft of his announcement, someone would walk it into Pauline, who was making soup in the kitchen. Several times, said one local supporter, she picked it apart and sent it back to her son. He eventually finished a version that passed her muster.

On the morning of Monday, March 1, as a small crowd gathered in a brisk wind on the steps of the Smith County courthouse in Carthage, Al Gore excused himself to go to a bathroom inside, where he threw up. He had prepared himself for this moment, but his balky stomach reminded him that he knew better than anyone what it meant. He was four weeks shy of twenty-eight, and the unanchored years, as Andy Schlesinger described them, were over. The role reversal that had begun in a canoe on the Caney Fork six years earlier was nearly complete. He was stepping up to run the family business.

With Tipper and two-and-a-half-year-old Karenna beside him, and his buddy Frank Sutherland writing the story for the *Tennessean,* he gave a brief speech vowing to fight for lower interest and electric rates and the reduction of "cruelly high" unemployment levels. Then he came to the heart of the matter. Gore said he didn't want people casting votes on the basis of his last name. "I want to speak on the issues, and the people of the Fourth District are perfectly capable of judging me on this basis," he declared.

Privately, Gore fretted that they were not. "I don't want people voting for me because I'm Albert Gore's son," he told Walter King Robinson, the old family friend and real estate partner. Robinson just shrugged and said, "That's probably the only reason they *will* vote for you."

Carthage Campaigner

ONE OF the few who claimed to be truly surprised by Al Gore's decision to run for Congress was his wife. Tipper Gore had told friends that her husband would never follow his father into politics, and she took him at his word that he intended to combine a law degree and his newspaper experience into some kind of writing career. Although most of the world saw public office as a certainty for Gore, she felt as if her life had been hijacked. "That was a bombshell," she said in 1987. "We were going in a very different direction." She had little of her in-laws' zeal for the political hunt, and certainly no appetite for a reprise of the smears and lies of 1970. But even she must have sensed at least some of the inevitability. Politics always rumbled in the distance, like the dog a few houses away that never stopped barking.

Her idea was to meet her husband halfway: she would campaign for him on her days off. Gore wanted her to be happy, but he also needed a full-time political spouse. Pauline had done nothing less for his father, and he expected the same. Jack Corn found himself mediating the dispute. He met the couple at the *Tennessean* one evening shortly after Gore announced his candidacy. "They were both very worried," he recalled. "He wanted to run for Congress, she wanted to be a photographer."

Corn sensed that Tipper was looking for a potential savior, someone to stand up for her budding talent, to shield her from a life of coffees she didn't want to attend and talks she didn't want to give. "I guess she knew she had to go with Al," he said. "But she wanted me to say, 'No, no, no, that would be the wrong thing to do. You're going to be great.'" But instead of trying to keep his promising young shooter, he helped Gore ease her out the door and onto the campaign trail. He promised that the job would be waiting for her if Gore lost the primary. For the moment, he told Tipper, "you need to be together, and you need to help him win this race." She agreed, reluctantly.

Corn had good reason to expect that she would be back in the *Tennessean* darkroom by late summer. Gore was hardly anyone's favorite to win the Fourth District primary. The rare open congressional seat created by Joe Evins's retirement had touched off a stampede. Tennessee had no runoff law that would force the top two vote-getters into a second race if neither won a majority. Whoever finished first on August 5 was the Democratic nominee. And with no serious Republican competition, the victor needed only to stay out of jail or the morgue to win in November. There were eight other candidates, several of them formidable competitors. T. Tommy Cutrer, a popular radio announcer at the Grand Ole Opry, had labor support. Rutherford County Judge Ben Hall McFarlin enjoyed a large following in the district's second largest county. But most of the smart money was on State Representative Stanley Rogers, the thirty-seven-year-old majority leader of the Tennessee House of Representatives and a protégé of House Speaker Ned McWherter. Rogers had spent years laying the groundwork to succeed Evins, accumulating a healthy war chest and support from the party establishment.

Even with a famous Tennessee name and connections at the state's dominant newspaper, Al Gore faced significant obstacles to starting up his first campaign. He had never been active in the local or state party, nor was there anything like a Gore machine on standby, ready to be oiled and popped into gear. His father was an indifferent organizer and fund-raiser, and his races were famously ad hoc enterprises. "For Albert, this is a twenty-first-century campaign," cracked one ally during the 1970 race. "Why, he even has a schedule."

For all his years of watching Albert and Pauline campaign, doing it himself was like struggling with a foreign language. Gore knew the basic vocabulary, but the grammar and idioms took time to master, and vomiting before the Carthage announcement didn't purge his anxieties. Tipper said it was "agony" to approach strangers and ask them to vote for her husband. "If I have to go to another tea, I think I'll explode," she told Eve Zibart (although it's unclear whether she was talking about her composure or her bladder). Being relatively new to

Tennessee also made her an easy mark for hecklers and wiseacres. One man demanded that she name all twenty-five counties in the Fourth District — an abusive question even for a seasoned pol. In May, Larry Daughtrey saw the Gores shaking hands at a shopping center in Mc-Minnville and thought they looked lost. "I don't think I've ever seen two more uncomfortable people in my life," he said.

Gore's first campaign was the only close race he ever ran in Tennessee. Had he been defeated, he might well have decided that politics truly wasn't for him. A look at how he won reveals the roots of an operating style that has remained largely intact for nearly twenty-five years: a relentless work ethic; tactical caution; passionate advocacy of worthy but low-risk issues; and a willingness to revise, or simply muddy up, politically inconvenient positions. His message reflected lessons absorbed from both of his parents. Gore identified with his father's New Deal liberalism, but the senator's 1970 defeat stood for him as a bitter lesson in the perils of staking out too many positions that challenged constituents' core values and beliefs. That meant running not on Albert Gore's legacy but at a safe distance from it, refining and homogenizing his message for an increasingly Republican state. Gore was also infused with a large dose of his mother's pragmatism, as evidenced by his pandering to Fourth District conservatives who loathed the senator. Al Gore honored his father by entering public life, but he honored his mother by doing what it took to win.

He started by making over his appearance, shedding the casual dishevelment of the Watergate-era investigative reporter. The only journalist Gore would ever again resemble was Clark Kent. His hair was trimmed, and the down-the-middle part migrated to the side. Self-conscious about his age, Gore tried to add some years by adopting the campaign uniform to which he would cling through six House and Senate races: blue suit (with trousers that were always short, to the exasperation of his wife and staff), a blue or white wing collar oxford shirt, and a red tie. The suit jacket stayed on even through broiling midsummer rallies.

"Rekindling the American Spirit" was the bland, feel-good bicentennial tag line of the Gore campaign. Some of his father's old issues popped up in speeches, like tax reform, lower electric rates, and pledges of eternal devotion to the TVA. But they were subordinate to a menu of consumer-friendly pitches designed to assure wary voters that while he might be Albert Gore's son, he was also his own man, and certainly no mutton-headed radical from Harvard. Indeed, Gore promised they would hardly know that Joe Evins, the legendary caseworker and pork-barreler, was gone. One of his commercials, produced by Memphis ad man Deloss Walker, showed an earnest young Gore looking into the camera and pledging that every Social Security problem, every snag in veterans' benefits, would be run to ground with seamless efficiency. The basic message, said Representative Bart Gordon, then a member of the state Democratic committee and the man who would succeed Gore in the House, was: "Don't worry, I'm not going to be a liberal. I'm going to work hard for this district just like Joe Evins."

More surprising — and dismaying to a few of his former newspaper colleagues — was his attempt to reinvent himself as a conservative on several hot-button issues. While Gore's *Tennessean* editorials were unsigned and generally reflected the consensus of the editorial board rather than an individual viewpoint, editor Lloyd Armour remembered him as well within the mainstream of the page's liberal politics. Yet as he read the news coverage of the campaign, Armour was struck by the gulf between Gore the editorialist and Gore the candidate. Gore told *Tennessean* reporter Alan Carmichel, apropos of no real issue in the race, that he believed homosexuality to be "abnormal." He also opposed additional gun registration laws in 1976, despite having written an editorial in which he decried the proliferation of cheap handguns. "It seemed to me he was trying to reposition himself," said Armour.

Gore bristled when reporters questioned him about his newfound conservatism. "I believe what I say," he protested to Carmichel. Privately, though, he was more candid. Frank Ritter, his old city editor, remembers confronting him during a visit to the paper. "He said, 'Look, I'm running in a district where people favor guns, and there's no way I can win if I take a position that indicates that I'm going to take away their guns. It's as simple as that.'" Local gun advocates were not exactly sold on their new best friend Al Gore. The Citizens Committee for the Right to Keep and Bear Arms endorsed T. Tommy Cutrer, noting that his posture "on all of the issues indicates a conservative philosophy consistent with the stand he had taken against the control of firearms." Gun owners' instincts were, of course, right. Gore would cast no major votes on gun issues in the House, but as a senator in 1990 he would support an unsuccessful attempt to ban assault-style weapons. A year later he voted for the Brady Bill, which required a five-day waiting period and police background check for handgun purchases. The 1991 version failed, but it finally passed in 1993 with the support of the Clinton-Gore administration.

Gore also stayed carefully in step with his district on abortion. "I don't believe a woman's freedom to live her own life, in all cases, outweighs the fetus's right to life," he told a Lincoln County audience one week before primary day. But as Gore's target audience changed, so did his position on reproductive choice. His turnabout on abortion remains the most dramatic shift of position in his career. Over his two decades in public life, he has transformed himself from a reliable "pro-life" vote in the House — compiling an 84 percent rating from the National Right to Life Committee — to vice presidential defender of President Clinton's decision to veto a congressional ban on "partial birth" abortions.

Gore began his House career as a strong supporter of the Hyde Amendment, which bans virtually all Medicaid funding for abortions. He even supported a version of Hyde that barred federal assistance in ending pregnancies that resulted from rape or incest, allowing payment only when the mother's life was at risk. In 1980 he voted to prohibit women employed by the federal government from choosing health insurance that covered abortion under any circumstance. "It is my deep personal conviction that abortion is wrong," he wrote to a constituent in 1984. "I hope that someday we will see the current outrageously large number of abortions drop sharply. Let me assure you that I share your belief that innocent human life must be protected and I have an open mind on how to further this goal." The following year he was one of seventy-four House Democrats who supported an unsuccessful amendment to the Age Discrimination Act of 1975 that would have defined "person" so as to include unborn children from the moment of conception. Gore later insisted that there had been a "misunderstanding" about the measure, sponsored by Michigan Republican Mark Siljander, and that it dealt only with "public hospitals and procedures in the third trimester." But Siljander, who lost his seat in 1986, said that it was explicitly designed to deny federal funds to any institution that performed abortions at any time. "I don't know how much clearer one can be," he said, than calling for an amendment that defines life as beginning at conception.

In the mid-1980s, Gore's position began to evolve. After reaching the Senate in 1985, with his eye more firmly fixed on a future in presidential politics, his votes took a more liberal cast. He opposed revocation of tax-exempt status for organizations that performed, financed, or provided facilities for abortions, and he voted against a requirement that minors obtain parental consent before receiving contraceptives at federally funded clinics. He also opposed confirmation of antiabortion Supreme Court nominees like Justice William Rehnquist (for chief justice) and Judge Robert Bork.

The elasticity of his record posed a problem during his first presidential race in 1988, especially since he was accusing other opponents, Representative Richard Gephardt in particular, of flip-flopping and pandering to special interests. The Siljander Amendment proved particularly inconvenient. "Since there's a record of that vote, we have only one choice," an unnamed Gore adviser told *U.S. News & World Report.* "In effect, what we have to do is deny, deny, deny. . . . We've muddled the point, and with luck, attention will turn elsewhere — or at least we'll be lucky enough so the thing doesn't blow into a full-fledged problem before Super Tuesday."

By 1990 Gore had come full circle, opposing Senator Jesse Helms's Siljander-like amendment to define "child" in the United Nations Convention on the Rights of the Child to include "the unborn at every stage of biological development." In 1992 he cosponsored the Freedom of Choice Act, which would have barred any strictures on abortion, even after the fetus was deemed capable of living outside the womb, if necessary to preserve the health or life of the mother. And as Bill Clinton's running mate, he endorsed Clinton's proposal for a national health insurance plan that would have covered abortions.

Gore has been hard-pressed to explain the transition. Grilled by Tim Russert and Lisa Meyers on *Meet the Press* as a vice presidential candidate in the fall of 1992, he repeated, a robotic seven times, "I believe a woman ought to have the right to choose." When David Frost asked that same autumn about his "sea change," Gore denied that any had taken place. He said he still regarded abortion as the taking of "innocent human life" but conceded that he no longer used such phrases in letters because they are "so loaded with political charge." He added:

I think that if, you know, I search my heart on what I really believe about this issue, it's the same now as it was then. And I think many of us have mixed feelings, because there are two questions involved, aren't there? The first question is how you feel about an abortion in a given set of circumstances. And the second question . . . is, who makes the decision? And regardless of how you and I might feel about the rightness or wrongness of a given decision in a particular set of circumstances, I believe the government ought not to have the right to go in and order a woman to accept its judgment about how to weigh the different aspects of the decision and order the woman to make the decision that government says she has to make instead of leaving the decision to her. I've always believed that.

Except, of course, when it came to low-income women with no economic resources of their own for medical care other than Medicaid. When Gore represented a conservative congressional district in Tennessee, the choice these women faced was to accept the government's judgment or risk their lives trying to end a pregnancy. His defenders in the pro-choice community argue that Gore's shift was a principled one, reflecting a shift in the dynamics of the debate from a focus on Medicaid funding to the Reagan administration's more far-reaching assault on abortion rights and a Supreme Court poised to overturn *Roe v. Wade.* "I'm not saying politics had no role," said Kate Michelman, president of the National Abortion and Reproductive Rights Action League (NARAL), who met numerous times with Gore as his position changed. But, she said, he genuinely "grappled with the issue," and Tipper Gore played an important role in moderating his view. "He was uncomfortable with the act of abortion," Michelman said. "But it takes time for someone to separate out their disdain for the act from what should be the rule of law."

Gore's tack to the right paid significant dividends in 1976. On July 6, he secured the endorsement of the *Nashville Banner,* a longtime antagonist of his father's. Although the Stahlman family had sold the paper to the Gannett chain four years earlier, it still retained some of the old prickly conservatism. But Gore won over the editorial board with his record as a reporter, his command of the issues, and an apparent willingness to distance himself from the liberalism of both Albert Gore and the *Tennessean.* The endorsement netted him critical — possibly decisive — votes in a close primary race. "It really solidified his base," said former *Banner* city editor Ed Manassah, now publisher of the *Louisville Courier-Journal,* "especially among conservative and moderate readers and in the business community." Gore's rightward tilt notwithstanding, the *Tennessean,* to no one's surprise, added its own enthusiastic endorsement.

The first campaign was a homespun enterprise, sustained largely by family and friends. The Gores converted their farmhouse into a headquarters, filling the living room with desks and leaflets. Nancy and Frank Hunger flew up from Greenville regularly to make calls and reenergize Albert Gore's old supporters. Volunteers who later formed the core of Gore's early congressional staff worked long hours. Two Carthage women with Gore family connections, Alberta Winkler and Melinda Mofield, answered the phones. Larry Harrington, a young law school graduate and nephew of one of Senator Gore's former aides, signed on to travel with the candidate (and later joined his congressional staff). Gore's Harvard classmate Ken Jost, his future legislative director, took a leave from the *Tennessean* to become campaign press secretary, setting up a combination office and bedroom in the Gores' glassed-in back porch with a sweeping view of the Cumberland Hills. His girlfriend, reporter Eve Zibart, stayed at the paper but came on weekends to cook, assuring the staff of at least one good meal a week. She also brought along a friend, an amiable former sportswriter for the *Banner* named Roy Neel, who went on to serve Gore for fifteen years as a congressional aide and vice presidential chief of staff.

At the suggestion of a family friend, Gore dropped by the office of Henderson insurance executive Johnny Hayes. Hayes was a sunny-natured good ole boy who once spent two years filling an unexpired term as a Sumner County commissioner; he had decided that they had been the most miserable years of his life. "People pickin' at you twenty-four hours a day," he said. But he had a knack for assembling money, and his favorite candidate had quit the race. Hayes liked Gore, even though he was one of the many politicians in the Fourth who regarded him as a long shot.

Hayes did what he could to find money, but it was difficult. "The funds just didn't come in," said Walter King Robinson, who served as finance chairman. He attributed the shortage to a backlash against the new campaign finance reform law passed in 1974. Robinson said he encountered many people who were leery of donating under the new system, which required more detailed record-keeping and government regulation. But part of the problem may also have been Albert Gore's residual unpopularity and voter ambivalence about seeing the Gore name return to Tennessee politics.

As a result, family and friends not only staffed the campaign but subsidized most of it. More than two-thirds of the $188,560 Gore spent (on both the primary and the general election) came from his own resources, principally a $50,000 bank loan and $75,000 out of pocket. The remaining $63,000 represented a network of supporters cutting across both generations of Gores, including Armand Hammer lieutenants like Occidental Petroleum President William McSweeney and Tipper's father, Jack Aitcheson. According to federal election reports, Gore's *Tennessean* friends Frank Ritter and John and Nancy Warnecke also chipped in with smaller amounts.

Later that spring the butterflies in Gore's stomach began to subside, and he felt more comfortable as a candidate. He would start before dawn and race to keep his schedule, using a CB radio in his car (his handle: "Carthage Campaigner") to avoid speed traps. On a good day he hit three county seats in the sprawling Fourth, which stretched from the outer-rim Nashville suburbs to the Alabama border. The traveling entourage was usually no larger than Harrington and reporters from the two Nashville papers, and the drill was the same in each town: visits to the radio station, the newspaper, and every "meat-and-three" (a roadside diner that served lunch specials of meat and three side orders) in the vicinity. With no inherited organization, Gore used a familiar tool to build one — a reporter's notebook. He or Harrington tried to jot down the name of everyone they met so that a follow-up note could be sent.

He filled out his deficits in polish and style with pure energy. Noel Clarkson, who shot the campaign spots for Deloss Walker, remembers Gore stopping the car, climbing through a barbed-wire fence in his blue suit, and jogging two hundred yards into a field to shake hands with a farmer on his tractor. "He was just a bulldog, a tenacious campaigner. He just flat was everywhere at every time," said *Nashville Banner* reporter David Lyons, who watched him climb a telephone pole to chat up a lineman perched at the top. In places where he knew he was behind, he visited and visited and came back again. One store cashier in Lewisburg, part of Rogers's stronghold, said that if he didn't know any better, he'd have thought Gore was running for mayor. Where there was lingering animosity toward his father, Gore worked even harder. "I saw people take his literature and stomp on it," Steve Armistead told the Copley News Service in 1988. "He wore people down. He'd go back four or five times."

A Gore stump speech in those days came complete with a corny, ice-breaking joke, like the Democratic kittens story. He was driving down the road the other day, he explained, and saw a sign that said, "Republican kittens for sale." A couple of days later, as he was driving by again, the same sign said, "Democrat kittens for sale." Well now, Gore would say, that made him stop. He pulled up and asked why the sign no longer advertised Republican kittens. "Oh," the man said, "they've got their eyes open now."

Many Tennessee voters saw a Gore different from the one later caricatured in Washington as "stiff." He reminded some old-timers, not of his father, but of Albert Gore's rival for national attention, Estes Kefauver, another awkward Ivy Leaguer who ingratiated himself with rural voters by listening carefully to their concerns. "He just embraced these people," Lyons, now a Nashville attorney, said of the younger Gore. "He didn't embrace them physically, but he was genuinely interested in what people had to say. And he didn't have an East Coast air about him. He may have been stiff, but he didn't have an appearance of, 'I'm better than you.' Didn't patronize, didn't sound condescending. He didn't sound like everybody thought he would sound — like Prince Albert."

Gore got good, often glowing, press. The *Tennessean*, while trying to be fair with space and play for other candidates, was clearly in the Gore camp. For many young reporters, the affinity was twofold. He was not only of their generation, he had actually been one of them. Even with the formality and the pandering to conservatives, they felt they were covering a kindred soul.

This pleasant rapport was disrupted by only one uncomfortable moment. Riding along with Gore between campaign stops, *Tennessean* reporter Alan Carmichel asked for his views on marijuana laws. Gore said he opposed legalization but endorsed proposals to reduce criminal penalties for first offenders. Then Carmichel asked whether he had ever smoked it himself. The question so flustered Gore, who was driving, that he pulled over to the side of the road and got out of the car for several minutes to consider his answer. When he returned, he said he wouldn't discuss it because he didn't consider the question appropriate. Carmichel withdrew it, he later explained, because he hadn't put the same question to Gore's competitors. Ken Jost, who was riding along with Tipper, described the couple as "indignant," especially because Carmichel hadn't asked the other candidates. "They thought it was unfair and that he wouldn't have asked that question of Gore except that he knew him," Jost said, "so he was taking liberties and being harder on him than he would have on somebody he didn't know."

Perhaps Carmichel — who later served as public affairs director for the TVA and did not respond to requests for an interview — couldn't resist asking because he had a good idea of what an honest answer might have been. Nor was he the only reporter in 1976 who was curious about Gore's drug history. David Lyons, Carmichel's competitor on the *Banner*, recalls that he asked similar questions and that Gore's off-the-record admission was, "I experimented with it." He characterized Gore's reaction to the inquiry as a wounded defensiveness — "Kind of like, 'Hey, I'm one of you. Do you really want to hurt me?'"

In the end, both reporters elected to let it drop. Carmichel said nothing until November 1987, when he recounted the incident to *Tennessean* reporters after Gore's admission during the presidential campaign that he had smoked marijuana occasionally as a student, soldier, and reporter. Lyons said that generational affinities kept him from pursuing the story. Gore *was*, after all, one of them. "It was a sensitive issue, and we were sensitive. He really got a free ride in '76."

There wasn't much difference between Gore and his principal opponent, Stan Rogers. Both were left-of-center Democrats, leaning to the right to win in a conservative district. Rogers's plan was to paint young Gore as an extension of his father. This time, however, it would not be Albert Gore's liberalism at issue, but his business interests. The old Cumberland populist was getting rich, and once again his friend Armand Hammer was involved, not as a partner, but as an employer.

Hammer used revenues from his Libyan oil concession in the late sixties (which he landed with the help of a multimillion-dollar bribe) to buy Island Creek Coal, then the nation's third-largest producer. But by the early 1970s he was unhappy with the profitability of some of the company's long-term sales contracts, including those with the Tennessee Valley Authority. "They had been entered into back when coal was very cheap, and they did not have proper escalation provisions. Hammer wanted to find some way to get the price up on these contracts," said Bill Allen, Gore's longtime Senate aide. Gore, with contacts developed from his years as a congressional patron of the TVA, was just the man for the job. He was practicing law with a Washington firm when Hammer hired him to represent Island Creek in the matter. According to Allen, Hammer was so happy with Gore's work on the TVA accounts that he gave him the whole company to run, naming him chairman in September 1972. By the early 1980s he was making more than $500,000 a year. Hammer's money took some of the sting out of Gore's humiliating loss to Bill Brock in 1970. Had he not been turned out of office, "I would not have made a little fortune for my family," he said, adding, with some exaggeration, "I would still be as poor as ever."

The price of energy was a hot political issue in 1976, and the TVA was under attack for rising electrical rates. Rogers seized on Albert Gore's connection to Hammer, depicting Gore Jr. as a young pawn of profit-hungry corporations. "Al Gore talks about jawboning the coal companies to reduce the price of electricity," Rogers said in a May speech. "All he has to do is jawbone his father at the breakfast table." But there was no real evidence suggesting that the younger Gore would be beholden to anyone. Rogers tried again, raising questions about payments for the zinc rights that Hammer had arranged. But since just about everybody in Smith County received money from zinc leases, that also went nowhere.

Rogers's biggest problem was that he was simply being out-hustled by Gore. He had more money but was running a flabby, old-style campaign, top-heavy with organizational endorsements from the teachers, the realtors, a smattering of unions, and his state house connections. "Stanley did it the old way," said Frank Sutherland. "He went to the courthouse, and Al went to the barns."

Most analysts called the race a dead heat in the final days. On primary night, Gore had planned to arrive at his Holiday Inn headquarters in Lebanon around 8:00 P.M. But at 9:00 he was still at home in Carthage, wary of showing up at his victory party a loser. He was clinging to a narrow lead around 9:30 when he and Tipper, joined by

Jost, got in the car to head across Interstate 40 for the thirty-minute drive to Lebanon. Though his future was teetering in the balance, Gore was calm and focused, roughing out ideas for a victory speech. "Who should I thank?" he asked. Jost nervously rattled off a long list of friends and supporters.

For a couple of hours, it looked like Gore had written the wrong speech. A few minutes after he arrived at the Holiday Inn, the returns came in from Coffee County, Rogers's home base. Gore's 3,000-vote lead had melted to 200; thirty minutes later it was down to 64, then Rogers edged ahead by 100. The Gores retreated to a private room and waited for the numbers that would tell the story — from their base in Smith and Wilson Counties. As Tipper paced nervously up and down the modest double room, Gore sat at the edge of a bed, arms folded and jacket on, quietly watching the news. At about 11:00 Smith and Wilson came through, bumping him up by 2,000 votes and into the lead for good. Rogers, who had a helicopter chartered to fly him to Nashville for television interviews as the victor, called a few minutes later.

Gore won by 3,500 votes out of 115,000 cast, taking 32 percent to Rogers's 29 percent. He benefited from the fragmented nine-candidate field, especially the presence of McFarlin, the Rutherford County judge who diverted several thousand votes that probably would have gone to Rogers. For his own part, Rogers believes that the final tally reflected pent-up remorse over turning Albert Gore out of office prematurely. "I think there was strong sentiment within the Democratic Party that they had let Senator Gore down," Rogers said. "A vote for the son was somewhat of a payback for what they had failed to do for the senator." Indeed, 1976 brought one other redemption of the Gore name. That fall Tennesseans booted Bill Brock out of office after one term and replaced him with family friend Jim Sasser.

It was close to midnight before Gore emerged to greet his small band of supporters, who had been subsisting through the long nerve-racking evening on Coke and potato chips. Despite the laundry list Jost had composed in the car, Gore knew who he wanted to thank first. "My family and I know the bitterness of defeat," he said. "I have a family that teaches you what public service is all about. That is what my family has taught me. I consider the office of congressman a sacred trust."

Primary night also marked the first campaign appearance of Albert Gore. His son had scarcely mentioned him publicly, but with victory now safely in hand, he was allowed to speak, and his thoughts were not about the House, but beyond. He gave the facts a little shave and a trim, but his meaning was clear: "You elected me to Congress when I was twenty-nine years old [actually thirty], and you elected Al at the age of twenty-eight," the senator said. "He's starting out one year earlier than I did, so maybe that means he'll go one step farther."

◆ 9 ◆

Bland Ambition

ON JANUARY 4, 1977, Al Gore stood on the floor of the House of Representatives and raised his right hand to become a member of the 95th Congress, reclaiming the seat his father had first won thirty-nine years earlier. Intent as he was on keeping the senator out of public view during the campaign, Gore could hardly deny him his victory lap after the election. The two men who galloped through the Tennessee countryside for the cameras in 1970 now rode side by side back into Washington. They wore nearly identical blue pinstriped suits at a reception in the stifling Rayburn Building dining room after the swearing-in, and each presided over his own receiving line of well-wishers. "Sweet vindication," the senator said, savoring his brief return to the spotlight, even though his son had run a campaign carefully trimmed of the dissident liberalism that had ended his career.

Gore had a stock answer for reporters who asked how he planned to follow in his father's footsteps. Albert Gore's legacy represented "a wonderful challenge for me," he said. In truth, the challenge wasn't always all that wonderful, but a mixture of burden, inspiration, and cautionary lessons, all of which shaped his son's legislative career. The senator urged Gore to follow the advice Cordell Hull gave him when he began — stay on the House floor and learn the rules. He heeded half of it, spending an hour a day for about a week studying floor procedure with a staff member from the Congressional Research Service. But Gore was also determined "to prove himself in a different way when he came to the House," said Roy Neel. He wanted to be known "as a person in his own right, not just his father's son. He did that pretty quickly."

He took meticulous inventory of his father's weaknesses and strove to ensure that they didn't become his. Where Albert Gore labored honorably but often without recognition in the shadow of Estes Kefauver during the 1950s and early 1960s, his son made visibility a priority. Following up on his senior thesis, which concluded that television coverage of the presidency had eclipsed the legislative branch, he joined the movement for opening House proceedings (and later the Senate) to radio and TV and made sure that he delivered the chamber's first televised floor speech in 1979. "It is a solution for the lack of confidence in government, Mr. Speaker," Gore said of video cameras in the House, high-minded spin from a freshman looking for a solution to his own lack of television exposure.

Like Kefauver, he understood the value of positioning himself at the center of a high-profile investigation. Gore developed a specialty in the big, dramatic oversight committee hearing, featuring witnesses and story lines guaranteed to draw press attention: babies sickened by nutritionally deficient infant formula, families desperately seeking organ transplants for loved ones, communities ravaged by toxic waste dumps, taxpayers ripped off by corrupt federal bureaucrats, and consumers exploited by rapacious corporate executives. Where his father was accused of indifference to home-state sentiment, Gore put himself on a punishing schedule of weekend travel back to the Fourth District. Other young House members of the post-Watergate era were also scooting home regularly, but few did it as relentlessly as Gore, who averaged more than one hundred open meetings a year in the twenty-five counties he represented.

He also drew on his years of observing congressional culture at the elbow of his father, who had paid a price for his clashes with Lyndon Johnson. This time Gore didn't follow his example: he generally obeyed the rules of the club, sticking to the party line and ingratiating himself with his elders. "He wanted to be a good soldier, and to the extent that he wanted to advance himself, he chose issues that wouldn't conflict with the team he was on," said Ken Jost, the former *Nashville Tennessean* reporter and campaign aide who became Gore's first legislative director. Gore hailed the House Democratic leadership of Tip O'Neill, Jim Wright, and Dan Rostenkowski as "extremely progressive" and "committed to reform of the institution of the House."

Gore was proud of his father's liberal legacy but worked assiduously to avoid the left-wing labeling that had hastened the end of his career. He dubbed himself a "raging moderate," a term he thought captured his carefully confined activism. Although widely viewed by voters as a moderate, his overall record leaned to the liberal side sometimes — decidedly liberal for a southerner, especially in domestic affairs. He was a reliable liberal vote on economics, taxation, and labor matters, and some of his legislative impulses resonate today as classic "big government" — a sharp contrast to the centrist New Democrat gospel that he has embraced as Bill Clinton's vice president. As a freshman, Gore supported creation of a new consumer protection agency. Spurred by the Arab oil crisis of the late 1970s, he pushed for a government-owned-and-operated synthetic fuels corporation, "a sort of TVA for synfuels," recalled former aide Eric Black. The idea was shelved as the energy scare blew over.

Yet Gore managed to foster a solidly moderate image by carefully choosing his issues and calibrating his level of political risk. He supported liberal government spending but rarely championed it. He took the same line with Democratic positions on volatile social issues like race, crime and punishment, poverty, and economic fairness. He was a patron of Tennessee tobacco farmers and defended their price support program, but he also worked with the health lobby to toughen the warning labels on cigarette packages. He walked the middle of the road on national security and defense issues, supporting the "nuclear freeze" movement in the early 1980s and at the same time helping to engineer a compromise with the White House to save the MX missile.

The issues on which Gore chose to be "out front" were likely to be worthy but narrow and highly technical. He was most engaged by policy discussions grounded not in emotion but in empirical evidence and rational argumentation. "I like problems with finite answers," he liked to say. His fascination with the future led him to organize hearings on the implications of genetic screening, the greenhouse effect, and the environmental consequences of nuclear war. He also devoted himself to a series of consumer-related matters like influence-peddling in the contact lens industry and television-viewing rights for satellite dish owners. These were all legitimate pursuits, and ones that made few lasting enemies. Colleagues noted his facility for assailing the assailable and fixing the fixable. Dan Glickman, another class of

1976 member and now a Gore ally as secretary of agriculture, told an interviewer in 1987, when he was supporting Dick Gephardt's presidential candidacy, that Gore "had a good knack for finding issues that were not terribly controversial."

Although he eventually became a star of the global environmental movement, he was no green giant in his House days. When Gore's concern for ecosystems was at odds with local economic concerns, he made sure to take care of business at home. The League of Conservation Voters (LCV) gave him a 60 percent for his eight years as a congressman, making him a friend but a tentative one, and hardly the environmental evangelist who would write *Earth in the Balance*. He supported two Tennessee Valley Authority projects scorned by the movement, the Tellico Dam and the Clinch River nuclear reactor. The $3.2 billion experimental breeder reactor was bitterly opposed by both greens and arms controllers, the latter arguing that the plutonium it produced could be diverted to weapons projects. Gore supported the project until its abandonment in 1983.

Brent Blackwelder, president of Friends of the Earth, remembers the day in 1977 when he lobbied Gore to support the Carter administration's attempt to eliminate a series of popular pork-barrel dam projects. The one in his district, the Columbia Dam on the Upper Duck River, was reviled by environmentalists as an endeavor that filled more construction jobs than unmet needs for flood control. "We need some leadership from home," Blackwelder said. "This is an inexcusable way to destroy a river."

The young freshman was sympathetic but unmoved. "What do you want me to do?" Gore replied. "Commit political suicide?"

The early encounter typified for Blackwelder what he saw as the central paradox of Gore, the continual gap between rhetoric and results. "He has as much knowledge as anyone I've seen," he said. "He really understands the details, and when you wanted to have an oversight hearing, he was great. But I can't think of anything where he would actually go out on the line with an amendment to challenge the status quo or change the dynamics of the debate." When environmentalists looked for a "go-to" person in the House to champion a tough issue, they worked through a long list of members before they got to Gore.

Finally, Gore's appearance reinforced the image of moderation —

he simply *looked* the part. His whole presentation exuded an old-fashioned rectitude: the studious manner, the dark suits, the strong, Dudley Do-Right jaw, the picture-book family. It all signaled a life that seemed straight as a string — the vigor of youth purged of the usual libidinous excesses and errors of judgment. Gore was "an old person's idea of a young man," as Michael Kinsley wrote.

Gore was never especially well liked on the Hill. As a colleague, he was an older version of the hard-charging, dynastically burdened Gore of St. Albans and Harvard, a man with no close enemies and no close friends. "There was a veneer, and it was hard to get through it," said Representative Henry Waxman of California, who served with him on the Energy and Commerce Committee. Fellow freshmen nevertheless recognized that his bloodlines, brains, and appetite for work made him a rising star. But his young-man-in-a-hurry style could be sometimes hair-raisingly literal. Late one afternoon in the early 1980s he and Representative Tom Luken of Ohio were attending a reception at the Four Seasons Hotel in Georgetown when their offices called with word that they had less than fifteen minutes to return to the House for a vote. Luken looked at Gore and said they had no chance in rush-hour traffic. "Watch me," said Gore, who jumped behind the wheel of his car and, invoking the tradition that allows members of Congress to break traffic rules while on official business, sprinted up Pennsylvania Avenue, past the White House, and over to Independence Avenue, slaloming between cars and hurtling past red lights. "We made it in something like six or eight minutes. I was trembling," Luken said.

Gore's competitive radar was always on, tracking potential rivals in a congressional class filled with members who believed they had dates with destiny. In 1981, over a Christmas season dinner with staff members at his Tennessee farmhouse, one aide casually asked about his long-term plans. Gore, three years away from election to the Senate and six from his first presidential campaign, talked about running someday for what he vaguely called "higher office," although there was no mistake about what office he meant. When someone asked who his most formidable rival might be, the aide recalled, he answered immediately. "Without missing a beat, he said, 'Dick Gephardt.' We didn't know anything about him. They never crossed paths at all. But in his mind, back in December 1981, he had picked Gephardt as the guy."

Gephardt was not a friend, but even Gore's few personal relationships in the House were colored by rivalry and ambition, played out over hard-fought pick-up basketball games in the House gym. The competition attracted other hungry newcomers like David Bonior, George Miller, and Norm Dicks. Gore was still in pretty good shape and quickly developed a reputation as a good, if overenthusiastic, outside shot. "People learned not to throw the ball to Al because they'd never get it back," said former Representative Les AuCoin of Oregon, another gym regular. Equally intense were the sessions of "horse": trying to match each other's tricky or difficult shots. One of Gore's specialties was a forty-foot carom off one of the gym walls and into the basket. "He was fascinated with doing this," recalled Bonior, who said Gore could make the shot about four times in ten.

Gore was drawn to other brainy, self-confident young men of whom much was expected. Tom Downey of New York's Long Island suburbs was an even more precocious political toddler than Gore, elected to the Suffolk County Legislature in 1971 at the age of twenty-two. They shared an impish sense of humor, wives who hit it off, voting records more liberal than the districts they represented, and a conviction that they were both smarter than just about anybody else around them. Tim Wirth of Colorado arrived in the House with a résumé polished to a gloss as fine as Gore's, having begun at Phillips Exeter, gone on to Harvard, and finished his education with a Ph.D. from Stanford. As he had done with Downey, Gore became both a friend and a competitor of Wirth's, sharing committee assignments with him and an interest in energy, the environment, and telecommunications policy.

Colleagues knew they could get under Gore's skin by talking up Wirth. After reaching the Senate, Gore came back to the House one day to discuss an environmental matter with Waxman, who said that he was glad to see that Gore cared, adding, "I thought Tim Wirth was the only one in the Senate interested in environmental issues." Gore laughed, but he took the competition with deadly seriousness. "There was always this tension between the two," said Waxman.

To guard against the criticism his father took for being "out of touch" with Tennessee, he tried to follow Joe Evins onto the pork-rich Appropriations Committee, sending the message to constituents that although Evins was gone, the flow of federal largesse back to the

Fourth District would continue uninterrupted. But even with his father lobbying the House leadership, Gore had to settle for a spot on the Interstate and Foreign Commerce (later renamed Energy and Commerce) Committee and its oversight and investigations subcommittee. It was a propitious turn of the wheel, one that brought him into contact with his first serious congressional mentor. John Moss of California was a maverick in the autumn of a distinguished career, a crusader against government secrecy and bureaucratic "news management" whose work had culminated in the 1966 passage of the Freedom of Information Act. The abrasive subcommittee chairman took an immediate liking to the foursquare young reporter from Nashville and gave him opportunities to run his own hearings, a gesture that astounded staffers. "He never gave the gavel to anybody," said the chief counsel Michael Lemov, "but Gore was special from the beginning."

Under Moss, Gore began to hone a slashing, confrontational style of questioning witnesses. "It was pretty strong and close," said former Representative Phil Sharp of Indiana. "There was a hostility, like you were on the stand. He would follow a line of inquiry and pursue, pursue, pursue." On May 15, 1977, he made his first splash on the evening network news by grilling representatives of the Velsicol Corporation, makers of Tris, a flame retardant used in children's pajamas. The company had stopped selling the substance in February, but tests as early as 1975 had shown that Tris caused tumor growth in animals. "Did it trouble you that the children of this country might have tumors, carcinogenic or otherwise, produced by the chemical that would be used in all this sleepwear?" Gore railed, his accent migrating below the Mason-Dixon line, as it often did when he was in high dudgeon. "Did that *truuuble yuuuu?*" Tris began a string of high-profile committee hearings for Gore in which Moss, his successor, Bob Eckhardt of Texas, and Interstate Commerce Committee Chairman John Dingell unleashed him for lines of tough questioning. "He described himself as Dingell's spear carrier," said Ken Jost. He displayed a knack for the tart turn of phrase that could be converted to headlines or quotes near the top of a news story. A month after the Tris hearing, he ridiculed Gulf Oil Corporation as a "corporate Patty Hearst" for participating — under duress, the company claimed — in an international cartel to force up the price of uranium, boosting electricity costs for millions of consumers, including TVA customers. The investigation eventually resulted in a multimillion-dollar cash settlement to TVA and other power suppliers.

One major probe, into the corporate dumping of toxic chemical wastes, afforded him an unexpected chance to demonstrate independence from his father. In 1978 chemicals from an abandoned underground dump seeped into basements and backyards in the Love Canal neighborhood near Niagara Falls, New York, turning trees and shrubs black and burning holes into kids' sneakers. More frightening, residents complained of an abnormal number of miscarriages and birth defects. The company responsible for the disaster was Hooker Chemical, which had become a subsidiary of Armand Hammer's Occidental Petroleum in 1968. Among Occidental's top executives was former Senator Albert Gore, now an executive vice president and director in charge of the company's Island Creek coal subsidiary. Although the pollution took place before the senator joined Occidental, the question of conflict of interest was close enough to worry some of Gore's staff. He considered recusing himself from the oversight committee's investigation but decided that the issue — and perhaps the opportunity to make his own mark — was too important. Later that year he cosponsored passage of the first Superfund bill, mandating a joint public-private effort to clean up the sites.

Gore reveled in his investigative role, and his energy and smarts made him a favorite of committee staff, who were accustomed to leading lesser-wattage members by the nose through complicated subject matter. He said that the only real difference between reporting and serving in Congress was subpoena power. "We're essentially investigative reporters," Gore told Carter Eskew, a young former *Nashville Tennessean* summer intern who came to his office to interview for the press secretary's job in 1980. Eskew declined Gore's offer but went on to become a friend and advertising consultant to his Senate races. Part of the 1992 consortium that handled commercials for the Clinton-Gore ticket, Eskew is now in charge of media and strategy for Gore's 2000 presidential campaign.

Gore garnered press attention with his oversight work, but he also converted it into a list of substantive legislative achievements. In addition to cosponsorship of the Superfund law, he authored the National Organ Transplant Act, which established a computerized network for locating, listing, and matching human organs with recipients. Gore also secured the Infant Formula Act of 1980, which established mini-mum nutritional standards for all formula sold in the United States.

As he did with his legislative program, Gore assembled his House staff with an eye to the future. He had brought with him three trusted Tennesseans from the campaign — Ken Jost, Marcia Webb, and Me-linda Mofield — but he needed someone with congressional expe-rience to run his cramped freshman office on the seventh floor of the Longworth Building. As Gore sifted résumés, wondering who to hire, it happened that someone had already hired him. Webb was sitting at her desk in early January 1977 when Peter Knight walked through the door and announced that he wanted to be Al Gore's chief of staff.

It was a characteristically aggressive move by Knight, a twenty-five-year-old accountant's son from Winchester, Massachusetts, who was as eager as Gore to make his mark in Washington. He was an econom-ics major at Cornell, and a punt-returning safety on the football team, before he landed an internship with Winchester's congressman, Tor-bert MacDonald. Knight did a brief stint after graduation as an analyst in the Justice Department's antitrust division before MacDonald, an old Harvard football player, brought him back as his administrative assistant in 1975. After MacDonald fell ill a few months later and died in May 1976, Knight ran the office, doing everything except going to the floor to vote.

With a new Congress and a Democrat, Jimmy Carter, in the White House, Knight wanted to hire on with someone likely to rise quickly in national politics. He checked with faculty at Harvard's John F. Ken-nedy School of Government, which runs an orientation program for new members, to see who they regarded as blue-chip prospects in the class of 1976. Three names came back from his queries: former St. Louis city councilman Richard Gephardt; Leon Panetta, a Monterey, California, attorney and former Nixon administration official turned Democrat; and Gore. Gore liked Knight's connections: his Massachu-setts background also offered an open line to the new speaker, Tip O'Neill, who had recommended him. After two interviews, Knight be-came the first person Gore hired in Washington.

Knight's presence caused a bit of a culture clash at first. Johnny Hayes got nervous when he called from Tennessee and heard Knight's Boston accent. It wasn't the best way, he thought, to signal constituents that Gore was in touch with concerns back home. "Peter," Hayes said, "whatever you do, let someone else answer the phone." To the Tennessee transplants still feeling their way around Washington, Knight was already the consummate insider. While Gore threw himself into his oversight hearings and base-building at home, it was Knight who became Gore's emissary to Washington's money and influence culture. Aides remember his affinity for the lobbyists who worked Congress, and his eagerness to establish relationships with them. "It was almost like he was in awe of the lobbyists that would come by the office," said Mike Kopp, a Murfreesboro newspaper reporter who joined the staff in 1981 as press secretary. Later, Kopp said, as Gore prepared for his first Senate campaign and began to build a serious fund-raising operation, it was Knight who led the way. "Peter would crack the whip," he said. "Until he ran for president, Al was very uncomfortable making political phone calls, asking for money, going to political events. That was just not his thing. Peter had the list and would come in and say, 'This is who you've got to call today.'"

Gore's other important addition to the operation was Roy Neel, an affable, low-key man with a talent for putting people at ease. He became the office's temperamental counterweight to Knight. When a mayor back in the district phoned asking for information about a federal grant, it was Neel, who grew up in Smyrna, Tennessee, who usually took the call.

Working for Gore could sometimes be difficult and rigorously unpleasant. Senior aides like Knight and Neel paint a benign picture, but former middle- and lower-level aides remember a boss who could be "a terror," as one put it. "His attentiveness and warmth ended with his staff," said one longtime former aide who worked for him in the House and Senate. Winning election didn't put to rest Gore's self-consciousness about his youth, and he felt compelled to act older than he was, sometimes taking a harshly authoritarian tone with a group of aides who were often young and inexperienced. When they took his calls from the road, staffers heard a familiar sigh of exasperation if they didn't immediately pick up on what it was he wanted. "He'd just get quiet, and you'd hear that sigh, and you knew you were on his shit list," said another former aide. Staff meetings could become excruciating Socratic affairs in which Gore kept digging until his questions exposed the limits of an aide's knowledge in a particular area.

An incorrigible micromanager, he even distributed the office mail for the first few months of his freshman term and tried to answer constituent letters himself, plunking an IBM electric typewriter down on his desk to bat out responses in his increasingly rare free moments.

As he had done in school and on the farm, Gore lowered his guard occasionally, letting a more casual, even goofy, nature slip into view. He unwound with aides at long Szechuan dinners in Chinatown or showed up at staff parties to drink a few beers, once wrapping a necktie around his head as he danced and cut up with Tipper. In line with his career-long fascination with (though not necessarily fidelity to) cutting-edge, private-sector management techniques, he took the staff to Coolfont, West Virginia, in February 1982 for a two-day retreat to build group cohesion.

Nowhere did Gore push harder than during his regular weekend trips back to the Fourth District — thirty-six-hour marathon dashes across middle Tennessee in which he sometimes held as many as six open meetings. Other House members did likewise, but few approached such outreach with Gore's obsessive energy. He attacked it like a precision-bombing campaign, keeping a district map in his office covered with pins marking the areas that had or had not been visited in the last year. The routine seldom varied: beginning with a late Friday afternoon flight to Nashville, the Washington contingent was met by a local staff member with a car, waiting to dash off to two meetings that evening and as many as four the next day. "Murderous," one former Tennessee aide described the pace. "You'd have to speed, take your life in your hands, to be fifteen minutes late."

The format of the ninety-minute programs — held in post offices, nursing homes, Elks lodges, and the backs of general stores — was the same, no matter how small the turnout (as few as two at one Smith County crossroads). Gore began with a brief overview of what was happening in Washington, then threw the meeting open to questions. Caseworkers stood by for those with Social Security or Veterans Administration problems. Gore's journalistic bent for explanation, tedious to aides and reporters, often held him in good stead with rural Tennessee audiences. At the height of the late 1970s energy panic, Eric Black remembers one angry constituent asking why the United States was exporting Alaskan oil to the Japanese. Gore was able to calm him by explaining how Alaskan oil was closer to end-users in Japan than to end-users in the United States and that by sending Alaskan oil to Japan, the United States was essentially swapping it for the Mexican oil coming to the lower forty-eight, at lower cost. "He put his hands up in the air to make a map of the three countries," said Black.

On the rare occasions when he took a vote that was unpopular in the district, Gore immediately hit the open meeting circuit to cool off bad feelings before they spiraled out of control. He faced testy questions at home when he became one of the few southerners in the House to vote against Ronald Reagan's massive 1981 tax cut, the centerpiece economic measure of an immensely popular president. As Gore explained at one gathering after another that the bill was filled with unfair loopholes and would explode the budget deficit, the rancor quickly faded. "He had a sense that if he made himself accessible and accountable, showed up a lot, and helped them understand why he voted in a certain way, then it would be okay," said former aide Steve Owens.

Gore credits one Tennessee meeting in the summer of 1980, a Murfreesboro auditorium full of teenage girls, with starting him on the path to his first major policy initiative. At a gathering of Girls State where students formed a legislature to pass their own laws, one member asked Gore how to end the nuclear arms race. He offered little more than boilerplate, a few watery clichés about how nations needed to work together. Gore asked how many of them believed they would see nuclear war in their lifetime. Nearly all the girls raised their hands. How many, he asked, believed we could change that if we really tried? Perhaps three or four responded.

Gore was stunned by their casually reconciled attitude toward Armageddon, he told aides later, and upset at his vapid response. His legislative pursuits suddenly seemed foolishly peripheral. Taking on the makers of cancer-causing chemicals in kids' pajamas was fine, but the threat it posed to their life expectancy shriveled when compared to the thousands of Soviet nuclear warheads aimed at them as they went to sleep every night. And yet he had spent no more than fifteen minutes taking part in the fierce arms control debates going on around him during his first four years in Congress.

The Girls State event stirred his own longtime nuclear anxieties, and memories of watching through his father's eyes as the world went to the brink during the Cuban Missile Crisis. Albert Gore warned in his memoirs about the race "to the top of the nuclear volcano" and the advent of multiple-warhead MIRV (multiple independently targetable reentry vehicle) missiles. After he lost his Senate seat, he became chairman of the Council for a Livable World, a disarmament lobbying organization.

Al Gore told friends about an especially vivid nightmare he had in the wake of the Murfreesboro meeting. The details have differed slightly in the retelling over the years, but in essence it involved the U.S. Army coming to Carthage High School to defuse a nuclear bomb placed under the bleachers of the gymnasium. The soldiers succeeded in deactivating the bomb and drove it away in an armored vehicle. But as they left, a friend told Gore that another bomb had been discovered and that it was up to him to defuse it. He crawled under the bleachers to deactivate the device, but he realized that he didn't have the tools or know-how for such a task and was terrified of setting it off accidentally. Gore dashed back to his farm on the Caney Fork River and gathered his family behind a smokehouse. Suddenly there was a brilliant flash followed by a fierce shock wave that collapsed the building onto their backs.

Gore resolved to become an arms control expert. How he became one, and why, reveals much about the mix of personal values and political self-interest that drives him. The Girls State episode and his own long-standing fears of nuclear holocaust were clearly motivators. But Gore was also facing the reality that if he wanted to be known for something more than policing tainted infant formula, he needed to commit to a high-stakes issue. He had an eye for nascent constituencies, and he recognized a potentially powerful one forming around nuclear angst in the early 1980s. There was a place in the debate for a moderate voice, he believed, one that bridged the chasm between the emerging nuclear "freeze" movement and the bellicose rhetoric of Ronald Reagan and his Cold Warriors. He asked House Speaker O'Neill and Representative Edward Boland, chairman of the House Select Committee on Intelligence, for a seat on the panel. That seat came through in January 1981, the beginning of his third term in the House.

Gore was entering the arms control world at a turbulent time. The Pentagon was increasingly concerned about the accuracy of Soviet intercontinental ballistic missiles (ICBMs) and the growing vulnerability of U.S. land-based missiles to destruction in their underground silos. Its weapon of choice to replace the aging Minuteman missile was the MX, also known as the Peacekeeper, a "silo-buster" that packed ten warheads to the Minuteman's three. In 1979 President Jimmy Carter, warned by the Joint Chiefs of Staff that they could not support the pending SALT II treaty without improvements in the "survivability" of the U.S. land-based arsenal, committed to the MX, proposing the purchase of two hundred missiles.

Critics argued that the MX was not only unnecessary — duplicating the nuclear deterrent already supplied by air- and submarine-based missiles — but dangerously destabilizing. It was a weapon designed not to deter war but to launch a successful first strike. Deployment of two hundred MX missiles could give the United States the means of achieving what the Soviets feared most, opponents said: a successful surprise attack. Complicating the MX issue were conflicts over how to deploy it in a way that would not leave it vulnerable to Soviet missiles. Carter favored a massive ten-thousand-mile "racetrack" through Nevada and Utah, a kind of doomsday shell game in which the missiles would be stashed in multiple shelters and moved periodically on railroad cars to thwart Soviet targeting. The plan, not surprisingly, was hugely unpopular in the West, and shortly after Reagan was elected he appointed a commission headed by Nobel physicist Charles Townes of Berkeley to come up with a better idea.

Gore knew that to be taken seriously by the nuclear "priesthood," he needed technical mastery that was beyond question. He asked Boland to recommend someone to teach him about arms control, and Boland had just the guy. Leon Fuerth was a rumpled, quirky, and surpassingly bright ex–foreign service officer from Queens, New York, who liked to relax by watching MTV late at night after his teenage daughters went to bed. He spent eleven years in the State Department, specializing in Soviet and Eastern European affairs, and as a senior aide to Boland's committee, he was responsible for oversight of covert action and arms control verification issues.

Fuerth was Gore's wonkish kindred spirit from day one, a man with "a Cray computer–like brain, a prodigious capacity for work, and tremendous self-discipline," said Deputy Secretary of State Strobe Talbott. No one interested Gore more than someone who could teach him something, and he became Fuerth's eager student. Fuerth was also utterly loyal, and phobic about contact with the press — the ideal staff man in Gore's world. His pragmatic and often hard-line views have exerted enormous influence on Gore's foreign policy outlook. Even now, as Gore's vice presidential national security adviser, said one former staffer, Fuerth is the only aide Gore considers his intellectual equal.

For more than a year — the winter of 1981 to the spring of 1982 — Fuerth tutored Gore in the bleak arcana of throw weights, hard-target-kill capabilities, and warhead-to-silo ratios. They met at least once a week, sometimes for four to five hours at a time, closeted in Gore's Longworth office or at the Intelligence Committee. Gore shrouded his new venture in the I'd-tell-you-but-then-I'd-have-to-kill-you style of Cold War secrecy, blocking chunks of time from his schedule but never fully explaining what he was up to, not even to his chief of staff. It would be ten months before he even introduced Knight to his arms control mentor.

Only those with useful information to offer were allowed into the Gore-Fuerth tutorials. James Woolsey had recently stepped down as undersecretary of the Navy in early 1981 when he received a call from Fuerth asking him to meet with the young congressman. Woolsey assumed it was about a naval matter, but Fuerth said that Gore wanted to talk about his work more than a decade earlier as an army lieutenant at the Pentagon. He had helped set up "Code 50," a Department of Defense computer model that simulated a nuclear exchange. When Woolsey entered Gore's office, he saw Fuerth and a young man in shirtsleeves who "looked like he had turned twenty," sitting at a plain, government-issue desk with a stack of IBM computer runs and a yellow legal pad.

There were no pleasantries. "Let me tell you the problem," Gore began. "I need to know the assumptions behind this model. I don't think I'd like the assumptions in Code 50 if I understood them." Gore wanted more information about the "survivability" of U.S. nuclear missiles, and so, for about forty-five minutes, Woolsey pieced together what he could remember about Code 50. As he got into a cab afterward, Woolsey, who served as director of Central Intelligence in the Clinton administration, realized that he had never had such a detailed technical discussion with a member of Congress.

The more Gore studied, the more superpower relations seemed to him like the affair of a pair of jealous lovers, with whom, he said, "a single bare fact can sustain a wild imagining" and "a small kernel of fear can sustain a large cloud of illusory fear." In strategic terms, the kernel of fear was that the other side could launch a successful first strike and still have missiles in reserve. Gore laid out his thoughts in a lengthy floor speech on March 22, 1982.

Americans were alarmed by the direction the arms race had taken, he said, and felt that their lives were in the hands of experts and ideologues on both sides who regarded nuclear war as winnable. "They are concerned that the direction we are headed in is only too clear: an unlimited, ungovernable competition with the Soviet Union to build new strategic weapons," Gore said, with "vast sums expended for what would in fact turn out to be diminished safety in the world. This foreboding is the stuff of which grassroots movements are made." The growing sentiment for a freeze was understandable, he said, but misguided and potentially dangerous. It was up to political leaders, Gore said, to "reach out and grasp their responsibilities" — to reclaim the arms control debate from this unelected establishment.

The centerpiece of Gore's proposal was not an original idea. It had been kicking around the arms control community for years and was certainly well known to Fuerth. In essence, it called for the two countries to convert all their multiple-warhead missiles to single-warhead. At the heart of the concept was the two-for-one rule of nuclear exchange — the assumption that it took two warheads to ensure the destruction of one. Within the flight time of an ICBM from the Soviet Union, an arsenal of single-warhead "Midgetman" missiles on mobile launchers could disperse over a wide enough distance that the Russians would have to commit their entire ballistic missile supply to destroy them. It gave both parties an invulnerable deterrent and eliminated fears of a first strike. Under Gore's plan, the superpowers would agree to a freeze on new weaponry while they negotiated a schedule for converting their multiple-warhead missiles to the single-warhead ICBMs. Research and development on the MX would continue, he said, but only as a hedge against the failure of talks. If negotiations succeeded, its deployment would not be necessary. The end-result was a safer world, albeit one that still had thousands of nuclear warheads. But Gore believed that removing the kernel of first-strike fear opened the door to deeper arms reductions and the possibility of vastly improved relations with the Soviets.

It's easy to see why the single-warhead ICBM appealed to Gore. For his purposes, Midgetman was the perfect weapons system, one that allowed him to split the difference in a critical debate over the future of the Cold War — and the survival of civilization. It was a weapon as carefully calibrated as his politics. Gore was a liberal, but not too much of one; Midgetman was a nuclear missile, but not too much of one. He could argue to the freeze and disarmament communities that he was trying to rid the world of the fearsome MX. At the same time, his advocacy as a southern Democrat of a new weapons system afforded him an invaluable national security credential. It gained Gore admission into a select club of defense intellectuals and insiders, no small thing for a young man who had watched his father move in the Kennedy administration's inner circle.

But despite a vigorous marketing plan that included op-ed pieces, speeches, and small breakfasts with national security journalists and columnists, the initial reaction to the rollout of Gore's plan was silence. Although Soviet officials expressed some informal interest — a U.S. delegation headed by Minneapolis Mayor Donald Fraser visited Moscow and received questions about "the Gore plan" — the proposal was for the most part like a missile falling in the forest with no one around to hear it.

Over the next year, however, a series of events put Midgetman back into play. One was the continued debate over to how deploy the MX in a way that minimized its vulnerability to attack. The Pentagon had considered no less than thirty-five different "basing modes," most of them representing escalating plateaus of lunacy. One scenario had them placed aloft in dirigibles. The Townes Commission reported back in the summer of 1982 with serious doubts about the security of the "racetrack" plan and suggested carrying the MX on aircraft or sticking them in deep underground bases; neither alternative was especially attractive. In November, Reagan recommended that one hundred MX be deployed in a "dense pack" — silos so close together that incoming Soviet missiles would blow themselves up and ensure the survival of some U.S. warheads. The following month, with the freeze movement gaining strength, the House voted to cut off money for the MX, on the grounds that no rational basing plan had been proposed.

The Midgetman got another boost in March 1983 when former Secretary of State Henry Kissinger, borrowing liberally from Gore — and those from whom Gore had borrowed — endorsed the concept in a *Time* essay. That same winter Reagan formed yet another commission, this one headed by former Air Force General Brent Scowcroft. Although its official mission was to review U.S. nuclear strategy, its real task was to craft a proposal to salvage the MX by reaching out to the House Democrats caught between the freeze movement and the defense community. Gore was one of a group of national security moderates, headed by Representative Les Aspin of Wisconsin, with whom the Scowcroft group closely consulted as it put together its findings.

The April 1983 report, written principally by James Woolsey, embraced Gore's proposal, recommending full-scale development of the Midgetman on a mobile launcher, with initial operation by the early 1990s. But it also recommended that one hundred MX missiles be deployed to meet "the short term needs for ICBM force modernization" while the Midgetman was readied, and that they be placed in the old Minuteman silos — the same silos whose vulnerability had triggered the original debate. The commission had solved the MX basing problem by effectively wishing it away. Despite their previous opposition to the MX, and their concern about its destabilizing potential, the moderates endorsed Scowcroft and began to build a bipartisan coalition in the House to release money for development and flight testing. Gore in particular, said Woolsey, "took to it like a duck to water."

Gore and his allies saw that the Scowcroft package was an opportunity, however imperfect, to prod Reagan into getting serious about arms control, and that a limited number of MX missiles was not too high a price to pay for getting the Midgetman. But Gore's thinking was wishful on two fundamental levels. Powerful voices within the administration, principally Defense Secretary Caspar Weinberger and his assistant for international security policy, Richard Perle, remained unremittingly hostile to the Midgetman and arms control in general. In their view, the Scowcroft panel was not calling for any real change in the administration's arms policy. Perle regarded Reagan's support for the MX as "quite broad and deep." Gore tried to nail down Reagan's position on the Midgetman in a May 2, 1983, letter he drafted on behalf of the House moderates, asking for specific assurances about the immediate development of the Midgetman. The answer was dismay-ingly vague, saying that the missile would be developed "on a high-priority basis."

To rally support, Representative Norm Dicks, another member of the Aspin group, arranged a dinner at the White House for wavering House Democrats. The idea was for Reagan to say explicitly that while the administration had to have the MX, he was serious about arms control. But he did nothing to make the moderates feel more secure about the Midgetman's future. The low point, Dicks recalled, was when Gore, flush with his newly acquired expertise, rose to ask Reagan a lengthy technical question about warhead-to-silo ratios. "You could see Reagan's eyes glaze over," he said. "I think maybe only Aspin and I and [Senator Sam] Nunn understood what the hell he was talking about." Reagan's response was a rambling, eight- or nine-minute talk that reflected no understanding of the principles involved. He then called on the head of his commission, "General Snowcroft," to help him with the answer. "We probably lost fifty votes," Dicks said.

Many House Democrats thought Gore had been euchred by the administration, which was using the Midgetman and the moderates to get what it really wanted — the MX — back on track. Others saw an ambitious young man caught up in the swirl of high-level consultations with the White House. Gore, it seemed, had been co-opted by the very community of insiders and specialists he had challenged in his 1982 speech. "It was heady stuff," said Les AuCoin, an outspoken critic of the MX compromise. "Al has always enjoyed being on the inside."

Two days of caustic and emotional debate preceded the vote on May 24, 1983. Proponents argued that killing the MX would send a signal to NATO allies that the United States was not committed to modernizing its arsenal and could undermine support for the deployment of Pershing II intermediate-range missiles in Europe. The opposition depicted the measure as a nuclear Tonkin Gulf Resolution — one that might someday back the country into its final war. They hammered away at what they saw as the glaring logical disconnect in the Scowcroft report: that to build a weapon to make the world safer (Midgetman), the United States first had to build one (MX) that was dangerous, destabilizing, and just as vulnerable to attack as the incumbent Minuteman. It was an uncomfortable spot for Gore, who was at odds with a majority of the Democratic caucus. He even found himself pitted against his fellow gym rat Downey, who didn't mention his friend by name but was unsparing in his disdain for those who had thrown in with the White House. "The theory is that we need to do something profoundly stupid to do something smart," said Downey. "I think on its face that speaks for itself."

When his turn came, Gore conceded that there was "an irony" in proposing to deploy a huge new missile bristling with nuclear warheads as a way of beginning to back away from the arms race. But he also pointed out that those who decried the destabilizing potential of the MX — its ability to provoke a Soviet first strike — also minimized the dangers posed by the highly accurate MX-type missiles that the Soviets had already deployed. "Do the opponents of this resolution really believe, do they *really* believe, that we are going to make an arms control agreement more likely if we eliminate this program?" He warned the White House that his vote for the MX was conditional — that if the administration equivocated on arms control talks with the Soviets, the money would be cut off. That brought a withering response from AuCoin, who said that weapons programs once started never fall off the funding train.

"If that is a bargain," said AuCoin, "all I can say is, to my colleagues on this side of the aisle who have entered into it, I am just pleased they are not negotiating with the Soviet Union."

Gore and the moderates prevailed, joining Republicans to revive the MX on a vote of 239–186. He continued to defend the missile through a series of legislative skirmishes, but the compromise he struck with the White House steadily unraveled over the next few years. The MX proved to be far more than a transitional weapon. The Pentagon never liked the smaller and more expensive Midgetman and tried hard to get rid of it in the 1980s. Its fate was finally sealed at the decade's end by budget crunches, competition for funding with other expensive weapons systems, like the Strategic Defense Initiative, and, ultimately, the end of the Cold War. Midgetman limped along in a low-priority research and development mode, achieving its first successful test flight in 1991 before George Bush canceled it outright a year later.

Gore's defenders say he stepped into a debate in which few people were making sense and developed a clear, workable approach to nuclear stability. Although he didn't kill the MX, he managed to limit proliferation of a dangerous weapon (only fifty were finally deployed) and came close to carrying out his vision for the Midgetman. The less enamored saw a hyper-ambitious young man who let his penchant for self-promotion and zeal for a place at the table outrun his judgment. Among his detractors was the head of the disarmament lobbying group that his father had once headed. "He was always looking for what I call smart-ass solutions, something no one else had thought of," said Jerome Grossman, executive director of the Council for a Livable World. "He was always looking to show a particular expertise. It was always a compromise solution. We had taken the position that new ICBMs would intensify the Cold War. His response was always to immerse himself in the details. We thought that was diversionary. He knows he's smart, and he wanted to show how smart he was."

❖ 10 ❖

Strange Blend

THE MIDGETMAN never made it past test flights, but it lifted Al Gore's profile in Washington. His reinvention as Arms Control Al won him recognition as an authoritative voice in a critical area of national policy, without triggering complaints from home that he was "out of touch." The regimen of weekend town meetings and judicious selection of issues inoculated him from the elitist image that had plagued his father at the end of his career. So politically untouchable was Gore that when the Tennessee legislature redrew congressional district boundaries after the 1980 census, adding two new House seats likely to go to Democrats, it took eleven strongly Democratic counties from under him and swapped them for the fast-growing and increasingly Republican suburbs of Nashville. Gore didn't lose a step — he ran unopposed for his fourth term in 1982 from the newly created Sixth District. He was on a roll — until he got the almost unbearable news about his beloved big sister.

Even before she was diagnosed with lung cancer that same year, Nancy Gore Hunger hadn't been well or particularly happy. Life as a Greenville, Mississippi, housewife had left her feeling lonely and stifled after her years near the center of the action in Washington. She had never found a career of her own, and while Frank Hunger put in long hours developing a successful practice as a civil trial lawyer, representing corporate clients like Chevron and Allstate Insurance in liability cases, she gardened, learned gourmet cooking, and pursued good works in the community. She remained close to brother Al, helping in his campaigns and fussing about the rapid proliferation of little Gores, the stated concern being that he and Tipper were overextending themselves financially. A second daughter, Kristin, was born in

1977; Sarah followed eighteen months later, and, in 1982, Albert Arnold Gore III. "How many babies is she going to have?" she complained to a close relative. She was a doting Aunt Nancy, though, and in her backyard she set up a beautiful dollhouse for the kids to play in when they visited. What she really wanted — children of her own — never happened.

She tried to interest Hunger in relocating to Washington, but he was committed to his Mississippi firm. "Greenville was a dead end for Nancy," said one Gore family member. "She was very unhappy there." In the early eighties she told at least one friend that she was considering a divorce. There were other health problems — high blood pressure, poor circulation, and, to the end, alcohol. At forty-four, the years of heavy smoking finally claimed their toll.

The Gore siblings dealt with the crisis characteristically: she insisted on the most aggressive treatment possible and started to take flying lessons; brother Al plunged into the details. Before rushing back to Nashville, where Nancy was hospitalized, he stopped at the National Institutes of Health for a briefing from pathologists. By that evening, when he saw James Fleming, a plastic surgeon and longtime friend who served informally as the Gores' family doctor, he was able to tick off the ten most common types of lung cancer. Fleming marveled at his facility with the subject, picked up literally on the fly. Gore spoke to Nancy's doctors on their level and scoured the medical world for new treatments that might help his sister. But time was running out: soon after diagnosis, surgeons removed one of her lungs, and the prognosis was poor.

As Gore struggled with his sister's illness, political fortune continued to break his way, his path cleared again by a favorably timed retirement. When he learned in January 1983 that Senator Howard Baker would not seek reelection in 1984, Gore put himself on a full-campaign footing, determined to scare off potential competitors by making victory seem inevitable. He kicked his weekend and congressional recess travel schedule into even higher gear, visiting all of the state's ninety-five counties at least once in 1983. Determined not to be outspent, as his father had been in 1970, he mobilized his Tennessee financial backers, until then the fund-raising equivalent of Maytag repairmen who had watched their candidate run three of four races with little or no opposition. Gore took one of his earliest benefactors, glad-handing Henderson insurance man Johnny Hayes, to the Democratic National Committee's finance committee meeting in Key Largo, Florida, so that he could get friendly with the party's deepest pockets.

Gore had sponsored legislation that limited candidates' ability to accept money from political action committees (PACs), but that didn't stop him from soaking up every PAC dime he could under the existing rules. He caucused with business PAC representatives, highlighting the votes he had made in their favor, like his no to expanded picketing rights for striking workers. "I am a strong supporter of PAC participation in the political process," he told *PAC Manager,* a newsletter for officials who administered business PACs. "I need to raise large sums of money, and I have enjoyed getting involved with the PAC community." Where his father had been singed by publicity from a fund-raiser at Teddy Kennedy's home, Gore kept his $500-a-head affair, cohosted by Tip O'Neill and Jim Sasser at the home of über-lobbyist Tommy Boggs, as low-profile as possible.

Business support streamed to Gore despite a demonstrably hostile voting record. (The U.S. Chamber of Commerce gave him a 30 percent rating for his eight years in the House.) By the end of 1983 he was sitting on a $1.1 million war chest (he would eventually raise and spend $2.5 million) and giving competitors a lot to think about before entering the race. Republicans looked hard for someone to head off another Senator Gore from Tennessee. Baker and President Ronald Reagan both tried to persuade Lamar Alexander, Tennessee's popular GOP governor, to make the race. But Alexander, who knew a juggernaut when he saw one, declined.

As he prepared to step up to the Senate, Gore entered the middle of another protracted debate, this one colored by his grief over Nancy. His history with tobacco had always been complicated — a strange blend of personal conviction, political calculation, and family dysfunction. All of it surfaced in his negotiations with cigarette manufacturers over new health warning labels. For most of his House career, Gore had said little publicly about the hazards of smoking. He took the conventional populist stance for a tobacco state member, framing the issue not as one of public health but of economic justice for the ten thousand farmers in his district who grew the crop. Most were

small family operators who depended on the cash, and the federal system of price supports, to stay afloat.

Taking care of tobacco was both pragmatic politics and a family tradition. When Gore's father was a young man, Main Street in Carthage
was impassable at harvest time as farmers waited in wagons and
trucks, sometimes for days, to haul their tobacco onto the floor of the
Upper Cumberland Loose Leaf Warehouse for auction. Strapped for
cash as a student, Albert Gore financed his first visit to Washington
with discarded tobacco that he cleaned up and sold for a profit. For
most of his life he held a federally regulated allotment that allowed
him to grow tens of thousands of pounds of burley each year on his
farm. Al Gore never grew it himself, but he learned the business from
his father and from farmhands during his Tennessee summers, and he
inherited a small poundage allotment with the farm that he bought
from Albert in 1973. (He then leased it back to the senator.) Interestingly, Gore, a stickler for reporting the smallest sums of income even
when not required by regulations, never listed the tiny bit of cash from
the tobacco lease on his congressional financial disclosure forms in the
1980s, electing instead to fold the money (estimated at between $140
and $350 annually, depending on market conditions) into his overall
revenue from "pasture leasing."

Around the same time his sister fell ill, Gore began laying the
groundwork for a stronger stand on smoking and health, sounding
out farmers at town meetings about the dangers of cigarettes. He
sometimes backed into the subject in a down-home way. Phil Ashford,
a former reporter for the *Memphis Commercial Appeal* who covered
Gore in the 1980s, said that a favorite Gore riff played on regional rivalry. "He'd say, 'Over in North Carolina, they grow so much of it they
have to pretend that it's good for you. Here in Tennessee, we've got
more sense than that.'" It's hard to know how many growers actually
agreed with Gore's formulation, but it put them on notice that the
health consequences of smoking had begun to matter politically.

Until 1983 the tobacco industry's lock on Congress ensured that
Gore never faced a meaningful vote on the issue. The climate changed
when the Energy and Commerce Subcommittee on Health, chaired
by Representative Henry Waxman, held hearings on the hazards of
smoking that detailed new research findings about the addictive qualities of nicotine. Waxman and his allies in the public health commu-

nity argued that in light of new scientific evidence, the warning label displayed on cigarette packages and advertising, unchanged since 1969 ("Warning: The Surgeon General Has Determined That Cigarette Smoking Is Dangerous To Your Health"), did little to convey the grave risks of tobacco use.

The result was a tough new bill that caught manufacturers by surprise. Waxman wanted a rotating series of warnings flatly stating that cigarette smoking was addictive and caused cancer and emphysema and disclosing the levels of carbon monoxide, tar, and nicotine yielded by each brand. Public health advocates regarded another provision of the Waxman bill as critical: that cigarette makers provide to the government the list of nontobacco additives used in the manufacturing process. As the tar and nicotine content of cigarettes fell, antismoking forces contended, these additives played a more important role and needed to be studied for their long-term effects.

The boulder in Waxman's path was John Dingell of Michigan, Energy and Commerce's powerful chairman. Dingell once told Matthew Myers, head of the Coalition on Smoking or Health, the antismoking lobby working with Waxman, that he simply didn't believe labels made a difference. The reason: his wife said that if the new warnings appeared on cigarette packs tomorrow, she would still smoke. Dingell's real agenda was his mutual protection pact with tobacco state legislators, his allies on critical auto industry matters like support for the Chrysler bailout or opposition to antipollution requirements for new cars. In exchange, he served as a defensive shield against regulatory pressures on the tobacco industry. There were also personal tensions between Dingell and Waxman, who had clashed bitterly on a recent round of air quality legislation. Waxman managed to get the bill out of subcommittee, but Dingell kept it bottled up in committee until the industry could work out a compromise to its liking. Despite his grassroots work on the hazards of smoking, Gore was reluctant to risk alienating tobacco farmers just before he ran his first statewide race. Even with his sister dying of lung cancer, he became one of several Democrats on Energy and Commerce who declined to line up with Waxman on the bill.

On a Friday morning in October 1983, Gore was the guest at a regular breakfast gathering of former Democratic committee staffers. They included Michael Pertschuk, the ex-chairman of the Federal Trade

Commission, who admired Gore's work on consumer issues and sounded him out about backing the Waxman bill. Gore, who "could wax nostalgic about the patriotic glories of tobacco farming," as Pertschuk recalled in a 1986 memoir, reiterated his political problem but wanted to be as helpful as he could given his situation. At Pertschuk's suggestion, Myers and his health coalition set up a meeting with Gore and Peter Knight in early November 1983.

Myers had only modest expectations for the session. He certainly wasn't looking for anyone to negotiate a compromise with the industry, and he was prepared to consider the meeting a success if Gore simply indicated that he wasn't an automatic no vote. "There were no reasons to believe he was anything other than a conventional pol from a tobacco state," he said. When they sat down, Myers told Gore that he understood his political predicament but wondered whether there was something the coalition could do to make support of the labeling bill more palatable. There were several possibilities, Myers said, such as giving Gore credit for opening a dialogue with the health lobby on tobacco price supports, which it had opposed. Myers was surprised and heartened by the response: If it came to a vote, Gore would be with him. "When push comes to shove, you will have me. I can't in good conscience ever vote against you," Gore said, adding that the coalition's willingness to help the farmers "is something that gives us a fair amount of meat to work with." Although nothing was settled, it was an encouraging meeting. They agreed to talk again in a week or so.

Myers was standing in his kitchen early that evening when the phone rang. It was Gore, who had called his office and tracked him down at home. He was pumped, Myers remembered, his voice sounding far more energized than it was at their afternoon meeting. He had been reflecting on their discussion, he said, and had become "angry" because he couldn't think of a good reason for the tobacco industry to be fighting something as straightforward as stronger health warnings. He and Knight had already taken it upon themselves to contact the Tobacco Institute, the industry's Washington lobbying arm, to ask whether there was room for compromise. It looked like there was.

Gore asked institute officials what they absolutely could not live with in the bill — not what they didn't like, but what they regarded as untenable. They expressed concern that the tougher labels could increase their exposure to product liability lawsuits. Myers said the health lobby's goal was not to open them to increased liability, and that the issue could be worked out. Gore was "absolutely euphoric," Myers said. "I think we've got a deal," Gore told him.

Myers never knew for certain what happened, how Gore had shifted in a few hours from "yes, if absolutely necessary," into a self-appointed broker. Gore may have decided that the political benefits of getting out in front of the emerging national antismoking movement outweighed the risks back home, especially if the farmers — who seemed to him increasingly ambivalent about cigarette smoking — were assured that their ability to grow tobacco and command a federally supported price would remain undisturbed. Both Myers and Knight said they weren't aware then of Nancy Gore Hunger's illness. But Myers now suspects that Gore's anguish compelled him to take the labeling bill on as a priority project. After that evening's conversation, it was clear to him that Gore was "personally invested in [the bill] and willing to take risks to make it happen."

The following week Myers received a less triumphant phone call, this one from Knight. Liability, it turned out, was only one of "about ten or fifteen additional things" that the manufacturers wanted addressed. It set the pattern for the next four frustrating months, as Gore and Knight repeatedly returned to the health coalition and extracted painful concessions only to learn at the eleventh hour that the industry had ratcheted the bar higher.

Some regarded Gore's negotiations less as a route to a deal than as a means of exposing duplicity and bad faith in the tobacco industry, which clearly hoped to kill the bill by stringing out the talks. But Gore didn't see it that way. "Gore looked at this incredibly naively," said one House aide who worked closely with the antismoking lobby. "Our strategy was to let this play out, let Gore get lied to, and let him come back to us."

In March 1984 Gore called Myers to announce yet another deal. "I think we're home free," he told him. This time the companies insisted that the warnings not be displayed as prominently as proposed by Waxman; the statement about carbon monoxide and tar and nicotine content also had to go; ditto any mention of addiction. Myers reluctantly signed off. But the next afternoon Gore called again, this time his voice "quivering, literally quivering," with rage. He had been told that the committee of tobacco executives reviewing the new version of the bill rejected it out of hand. Some officials, he was given to understand, turned it down without even reading it. "Gore was so angry that he just couldn't speak, practically," said Myers. When Gore encountered the chairman of the Tobacco Institute, Horace Kornegay, in a Capitol hallway shortly after the latest abortive deal, he exploded. Knight told Waxman aide Rip Forbes that it was "the only time he could ever remember seeing Gore totally lose control, and just start screaming at Kornegay for basically having screwed them." Gore, who had been keeping Dingell and Representative Charlie Rose of North Carolina, a key congressional ally of tobacco, posted on his progress, reported that the industry's conduct had become intolerable.

For Dingell, the issue was no longer about dubious health warning labels but about a member of *his* committee getting jerked around by parties negotiating in bad faith. After hearing from Gore, he unleashed his abrasive committee staff director Mike Kitzmiller, known around the House as "John Dingell's killer." Kitzmiller delivered Dingell's message to the cigarette manufacturers: make a deal with Gore in the next twenty-four hours or the chairman would vote Waxman's original bill out of committee.

Even after angering Dingell, Kornegay and the tobacco companies tried to roll the House Democrats, making one last attempt to scuttle the bill in the Senate. They succeeded in getting Senator Wendell Ford of Kentucky, apparently unaware of all that had gone on in the House, to place a "hold" on the bill. Gore tried reaching out to Ford, with disastrous results. "Al called Wendell to see if he couldn't help them work this problem out. And Wendell went off at the cork," said Kitzmiller. "He said, 'You run your [expletive deleted] business in the House and let me run my business in the Senate. Don't you ever call me, you young whippersnapper.'" Kitzmiller told Pertschuk there were several points in the bill's tortured history where Gore's intervention hurt more than it helped. "I told Gore himself that I was tired of going around after him with a pooper-scooper and cleaning up," he said. "Gore's always going to solve everybody's problem and always makes messes."

Gore had been played for a fool by Big Tobacco. Like his dealings with the Reagan administration on the MX missile, his negotiations on health labels revealed a streak of credulousness about those at the table with him. Even one loyal longtime staffer conceded that Gore "was the kind of guy you'd like to have sitting across from you at a poker game." Still, his persistence set the industry up for a thrashing by Dingell. His doggedness, combined with Dingell's muscle — and the industry's fear of harsher, more punitive antitobacco legislation in the pipeline — finally closed the deal. The Comprehensive Smoking Prevention Education Act, signed by President Reagan on October 12, 1984, was essentially Gore's watered-down version of Waxman's original. The warnings were smaller and purged of any mention that cigarette smoking was addictive. Where Waxman's text stated flatly that cigarettes cause cancer, the final version restored "Surgeon General's Warning" as a preface, which cigarette makers regarded as more protection against liability suits. Companies still had to turn over a list of nontobacco additives but did not have to specify the quantities or the individual brands in which they were used — and the inventory would be kept under lock and key, available only to government researchers. Still, stiff language remained in the four rotating labels, including one warning pregnant women who smoked of possible prematurity and low birthweight.

More important, the bill was a watershed for an industry accustomed to flattening its congressional opposition, and it prepared the ground for the broad legal and legislative offensives that antismoking forces launched in the 1990s. "Al Gore was the first member of Congress from a tobacco state to take on the tobacco industry on health issues in any meaningful way," said Myers. "Whatever else you think of the guy, in 1983 that was not something that was good politics, and it was something that took real personal courage." The cigarette makers would also pay a steep price for their cavalier treatment of Gore. Memories of their double crosses, as his sister lay dying, kindled a hatred that grew more visceral through the years. As vice president, he allied with FDA chief David Kessler and Clinton pollster Dick Morris to build the case for the administration's regulatory assault on tobacco, one that included sharp limits on its ability to sell and advertise cigarettes to minors. "They're killers, they're killers," he muttered, "beet red and shaking," as the *Washington Post* described him at one 1995 White House meeting.

Even as she lived on one cancerous lung, Nancy Gore Hunger was unable to stop smoking. She grew weaker in the spring of 1984, lost her hair from chemotherapy, and fell into a depression, but she still craved cigarettes, asking Jimmy Fleming to slip them to her while she was treated at Vanderbilt Hospital. There were graces at the end — she and Frank Hunger reconciled their differences. Because she was barely able to walk, Hunger literally carried her everywhere, strapping her into his small plane for the trips from Greenville to Nashville for medical care. Before she died, she told her old Vanderbilt roommate Nancy Fleming that the quality of her final two years would never have been what it was without Hunger. Determined to help her brother get to the Senate, she willed herself out of bed and put on a wig to attend his campaign kickoff at the Nashville airport on May 30, 1984. It was her last public appearance. Six weeks later, on July 11, Gore was campaigning in east Tennessee when he received word that she was failing rapidly, and he sped back to Nashville. Later that evening, the woman media adviser Bob Squier called "the biggest of big sisters" was gone. "She was a terribly important part of Al's life," Tipper Gore said later. "She was a mediator, adviser, powerful supporter, and loving critic."

All of which makes the behavior of Gore and his family in the years following her death difficult to understand. Rather than purging their connections to tobacco, their dealings became a patchwork of hypocrisy and denial — beginning with the mixed signals Gore sent to friends about the cause of his sister's death. One longtime family friend said that on July 13, 1984, as the graveside funeral service at Smith County Memorial Gardens in Carthage broke up, Gore "put his arm around my shoulder and said Nancy's death did not come about from smoking tobacco." Another friend, Nancy Fleming, said that she was told by the family that "the cancer in her lung was not the kind generally associated with smoking, and may have originated at another site."

Gore was cushioning the pain of his loss by reaching back into his newly acquired expertise on the pathology of cancer, but his claim wasn't accurate. It was true, according to Jimmy Fleming, that Hunger's lung cancer was neither the small-cell nor squamous-cell type most frequently seen in smokers. It was an adenocarcinoma — less common but still clearly associated with smoking. Fleming also said that Hunger's medical team "looked at the possibility" that her cancer had metastasized into the lungs from another organ but ruled it out.

Grief over his sister's death did nothing to diminish his enthusiasm for tobacco farming. Making money by growing tobacco, and profiting from its sale in the form of cigarettes, remained on opposite sides of a firm moral partition in Gore's mind. By the fall of 1984 he was actively soliciting the votes of tobacco farmers in his Senate campaign and promising continued allegiance, devoting an entire day in October to talk about his pro-grower record. Four years later, campaigning in North Carolina before the 1988 Democratic presidential primary, he assured a crowd of farmers: "Throughout most of my life I raised tobacco. I want you to know that with my own hands, all of my life, I put it in the plant beds and transferred it, I've hoed it. I've chopped it. I've shredded it, spiked it, put it in the barn and stripped it and sold it."

Gore was right when he suggested that he was one of them. It was not until 1991, a full seven years after Nancy's death, that he and his father sold their tobacco allotments. Both father and son fudged the facts on this point. Gore told Tennessee reporters that he gave up the allotment in 1989. Albert Gore said that he sold his after Albert III, then about age four, visited the family farm and watched as the senator irrigated a field. "Granddad, what's that plant you're watering?" the little boy asked. "Tobacco," Gore answered, adding that he "looked at me in astonishment." Then his grandson said, "Isn't that what killed Aunt Nancy?" Gore said the moment "drove it home," and that he immediately quit the tobacco business. The problem with this poignant anecdote is that Albert III turned four in October 1986, five years before the allotment was actually sold.

Nor did Nancy's loss, or his experience with industry double-dealing in the warning label negotiations, slacken Gore's appetite for campaign contributions from Big Tobacco. From 1984 to 1990, Gore accepted nearly $15,000 from the industry — not exactly a windfall, but enough to raise questions about his real sentiments. Although he supported antismoking messages, especially those aimed at the young, he also joined eighteen other senators in urging the Bush administration's trade representative to pressure the government of Thailand to allow sales of U.S. cigarettes.

The 1984 Senate campaign went dark for several days after Nancy's death, and when Gore returned he was distracted and depleted. Journalists barnstorming the state with him saw a candidate bounding from one event to the next as if nothing had happened. But those up close saw that he was off his game, especially in his usual attention to micromanagerial detail. "He was someone who always said, 'I can do that — I can sign these one hundred letters, I can write these fifty notes,'" said one traveling staffer.

In time he bounced back, and in the process his grief brought him closer to Frank Hunger. The soft-spoken Mississippian was no political animal, but he would become a constant presence, at Gore's side in every campaign, emerging as one of his closest friends and confidants. One former aide said that reaching out to Hunger helped him keep Nancy's memory alive. "He was clearly looking at Frank for that connection," the ex-staffer said, "as a sort of constant reminder that Nancy was there."

Although Gore was struggling, it didn't much matter in 1984. His GOP opponent was State Senator Victor Ashe of Knoxville, whose campaign mascot was a fierce-looking bulldog that symbolized tough-mindedness and tenacity — although not, evidently, tactical smarts. After prodding Gore to release personal financial records, Gore happily complied, showing his net worth to be one-third of Ashe's ($1 million to $360,000).

Even with the anemic competition, Gore ran scared. He waged a cautious, ball-control-offense of a campaign designed to distance him from the top of the doomed national ticket headed by former Vice President Walter Mondale. One Washington-based Gore consultant said it was "a point of pride to Gore himself" that he got through the race without being photographed within arm's length of Mondale, who was headed for a landslide defeat in November at the hands of Ronald Reagan. So completely did he airbrush the liberal Minnesotan from his message that at a September 30 debate in Jackson, Tennessee, Ashe offered five dollars to charity for Gore to merely utter the words "Walter" and "Mondale," an offer he declined. When Ashe renewed the invitation a week later in Knoxville, upping the ante to ten dollars, Gore turned the gag around. He finally spat out the name and dedicated the money to charity in the names of Victor Ashe and Walter Mondale.

In painting Gore as an avowed liberal in moderate sheep's clothing, Ashe tried to cast the race as a battle between the "Mondale-Gore" and "Reagan-Ashe" tickets, but it never washed. Gore spent most of his time detailing the moderate aspects of his House record: twelve hundred open meetings, safer infant formula, crusades against toxic waste and the uranium cartel. He particularly emphasized his common ground with Reagan on national security issues, reminding Tennesseans of his support for the MX missile, the administration's sale of Stinger missiles to Saudi Arabia, and the deployment of an additional aircraft carrier to the Persian Gulf to monitor the Iran-Iraq War.

The Gore campaign's caution and moderation extended to style as well as substance. His guard was always up, ready to fend off the smallest potential embarrassment. If his driver sped to stay on schedule, he hunched down when they passed other cars so that motorists couldn't see that their Boy Scout of a prospective senator was a traffic scofflaw. Tennessee political reporters accustomed to kicking back over beers with a candidate after a long day on the road found that they were drinking only with each other.

Gore also had some strange ideas about appropriate behavior with women journalists. When Carol Bradley, who covered the race for the *Nashville Banner,* emerged bleary-eyed from her motel room in the mornings after a typically short night, the first person she often encountered was Gore. "I'd open my door, lugging my suitcase and Radio Shack computer, and he would rush up and grab them and give me a kiss on the cheek. It was kind of embarrassing," said Bradley, who added that other women covering Gore got the same treatment.

Gore succeeded in keeping the press at bay, but not his father. The old senator was at the campaign kickoff on the steps of the Smith County courthouse this time, watching the grandchildren pass out old red-white-and-blue Gore buttons from his 1952 race. His son borrowed, nearly verbatim, the phrase his father had employed in stump speeches against Kenneth McKellar thirty-two years earlier. Avoiding any mention of his opponent by name, he said: "The central issue is who can best serve Tennessee in the U.S. Senate." (Albert's 1952 refrain was, "I raise but one principal issue. Who is best fitted to serve the state and nation in the U.S. Senate for the next six years?") Still, Gore remained ambivalent about the associations that a highly visible Albert Gore might rekindle for voters, especially the old liberal tag. Just as in 1976, he decided that the safest place for the senator was away from the cameras and microphones. Yet, against the advice of his consultants, he insisted on retaining Albert Gore Jr. as the name on all of his advertising and literature, determined that he not be seen as running away from his family identity.

Gore's official line depicted his father as a trusted adviser and mentor, but serious tensions were visible. Over dinner after a day of campaigning, a reporter from a major eastern newspaper watched incredulously as the elder Gore badgered and belittled his son. "Whenever Gore would say something, his father would say, 'You don't know anything about that. This is how it works.' It was humiliating. Gore never disagreed with him. He just sat there and took it."

And despite Gore's wishes that Albert would stay out of the limelight, the old senator couldn't resist giving a self-aggrandizing breakfast interview to the *Banner*'s Carol Bradley the morning after election day, casting himself as the campaign's principal adviser and launching into an extended discussion of the private counsel he had given his son. Most of it was innocuously conventional wisdom: smile during debates, pick issues that appeal to moderate Republicans and independents. But Bradley later heard that Gore was "furious" at his father for agreeing to the interview — and, she suspected, for the senior Gore's suggestion that they had even needed a strategy for disposing of Ashe. They probably didn't. Gore ran two points ahead of Reagan in Tennessee, taking 61 percent of the vote to Ashe's 34 percent, the worst showing by a Republican senatorial candidate in the state in twenty-five years.

Albert Gore had taken his old Senate chamber chair with him when he was pushed into retirement, and the time had come to dust it off. He and Pauline were thrilled to see their son claim it — for a while. At the January 2, 1985, swearing-in ceremony, Albert leaned over to Martin Peretz, his son's Harvard instructor, and said, "This is the beginning."

♦ 11 ♦

Lyric Opera

I T MAY have been a boyhood haunt as familiar to him as a neighborhood playground, but Al Gore was never really at home in the Senate as an adult. Its clubby culture of accommodation, built on personal prerogative and collegial connection, left him an outsider for most of his eight years there. He was never, as one former senior aide to the Republican leadership said, "the guy you went to" to secure votes from the other side of the aisle. The slow, often painstaking work of building legislative coalitions seldom engaged him. Gore preferred what one adviser described as "the bank shot" — moving public opinion through oversight hearings and disclosures of information as a way of preparing the ground for legislation.

His style was better suited to the scuffling, entrepreneurial mix of the House, where raw ambition was treated with a little more tolerance and a sharp-elbowed newcomer could carve a niche for himself. "In the House there was a sense that if you worked really hard, and you pushed really hard, and you had the arguments on your side, that you could get a lot done," said Peter Knight. "I think he felt it was hard to get things done in the Senate." In a body where nearly all ninety-nine other members looked in their bathroom mirror on at least one morning and saw a potential president, Gore's young-man-in-a-hurry manner often grated. "There was an intolerance and an impatience in the institution, so people would fuck him," said another longtime adviser. "It's easy to marginalize people there." Easier still with the Republicans in the majority, as they were during his first two years.

Gore brought to the Senate his portfolio of House issues, anchored by arms control, the environment, and legislative oversight. He continued to try to protect the MX missile from its enemies and joined the twelve-member Senate observer group that monitored the re-sumption of arms control talks in Geneva in 1985. After the Chal-lenger shuttle disaster in early 1986, he was the Senate Commerce Committee's sole opposition to the return of NASA administrator James Fletcher, who had vastly underestimated the cost of the shuttle program when he oversaw its creation in the 1970s. His investigative instincts helped unearth damaging disclosures about the space agency, where margins of safety had eroded dangerously. With the help of an enterprising aide who had contacts in NASA, he uncovered data showing that the number of staff devoted to quality control had de-clined 71 percent in fifteen years.

More often, though, he struggled to re-create the kind of impact he had made in the House. An avid reader of Alvin Toffler's work (*Future Shock, The Third Wave*) on how rapid technological change may affect future generations, Gore collaborated with another big-think futurist, Representative Newt Gingrich of Georgia, on a bill to establish an Office of Critical Trends Analysis, tasked with looking around the cor-ner for the next economic or environmental crisis. Although modestly budgeted at $5 million, the idea was scorned as an attempt at big gov-ernment–style central planning and earned more hoots than votes. He coauthored a series of civil service retirement reforms, but for the most part he felt stymied and could often be found back in the House gym, playing basketball with Downey and the old crew. Over dinner one night in 1985 with aide Steve Owens, he seemed to harbor real re-grets about leaving the House. "Sometimes I wonder whether this was such a smart move," Gore said.

Reaching the Senate also meant stepping into the heart of his fa-ther's legacy, and it seemed to place new pressures on Gore. At thirty-six, he was not quite the youngest senator (Don Nickles of Oklahoma was nine months his junior, with four years' seniority), but sitting in the same chamber with men who had served with his father deepened his impulse to act older. The transition bred even more rigidity into a political style that had never been especially fluid. Former vice presi-dent and Senate colleague Dan Quayle noticed Gore's habit of taking a large gulp of air before coming up to shake hands, puffing out his chest to make himself look more formidable. Eve Zibart saw her old Nashville friend become "more serious, more calculating, and an ex-pert at hiding his true nature." His hair got shorter, his suits even more conservative, and his tolerance for imperfect staff work sank to zero. There was the sense among the old Tennesseans in the office that the stakes had suddenly grown higher, and that the House years had been a dress rehearsal for a bigger production that had just begun.

Gore's notion of a senatorial image did not include a declaration of war against lurid rock lyrics, with his wife as commanding general. Tipper Gore's mobilization against "porn rock" was as much about her need to establish an identity in the larger world as it was to protect children from raunchy music. Politics was not the life she had chosen. She had deferred the pursuit of two prospective careers — in psychology and photography — to help her husband find his place in public service, and she had also endured an emotional crisis during his Vietnam tour.

When the Gores returned to Washington after the 1976 election, they had bought Verda Carlson's Tudor home in Arlington for $208,000. Located just a few minutes from National Airport, the place made logistical sense, facilitating his weekly commutes to Tennessee. But moving back to the house where Tipper grew up had also been a hopeful act, as if she were taking a second shot at a happy childhood. She wanted to fill the place with children, six if they could.

But Washington schedules can "put a strain on the most blissful marriages," she would later write. Gore defined himself almost exclusively through his work, and it often squeezed his family life to the margins. "It was, 'Could I work twenty-four hours a day, please?'" Reed Hundt said in describing his friend's career zeal. While Gore stayed late for votes in the House and held Tennessee town meetings, the burden of serial pregnancies and care for four small children fell principally to Tipper. She missed photography and tried to keep her hand in, building a darkroom after Sarah was born and shooting occasionally for the *Tennessean* on trips back to Carthage.

She also helped form the Congressional Wives Task Force, a group of spouses who wanted some recognition for their thinking on substantive policy questions. "It gave us our own identity where it was very hard to carve it out," she said, "because in Washington, the senator or congressman — that is it. Even at parties you are sort of given this deprecating attitude." The group staked out issues that presaged the rock music fight, studying television violence and its effect on chil-

dren and urging stricter controls on video advertising aimed at minors. But "most of the time," she said of the early congressional years,
"I just stayed home with the children."

Like other major chapters in the Gore canon, the lyric campaign began, as Tipper Gore has described it, with a bracing moment of personal revelation. In December 1984, eleven-year-old Karenna, a fan of
the artist formerly known as Prince, asked her mother to buy his *Purple Rain* album. At home, mother and daughter listened to a song
called "Darling Nikki," which included the verse:

> I guess you could say she was a sex fiend.
> I met her in a hotel lobby masturbating with a magazine.

The album rocketed to the top shelf in the Gore home, away from
Karenna's reach. During the same period, as Tipper remembers it,
Kristin and Sarah, ages eight and six, respectively, began to ask questions about things they had seen on MTV videos. When she sat down
to watch with them, Tipper Gore said she was stunned by what she
saw — a world of casual violence, brutality toward women, sadomasochism, drug abuse, and glorification of satanism and suicide. Much
of it, in her view, was generated by heavy metal groups like Motley
Crue, whose "Looks That Kill" video featured scantily clad women
caged by men dressed in studded leather, and Def Leppard's "Photograph," which offered a dead woman bound in barbed wire. The teenager who had inscribed "Rolling Stones Forever" on her old boyfriend's 45rpm of "Get Off of My Cloud" was now an anxious mother
of preadolescents. "These images frightened my children; they frightened *me!*" she wrote in her 1987 book *Raising PG Kids in an X-Rated
Society.*

Susan Baker was at a similar crossroads in early 1985. The wife of
Treasury Secretary James Baker also struggled with the isolation created by a seldom-seen Washington spouse. "My heart felt deserted,"
she later said of that period. "So I looked to God for answers. I found
other women in Washington who also needed company for the same
reason." One of them was Tipper Gore. As it happened, Baker was also
disturbed by the music her kids were listening to, especially the Ma-
donna songs on the radio that her seven-year-old daughter favored.
She had already enlisted several women who wanted to do something
about it, including Pam Howar, the wife of a Washington construction

executive, and Sally Nevius, a former dean of admissions at Mount Vernon College whose husband had been chairman of the District of Columbia city council.

Attempts to cleanse rock and roll had a long and dubious history, beginning with anxiety about Elvis's pelvis, through Vice President Spiro Agnew's denunciation of lyrics that glamorized drug use. The recording industry traditionally treated such complaints with a flick of the fast-forward switch. In 1984 the National PTA, also concerned about explicit lyrics and videos, sent a letter to thirty record companies and their trade group, the Recording Industry Association of America (RIAA), suggesting the creation of a panel including consumers, artists, and industry representatives to establish standards for determining which records might need a parental warning label. Of the thirty companies queried, seven responded, none favorably.

Gore and Baker forged ahead, forming the Parents Music Resource Center (PMRC) in the spring of 1985 and inviting everyone they knew to an inaugural meeting at St. Columba's Church in Washington on May 15. The women arranged for Jeff Ling, a onetime rock musician and youth minister at a suburban Virginia church, to present a slide show illustrating rock's pornographic excesses. More than 350 attended, and two weeks later a letter signed by sixteen wives of congressmen and senators landed on the desk of RIAA President Stanley Gortikov.

In a series of letters and meetings, the PMRC petitioned record makers for "voluntary self-restraint," proposing a categorical rating system similar to the one employed by the film industry. And like the PTA, they wanted record makers to develop uniform guidelines for classifying the explicit content of new music. Lyric sheets, either on the album cover or in a master file at all record stores, should be available, they urged, for parents to preview before purchase. The group also asked that record companies reassess their contracts with artists who used violence, drugs, or explicit sexual behavior in concerts where minors were admitted.

"The Washington Wives," the condescending shorthand frequently used to describe them, attracted press by the busload. The National PTA boasted a membership of 5.6 million, but it didn't have what the PMRC had: a cadre of women, married to cabinet secretaries and members of Congress, who had spent years watching their husbands work the press to advance their agendas. Suddenly columnists from George Will to Ellen Goodman to Mike Royko hopped onto the story, as did local newscasts all over the country, seizing the opportunity to run clips of all the videos the women found objectionable. In a string of interviews, Tipper reprised her "Darling Nikki" epiphany while Baker took particular exception to "Sugar Walls," Sheena Easton's million-selling ode to female arousal, also written by the artist then known as Prince:

> The blood races to your private spots
> Lets me know there's a fire
> Can't fight passion when passion is hot
> Temperatures rise inside my sugar walls.

"And you should hear the way she sings those lyrics, using this very sexy, erotic voice," Baker told the *Los Angeles Times,* putting extra emphasis on the word *erotic.* "Well, you don't have to be much older than ten to know what that means." Even Bruce Springsteen couldn't evade the PMRC smut-sweep. Howar singled out "I'm on Fire" for celebrating promiscuous sex.

It wasn't the moral power of the PMRC's arguments, or pressure from its aggressive media campaign, that forced the industry to take it seriously. It was political self-interest, driven by a fear of women whose husbands would be voting on legislation in which record makers had a vital stake — intellectual property issues like piracy, copyright violation, and home recording. "We had to be cognizant of those realities," said Gortikov, who set up negotiations with the PMRC that summer.

He considered much of what the group wanted to be utterly unrealistic. Record companies had little control over artists' deportment in concerts; Gortikov suggested that the best preventive was a parent saying, "No, you can't go." Nor could record makers commit to placing in stores lyric sheets to which publishing companies generally owned the rights. A Hollywood-style rating system was workable for the three hundred or so films released every year but was wildly impractical, in Gortikov's view, for an industry that generated twenty-five thousand new songs annually. As for specific, industrywide guidelines, "No star panel is going to be able to make endless laundry lists of unacceptable words, let alone characterizations, that can tidily apply to every future lyric written," he wrote to Pam Howar. "There are just no 'right-wrong' characterizations, and the music industry refuses to take the first step toward a censorship mode to create a master bank of 'good-bad' words or phrases or thoughts or concepts."

By late summer artists were starting to speak up, trashing the PMRC for highlighting the excesses of a few marginal rock groups. Danny Goldberg, then president of Gold Mountain Records, formed the "Musical Majority" to fight what he and others regarded as a blatant attempt at censorship. Frank Zappa published an open letter in *Cash Box* magazine calling the PMRC's case "totally without merit, based on a hodge-podge of fundamentalist frogwash and illogical conclusions."

But the women were not without sympathizers in the industry. One of the PMRC's early financial benefactors was Beach Boy Mike Love. Motown legend Smokey Robinson went on record against "musical pornography," and Paul McCartney told *Rolling Stone:* "Let's say a really great group emerged . . . and they came out with a really great album and turned a lot of people on to Satanism. There's got to be a point where you're gonna say, 'Look, guys, we're all for artistic freedom, but maybe we just don't want de debbil trampling across America.'"

Hoping to shut down the controversy before the women picked up more support, Gortikov led nineteen record companies, covering about 80 percent of the business, into a proposed deal with the PMRC in the summer of 1985. On albums that, in the companies' view, carried graphic content, record firms agreed to place a label that read, "Parental Guidance — Explicit Lyrics." But the PMRC rejected the offer, arguing that to leave such rating decisions to individual record labels would mean uneven standards and confusion for consumers.

Some grassroots movements work for years to land a congressional hearing as a forum for their views, but the PMRC was no ordinary movement. Its membership included Sally Danforth and Peatsy Hollings — the wives, respectively, of the Senate Commerce Committee's chairman and its ranking Democrat. Missouri Republican John Danforth had misgivings about wading into the issue, principally because no specific legislative proposal was under discussion; nor could there be without raising the possibility of government censorship. Perhaps more in the interests of domestic comity than good public policy, he scheduled a one-day session for mid-September.

Al Gore loved nothing better than a seat behind a microphone at a news-making committee hearing. But the five-hour session on rock lyrics was one he might have been happy to skip. It was nearly impossible to move in room 253 of the Russell Senate Office Building on the morning of September 19, 1985. The overflow crowd spilled into the corridor, and Danforth will never forget counting seventeen cameras in place to record the events. "It was unbelievable," he said. What those present witnessed was one of the great moments of absurdist Washington theater, featuring Senator Paula Hawkins screening Van Halen's "Hot for Teacher" video, the PMRC's Ling reciting lyrics to a song called "Golden Showers," and Nebraska's James Exon asking Frank Zappa whether he had ever performed with Glenn Miller or Mitch Miller. (It turned out that as a grade-schooler Zappa took music lessons from Mitch Miller's brother.)

In a sanctimonious opening statement, Al Gore expressed disappointment that the record executives invited by the panel were no-shows, electing to let the RIAA's Gortikov do their talking. "I think that they should take a look at what their companies are doing and just ask themselves whether or not this is the way they want to spend their lives, if this is the way they want to earn a living," he said. Tipper Gore, perhaps cognizant of the heat she and her husband were both attracting, was careful to stay off the moral high horse. The timid political novice whose stomach once did back flips when she had to give a five-minute talk to the Rotary Club was considerably more confident now. Freedom and responsibility, not censorship or federal intervention, were the issues. "Clearly, there is a tension here, and in a free society there always will be," she said. "We are simply asking that these corporate and artistic rights be exercised with responsibility, with sensitivity, and some measure of self-restraint, especially since young minds are at stake."

But musicians saw more malignant agendas at work and exercised little self-restraint and less sensitivity in saying so. Zappa, praised as a "true original" by Gore, who counted himself a fan, accused the Gores of crusading against heavy metal to free up more record-store rack space for the Nashville-based country music industry. And that wasn't all:

The establishment of a rating system, voluntary or otherwise, opens the door to an endless parade of moral quality control programs based on certain things Christians do not like. What if the next bunch of Washington wives demands a large yellow "J" on all material written and performed by Jews, in order to save helpless children from exposure to concealed Zionist doctrine? . . . The PMRC has concocted a Mythical Beast and compounds the chicanery by demanding "consumer guidelines" to keep it from inviting your children inside its sugar walls. Is the next step the adoption of a "PMRC National Legal Age for Comprehension of Vaginal Arousal"?

The proceedings bottomed out with the arrival of Twisted Sister's Dee Snider, who bellied up to the witness table in dark glasses and a sleeveless black T-shirt. One of Snider's songs, "Under the Blade," had been condemned by the PMRC for its celebration of bondage and rape:

> It's not another party head
> This time you cannot rise
> Your hands are tied
> Your legs are strapped
> A light shines in your eyes
> You faintly see the razor's edge.

Snider, describing himself as a Christian and a family man who did not drink, smoke, or do drugs, charged Mrs. Gore with "character assassination" for falsely accusing him of marketing a T-shirt showing a woman spread-eagled and in handcuffs. He also insisted that his song was actually about fear of surgery, inspired by the anxiety of a band member awaiting an operation to remove throat polyps. "I can say categorically that the only sadomasochism, bondage, and rape in this song is in the mind of Mrs. Gore," said Snider.

While other committee members were angered by the personal dig at a senator's wife, Gore hung back, saying nothing in direct rebuke when his turn for questions came. Instead, he tried to discredit Snider through a series of interrogatories about "Under the Blade." ("Have you ever had surgery with your hands tied and your legs strapped? . . . Is there a reference to the hospital in the song?") When Gore asked about the name of the group's fan club, SMF Fans of Twisted Sister, Snider acknowledged that it stood for Sick Mother Fucking Fans. "Is this also a Christian group?" Gore asked. "I do not believe profanity has anything to do with Christianity, thank you," Snider replied.

Despite the constant assurances from the PMRC and its friends on the committee that they opposed censorship, the proceedings carried the unmistakable chill of official sanction. "These hearings seem designed not to warn parents about content so much as to warn persons in the recording industry . . . they must either 'voluntarily' alter their product or face new statutory or regulatory initiatives. The threat of forthcoming censorship is palpable," ACLU legislative counsel Barry Lynn wrote to Danforth.

The PMRC backed off six weeks later, dropping its insistence on uniform industry standards and a categorical rating system for explicit lyrics. The group announced that it would accept the RIAA's omnibus "Explicit Lyrics — Parental Advisory" sticker, leaving it to record companies to decide which albums should be so designated. The PMRC also agreed to stand down from its aggressive media campaign for one year. But industry compliance with the labeling agreement was spotty, and the companies, left to design their own advisory logos, made them too small to be easily noticed or blended them into the artwork on the cover.

Tipper Gore's battle with the music industry was only a partial victory, but it positioned her to fight a wider war. Her work caught the eye of Michael Lawrence, senior editor at Abingdon Press, a division of United Methodist Publishing House in Nashville, who encouraged her to consider a book — one that expanded the discussion beyond the rock lyrics to the broader impact of popular culture on children. *Raising PG Kids in an X-Rated Society,* published in April 1987, was both a parental how-to on shielding kids from pernicious messages in music, television, and print and a genuinely indignant, if cumbersomely worded, personal defense. "There is a responsible, non-fanatical, growing concern over pornography that can't be pinned on outdated images of prudish misfits attempting to Lysol the world," she wrote. "As parents we have a special duty to establish a moral imperative for our children."

Some of the advice is helpful, if a tad obvious ("Talk about popular groups with your children. Listen to their likes and dislikes. Teach them that they don't have to patronize musical groups that exploit women and commercialize violence"), and there's a prescient section (for 1987) on the dangers of pornographic materials available online. But other recommendations are just plain naive: "Help your child make musical choices that are positive. Go with him or her to the rec-

ord store, examine the albums, discuss the groups," she urges, perhaps forgetting how few adolescents would be interested in such an
excursion with a parent. Much of the book, written with the help of
Gore consultant Carter Eskew, has the feel of a 140-page Lexus/Nexus
search that scoured the landscape for every over-the-top splatter film,
rock video, or heavy metal album that reinforced her arguments. (The
illustrative examples were so graphic that the book carried its own parental advisory.)

Neither Gore was prepared for the pounding their public images
took as a consequence of the lyrics campaign. For a politician who
picked his fights with meticulous care, having a huge one picked for
him by his wife was a shock to the system. One close friend remembers him expressing "nothing but pride" about her new cause, but it
created serious political problems. Some aides fretted that his daughter's encounter with a Prince record would turn him into the senator
formerly known as a presidential contender, landing him on the side
of concerned parents but at odds with critical liberal constituencies
inside the party. Tipper-bashing reverberated through Gore's 1988
presidential campaign, throwing a chill over fund-raising on both
coasts. "There is no possibility . . . that I will support with my money,
my vote, or my persuasiveness a candidate with a wife named 'Tipper'
who crusades against rock lyrics," Democratic contributor Peggy Kerr
of New York wrote to the Gore campaign after she was solicited in the
summer of 1987. "Should the Senator get a divorce, please let me
know, and I will cheerfully consider a campaign donation." Hollywood, traditionally a deep pocket for liberal Democrats, was especially
hostile toward Gore, despite a friendly voting record on recording industry interests (Nashville's country music community was an important constituency), including a key role in killing a measure that
would have made it more difficult for composers and songwriters to
collect royalties. Others saw the porn rock war as a drain on the energy
and allure of a thirty-nine-year-old candidate who should have been
a Kennedy-esque magnet for young voters. Even *The New Republic*
vented its frustration. "Having a wife who has made herself the surgeon general of rock 'n' roll makes Gore a faintly ridiculous figure,
like the Ralph Bellamy character in 'His Girl Friday,'" wrote Hendrik
Hertzberg. "In some subtle and no doubt deplorable way, it unmans
him."

For Tipper Gore, her birth as a public figure was a trauma from which she never quite recovered. After eight relatively quiet years as a congressional spouse in suburban Virginia, she found herself pinned down in the culture war's crossfire, enshrined as everything from "Asshole of the Month" in *Hustler* to one of *Esquire*'s 1988 "Women We Love" ("So she doesn't like Twisted Sister. Big f —— g deal"), joining Robin Givens Tyson, Mary Beth Whitehead, Katarina Witt, and Shirley MacLaine. With the PMRC she fell into the same kind of schism between public identity and private personality that trapped her husband. Her media caricature — the prissy blond housewife with the little girl's name who wanted to steam-clean popular culture — eclipsed the spirited, humorous, charmingly earthy woman whom friends said they knew. Although her moralizing may have grated at times, she came to the issue not as a conservative cultural warrior but as a liberal feminist angry about the mass-marketed degradation of women.

Her spirits bottomed out at a September 1985 forum in New York sponsored by the National Association of Recording Arts and Sciences. Naively expecting a reasoned discussion, she walked into a three-hour ambush highlighted by a harangue from singer Wendy O. Williams, who suggested that the concern about lyric content came from fears about her own children wanting to masturbate. "When is it all right for a child to masturbate . . . Mrs. Gore?" Williams asked, not the kind of query that the campus Young Democrats in Knoxville lobbed up to the plate. As she limped back to Washington that night, she was stranded at La Guardia by bad weather. "I had never felt so alone," she later wrote. "I longed for the familiarity, love and comfort of home. How had I gotten myself into this situation?"

Over the next several years a double-album's worth of "greatest hits" denounced her in the most scalding terms, like Ice-T's "Freedom of Speech":

> Think I give a fuck about some silly bitch named Gore?
> Yo PMRC, here we go, raw
> Yo Tip, what's the matter? You ain't gettin' no dick?
> You're bitchin' about rock 'n' roll, that's censorship, dumb bitch.

As the presidential primary season neared, the Gores decided that it was time for some strategic backpedaling. While publicly standing firm, they privately sought to appease Hollywood interests whose campaign largesse they needed. On October 28, 1987, they sat down to an off-the-record lunch in the Los Angeles dining room of the entertainment giant MCA, hosted by music group chief Irving Azoff and a delegation of aggrieved industry figures, including television producers Norman Lear and Michael Mann, Don Henley of the Eagles, record executive Danny Goldberg, and entertainment lawyer Lee Phillips, whose clients included Prince. The meeting was put together by California lawyer and Democratic fund-raiser Mickey Kantor, a native Tennessean who later served as President Clinton's trade representative and Commerce secretary.

But the Gores' plan to do a little discreet groveling quickly unraveled into a fresh embarrassment. A transcript of the surreptitiously taped gathering, leaked to *Daily Variety*, showed that while they defended the labeling agreement with the RIAA, both disavowed the Commerce Committee hearing. Gore pleaded lack of stature, arguing that as a lowly "freshman minority member of the [Commerce] Committee" he had no power to head off the spectacle. "I did not ask for the hearing. I was not in favor of the hearing," he said. But according to at least one former colleague, Gore was once again playing loose with the facts. Paula Hawkins said that Gore approached Senator Ernest Hollings to lobby for the hearing. Mrs. Gore was already on record as having placed the responsibility for the committee spectacle elsewhere; in *Raising PG Kids*, she claimed that "both he [Gore] and I had reservations about it." Danforth, however, remembers both Susan Baker and Tipper Gore actively joining his wife Sally in pushing for congressional attention.

But the entertainment execs were not mollified, and what started as a summit deteriorated into a reeducation session. "Are you familiar with blacklisting and how it happened?" Goldberg lectured. "It's not about the First Amendment. It's about when government officials or people close to them start criticizing entertainment." Azoff suggested that the PMRC might defuse some of the ill will if it dropped "Music" from its name and called itself the "Parents Entertainment Resource Center," or simply the "Parents Resource Center." Tipper Gore promised to take up the idea with the PMRC board. As the *New York Times* archly noted two weeks later on its editorial page, "The lunch thus illustrates how a political campaign fosters understanding for other people's views."

The rock issue opened up a "huge division of opinion" inside Gore's 1988 campaign, said former press secretary Arlie Schardt. Some aides contended that Tipper was a liability who needed to be kept in the background. "[Gore's] advisers were saying to him, 'Please rein her in. This is killing your campaign,'" she wrote later. On an early trip to Iowa, just "one or two" people showed up at a coffee. "The organizers told me they just couldn't get anyone to attend because everyone thought I was for censorship."

Her attempt to win some respect and make a contribution became a quest to convince voters she wasn't some rock and roll Carrie Nation. Instead of talking about what kind of president her husband would make, she explained again and again that she did not advocate censorship. In California one Gore fund-raiser assembled a nine-page "Tipper kit" for visiting reporters, with articles spinning the story her way. She opened up her record collection to reporters, showing them her Grateful Dead albums, making sure they knew she was an early Springsteen fan and a high school drummer. "You're talking to someone who truly understands rock music," she said. "We are liberal-minded people." Even Karenna, who started it all with "Darling Nikki," put in her time on damage control. Campaigning with her father on the streets of New York's Little Italy in the spring of 1988, the fourteen-year-old pronounced her mother "the most misunderstood woman in America," adding: "You know, she's just an easy target, she really is. 'She's a bored housewife,' you know. 'Wife of a Senator.' I mean, it's really unfortunate what's happened. I think it's really unfair."

By 1990 Tipper Gore was in full retreat from the issue, even collaborating with the industry to roll back some of the grassroots activity inspired by the PMRC, which included mandatory labeling bills pending in nearly two dozen states. She traveled to Missouri to plead the record makers' case before the legislature and successfully lobbied Louisiana Governor Buddy Roemer to veto a labeling bill that had already passed. Although mandatory labeling was the kind of de facto censorship that Tipper Gore never had in mind, it was, ironically, the brushfires at the state level that forced the RIAA to get more serious. That same year it adopted a standard, uniform design for the advisory logo and tightened up on compliance.

But by then Tipper Gore had turned in her rock police badge. When

Al Gore joined the Democratic ticket two years later, she remained conspicuously silent during the wide debate over violent rap lyrics. As she changed her tune, the music industry took the Gores off probation. Danny Goldberg, one of their inquisitors at the MCA lunch, helped two of his clients, Bonnie Raitt and Nirvana, organize a fundraiser for the Clinton-Gore ticket, although he acknowledged that he was motivated more by the prospect of another four years of George Bush than by any great fondness for the vice presidential candidate and his wife. Less than two months after Gore moved into his West Wing office in 1993, Tipper quietly resigned from the PMRC. As if to complete the circle, Frank Zappa's widow, Gail, donated $240,000 to the Democratic National Committee during the 1996 campaign, sending her checks directly to Clinton-Gore chairman Peter Knight.

The porn rock fight didn't drive Tipper Gore from public life, but for a time it pushed her back from the front lines of the culture wars, and she adopted some of her husband's strategic caution. Pop culture and its impact on children remained an interest — she actively supported the administration's V-chip legislation, which gave parents the technology to block questionable television programming — yet her support in this area was subordinate to a broader, and less contentious, portfolio of issues like homelessness, mental health, and "family" concerns. In May 1999, however, the shootings at Columbine High School in Littleton, Colorado, filled the debate about kids, guns, and popular culture with a new urgency. It also reintroduced — and perhaps in some sense vindicated — Tipper Gore as someone with a serious message. In Littleton's aftermath, she stepped up her role as an advocate for improved mental health care and an end to the stigma attached to those with emotional disorders. She also spoke publicly for the first time about her own treatment for depression after Albert III's near-fatal car accident in 1989.

Still, of the foursome that shape the public face of the Clinton administration — the president, Hillary Clinton, Gore, and Tipper Gore — she remains the most ambivalent about the risks and rewards of political life. Although she says she is no longer in treatment, some friends see an unquiet soul, one that would be happiest if her husband became a university president or a full-time author. "Tipper can have some pretty dark moods," said one longtime family friend.

After the years of excoriation by the rock world, it's worth noting that she remains a fan. In 1997 an old campaign aide spotted her in the audience at a Tina Turner concert with one of her daughters, happy and completely at ease dancing to the music as Secret Service agents stood vigil on each end of the aisle. But there are still moments when she works too hard to distance herself from the episode, until it is difficult to know which persona is truly her and which is part of the ongoing hipness campaign.

Asked in a 1996 interview about the reading the vice president kept on his nightstand, she said, "Are you kidding? He's living with me. You think he's going to read a book at night?" sounding like a cross between Mae West and Barbra Streisand. To a question about a Gore presidential race in 2000, she answered: "We are focused on this election, not the next one. You cannot allow yourself to think about the next election. . . . I don't even think about it. Not now. It's premature . . . it's premature evaluation!"

◆ 12 ◆

The Warm Puppy Principle

O N JULY 18, 1986, Al Gore sat down with Washington talk show host John McLaughlin for a taping of his *One on One* interview show. Toward the end of a half-hour discussion about the Salt II treaty and the Nicaraguan contras, McLaughlin asked a question, couched in his usual bombast, about the 1988 presidential race.

"You've got the magical name — Al Gore. Your father was in Congress for thirty-two years. You've got character. You've got no clay feet, no skeletons showing. You're intelligent. You're well informed. You've got a Vietnam War record. You've been an investigative reporter, and you've got religious coloration too. For one year you were a divinity student, and you're a devout Baptist. You're almost too good to be true. Are you too good to be true?"

"Well, I don't know . . . " Gore said.

"I mean, what's going to happen to you? You say you have no aspirations for a national career," McLaughlin persisted.

"I'm trying to do the best job I can as a senator."

Notwithstanding his hedging, the question of a presidential candidacy was never an "if" for Gore, only a "when." Yet even a politician of his genetically engineered ambition had good reasons to conclude that 1988 was not his year. He was thirty-eight years old, not even halfway through his first Senate term. While he had made a name for himself as an arms control expert, he was not identified in the public mind with the kind of "kitchen table" economic issues that usually provide the foundation for a run at the White House. He also felt certain that New York Governor Mario Cuomo was going to get into the race and instantly become the preemptive favorite for the nomination. His wariness about running even trickled into his subconscious that summer. Over dinner one night he told writer Leon Wieseltier, a friend from Martin Peretz's *New Republic,* of a dream in which he was working outdoors and came across a tree that needed moving, but he put it off. The tree, Gore told Wieseltier, was a run for the presidency.

But the buzz around Gore grew steadily more audible as the presidential season approached. After Walter Mondale's forty-nine-state loss in 1984, many Democrats yearned for a candidate who couldn't be spray-painted by the GOP as a tax-and-spend liberal. There was broad sentiment for a centrist — or at least someone who seemed like a centrist — capable of reaching out to disaffected southern whites who had turned to Nixon and Reagan. Two of Gore's Senate colleagues, Sam Nunn of Georgia and Dale Bumpers of Arkansas, popped up most frequently in the speculation, but Gore was also invariably one of the Mentioned. Jay Rockefeller of West Virginia, one of Gore's few friends in the Senate, touted him to Charles Peters, Nancy Gore's old Peace Corps pal who was now publisher of the neoliberal *Washington Monthly.* The result was a profile that became the magazine's November 1986 cover, a piece by John Eisendrath ("The Longest Shot: Measuring Al Gore Jr. for the White House") filled with praise for his work in arms control and legislative oversight. So effusive were the reports from Rockefeller and Eisendrath that Peters set up a lunch to check out the kid brother of his late colleague. He was dismayed when Gore spent most of the occasion diagramming ballistic missile throw weights. "On the whole, I admire Al," said Peters. But one lunch, he felt, was more than enough. Like many others over the years, he was engaged by the ideas, but bored by the man.

Gore's view of the race started to shift over the Christmas holidays in Tennessee. Albert Gore quietly pulled his son aside during a family dinner to tell him he was uniquely positioned to win the Democratic nomination and the presidency. The new Super Tuesday primary, taking in twenty southern and border states, was a potential windfall for the right Democrat from the region, the elder Gore said. Americans tended to seek presidents who compensated for perceived weaknesses in their predecessors, he added, electing a young Jack Kennedy after an aging Dwight Eisenhower, or a righteous Jimmy Carter as a corrective to the Nixon-Ford years. Voters were poised to do the same, the senator believed, now that Ronald Reagan was headed back to California.

At first his son was dismissive and a little overwhelmed. It was one thing to get some flattering press, and quite another to hear the ultimate authority figure in his life tell him that this was his moment. "That's frightening," he said. "You can't mean it. Absolutely not. No!"

But the old senator was stone serious. Left unsaid by both men was another, more personal, calculation. Albert Gore turned seventy-nine the day after Christmas, and this was likely to be his only chance to see his son enter the White House. Mortality, more than an electoral map, drove his view of the race, as it did, at least in part, his son's attempt to become the youngest major party presidential candidate since William Jennings Bryan. "He had a naked, desperate desire to see his boy be president," said Arlie Schardt, Gore's 1988 campaign secretary.

Gore returned to Washington in early 1987 still insisting that he was not in the hunt. But the question took a dramatically different cast on February 19 when Cuomo backed out of the race. Nunn and Bumpers remained possibilities, although neither seemed to be doing what was necessary to mobilize a presidential campaign. Cuomo's departure and the Christmas talk with his father combined to tug at his competitive instincts. He asked an aide to begin a file of press clippings on Gary Hart, now the front-runner, and the ambitious young chairman of the National Governors' Association who was raising home-state seed money for a race, Bill Clinton of Arkansas. The reasons against running that had seemed so sound just a few weeks earlier — age, competition, issues — started to feel less compelling. Absent Cuomo, the rest of the probable field looked distinctly mortal. Clinton was an unknown quantity, but Hart, Joe Biden, Paul Simon, and Dick Gephardt were all colleagues and he had seen their moves. Former Arizona Governor Bruce Babbitt and the Reverend Jesse Jackson were no real threats. And Michael Dukakis, the Massachusetts governor, had no grounding in what Gore believed to be the critical issue facing the country.

He was convinced that with Mikhail Gorbachev's rise to power, U.S.-Soviet relations were at a historic crossroads. His arms control expertise, with the Midgetman as a centerpiece, could help end the nuclear arms race. Wasn't saving the world reason enough to run?

As spring neared, the *Washington Monthly* piece had set off a Gore boomlet within the city's journo-politico community. *Newsweek* declared "Gore Chic" a Washington phenomenon. James Reston of the

New York Times pronounced the former summer copy boy unjustly overlooked and perhaps the most promising young man in the Senate: "He's too young at 38, the 'experts' say, forgetting in this 200th anniversary of the Constitution that it was written by Alexander Hamilton when he was 30, James Madison when he was only 36 and John Adams when he was 37." (In a note to Reston later that year, after he entered the race, Gore thanked him for the encouragement, and especially for minimizing concerns about his age. "I'm glad your column early on got me into it [or *helped* get me in, at least]. As for the so-called 'stature gap,' remember that in 1960 there was talk of Stevenson getting in up until near the end. Even Truman publicly questioned JFK's stature. But the campaign dealt with that question effectively. I feel the same thing happening now.") Gore began to fall prey to what Roy Neel called "the warm puppy" principle of deciding whether to run for president. "Once you start thinking about it," Neel said, "you take the puppy home and you can't live without it. Problem is, you forget the puppy is going to pee on the rug. Al always knew that someday he would run. Once he began to think it was doable, I suspect he may have rationalized some of the negatives away."

Still, Gore knew that before he could save the world, he would have to find someone to pay for the crusade. Even the old senator, for all his pieties, depended on figures like Armand Hammer for some of his funding. Gore needed his own underwriter, and one of his first calls was to Nathan Landow.

A developer in Bethesda, Maryland, who looked as if he had escaped from the pages of a Damon Runyon story, Nate Landow took a correspondence course in blueprint reading as a young man, borrowed money from relatives, and parlayed it into a fortune building and managing apartment houses. There was a hint of menace under the perpetual tan and the pugnacious charm, the manner of a man for whom the only right answer was yes. "Nate walks into the room, and it becomes Nate's room," said one Democratic Party official. He raised millions for Jimmy Carter in 1976 and was considered a shoo-in for an ambassadorial post until the story of his business relationship with Joe Nesline, a Washington gambler with ties to Meyer Lansky's organization, landed in the papers. Landow was never charged with any wrongdoing, but politicians who found their way to his door knew they weren't dealing with a champion of good government. He would turn up on the margins of several scandals of the Clinton-Gore era, including the Paula Jones case. Independent Counsel Kenneth Starr investigated whether he helped obstruct justice by urging former White House volunteer Kathleen Willey not to tell Jones's lawyers that Clinton had groped her. Again, he was never charged.

Landow served as Mondale's finance chairman in 1984 and was determined not to pour cash into another Republican landslide. So he formed IMPAC 88, an alliance of forty-five Democratic money men determined to find and bankroll a salable candidate. Landow hired former Carter pollster Patrick Caddell to prepare a memo sketching the archetypal Democrat for 1988. Mr. Right was an "inside insurgent," Caddell wrote, someone who embodied generational change in a year when 60 percent of the electorate was under the age of forty, but not so threatening as to be considered an "outsider." Landow didn't know from outsiders and inside insurgents, but he knew political horseflesh, and he sensed that Gore was the guy. He had been keeping an eye on the young Tennessean since he reached the Senate. When Landow saw Gore at a party in early 1987, he said, "If you decide to do anything at the presidential level, I would like to work with you."

Gore knew Landow's track record with money and took the offer seriously. On February 25, less than a week after Cuomo's exit, he invited Landow and another IMPAC member, Daytona Beach attorney Bill Crotty, to lunch at his parents' apartment in the Methodist Building on Maryland Avenue, across the street from the Capitol. Over soggy chicken salad sandwiches, Gore asked about his prospects for financial support. Both men were bullish on Gore, but it was late, they said. Each IMPAC member was free to underwrite whomever he wanted, and a number had already made commitments to Biden, Gephardt, and Hart. Many were "on hold," waiting to see whether Bumpers was going to run. The group's next scheduled meeting in Washington was March 19, and Landow suggested that Gore come to speak. Gore and Knight prepped for the event as if it were a presidential debate. These were "the legendary figures of the Democratic fundraising community," as Peter Knight reverently put it, and their reaction could help Gore launch a presidential candidacy.

He shook every hand when he strode into the dining room at the Grand Hotel that evening, then warmed up the money men with a couple of well-worn jokes, one a divinity school story about unscrewing the inscrutable. After a few remarks about competitiveness, telecommunications, and the highway system his father helped to build, Gore cut to the chase. For twenty minutes he spoke in a slow, preacherly cadence about how the country needed a president who knew how to lead it out of the arms race. "Nuclear war is not inevitable," Gore said. "I don't believe that." Afterward Landow wandered the room and found the makings of serious support. He looked like a president, many of them thought. They were also drawn to him because of what he did not resemble: a prickly northeastern liberal like Dukakis, or an overheated motormouth like Biden. "He's it! He's the one!" exulted Austin businessman Buddy Temple, waving a finger in Gore's direction. Landow agreed. "He looks like a president, not some kind of wimp! I could understand what he was talking about. If he could make me understand arms control, he could make anyone understand it. That age? Don't bother me at all."

Gore had always gotten more than his share of lucky breaks in planning his next career move. Two well-timed retirements (Joe Evins and Howard Baker) had smoothed his way into the House and Senate. Now it seemed to be happening again. The day after his IMPAC meeting, Dale Bumpers announced that he wasn't running. Knowing that much of his audience the night before had been holding out for the eloquent Arkansas country lawyer, Gore called Landow and asked for a second crack at IMPAC. How soon could he get them back to town?

"Al, they just left," Landow said. He promised to turn them around as quickly as possible.

While Gore was anxious to close the sale with IMPAC, he continued to discourage speculation about a candidacy. Four days after his pitch to the fund-raisers, he told the *Nashville Banner*'s senior political writer, Mike Pigott, that his only interest was in remaining a senator and that his head hadn't been turned in the least by all the talk. "Every once in a while someone mentions it," Gore said nonchalantly. "But it hasn't affected my thinking on it." On March 27, four days after speaking with Pigott, he was back in front of IMPAC. With Bumpers out, seventeen members promised to raise $250,000 apiece for Gore, more than $4 million. It wasn't enough to sustain a campaign, but adequate to get it started — and a marker of legitimacy that could attract other money. Gore asked for two weeks — until April 10 — to make a final decision. Landow and company agreed, but warned that his backing would start to peel away if he dithered.

Once again a sudden, though hardly unexpected, change of career plan took Tipper Gore by surprise. She had seen all the stories but again chose not to recognize the signs in plain view. As in 1976, she was absorbed in her own plans. She had scheduled an April book tour to promote *Raising PG Kids in an X-Rated Society.* When Gore told her he had set an April 10 deadline to decide on a run for the Democratic presidential nomination, she was stunned. "Shock therapy — you continue to do it to me," she told him. She argued that he needed months, not days, to weigh such a huge decision. But Gore had no choice: the IMPAC meter was ticking. Moreover, he had seen the run/don't-run dilemma turn into a quagmire for other politicians, paralyzing and ultimately diminishing them. He was determined that his deliberations would be crisp and timely.

Gore spoke to scores of people over the next two weeks: friends, congressional colleagues, staff, political consultants, and former combatants like Mondale, who offered a grimly candid assessment of the hardships that a campaign would pose for his young family. He brought his kids into the loop at a family meeting in their Arlington living room, and they had their own singular concerns. "When is Social Security going to start following us around?" asked eight-year-old Sarah.

The issue that preoccupied Gore was his age. He had turned thirty-nine on March 31, making him four years younger than Jack Kennedy when he ran. He had no doubts about his ability to do the job — his robust self-regard left no room for that — but wondered whether the public would take him seriously. "Is it too soon?" he asked Eve Zibart. Even those closest to him weren't sure where he was going to land. Media consultant Bob Squier invited the Gores and partner Carter Eskew down to his winter retreat near Sarasota for a weekend of sailing and tennis. Although the getaway had been offered as a respite to help Gore clear his head, the two ad men couldn't resist pressing the question. They had T-shirts made up to say, "If Not Now, When? If Not Me, Who?" There were hours of open-ended talk, but no decision.

On Thursday morning, April 9, twenty-four hours to deadline, Gore stopped by his parents' apartment on the way to the office. Just as he had during other visits, he sat in the living room, surrounded by Pauline's tasteful antiques and the memorabilia of a political lifetime, and marched through the litany of reasons why running was the wrong choice. The old senator remained gung-ho, but Pauline hung back. She explained in an interview with *Newsweek*'s Lucille Beachy several months later: "I think if you do your job bringing your children up well enough, when they reach that stage and age, they're better equipped to make that kind of decision than you are. If they're not, you haven't done your job well. Fortunately or unfortunately, my husband doesn't have that same feeling. He urges or inhibits, one or the other." Gore left without revealing his plans. But he had mounted such a convincing case for standing down that Albert thought his son had indeed talked himself out of it, and he flew back to Tennessee later that day. Pauline said later that what her husband had taken for no was something else: "I think my son had to establish that it would be his campaign and that he'd be doing it his own way."

Gore woke up before dawn the next day and called Tipper, who was out on her book tour. "I've pretty well decided to run," he said. She canceled the rest of her itinerary and raced back to Washington. Around 9:00 A.M. he told Knight, who laid on a midafternoon press conference. Pauline, who had stayed behind at the Methodist, picked the kids up from school early and made sure they were wearing nice clothes. Finally, at 11:00 A.M., twenty-five years to the day that he listened in on Jack Kennedy, the phone rang at the farm. "Dad, it's a go," Gore said. The old senator let out a whoop, he said later, "like a banshee Indian."

Later he told his father of another decision, one the elder Gore would also support. When his candidacy became official that summer, the name adorning his signs and literature would be Al Gore, not Albert Gore Jr.

◆ 13 ◆

Rolling Alamo

A L GORE now concedes privately what Democratic primary voters figured out pretty quickly in 1988: he wasn't ready to be president. One former campaign adviser, who later worked in the Clinton White House, says that Gore readily acknowledges that, in retrospect, "he didn't know what the job entailed" and that he "knows now he needed some maturing experiences."

The announcement of his candidacy on April 10, 1987, captured the essence of the unfocused and maladroit campaign to come. He had to backtrack after declaring that when Ronald Reagan left office, voters might want "to turn to youth, vigor, [and] intellectual capacity," an indelicate (although not indefensible) suggestion that the Great Communicator had slipped mentally. Most telling was the substance of his message, scribbled on yellow legal paper. It wandered from arms control and the environment, to AIDS and Alzheimer's, to 100 percent literacy and men on Mars by 2000 — all sounding equally urgent. "What is the national priority?" a befuddled reporter asked.

"The arms race, and making America competitive, and cleaning up our environment, and creating the best education system in the world. Those are the four top," Gore said.

His formal kickoff speech ten weeks later, on June 29, 1987, under a blazing June sun at the steps of the Smith County courthouse in Carthage, where he and his father began all their races, was an even lengthier laundry list. He didn't mention nuclear security, the ostensible inspiration for his candidacy, until the thirty-second of a thirty-nine-paragraph address. Instead, he staked out the moral high ground against the Reagan administration, which was enmeshed in the Iran-contra scandal. "My first promise to the American people is something I can carry out without any action by Congress," he said. "Any government official who steals from the American people or lies to the United States Congress will be fired immediately."

Gore never converted his passions into a coherent, compelling rationale for a candidacy. He changed messages as often as he did the rickety charter planes that carried him from state to state, backing away from the arms race and environmental renewal when handlers told him they weren't resonating in the polls. He morphed from national security expert to friend of working families to defender of Israel. This wasn't a felony, nor was it necessarily bad politics. But it was politics as usual from a man who presented himself to the world as something new.

In the glare of his first national primary campaign, his self-consciousness about age deepened. Gore viewed solemnity as his only protection against the ravages of youth, and he refused to risk the slightest departure from his blue-suited blandness. Even the new ties that Tipper slipped into his luggage to jazz up his appearance went unworn as he continued to favor his usual nondescript red. Political pros who had seen a quick, clever, and poised candidate in his Tennessee campaigns were baffled. "In his Senate race, Al Gore was the best candidate we ever worked with," said one former consultant. "Then he ran for president, and this guy just tightened up."

The same problems Gore struggles with in the 2000 incarnation of his candidacy were writ large in 1988. Aides despaired at how to make public some of the private Gore who resided off the record on campaign planes and at dinners, a more relaxed, even subversively funny man who enjoyed long evenings of talk fueled by Calvados and espresso, who broke into song (*La Bamba* during a storm-tossed plane flight) and liked to explain how to hypnotize a chicken (hold the bird's head down and move your finger in the dirt in front of its face). Page Crosland, a former aide to Tipper Gore, remembers visiting the family's Arlington home on a rare campaign day off when Gore, dressed in blue jeans and a plaid workshirt, put his favorite George Strait song, "All My Exes Live in Texas" ("That's why I hang my hat in Tennessee"), on the stereo and started dancing. Gore the wooden candidate was gone, Crosland thought. "It was just this rugged, funny, exuberant man," she said, "dancing around the living room and singing along with George Strait."

It probably didn't help Gore's confidence to have the old senator constantly looking over his shoulder. Testing the waters in the South in the spring of 1987, Gore traveled to North Carolina, Alabama, and Georgia, where he spoke to audiences of party activists. The Dixie swing attracted little notice in the press — just one reporter, Scott Shepard of the *Atlanta Constitution,* tagged along. But when the trip ended in Atlanta and Shepard, the paper's Washington correspondent, dropped by the *Constitution,* editor Bill Kovach called him into his office. Kovach, an old family friend, asked for a report on Gore. So-so in North Carolina and Georgia, pretty good in Alabama, Shepard said. Kovach then dialed a phone number and handed the receiver to Shepard. On the other end of the line was Albert Gore, eager to hear how his boy had done.

Gore entered presidential politics at a moment when the rules of engagement between candidates and journalists were changing dramatically. In May 1987 Gary Hart, the Democratic front-runner, was driven from the race after the *Miami Herald* exposed his affair with Donna Rice. The personal had suddenly become political, and off-hours conduct once considered out of bounds was now fair game. "Character," or, more precisely, private behavior, had come of age as a criterion for judging presidential worthiness.

It seemed that Gore had little to worry about on the infidelity front. His seventeen years with Tipper had seen the usual ups and downs, and as a man who married at twenty-two, he had occasionally cast a mildly envious eye, said one bachelor friend, at the freedom that single people seemed to enjoy. But there was no evidence that he had ever broken his wedding vows.

When Hart reentered the race briefly in late 1987, arguing that a candidate should be judged by public contributions, not private behavior, some advisers urged Gore to make an issue of personal morality. But, according to Reed Hundt, he shut them down. "He never liked it, and he never bought into it," Hundt said.

Although reluctant to exploit the matter, Gore made it clear privately that he disapproved of Hart, and that he believed that public leadership and private morals were not separable. Over the Christmas holiday he wrote to *New York Times* columnist James Reston, who had been sharply critical of Hart in a December 25 piece. Reston had quoted Walter Lippmann, who said that those who hold positions of public trust are "the custodians of a nation's ideals. . . . They are unfaithful to that trust when by word and example they promote a spirit that is complacent, evasive and acquisitive." Gore praised Reston for a "particularly insightful" column, especially the Lippmann reference. "It reminded me of a favorite quotation of mine from Aristotle," Gore wrote, "'Virtue is one thing.' It is not to be compartmentalized for public life and seen as entirely separate from the rest of one's life."

A decade later, as Bill Clinton's vice president, Gore would again be forced to confront the issue of private conduct in public office. He would have a significantly different response from the one he shared with Reston.

On one level the new culture of personal inquiry was innocuous enough. It often meant questions from local television reporters about his favorite color (blue), favorite food (Tex-Mex), and favorite ice cream (cookies and cream). But as Hart self-destructed that spring, the *New York Times* Washington bureau chief, Craig Whitney, wrote to each candidate requesting their consent to what amounted to a journalistic strip search. Some of the information the *Times* sought — birth certificate, marriage license, criminal or civil court cases in which he had been a plaintiff or defendant, lists of close friends — could have been acquired with some basic reportorial shoe leather. Other items the paper requested broke uncomfortable new ground: medical records, including those of treatment for mental illness, military documents exempted from the Freedom of Information Act, and a waiver of privacy rights that would have enabled *Times* reporters to peruse investigative files that might have been prepared by the FBI.

The Gore camp spent weeks scrambling for the information and then deliberating over how much of it should be handed over. "Try not to respond at all until follow-up calls come," one top adviser urged in a memo. "Tell 'em to screw off," Tipper Gore told another aide tasked with canvassing viewpoints among members of the inner circle. The candidate was only slightly more cooperative. In the end Gore elected to provide some of the basic data but refused to waive his privacy rights. A draft of a June 15 letter to Whitney said: "As a former investigative reporter myself, I found some of your requests to be unreasonable and inappropriately personal."

It was, ironically, embroidered claims about his reporting career that led to Gore's first major "character" lapse as a candidate. On a late September trip through Iowa, he told the *Des Moines Register* that at the *Tennessean* he had got "a bunch of people indicted and sent to jail." The "bunch" in question were two Metro Councilmen charged with bribery in zoning cases: Morris Haddox, indicted and acquitted, and Jack Clariday, convicted and given a three-year suspended sentence. Interestingly, it fell to the *Commercial Appeal* of Memphis, not John Seigenthaler's *Tennessean,* to correct the record. Gore apologized, calling it "a careless statement that was unintentional."

Gore had his defenders — no less a liar than Richard Nixon, his father's old nemesis, wrote to offer his support. "Incidentally," he told Gore, "don't be discouraged by the flack you are getting about possibly exaggerating your achievements as an investigative reporter. After all, what you said was essentially true. No one can claim that you did not produce results which is all that matters."

Competitively, Hart's exit was good news for Gore, but with his late entry into the competition, his campaign was still the political equivalent of an expansion baseball team — left to stock its roster from a shallow pool of rejected or overlooked talent. At Landow's suggestion, Gore hired former Cuomo and Mondale aide Fred Martin as campaign manager. Like his employer, he was young (thirty-four), credentialed (a Harvard Ph.D. in American history), and inexperienced in the management of a presidential primary campaign.

Both also agreed that as the last and youngest to enter the race, Gore needed to prove right away that he belonged, and they saw the primary campaign's marathon schedule of debates (actually closer in format to panel discussions) as an opportunity. They believed that his ability to master detail, argue a position, and dominate as he had in some of his oversight committee hearings would help him break out in a field of candidates derisively dubbed "the Seven Dwarfs."

Gore prepared exhaustively but muffed the first question he ever got in a presidential forum, during an edition of William Buckley's *Firing Line* broadcast from Houston on July 1. It was an old chestnut: which presidential portraits would he hang in the Cabinet Room? He named Wilson, FDR, and Kennedy, who were "personal heroes," and said he would add Tennessee's two elected presidents, Andrew Jackson and James K. Knox. James K. Knox? He had hoped to make a cute little point by mentioning James *Polk,* the young Tennessee dark horse who made it to the White House. But a nervous Gore used his middle name instead.

He recovered to get the better of Buckley in a sharp colloquy over the proposed "Star Wars" defensive shield, which Gore opposed. But Robert Shogan of the *Los Angeles Times* called it his "one moment of passion." A focus group of Iowa Democrats watching the debate rated Gore dwarf number six out of the seven.

He searched through the summer and fall of 1987 for ways to differentiate himself from the pack. In late September he and Martin launched the first in a series of reinventions: Al Gore, national security candidate, the only one willing to use force to protect America's vital interests. Gore was not the typical post-Vietnam Democrat, skittish about any discussion of fighting as a means of reaching political objectives. He was a recognized player in the arms control debate and collaborated with the Reagan White House on the MX missile compromise. He had supported the Grenada invasion and the flagging of Kuwaiti tankers in the Persian Gulf and opposed a ban on ballistic missile flight tests favored by many Democrats. With Sam Nunn officially out of the race (as of August 27), there was an opening for a candidate with a more moderate message on defense. And it was all a natural extension of the nuclear security issues he really wanted to talk about. "The politics of retreat, complacency, and doubt may appeal to others, but it will not do for me, or for my country," he announced in a National Press Club speech in early October.

But Gore was maximizing what were essentially marginal differences between himself and the competition. On major defense issues he was solidly in the Democratic mainstream. He had supported the nuclear freeze and sharp limits on Star Wars spending, opposed funds for two new aircraft carriers and, until the campaign, most aid to the Nicaraguan contras. The Council on National Defense, a pro-Reagan political action committee, using a zero to 100 scale (100 meriting a "Golden Eagle") gave Gore a 27 in 1985 and a zero in 1986. Over his ten years in the House and Senate, the American Security Council placed him under 50 percent.

One tactical objective of the national security theme was to signal that Gore wasn't beholden to politically influential peace activists in Iowa. But STARPAC (Stop the Arms Race Political Action Committee), the state's leading peace group, thought Gore checked out just fine, approving of his stance on eight of ten major issues they had asked about in a questionnaire. It was a classic split-the-difference Gore exercise, an attempt to woo southern conservatives without alienating traditional dove constituencies on the left, and it seemed to pay off. Gore rose into double digits in most southern state polls, usually running a close second behind Jesse Jackson. Gore's competitors were alternately irritated and amused by his new positioning. "Maybe the next debate should be between the old Al Gore and the new Al Gore," said Dick Gephardt.

In picking a phony fight with peace activists in Iowa, Gore was coating political reality with a veneer of virtue. He had no prospects there. Gephardt had all but taken up residence, and Dukakis had Gore outstaffed and outspent. Getting into the game would have taken at least another $1 million that was better spent elsewhere, like New Hampshire and the Super Tuesday South. He would bow out of Iowa with a flourish at the Jefferson-Jackson Day dinner in Des Moines on November 8, trashing a nominating process that gave one early state such a loud voice and yet produced liberal nominees incapable of carrying the state in November. But his strategic retreat from the heartland was eclipsed by the two most turbulent days of his campaign.

With Hart's departure, Gore knew that if sex was on the table, then drugs weren't far behind. Earlier in the fall, he had been questioned on the subject by two reporters with papers outside Tennessee. He deflected the queries as he had in 1976, with off-the-record protests that the issue wasn't "relevant," but it was clear that the rules that had given him a pass eleven years before were being rewritten. He decided it was time to get out in front of the story before more journalists started poking around. In mid-October the phone rang at John Warnecke's house in San Mateo, California.

Warnecke had turned his life around since the hard-partying Nashville days. Clean and sober for eight years, he had remarried and had two small children and was working steadily, first for his father's architectural firm and then as a salesman for Metropolitan Life. He and the Gores had remained friends, getting together for dinner when Warnecke came to Washington on business or when Gore flew to the Bay Area to raise money.

Peter Knight was on the line when Warnecke picked up, and he sounded nervous. The press wanted to make an issue of Al's smoking, Knight said. "Tell them it's personal, it's none of their business. Don't talk to them." Warnecke didn't appreciate Knight's attempt to script him. For one thing, the lines seemed tactically dumb. He didn't ask Knight who else was on the call list but suggested that if everybody in Gore's life who might have seen him use marijuana said it was "nobody's business," it was only "an invitation to more investigation." Stonewalling also cut against the grain of his recovery. The twelve-step philosophy that had lifted him out of drugs and alcohol demanded total honesty with himself and others. The conversation ended cordially, but inconclusively. Knight said he didn't recall the conversation. "I'm not saying it didn't happen, but I don't remember it," he said.

A few minutes later Tipper Gore called and put her husband on the line. He was calmer than Knight but delivered the same message. "He told me to tell reporters that this was a personal matter. I told him you couldn't raise a bigger red flag." This ten-minute talk also ended on a friendly note but again without resolution. Within an hour Gore was on the phone again, his tone more emphatic, intent on securing Warnecke's cooperation. "The press has no business prying into my personal life," he said. Warnecke made one last attempt to dissuade him, arguing that a forthcoming answer would shut the story down more quickly. "You can't treat reporters that way," he said, but his old newsroom colleague wouldn't budge. Warnecke was stunned and angered that a friend would put such pressure on him. But he also didn't want to do anything to hurt him. He decided that if reporters called, he would go along with the stonewall Gore wanted.

The journalistic reefer madness that Gore feared became a reality on Thursday, November 5, when Supreme Court nominee Douglas Ginsburg acknowledged that he had smoked marijuana once as a college student and on "a few occasions" as a Harvard Law School professor in the 1970s. He withdrew his name from consideration the next day, but the admission handed campaign reporters a natural peg on which to hang drug queries. Between campaign stops in Alabama, Gore was on the phone with Martin, who wanted him to cancel his weekend appearances and come back to Washington to discuss possible responses. But Gore was adamant about keeping the schedule. He ordered Martin and other senior staff to meet him in Miami, where he was due late that evening for a speech the next morning to the state Democratic convention.

When he walked into the Fontainebleau Hilton lobby, a gaggle of reporters surrounded him to ask whether he had ever smoked. He said he would talk to them later. As the Gore high command — which included Martin, scheduler Dick Deerin, press secretary Arlie Schardt, and Albert Gore, who was in the state whipping up the senior citizen vote — gathered in their sixteenth-floor suite, the issue was no longer whether the candidate should acknowledge smoking dope, only the substance and mechanics of the admission. They scheduled two press conferences, one early the next morning in Miami and the other later in the day in Des Moines, where he was set to speak at the Jefferson-Jackson Day dinner. The plan was to tell the truth, or at least Gore's version of it. He had smoked occasionally as a student, soldier, and reporter, he hadn't touched an illegal substance since entering public office, and he and his wife were among the tens of millions of young men and women in their generation who had done the same.

As they talked deep into the night about the next day's official line, Albert Gore grew angrier. The man whom Nancy Gore had called "the Baptist" considered marijuana "pretty high up on the list of bad things to do," Deerin said. "He thought the statement should be more apologetic than explanatory." Gore, always respectful of his father, especially in front of others, finally lost his patience. "This is the truth, Dad! I've got to deal with this," he said. "You're not being helpful." The discussion grew heated enough that Deerin eased the old senator out of the room and downstairs for a cup of tea.

At 8:45 A.M. on Saturday, on three hours' sleep, Al Gore stepped in front of a roomful of reporters and described his marijuana consumption as "infrequent and rare." He said that he first tried it as a Harvard junior, and that "at the beginning of my senior year, I tried it a few more times. Then I got absorbed in my studies and after that point it was extremely rare, extremely rare." He filled his account with lawyerly stipulations worthy of Bill Clinton: never bought it, never smoked it while on duty in the army, never tried anything stronger, never supported decriminalization. Unlike Clinton, Gore inhaled, but he was determined to leave the impression that he never enjoyed it. "When I was twenty-four, I decided it was wrong for me," he said. "When I became a man, I put away childish things." Gore still challenged the relevance of the issue but said he wanted to "unburden myself rather than wrestle with it in private because I want to be honest about it."

Gore reprised the message in Des Moines that evening, eclipsing his speech assailing Iowa's role in the nomination process. In the next day's papers, Gore supporters argued that he deserved big points for his candor. "Al Gore is the first real political leader of his generation — these baby boomers — to come clean on the 60s. It's an indication of his honesty," Bob Squier proclaimed.

The *Tennessean,* one of Gore's employers when he was lighting up, was obliged to check out the veracity of his "infrequent and rare" explanation. When reporter Jim O'Hara called that weekend, Warnecke didn't stay with Gore's preferred script about the sanctity of his personal life. Instead, he told what he thought was a more nuanced, authentic-sounding lie. There was no mention of the long hashish-filled evenings, or the road trip to Memphis, or Gore's paranoia about getting caught. "I can remember only one specific time, and I think it was right after he got back from Vietnam in 1971," Warnecke said in a front-page piece that ran November 10. "Once he was into life back in the States, I just never saw him involved in anything like that. The many times I was around Al this was not a big thing." O'Hara didn't push him very hard, Warnecke remembers.

He was the only person in the article, based on more than forty interviews, who acknowledged seeing Gore smoke. Many of those quoted in the piece were older colleagues or figures unlikely to have partied with Gore, including Vanderbilt Divinity professor Jack Forstman and *Tennessean* managing editor Wayne Whitt. Those in his immediate social circle either had nothing to say or were missing entirely. Warnecke's ex-wife Nancy, who still worked at the paper, said: "Al has spoken for himself, and I have no comment." Three others, unnamed former staff members, declined to respond to questions, citing, per Gore's talking points, his right to privacy.

The story quickly receded, pushed off the media's radar by Gore's carefully trimmed version of the truth and a clean bill from the *Tennessean.* Yet Gore considered Warnecke's revision of the past, reducing his drug use to a single innocent-sounding episode, a betrayal, and it effectively ended the friendship. Although Warnecke remained in touch with Tipper — his stepson interned in her office a few summers ago — he hasn't spoken to Gore since 1987. The subsequent years have been difficult: his second wife, Linda, who also struggled with drug addiction, committed suicide in 1991. Warnecke, who has battled with depression most of his life, was treated for a severe episode following her death and remains on disability from his job at Metropolitan Life. He said that his decision to correct the deception he left in the record grew out of the psychotherapy he's received over the last couple of years. "At first it didn't bother me," he said. "But as the years have gone by, I felt very bad that I lied to my own paper, lied to a fellow reporter. At the time I looked at it as spin." The issue is not smoking dope, he said, but the measure of a man who would browbeat a friend into covering up. "It's not something that you ask your friends to do."

Opting out of Iowa raised the stakes for Gore, in New Hampshire and especially in the Super Tuesday South. North Carolina seemed like an especially good prospect, adjacent to Tennessee and full of tobacco farmers, whose language Gore spoke. But he trailed Jesse Jackson there in the fall of 1987 and needed money and friends to help him claim the state's eighty-two delegates. He found them in an alliance with a notorious industrial polluter.

For three generations, Champion International had operated a paper mill along the banks of the Pigeon River in western North Carolina. Thousands of tons of wood chips rolled in by box car each day to be cooked to pulp, bleached, and transformed into juice cartons and fast-food soda cups. The process, which requires millions of gallons of water, turned the Pigeon from a crystalline mountain stream into a warm, coffee-colored soup by the time it left Champion's plant in downtown Canton, North Carolina. On some days the river smelled "like rotten eggs crushed in a waterlogged sneaker," as the *Winston-Salem Journal* put it.

Although Champion was Canton's meal ticket, its pollution stunted the growth of downstream communities in eastern Tennessee; the town of Hartford, for instance, was once nicknamed "Widowville" by grieving residents for what they saw as suspiciously elevated rates of cancer among those living near the river. (State epidemiologists said the rates were not abnormal.) More than an economic deadweight, the river is a cultural and psychological barrier. "It's set the tone we have here. It's just defined us as a trashy community," said Philip Owens, a garrulous, chain-smoking attorney and juvenile court judge whose office looks out over the Pigeon as it courses through downtown Newport. "How much pride can you have when you have an open sewer running through town?"

In Gore, Cocke County residents thought they had a powerful advocate for a cleanup of the Pigeon. When he reached the Senate, he quickly emerged as an outspoken critic of Champion and lax North Carolina regulators. "This issue is of the utmost importance to me," he wrote to EPA regional administrator Jack Ravan on July 9, 1985, in one of a series of increasingly indignant letters demanding that the agency intervene. "Instead of seeking to protect the Pigeon River, the State [of North Carolina] has unashamedly persisted in dragging its feet and has obstructed the effort to clean the river up. It is now the EPA's duty to act — and to act swiftly," he said in a letter several months later dated November 8.

His pressure began to make a difference. The EPA moved to strip North Carolina of its authority to regulate the mill in late 1985. On December 1, 1986, U.S. District Judge David Sentelle rejected a legal challenge to the EPA's enforcement powers from Champion and North Carolina officials. On a visit to Cocke County that month, Gore called the ruling a great victory. "I look forward to the day when the Pigeon River will flow clear, pure, and clean," he said.

The EPA announced in early 1987 that if Champion wanted to renew its permit to dump waste in the Pigeon, it had to observe a new, more rigorous water quality standard. A half-mile from the plant's discharge pipe, the river had to be running at fifty color units (CUs), or about the shade of ginger ale. Not great, but potentially a dramatic improvement. Gore once again led the parade for the EPA, applauding fifty CUs as "positive and responsible." He also warned federal regulators to get ready for a fight. "Knowledge of the history of this case makes me concerned that there very well may be resistance to the requirements of this permit, particularly the color unit limitations, from Champion. I strongly urge EPA to steadfastly adhere to the standards which have been established. . . . The public interest demands no less," he wrote to Ravan on February 9. A month later, on March 11, he told Ravan: "It is only by including the 50 color unit limit in the permit that the Pigeon River can ever adequately be protected from continued pollution by Champion." Gore was right about Champion's reaction to the crackdown. Two weeks after the EPA's announcement, the company said that approval of the new permit would force it to close the mill, throwing twenty-six hundred people in the Canton area out of work.

Champion was also working behind the scenes to soften up Gore. In a memo of March 19, 1987, Champion's attorney Ben Bilus outlined an elaborate lobbying strategy to change Gore's position. Part of it involved North Carolina Senator Terry Sanford, a major supporter of the company, having a candid talk with his colleague from Tennessee. Paraphrasing the views of another Champion official, Bilus wrote: "The bottom line for Gore is that he wants to be president and that, when he runs, he'll need a solid Democratic south and he'll need the help of the Democratic senator from North Carolina, Senator Sanford."

Sanford, in an interview with *Newsweek*'s Michael Isikoff before his death in 1998, confirmed that Champion officials had asked him to intervene with Gore, but he didn't recall any details of the conversations. However, he said he could "absolutely guarantee" that presidential politics did not enter the discussion. "We were dealing on the merits."

As North Carolina loomed larger in Gore's presidential plans, "the merits" shifted from the needs of his east Tennessee constituents to primary voters on the other side of the state line. He found a valuable partner in Representative James Clarke of Asheville, an influential North Carolina Democrat whose Eleventh Congressional District included the mill. Gore was scheduled to speak at a November 14 fundraiser for Clarke when, on Saturday, October 31, the *Asheville Times* carried a story describing yet another Gore letter to the EPA attacking Champion. Clarke's staff faxed a copy of the article to Sanford's office, and Clarke, for his part, told reporters it would be "very difficult" to have Gore speak at the fund-raiser if he wasn't considering "the economic welfare of our people." Gore faxed a letter to Clarke the same day, expressing "regret" for the "misunderstanding" and said he was committed to a "common sense" solution. "I believe we can clean up the river without losing a single job," Gore wrote.

Four days before the Clarke fund-raiser, Gore wrote once again to the EPA — this time not as an advocate for east Tennessee but as an emissary for Champion. Where he had once urged the agency to "steadfastly adhere" to fifty CUs as the only standard that would ensure a clean Pigeon, Gore was now conveying a new offer from the company, presented to him by Jamie Clarke: a less stringent CU level of eighty to eighty-five. Gore endorsed it as "the starting point for new negotiations" with the company. Gone was the slashing rhetoric about intolerable foot-dragging by the mill and North Carolina regulators and demands that the EPA stand its ground. "I remain committed to working with all parties to produce a solution which effectively balances the economic needs of the region with the goal of a clean Pigeon River," Gore wrote.

Gore's softer line on Champion unlocked critical support in North Carolina. He was hailed as a local hero, "a new ally," said an *Asheville Times* editorial. Clarke, who subsequently arranged at least two meetings between Gore and a Champion vice president, said: "We've educated Senator Gore on the problem and told him we expect him to help us. It's my experience in life, particularly in politics, that you scratch my back, I scratch yours." Sanford and former Governor Jim Hunt, the state's most prominent Democrats, endorsed Gore and on January 17 sponsored a fund-raiser in Winston-Salem that generated $110,000. The funds helped ensure that Gore carried North Carolina on Super Tuesday. Canton attorney Pat Smathers, Gore's campaign chairman in the Eleventh Congressional District, told reporters on primary night that Gore's attitude adjustment was "why he ran so well" in the western end of the state.

Cocke County residents never forgot Gore's duplicity in 1988. He spoke all over the country in bold terms about the need for environmental renewal. "The environment is under siege from industrial civilization," he said at a November candidates' forum on Boston television just days after his reversal on Champion. At a debate in south Texas, he pronounced himself "passionate" about cleaning up the Rio Grande. "You could put 'two-faced son of a bitch' in Webster's Dictionary and put Al Gore's name beside it," said Phil Owens.

The regulatory wrangling dragged on for years, and the Pigeon has gotten only marginally cleaner. In 1996, after North Carolina renewed the mill's pollution permit without requiring any further improvement in the Pigeon's water quality, a citizens' group called the Dead Pigeon River Council contemplated a special gift for Gore — a billboard denouncing him as a sellout. The protest, which came on the heels of a presidential reelection campaign in which the Clinton-Gore ticket barely carried Tennessee, got the vice president's attention. He asked EPA administrator Carol Browner, his former legislative director, to consider toughening the permit. Champion put the mill up for sale in October 1997, and in the spring of 1999 it was bought by the local paperworkers' union. Perhaps under a new owner the Pigeon will run, as Gore once predicted, "clear, pure, and clean."

*   *   *

Gore knew that winning in New Hampshire, Dukakis's backyard, was not possible. But he had hoped to pull off a February surprise with a better-than-expected second- or third-place finish. He came in fifth. The poor showing, combined with a predestined seventh in Iowa the week before, sent the campaign into a competitive and spiritual funk. Super Tuesday, on March 8, was when he intended to win most of his early delegates. But getting there had turned into a long and difficult underwater swim. He was out of sight, running out of air, and nowhere near breaking the surface.

The early losses put even more pressure on a campaign riven with internal tensions and rivalries. The Gore organization was no ordinary campaign — it was a political family gone to war, and major decisions were made collectively, and privately, by the Gore clan. The influence of the family — Albert, Pauline, Tipper, and Frank Hunger — was often like a distant astronomical phenomenon: impossible to see but clearly exerting great force. One former consultant said that questions put to Gore by the staff often fell "into the black hole of 'I'll think about it.'" Later, he said, "he comes back with a decision and it's hard to know who did it."

Aides learned to tread carefully around Albert and Pauline — "Senator Sir and Senator Ma'am," as one campaign veteran called them. They railed about the quality of the field operation, and their complaints resulted in firings and shufflings of midlevel operatives, according to one former senior staffer. Aides found the old senator's advice dated, impractical, or simply irrelevant. He returned from senior citizens' events in Iowa and Florida urging that the campaign pour money and staff into those states, where Gore had no prospects. One former staffer recalled that the senior Gore "would take me out to lunch and tell me, 'This is how you win a state.'" She'd listen, politely, she said, because there was little choice. Pauline's counsel was often considered hard-headed and pragmatic, especially the way she encouraged her son to loosen up in debates. Although she did not attend strategy sessions as often as Albert, when she spoke the room grew noticeably quieter. "There was a pause in the action while people thought about what she said," said Arlie Schardt, "and there was something even a little intimidating about how she spoke."

Tipper Gore waged her own rearguard action against the staff, holding Sunday evening rump sessions back home in Arlington with family friends to discuss ways of jump-starting Gore in the polls. According to Schardt, Tipper urged that Martin be fired and even tried to line up a replacement. But her principal concern was keeping the family together through the long slog of the primary season. She campaigned for brief stretches — rarely more than three days at a time — before returning home for a week or ten days, caring for the children and wedging in radio interviews by phone to promote her book. She complained bitterly to scheduler Dick Deerin about Gore's grueling itinerary, and tried to keep the kids in at least cursory touch with their father by putting each of them on the plane with him for short trips. But the attempt to make the campaign family-friendly was short-lived. One aide still shakes his head at the memory of nine-year-old Sarah, who seemed lost in the hurly-burly of a swing through the Midwest. "She was just shunted aside," he said.

Most presidential primary campaigns are barely controlled disasters, improvising on the fly from state to state, but Gore's seemed especially unprepared and sometimes snake-bit. Young, inexperienced staff bobbled basic logistics. Charter flights turned into hair-raising odysseys with flames shooting out of engines. On one December trip over Texas, the cabin was hushed with tension as pilots fought to keep the aircraft from going into a roll when the electrical system controlling the trim tabs failed. While most passengers were deliriously grateful to be on the ground in one piece after an emergency landing in Waco, Gore's first reaction was: "Get another plane so we can get to Lubbock."

As Gore staggered out of New Hampshire in February 1988, three other especially ominous problems loomed. The first was money: for all the drum roll and hype, only about half of the seventeen IMPAC members who committed to him actually raised the cash they had promised. Nate Landow had single-handedly managed not only to leave Gore short of funds but to create the lingering image that he had been bought by a small group of rich guys trying to elect the next president. Hollywood, an important resource for Democrats, locked Gore out of its box office in opposition to Tipper's rock lyric crusade. He had to borrow $1 million to cover his Super Tuesday expenses, one-third of it from Tennessee banks with close business and political ties to his family.

His second problem was message. After a brief bump in the polls, it became clear that Gore's national security and environmental themes were not catching on. In early 1988 two newcomers to Gore's circle, a young Rhodes scholar from Idaho, Bruce Reed, and a refugee from the Hart campaign, Washington attorney-lobbyist Jack Quinn, coauthored a fifteen-page memo encouraging him to recast the campaign with more traditional Democratic themes. "The people are ready for a dose of responsible indignation on the question of economic fairness," they wrote. Instead of sticking to the ideas that inspired him to run, Gore followed the lead of staff who had their eyes on the polls. Enter Al Gore, class warrior, ready "to put the White House back on the side of working families," as the new mantra went. It became the basis for a batch of soak-the-rich television spots that were dramatically different in spirit from the pro-business themes Gore has embraced since becoming vice president. "The bigger the corporations get in this country, the more lopsided our economy becomes," said Gore, his voice accompanying a graphic of Chrysler Chairman Lee Iacocca and a reference to the $20 million he made in 1986, juxtaposed with images of laid-off autoworkers. "Let's make them put people over profits."

His third problem was Dick Gephardt. Gore had hoped to go into Super Tuesday with Dukakis and Paul Simon — two Yankee liberals — as his principal competition. But Gephardt, the winner in Iowa, finished a solid second behind Dukakis in New Hampshire. It meant that Gore had to go south contending with a border state (Missouri) candidate who could also appeal to moderate whites. A strong showing by Gephardt would demolish the operating premise of Gore's campaign — that his strength in the South made him the strongest candidate for the party in November. On primary night in New Hampshire, Gore spoke by phone to Martin and his father. On this point they all agreed: Gephardt had to be taken out of the race.

The air war against Gephardt was the culmination of years of competitive tension between two men groomed from day one to succeed. Gephardt wasn't born to power and privilege — he was the son of a St. Louis milkman — but like Gore, he was also "a mother's idea of a perfect kid," as Richard Ben Cramer wrote in *What It Takes*: an Eagle Scout, a mainstay at Christian leadership camp, and a high school nerd. They came to the House together in 1977, and each climbed the ladder in his own way — Gore with arms control, the environment, and oversight hearings, Gephardt by a more conventional ascent into the House Democratic leadership. The two kept their distance personally as well as professionally, both aware that they would eventually square off in a presidential primary. Each viewed the other as a panderer and a phony, and each was in some measure right. As a candidate, each had done reconstructive surgery on his record — Gore by channeling Scoop Jackson and Sam Nunn to become a national security hawk, and Gephardt by campaigning as a populist against the excesses of Reaganism after voting for his 1981 tax cut. Gore liked to tell friends the story of sitting next to Jesse Jackson at a candidate forum, listening to Gephardt talk for the umpteenth time about the importance of hard choices, and how they were like the castor oil his mother gave him as a child. "Your mother give you castor oil, Jesse?" Gore asked one day. "No," said Jackson, "but I wasn't full of shit all the time."

Their colloquies in debates grew increasingly barbed. Gephardt sneeringly described Gore as a "backbencher." Gore asked, "How can you ask to lead the Democratic charge when you agreed with the centerpiece of the Reagan mistake?" Gephardt's campaign manager, Bill Carrick, launched a barely coherent tirade when asked about the prospect of taking on Gore in the South. "I can't wait. It's blood lust. Let me at him. I hate all of them. I think they are the phoniest two-bit bastards that ever came down the pike, starting with Al Gore, moving through boy-wonder ex-wordsmith, the mosquito who roared [Fred Martin, Gore's manager]. They are just a [expletive] bunch of meddlesome bastards." At a League of Women Voters debate in New Hampshire on February 13, Gephardt offered a halfhearted apology on Carrick's behalf. "I'm sure Bill Carrick is apologetic to you and will say that to you."

"Are you?" Gore shot back.

"Of course, Al, of course," said Gephardt, his face deep frozen in a contemptuous smile. "You're my friend." The audience broke up.

Gore pounced on him in Dallas five days later with a riff that became a sixty-second spot.

> Standing up to pressure is something the next president is going to have to do. And I'm gonna lay it on the line here, Dick. Now look, you voted against the minimum wage. . . . Now you say you're for it. You voted against the Department of Education, now you say you're for it.

You voted for tuition tax credits, now you say you're against it. You voted for Reaganomics, now you say, well, where are you this week on Reaganomics? I'm not sure.

Gore even had the crust to go after Gephardt on abortion, though his own record zigged and zagged. "You gotta be willing to stand your ground and be consistent," Gore said, as wild applause broke out. Other Gore spots that aired throughout the South used a newspaper op-ed headline that called Gephardt a "populist hypocrite." "Dick Gephardt. As a candidate he'll say or do anything to get elected. What about as president?" said the ominous-sounding narrator.

Gore's search-and-destroy mission didn't single-handedly sink Gephardt. He had his own money troubles and was also taking a pounding on television from Dukakis. He managed only one victory on Super Tuesday, at home in Missouri, and hung on for another month before calling it quits after a third-place finish in the Michigan caucuses. For Gore the big regional primary was more fruitful, but not the bonanza he had counted on. Fred Martin believed that for Gore to stake his claim as champion of the new South, he needed to win at least eight or nine states. He won seven in the border South and West (North Carolina, Tennessee, Kentucky, Arkansas, Oklahoma, Nevada, and Wyoming on March 5). As *Newsweek*'s Peter Goldman wrote, the Super Tuesday numbers reflected two new Souths — Gore's and Jesse Jackson's. Gore had conceded the black vote to Jackson but discovered too late that there simply weren't enough white votes left to go around.

Jackson tore a swath through the old Confederacy, taking Virginia, Georgia, Alabama, Mississippi, and Louisiana. His historic victories that night were one of two stories that shrunk Gore's solid performance to a footnote. George Bush had blown out Bob Dole, effectively ending the race for the Republican nomination; the rest of the press's attention was fixed on Dukakis's victories in Texas and Florida. But the Gore clan, gathered at the Opryland Hotel in Nashville, was euphoric, convinced that their southern strategy had paid off. As the campaign headed north, new money and press attention would surely come flowing in their direction. "Arlie! Arlie!" a red-faced Albert Gore hollered to press secretary Arlie Schardt at a celebration in the hotel ballroom. "That boy is going to be president!"

The family got a snapshot of reality later when they gathered upstairs for a special edition of *Nightline*. Twenty-five minutes went by before Peter Jennings happened to mention to Ted Koppel that Gore's finish constituted "a minor surprise." About 1:00 A.M., the Gores met with Martin and other aides to discuss a plan, but the campaign was essentially over: they had bet everything on a Super Tuesday tide lifting their boat. Yet the adrenaline rush from victories in six states left the candidate and his family with an illusory sense of triumph and a bloated idea of their real prospects. "It was insane," said one senior aide, who watched Gore become consumed by denial.

Martin wanted to play for time and survival, staying out of the big, expensive battleground states like Illinois and competing in smaller places, perhaps Wisconsin and Indiana. Later, after they regrouped, they could take Dukakis on head to head in California. It was an equally wishful scenario, but one that wouldn't drive them as deeply into debt. Martin also had a deal with Paul Simon's camp, one on which Gore had signed off. In exchange for Simon staying out of big Super Tuesday races like North Carolina, Gore would not seriously contest Illinois. But spurred on by his parents and swept up in the headiness of the moment, Gore reversed himself. Serious presidential candidates competed in Illinois, he said, they didn't tiptoe around it. It was a decision that had the fingerprints of Senator Sir and Senator Ma'am all over it. Martin was overruled.

But Gore was no longer a serious candidate, and he disappeared in Illinois, drawing 5 percent of the vote on March 15. Through March and into April the campaign became "a rolling Alamo," as one Dukakis staffer put it, going everywhere and winning nowhere — from Kansas to Puerto Rico to Michigan to Connecticut to Wisconsin. Running on pure fumes and hubris, Gore decided to make his last stand in New York on April 19.

He found himself in an unfamiliar and disorienting position in the spring of 1988 — with his back to the wall. After a decade of mostly powderpuff competition in Tennessee races, Gore had been bloodied and embarrassed as a presidential candidate. For some politicians — Bill Clinton stands as the most remarkable example — desperation unlocks fresh reserves of energy and resolve. Gore merely looked mean-spirited and panicky as he flailed away, buried in single digits far behind Dukakis and Jackson. He pandered to New York City's big Jewish vote, denouncing Jackson (memories of his 1984 "Hymietown"

Gore's parents called him "Little Al," and he was eager to show them that he could pull more than his own weight, even at age four.

KNOXVILLE NEWS-SENTINEL

Pauline Gore was widely considered the family's most astute politician. Some staff members referred to the couple as "Senator Sir and Senator Ma'am."

Wedding day, May 1970. Seven months later, during their first Christmas together, Gore shipped out to South Vietnam. The separation hit his young bride hard.

Gore never forgot election night 1970. His father's defeat left him careful to avoid being labeled a liberal when he began his own political career.

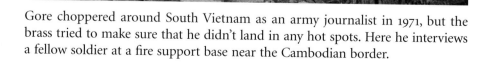

Gore choppered around South Vietnam as an army journalist in 1971, but the brass tried to make sure that he didn't land in any hot spots. Here he interviews a fellow soldier at a fire support base near the Cambodian border.

With Tipper and three-year-old Karenna on primary night 1976. The only close race Gore ever ran in Tennessee was his first, in which he narrowly won the Democratic nomination for the congressional seat his father once held.

Despite Gore's bloodlines, the Senate was never a comfortable place for him. Here he waits outside the chamber for a session to begin in 1985.

BILLY EASLEY/NASHVILLE TENNESSEAN

Gore uncovered a city hall bribery scandal as a Nashville reporter, but he got caught exaggerating the results when he ran for president in 1987.

IRA WYMAN/SYGMA

Shown here with Michael Dukakis, the eventual winner of the 1988 race, Gore counted on debates to distinguish him from the competition, which also included Paul Simon, Jesse Jackson, and Bruce Babbitt.

Gore's environmentalism intensified after his 1988 defeat. Early in 1989, he traveled to Antarctica to investigate global warming and damage to the ozone layer.

Clinton and Gore were packaged as political buddies, but the hype papered over real tensions between their camps during the 1992 campaign.

Gore's failure to aggressively rebut Vice President Dan Quayle's attacks on Bill Clinton's character during a 1992 debate caused a brief rift with the first-couple-to-be.

Gore relished his role as computer-geek-in-chief. In February 1996 he helped celebrate the fiftieth anniversary of ENIAC, the world's first computer.

San Gabriel Valley Tribune/Sygma

The vice president insists that he didn't know his visit to the Hsi Lai Buddhist Temple in California resulted in thousands of dollars in illegal contributions, but the event epitomized the "money talks" ethos of the 1996 campaign.

Associated Press/Ruth Fremson

Gore gets points for enthusiasm, if not for form, during his dance with the country singer Billy Ray Cyrus at the 1997 Southern Inauguration Ball.

Gore sounded like a criminal defendant in March 1997 when he argued that there was "no controlling legal authority" to prevent him from placing fund-raising calls from his West Wing office. That same month he caught more flak for toasting a business deal with Chinese prime minister Li Peng, known as "the butcher of Tiananmen."

The shirt was loud enough, but it didn't keep this group of Honolulu school-children from thinking about taking a nap as Gore discussed educational issues in August 1998.

Call it the vice presidential stare: Gore perfected it during his count-less appearances at Clinton's side, like this one at the White House in October 1998.

Clinton appreciated Gore's loyalty, including his often spirited introductions, but he was also amazed by Gore's lack of political instinct.

slur were still fresh) for his embrace of Yasser Arafat and assailing front-runner Dukakis as "absurdly timid" for not confronting him. "I categorically deny [Jackson's] notion that there's a moral equivalency between Israel and the PLO," he said. "In a Gore administration, no one will have reason to doubt America's commitment to the survival and security of Israel." He supported Israeli Prime Minister Yitzhak Shamir in his rejection of the newest White House proposal, a land-for-peace plan endorsed by some of the Senate's most stalwart supporters of Israel, including New York Senator Daniel Patrick Moynihan. And after a long campaign season of peaceful coexistence, he went after Jackson personally, telling the Association for a Better New York: "We're not choosing a preacher. We're choosing a president. The Oval Office is a whole lot more than a pulpit."

Five days before the primary, Gore's plane was ready to leave Washington for New York when he took a call on his cell phone and a big smile lit his face. It was New York City Mayor Ed Koch, calling to say that he planned to endorse him. "Ed, that's wonderful. That's a very courageous thing to do," said a delighted Gore. Within forty-eight hours Gore would wish that Koch had lost his number. With the possible exception of his 1996 fund-raising luncheon at the Hsi Lai Temple in Los Angeles, "The Koch Show," as he ruefully described it later, was the single most debilitating political encounter of his career. Gore had hoped that Koch's endorsement would give his campaign a desperately needed New York imprimatur. Instead, he found himself hitched to a polarizing figure, a mayor considered hostile to blacks in a deeply divided city where the mix of race, crime, and politics was always explosive. Four months earlier, three white teenagers had been convicted of manslaughter in an attack on a twenty-three-year-old black man in the Howard Beach section of Queens. The victim, Michael Griffith, was killed by a car as he fled a gang of whites. In June 1987 a jury acquitted "subway vigilante" Bernhard Goetz of the attempted murder of four black youths.

Gore had eagerly courted Koch despite his shrill and ugly attacks on Jackson (Jews would be "crazy" to vote for him given his pro-PLO stance, or a Jackson presidency would put the country "in bankruptcy in about three weeks"). By the time Gore realized the backlash that was forming against Koch's demagoguery, it was too late. He was stuck with him, like a piece of chewing gum on the sole of his shoe. "We couldn't get rid of the guy. Everywhere we went he would go on this tirade about Jackson," said Arlie Schardt. "It made us look like the campaign was racist." Gore began to look less like a president than a well-dressed Jethro Clampett, led around by the nose from borough to borough as Koch pursued his vendetta against Jackson.

When Gore managed to shed himself of Koch for a few hours, he seemed flummoxed by the city. One morning he planted himself at the top of an escalator at the Madison Square Garden subway station for a little rush-hour hand-shaking, a New York campaign tradition. But bad advance work put him in the wrong spot, and the few people who did want to stop and say hello ended up blocking others who wanted to get to work. "Move away! Move away!" snarled one woman. "You just lost anyone who was going to vote for you."

He took one last shot at undermining Dukakis — by painting him as a liberal soft on crime. Gore's case in point was a Massachusetts state prison program that granted furloughs to convicted murderers with life sentences. In 1987, an inmate on leave named Willie Horton bound and slashed a Maryland man and raped his wife. Although the Bush campaign, which used the furlough issue extensively against Dukakis in the general election, disingenuously credited Gore with unearthing it, this was no great feat of enterprising opposition research. The program's problems had already received extensive press attention. A Massachusetts newspaper, the *Lawrence Eagle Tribune,* had won a Pulitzer Prize for a series exposing its lapses. *Newsweek* and *Business Week* had both done pieces in early 1988. Dukakis antagonists in Boston sent out material that found its way to Gore's Crystal City, Virginia, headquarters, where deputy campaign manager Thurgood Marshall Jr., son of the legendary civil rights lawyer and Supreme Court justice, oversaw the research operation. That spring Marshall and his assistants briefed Jack Quinn, who was in charge of debate strategy and preparation, on the story. Quinn, as one campaign aide remembers it, was "pretty fired up." The Horton story was placed on the campaign's internal "New York Issues Schedule" as part of a plan to illustrate Gore's commitment to middle-class concerns. "With *Time* charging that 'Gore lurches from issue to issue,' we feel surer than ever that you have to show concretely and coherently what you mean by putting the White House back on the side of working families," aide Bart Gellman wrote to Gore on April 4. "A continuing flurry of tactical hits is essential to staying in the story line." At a debate scheduled for April 12, Gellman added, "you can pick a fight on drugs and crime with Dukakis [furlough]."

Gore surely knew that substantively it was a bogus issue. The federal penal system seldom handled murderers, and the program was actually started under Dukakis's Republican predecessor. But Dukakis was selling himself to voters as a skilled manager, and Willie Horton was clearly a management problem. "You've been the principal advocate and defender of a program in Massachusetts that has just been canceled over your objections by the legislature that provided for weekend passes for convicted criminals, including those convicted of first-degree murder who are serving life sentences without parole," Gore said. "Two of them committed other murders while they were on their passes. If you were elected president, would you advocate a similar program for federal penitentiaries?"

Gore never mentioned Horton by name, nor the fact that he was black, but he didn't have to. In a city where white fears about violent crime often had a black face, Gore's question sent an unmistakable message to white voters: Dukakis was not just soft on crime, he was soft on *blacks* who committed crimes. It made little difference — voters had stopped listening to Gore weeks before. In New York the conventional wisdom had already metastasized: a vote for Gore only strengthened Jackson and bruised the presumptive nominee Dukakis.

The early numbers on primary night only made the end official — staffers in Crystal City had been packing boxes for days. Gore was on his way to an anemic third place, with 10 percent of the vote, when he called around to some of the elders in his inner circle. Tennessee Governor Ned McWherter said that he was proud of Gore, but that when "reality raises its head," it's best to congratulate the winner and "go get a shoeshine." Around midnight, after he conceded, Gore went to Jackson's hotel suite to apologize for Koch. Then he partied with his staff, shouting himself hoarse with his Ed Koch imitation, braying, "Hi, everybody!" as Koch did when he campaigned on New York's streets.

The whole Gore clan was there with him in the 1812 Room of the Russell Senate Office Building when he officially folded his candidacy two days later, on April 21. He had turned forty three weeks earlier, and this was not the way he wanted to begin middle age. He glanced over at his father before he began. "I was doing great until I turned forty," he said, his voice still weak and scratchy from primary night in New York.

The 1988 Gore presidential campaign broke up later that night with a party at the Fifth Column in Georgetown, where the now ex-candidate took his tie off, rolled the sleeves of his blue Oxford shirt to the elbows, and danced, as Secret Service agents looked longingly at their watches. Later, as he sat at the bar and drank a beer, Tipper came over and put her arms around him and rested her head on his shoulder — affection, exhaustion, and relief all bundled into one gesture. They held each other quietly for a few minutes and then went back to the dance floor, before leaving a little after 1:00 A.M.

Considering the fatal flaws of strategy, message, funding, and personnel, his bottom line was substantial: seven states, four hundred delegates, three and a half million votes. But Gore knew better. He hadn't just lost, he had embarrassed himself and his family. "Horrible," he said, when the husband of an old Tennessee friend asked about the experience.

But would he do it again, the friend's spouse asked. Gore didn't hesitate. "Oh, yeah," he said.

◆ 14 ◆

Into the Ashes

AL GORE returned to the Senate chastened and subdued in the spring of 1988. He was more than $2 million in debt and facing a senatorial reelection race in two years. His demagogic endgame in New York had tarnished his stature in the Democratic Party. African American leaders in Tennessee were especially angry about his Jesse-bashing collaboration with Ed Koch. But even friends like Tom Downey thought a little comeuppance might not necessarily have been a bad thing for a man who approached life as if he were always the smartest person in the room. "Getting your ass handed to you helps you realize you're not perfect," he said.

Gore did his share of moping in the first few months after his withdrawal, displaying little of the old zeal for spotting an issue and hopping on. The press's new character consciousness had left him even more cautious than usual about his personal conduct. One Friday night that spring, with school out and Tipper and the kids in Tennessee, Eve Zibart invited him to her home in Washington Grove, Maryland, where she lived with her husband. Bring your swimming trunks, she said, for a dip in the small lake nearby. But Gore arrived the next day without them. He explained that even though he had known Zibart for more than a decade, he could no longer swim in the company of another woman without his wife. "He said it was too risky, too tricky to explain," said Zibart.

Gore began his postcampaign reentry with an elaborate round of critiques, inviting staff, friends, and contributors to talk frankly with him about what had happened in 1988. "He said, 'Let's go around the room and everybody tell me the things I did wrong,'" said Reed Hundt, who helped put the sessions together. Gore got an earful.

Much of what he would hear again when his 2000 campaign began sluggishly: that he was wooden and remote with voters and needed to relax and let them see his more informal side; that his obsessive micromanagement made it impossible for subordinates to do their jobs. "It was painful to listen to," Hundt said. Gore disputed little of what was said, although it brought no immediate change in his behavior.

While friends were calling attention to matters of heart and soul, Gore retreated to what was most comfortable — his head. He felt that as a candidate there were too many gaps in his knowledge of important issues, and he asked aides to set up what amounted to Gore University, a series of late-afternoon office tutorials with top scholars and experts in areas like technology, economics, and Asian affairs. These were no casual drop-bys: a syllabus of advance reading was prepared for each one- to two-hour session. They were the kind of deep-think-athons that Gore, who considered himself as much a teacher and researcher as a legislator, relished.

But it was the $2 million-plus campaign debt that Gore regarded as the most serious issue facing him, one that posed a direct threat to his future. It would only become harder to pay off the longer it stayed on the books and stood as a glaring reminder of his failure in 1988. Peter Knight drew up a plan for retiring it within ten months, but Gore wanted it done in ten weeks — in time for the Democratic convention in Atlanta. A show of financial muscle after losing the nomination would send the right message — that his future in the party remained bright. He and Knight launched the "40–40" program — mobilizing forty fund-raisers committed to raising $40,000 each. Some of the 40–40 benefactors were IMPAC veterans; others were new contributors who thought Gore was bound to run again and were interested in the political equivalent of buying a good stock when the share price was low.

Whatever qualms Gore had earlier in his career about hustling money disappeared as he pursued 40–40. From April to July he worked the phones, pressing donors for cash with the same vigor that would earn him the dubious title of "Solicitor-in-Chief" at the Clinton White House in 1995 and 1996. Anxious to wrap it up before Atlanta, he called Landow for constant updates. "He'd say, 'How ya doing, Nate? You got it yet?'" said Landow. By midsummer the debt was gone, and to thank his backers Gore threw a July 14 gala at Governor Ned McWherter's mansion in Nashville, with Johnny Cash and Tommy Lee Jones as the entertainment.

Moving so aggressively to retire the debt also advanced another agenda: the vice presidential nomination. Gore was interviewed three times — twice by Dukakis and once by his campaign chairman Paul Brountas. The governor's first choice was actually New Jersey Senator Bill Bradley, who said he wasn't interested, and his second was Representative Lee Hamilton of Indiana, who was a highly regarded foreign policy expert but lacked marquee power. Gore's name eventually landed on a short list that included John Glenn, Lloyd Bentsen, and Dick Gephardt. For the record, Gore displayed the appropriate indifference. Behind the scenes, his body language was somewhat more receptive. "He was interested," recalled Dukakis, "although he wasn't panting after it." Still, just before Gore's early July visit to Dukakis's home in Brookline, Massachusetts, aides talked up the Nashville celebration and the success of the 40–40 program with reporters, hoping to give Gore's stature a boost as Dukakis made his selection.

Only Bentsen and Glenn — Washington eminences who offered heavy counterweight to Dukakis's state-house background — remained in play at the end, with Bentsen the final choice. Even if Dukakis had wanted Gore, it's doubtful whether he could have gotten him. Gore's deficits in the black community were more intractable than his campaign debt, and opposition from the Jackson camp would have quashed the deal. Gerald Austin, Jackson's campaign manager, warned that Gore's selection would be an "outrage." Gore was booed when he joined Jackson for a rally at a Baptist church in Nashville on the Friday before the convention. In Atlanta several Jackson delegates from Tennessee demanded that he and Jim Sasser cast their votes (they were also delegates) for Jackson, and they made it clear that their decision would be remembered on Election Day 1990. One Memphis delegate demanded that Gore publicly ask for Jackson's forgiveness. Representative Harold Ford, whose Memphis organization controlled a critical bloc of African American votes, told a press conference that he had no intention of asking either senator to commit to Jackson, and that it was up to them. The tensions unraveled with a scene in Governor Ned McWherter's hotel suite: Gore, listening to a tape of Ford's comments, yanked the cassette from the machine, angrily threw it on the bed, and demanded an apology, insisting that Ford had threatened him.

It was a generally sour week for the Gores, who once thought Atlanta might be a moment of triumph. When Tipper's entourage was blocked by security from entering Omni Arena one night because they didn't have the proper credentials, she reamed out former aide Larry Harrington, who had moved over to the Dukakis campaign as southern coordinator. Journalists found Gore distant, defensive, and devoid of passion. *Boston Globe* reporter Curtis Wilkie, meeting with him in his hotel room, saw a young man still burdened by what David Halberstam called "the general's son syndrome" — the stress that came from a sense of obligation to his father. When Wilkie asked him which books he valued, Gore opened his briefcase and produced a copy of physicist Stephen Hawking's *A Brief History of Time*. He also mentioned Shakespeare and Erik Erikson, but not a word, Wilkie said, about any of the novelists who had written so evocatively of his own generation, like Robert Stone, Richard Ford, and Bobbie Ann Mason. "It sometimes seems that he really isn't a part of his generation," Wilkie wrote.

What began as a spring and summer of discontent grew into a broader midlife examination. It wasn't just his failure as a presidential candidate that troubled Gore, but the *way* he failed. When the polls showed no movement and the press no interest, he downplayed his keystone issues, arms control and the environment, to talk about things that mattered less to him. "I began to doubt my own political judgment," he wrote later in *Earth in the Balance*, "so I began to ask the pollsters and professional politicians what they thought I ought to talk about. As a result, for much of the campaign, I discussed what everybody else discussed. . . . The harder truth is that I simply lacked the strength to keep on talking about the environmental crisis constantly whether it was being reported in the press or not." Friends say his remorse about the campaign triggered a serious reassessment of what it was he really wanted to accomplish as a politician and a man. Gore had looked inward before, as a twenty-something Vietnam veteran and divinity student in Nashville. But taking stock at age forty involved a much more painful descent — one that forced him to examine not only the substance of his politics but the psychological costs of a political life and the unhealed wounds sustained from growing up in an avowedly political family.

His reappraisal led to a renewed focus on the issues that captured his imagination, like high technology and the environment. On May 18, 1989, he introduced the National High-Performance Computer Technology Act, a five-year, $1.7 billion program to expand the capacity of the information highway to connect government, industry, and academic institutions. Signed by President Bush in 1991, the bill required the Pentagon's Defense Advanced Research Projects Agency (DARPA), which operated a computer network that was a forerunner to the Internet, to support research and development of advanced fiber-optics technology, switches, and protocols for an improved national computer system. The measure also directed the National Science Foundation to assist colleges, universities, and libraries in connecting to the new network. While Gore is not, as he suggested in 1999, the father of the Internet, he can credibly claim credit as the wealthy uncle who stepped up to provide funds at an important moment. In the spring of 1989, when few public officials grasped the profound changes that new information technology would bring, Gore saw them plainly. "I genuinely believe that the creation of this nationwide network . . . will create an environment where work stations are common in homes and even small businesses," he told a House committee in the spring of 1989.

Although Gore had always been active on issues like toxic-waste dumping and was an early voice of warning on the dangers of global warming, other members, including Republican John Chafee of Rhode Island and Democrats like Daniel Moynihan and Tom Harkin, sported more environmentally friendly voting records during Gore's first four years in the Senate (1985–88). But as 1988 wound down, Gore mounted an aggressive new effort. "He said to himself, 'Look, I'm a public official. I've got to be here for a reason,'" said Hundt. "I have to make sure I'm focused on it." He wrote an essay for *Time*'s "Planet of the Year" issue and started contemplating a book about the environment. He traveled literally to the ends of the earth to bear witness to what he considered global threats, framing themes and lines of argument that he would explore four years later when he wrote *Earth in the Balance*. At the South Pole he watched scientists extract tiny oxygen bubbles from ice core samples to document rising levels of carbon dioxide and other "greenhouse gases" produced by the burning of fossil fuels that trap the sun's heat in the atmosphere and are likely to raise global temperatures in the next century. Also within the polar ice was evidence of man-made chlorofluorocarbons (CFCs) (found in refrigerants like freon), which had begun eating a hole in the ozone, a layer of oxygenlike gas in the stratosphere that shields the planet from deadly ultraviolet-B radiation.

In January 1989, he joined a congressional delegation on a dramatic trek to the Amazon with Smithsonian biologist Tom Lovejoy to investigate the plunder of the Brazilian rain forests, whose millions of acres provide a vital source of oxygen for the planet and habitat to thousands of species of plants and birds. With Senate colleagues John Heinz and Tim Wirth, he held hearings at a cathedral in the Brazilian provincial capital of Rio Branco, near the rubber plantations where labor organizer Chico Mendez had been murdered just a few weeks earlier, almost certainly the victim of landowners determined to clear the forest for cattle ranching.

Later they jeeped 125 kilometers into the jungle to camp and hike under Lovejoy's supervision. The group bathed in streams and slept in common tents where, in addition to ticks, weevils, and mosquitoes, they endured Gore's lusty snoring. Just to heighten everyone's comfort level, Heinz passed around literature about an Amazon resident called the candy roo — a waterborne parasite that detects and follows a swimmer's urine stream to its source, then lodges itself in the urethra by bristling its spines, producing exquisite pain. Gore avoided such a fate, but Lovejoy later said, "If you want to make the vice president blush, mention the candy roo." But it was the rain forest's mysterious beauty that left a lasting impression on Gore. "We know more about outer space than we do about the Amazon," he said in wonderment one evening to Representative Gerry Sikorski, another camping partner.

When he returned to Washington, he introduced a package of proposals titled to evoke the urgency of a national security issue. He called it the Strategic Environmental Initiative, after the Strategic Defense Initiative (or Star Wars program). It called for a complete phaseout of CFCs within five years, massive reforestation programs, large-scale recycling, and development of alternative energy sources. Portions of this program were adopted a year later.

At the heart of Gore's newly energized environmental conscious-ness was global warming. It had interested Gore since Roger Revelle's lectures at Harvard; he had held some of the first congressional hear-ings on it (featuring Revelle and Carl Sagan) during his tenure as chairman of the House Science and Technology Oversight Subcom-mittee. But as the eighties ended and scientific evidence mounted, his sense of urgency escalated into a crusade. It was the rare visit to Gore's Senate office that didn't include a presentation on the planetary con-sequences of rising temperatures. And those stopping by didn't neces-sarily have to be opinion leaders or members of key committees. Gore's St. Albans classmate David Bartlett remembers dropping in one day for what he thought would be a pleasant few minutes of catching up on family and mutual friends. He found himself on the office floor for forty-five minutes, poring over charts of polar ice core samples. There was nothing cold or academic about it, Bartlett said. Rather, it was Gore's idea of casual fun — what one might expect of a dinner host insistent on showing a few too many slides of a recent vacation to Fiji. At La Guardia Airport one day waiting for the shuttle back to Washington, Gore ran into *Nightline*'s Ted Koppel and invited him to grab a cup of coffee. Before it was done, Gore was using a nap-kin to sketch out his concerns about depletion of the ozone layer.

Gore's nightmare was not the specter of a world sweltering in per-petual summer, but the possibility suggested by the research that a rise of just a few degrees in the earth's temperature could throw the planet's weather system out of kilter. The key was Antarctica. Home to 90 percent of the earth's ice, it's a giant planetary cooling machine that distributes its chill through prevailing winds and ocean currents. Sur-rounding the continent are extremely cold ocean waters that absorb more carbon dioxide than the world's rain forests. Carbon dioxide from automobiles and industry accumulates in the atmosphere and traps the sun's heat, causing the Antarctic seas to get warmer, thus lim-iting their ability to absorb carbon dioxide and perhaps hastening the breakup of the West Antarctic ice shelf, which could lead to disas-trous coastal flooding. Rising temperatures in the Antarctic would disrupt a long-standing equilibrium in temperatures at the poles and the equator, altering the distribution of heat and cold. Scientists fear the change could create new weather patterns, causing widespread drought, heat waves, and severe storms.

Gore's rhetoric in describing the global consequences of inaction has had a dramatic, even apocalyptic edge. "The real question is whether the world's political system can find a new equilibrium before the world's climate system loses its current one," he wrote in *The New Republic* in late 1988 after returning from the South Pole. "Even now, the winds of change are approaching hurricane force." Rolling back the greenhouse effect was part of what he called a new "sacred agenda": making the rescue of the environment a worldwide priority.

As the name implies, the sacred agenda reflects Gore's spiritual beliefs about humankind's stewardship of the Earth. During this same period he helped launch a coalition of spiritual leaders to mobilize churches on environmental issues. His involvement grew out of a long conversation with theologian Paul Gorman on a flight back from a 1990 environmental conference in Moscow. A group of thirty-four scientists, headed by Carl Sagan, had just drafted a letter to the world's leaders asking for their help in reversing environmental decay. Gorman, vice president of public affairs and advocacy at St. John the Divine in New York, remembers Gore expressing regret that "he had never seen a religious leader testify on the environment" before Congress. Gorman said he too had been struggling for years with the spiritual community's skittishness toward green issues as pagan or antireligious, glorifying creation rather than the creator. He felt "called" to make the environment a social justice issue for churches. Gore, whom Gorman had never regarded as a big player on the environment, told him he was working on a book about ecology and spiritualism and said, "If I can do anything to move this forward, get in touch with me. I can't think of anything that's more important to me at this moment."

Gorman said Gore was as good as his word and deserves much of the credit for bringing together religious and scientific leaders two years later to form the National Religious Partnership for the Environment, whose members include four major umbrella organizations (the U.S. Catholic Conference, the National Council of Churches of Christ, the Coalition on the Environment and Jewish Life, and the Evangelical Environmental Network, although not Gore's own Southern Baptist Convention). "If he achieves nothing else in his life," said Gorman, "he will have helped catalyze a profound development in human civilization — the moment religious life recovered its lost relationship with creation."

Like his decision to enter the nuclear priesthood, his effort to acquire a deeper shade of green coincided with polling that suggested it was good politics. In both global and vividly personal terms, Americans were growing more anxious about humankind's impact on its home. A series of disasters in the mid and late eighties underscored the fragility of the planet's environment and its vulnerability to catastrophe. The April 1986 explosion of a nuclear reactor at the Chernobyl power plant in the Ukraine spread a cloud of radioactive gas over ten thousand square miles of northern and eastern Europe. In the hot, drought-stricken summer of 1988, as medical waste and dead dolphins washed onto U.S. beaches, NASA scientist James Hansen told a Senate subcommittee that the earth had warmed more than two degrees Fahrenheit in the last century. Rising levels of carbon dioxide, he warned, could lead to a temperature increase of more than eight degrees by 2050. When the tanker *Exxon Valdez* ran aground in early 1989, it spilled 11 million gallons of crude oil across one thousand miles of Alaskan coastline, killing hundreds of thousands of fish and birds.

Nearly eight years of policy set by Reagan administration appointees like Interior Secretary James Watt and EPA Administrator Ann Gorsuch had left increasing numbers of Americans feeling as if the government were at war with the environment rather than protecting it. In the fall of 1987, according to one poll, 32 percent of Americans believed that the environment was in worse condition than it had been five years earlier. A year later 46 percent said it had deteriorated.

Gore's resurgent environmentalism aggravated competitive tensions with another ambitious young senator who aspired to be the movement's preeminent voice in Congress — Tim Wirth. The two had argued for years on regulatory issues. In the House, Wirth, a Coloradan, pushed for decontrol of oil prices, which Gore opposed. Later, in the Senate, Gore's successful fight for reimposition of government controls on the cable industry again pitted him against Wirth, whose state was home to powerful cable operators like TCI's John Malone. Sharing the same page proved to be even more awkward.

Some greens regarded Wirth as the more steadfast advocate, but Gore began to compete with him by aggressively courting pro-environment constituencies. The situation festered until they had what Gore later called "an extremely candid" discussion. "We were in danger of getting in each other's way as we made similar points on the same issue," Gore wrote in *Earth in the Balance*. In Gore's version of the conversation, the two agreed that they needed to put aside petty differences and "to work together whenever it was productive." Since then, said Gore, "we have worked closely together." Wirth's account is more revealing. He said he found Gore's ambition to be so suffocating that he finally told him that he was not a competitor. "Al," Wirth said, "I don't want to be president of the United States." With *that* assurance, according to Wirth, the relationship improved markedly.

The more turbulent part of Gore's midlife reassessment took place privately. For the first time the "real little politician" of the Fairfax began to explore the emotional costs of meeting the grand expectations set by his parents. He said he had "never been on a couch," although his personal issues made him an ideal candidate in the late eighties. Gore, who regarded swimming with a woman other than his wife as too risky, must surely have concluded that therapy carried even greater exposure to career damage. That began to change one day in the early spring of 1989 when he entered an office in a small strip development on the outskirts of downtown Knoxville for an appointment with Dr. Lance Laurence, a clinical psychologist and University of Tennessee professor.

Legislation, not therapy, was on the agenda. Laurence had raised money for Gore in 1988, under the auspices of a political action committee, Psychologists for Legislative Action Now. The shrink PAC was seeking improvements in Medicare coverage for mental health services, and Gore, always eager to keep donors happy, had agreed to come discuss cosponsorship of a bill, introduced by Senator Jay Rockefeller, to meet some of their goals. That, so far as was known by Laurence and his five therapist colleagues sitting in, was the meeting's purpose when Gore settled into the blue reclining rocker in his office.

The official business took about a minute. Gore said he was sold on Rockefeller's bill and would be happy to cosponsor it. Then he asked, "Why don't you tell me something about yourselves?" When one of Laurence's colleagues mentioned that he was a former minister, it launched Gore into a ninety-minute discussion that ranged over broad areas of philosophy, religion, and psychological issues of identity, intimacy, and family dysfunction. It was obvious to Laurence that

Gore was a man looking for answers about himself. "It was a search for his own meaning, not just an intellectual exercise," he said. Gore struck him, he added, "as a guy who was too alone, and maybe not getting enough personal relating."

One theme he vividly remembers Gore touching on was fathers and sons. He discussed the writing of Robert Bly, who had used the Grimms' fairy tale "Iron John," about a wild man of the woods who guides a young boy into adulthood, to discuss the effects of emotionally remote and absent fathers. Listening to the most famous political son in Tennessee holding forth on Bly and other New Age writers left Laurence and his colleagues stunned.

Before the meeting broke up, Gore asked Laurence if he could recommend some books. The request began what one close friend of Gore's called "psychoanalysis by correspondence course." Laurence's suggested reading would resonate with Gore for years. The selections included two 1970s works by therapists examining the psychic wounds left by abusive parents: Alice Miller's *Drama of the Gifted Child* and Allen Wheelis's *How People Change*. Wheelis's slender volume, slightly over one hundred pages, is a meditation on the freedom achievable through therapy for those committed to working hard at it. The book's centerpiece surely stirred emotional embers within Gore. Wheelis describes his struggle with anxiety attacks triggered by lingering memories of being a "psychological slave" to his disparaging, emotionally distant father, who forced him to spend a whole summer on the family farm clearing several acres of grass using a hand razor.

Miller's work explores the damage done by parents who love their children only in proportion to their compliance with expectations or conceits. The constant accommodation leads to what Miller calls the "as if personality": the child "develops in such a way that he reveals only what is expected of him and fuses so completely with what he reveals that one could scarcely guess how much more there is to him behind the false self. He cannot develop and differentiate his true self, because he is unable to live it." The "gifted child" of the title refers not to good grades or high IQ, but to the strength demonstrated by those who "survived an abusive childhood thanks to an ability to adapt even to unspeakable cruelty by becoming numb," an idea Gore later incorporated into his own writing and speaking. Miller says that those who spend their childhood adapting to parental ideals often go on to great success and acclaim as adults but end up losing touch with their own personalities, struggling instead with the "false self" that they present to the world. The first major setbacks or career disappointments, Miller writes, can bring many high flyers crashing to earth. "These dark feelings will come to the fore as soon as the drug of grandiosity fails, as soon as they are not 'on top,' not definitely the 'superstar,' or whenever they suddenly get the feeling they failed to live up to some ideal image and measure they feel they must adhere to," says Miller. In therapy, "the small and lonely child that is hidden behind the achievements wakes up and asks, 'What would have happened if I had appeared before you sad, needy, angry and furious? Where would your love have been then?'"

Drama clearly moved Gore — he gave copies to Carter Eskew and other friends. He also met with Laurence on trips back to Tennessee, not as a patient, Laurence said, but to talk about the psychological concepts he wanted to incorporate into *Earth in the Balance.* Traveling between town meetings on taxation and Social Security and veterans' benefits, Gore communed with Laurence about connection, disconnection, and narcissism. "He'd get back into the car after his political thing and just pick right up and talk," he said. Gore has been loathe to discuss any of this personally, telling the *Washington Post*'s Katherine Boo, who first reported his enthusiasm for Miller's book, that Washington was a place where "any mention of an inner life, the spirit, the heart, is greeted with guffaws and snickers and even ridicule." He did acknowledge:

> It's real easy in the profession of politics to lose yourself in presenting yourself to others, and I think a lot of people do. I think the profession draws to it some people who have a clear understanding of the difference between the medium and the message . . . but I think it draws others who get lost in the profession itself and in the forms of politics, the methods of politics. I became more aware of that danger when I really stopped to think about it long and hard.

Gore's inner search took a wrenching turn early on Monday evening, April 3, as he and Tipper strolled out of Baltimore's Memorial Stadium with their six-year-old son, Albert III, after watching the Orioles beat the Red Sox in extra innings to win their 1989 home opener. They were getting ready to cross Hillen Road, a four-lane street several blocks east of the stadium, when, witnesses told police, Albert suddenly pulled free of Gore's hand and darted into the roadway.

He made it across the two northbound lanes, but in the third lane a 1977 Chevrolet driven by twenty-two-year-old Jasper McWilliams smashed into his left thigh. Williams was not speeding, but the force of the collision, as Gore described it later, using the detached language of an engineer, "torqued" his son's body onto the car's hood — breaking a rib, rupturing his spleen, and bruising his kidneys and pancreas. The impact knocked him twenty feet in the air, and when he landed he broke his collarbone and right shoulder blade, collapsed a lung, and suffered a concussion. He skidded along the pavement for another few feet, receiving second-degree burns as the asphalt tore at the skin on his right arm and the side of his head.

When the Gores reached him, they said later, he was lying motionless in the gutter, without a breath they could hear or a pulse they could feel.

Albert and Pauline were at the Gores' Arlington home with the girls, waiting dinner, when the phone rang. Pauline assumed Al was calling to let her know they were on their way home. "He tried to be as calm as he could," Pauline remembered. "He said, 'We've had an accident, Mother. Don't get too excited, but he is badly hurt.'" Gore told her that two nurses from Johns Hopkins, Victoria Costin-Siegel and Esther O'Campo, "breathed life back into him." Pauline wanted to bring everyone to the hospital, but Gore said it would be best if they didn't. So that night they sat and prayed with their granddaughters, and Pauline said she will never forget ten-year-old Sarah, her face contorted with all her strength to keep from crying. She tried her best at the hospital the next day, too, when the children were asked not to show any emotion at the sight of their little brother, battered, burned, and breathing with a respirator. Albert was not immediately out of danger: forty-eight hours after the accident, he was still bleeding internally and needed surgery for doctors to pinpoint the source. They ended up removing more than half of his spleen.

Gore put his Senate business on hold to spend his days and nights in Albert's room at the Johns Hopkins Children's Center. He came back to the floor just once during the first two weeks — to vote for an increase in the minimum wage — before streaking back to the hospital with a police escort. Albert finally came home in late April in a stom-ach-to-toe body cast, and the Gores converted the dining room into a bedroom, where they took turns spending the night at his side in a sleeping bag. The cast came off in a month, but he needed more sur-gery in July to repair nerve damage in his right arm. It took more than a year — and many driveway games of catch with his father — before the little boy who loved baseball had his arm strength back.

The near-catastrophe hit Gore like a lightning strike. For a man who kept such a tight grip on everything in his life, losing hold of his son's hand at the curbside and watching him almost die was haunting. "I had him," he told a Tennessee aide as he rode through the state one night. "*I had him.*" As he stood vigil at Hopkins, his midlife funk cas-caded into a full-blown crisis. "I felt as if my life had grown . . . super-critical," he wrote later, borrowing yet another scientific term to de-scribe an emotional event, this one from physicists who had studied how individual grains of sand move in an avalanche. He leaned on his Baptist faith, deepening his prayer life during Albert's convalescence. "I know he believes part of Albert's healing came from prayer," said Lorraine Voles, his former vice presidential communications director. "He really thought the power of prayer helped to heal his son."

Friends and colleagues reached out to support Gore, but he said later that what moved him most was the support and prayer offered by scores of people he had never met, those who offered their own stories of crisis and loss. It freed him, he said later, to grieve in a way he never had before. "I don't know what barriers in my soul had prevented me from understanding emotionally that basic connection to others until they reached out for me in the dark of my family's sorrow," he said in a speech at Harvard five years later. "But I suppose it was a form of cyni-cism on my part." Less cynicism, perhaps, than fear of dropping the mask of the relentlessly correct little boy determined to meet every-body else's needs. The new connection "gave me permission to fully realize my grief and go, in Robert Bly's words, 'into the ashes,'" Gore wrote, using a phrase from *Iron John* describing rituals of symbolic death and rebirth.

For a brief period at least, his therapy by correspondence course became the real thing. He and Tipper sought family counseling at Hopkins to cope with the trauma of the accident and the stresses posed by Albert's lengthy rehabilitation. The sessions forced larger marital issues into open view, especially the toll that Gore's relentless careerism had taken on the family. He was turning into another absentee senator-father, and Tipper insisted that he change the way he did business. She also acknowledged that she needed to do the same. "Albert's accident stopped us cold," she wrote in 1996. "It caused Al and me to reassess the way we allotted our time and to think about what our kids really meant to us."

The aftermath of the accident also led to Tipper Gore's treatment for depression. In the spring of 1999, as her husband prepared to run for president again, she spoke publicly for the first time about her struggle with the disease, saying she wanted to encourage young people coping with depression to get help. She said her treatment, which included a regimen of antidepressants, was "something that was separate" from the family counseling at Hopkins and that it "happened later," although exactly how much later she will not say. A meeting with a social worker friend confirmed that she was showing depressive symptoms, she said; she was told that her illness "was probably a result of [an] accumulation of things that had happened in my life." She didn't elaborate, but it isn't hard to see how the circumstances of her life could have cascaded into an emotional crisis. The hereditary vulnerability caused by her mother's illness, the stillborn careers, long hours of parenting without a husband's help, the sometimes vicious characterization of her as a prissy housewife out to sanitize pop culture, the strains of the 1988 campaign, and finally, Albert's accident, all prepared the psychological ground.

In response to the near-loss of Albert, and perhaps to his wife's depression, Gore became more conscientious about blocking out time on the schedule for the kids' school games and birthdays. He also worked at becoming a nicer boss, and in the accident's wake some aides saw fewer flares of temper and less compulsion to act older than he actually was. He made, said one former campaign consultant, "a much more conscious effort, in his own methodical way, to be sensitive to people."

Part of Gore's idea of reaching out, however, was to hire a professional facilitator. Jane Hopkins was a Richmond, Virginia, management consultant and organizational psychologist he met through former Virginia attorney general Mary Sue Terry. A soft-spoken woman in her midforties, Hopkins had worked with companies in the private sector to foster better communication among managers, and in 1989 she became a kind of one-woman personnel office in Gore's Senate operation, smoothing jurisdictional disputes, reviewing job candidates, and serving as a go-between for Gore and his staff. "She can explain him," one ex-aide said of Hopkins, although some staff viewed her as something of a spy, keeping Gore informed about grumbling or other seditious activity in the ranks.

Despite his attempts to become more sensitive and communicative, Gore remained an elusive figure, sometimes even to his wife. She fumed when he blindsided her with plans or threw her into events without what she felt was adequate preparation. He seemed to have trouble assimilating the idea that the rock lyrics episode had made her a public figure in her own right, and years later he sometimes still treated her as an ornamental political spouse, available to simply show up at events and smile adoringly. In early 1990, as the couple rode from Nashville to Chattanooga for the first in a series of fund-raisers for his senatorial reelection campaign, Tipper began asking the aide who was driving them questions about the three-day itinerary. "It was clear she didn't know much about it," said the staffer, "and as she asked more questions of me, [Gore] tried to placate her, like, 'Don't worry about all these questions, we've got it under control.'"

Tipper, seated in back while Gore rode in front with the aide, blew up. "I'm down here for three days, I'm going to these events. I'm trying to get information," she said. "You keep your mouth shut! I've got to find out who's going to be there because these are people I have to deal with all the time also."

Gore tried to calm her down. "We do these fund-raisers all the time, it's not rocket science," he said.

"That's how you always interpret it," she snapped. "That's what I'm sick and tired of. That's why I'm not prepared. That's why you have expectations of me and I can't meet them."

"You do great, honey, everything's fine."

Gore promised to do a better job of keeping her in the loop, and the spat subsided. Then, as their car tooled south on Interstate 24, Al Gore fell asleep.

◆ 15 ◆

Gore in the Balance

AFTER pledging to make his life less career-centered and more family-friendly, Gore embarked on one of the more career-centered, family-unfriendly pursuits imaginable — writing a book. He had contemplated writing a book about the environment since the 1988 campaign, but the emotional fallout from Albert's accident, combined with his own midlife turbulence, elevated the project into something more personal. This would be more than an earnest treatment of a pressing policy issue — it would be part of his therapy. In the summer of 1990, with the help of New York literary agent Mort Janklow, Gore signed a contract with Houghton Mifflin to write *Earth in the Balance.*

Once he had been reelected in November to a second Senate term against minimal opposition, Gore holed up in his parents' Methodist Building apartment and produced a 711-page draft (whittled by editor John Sterling to slightly over 400) by mid-1991. He had a running start — portions of the manuscript came from speeches and op-ed pieces he had already written, and he was aided by a full-time researcher and a hefty supporting lineup of scholars, including the Smithsonian's Lovejoy, Michael McElroy, chairman of Harvard's Department of Earth and Planetary Sciences, and Nobel Laureate chemist Sherwood Rowland. He wrote nights, weekends, and in whatever holes his official schedule created, keeping such odd hours at the Methodist that Alabama Senator Howell Heflin, who also had an apartment there, took him aside and expressed his concern about what his young colleague was up to. "I'm worried about you, son. You go home and see your family," he counseled.

Politicians with presidential aspirations usually play it safe when putting words to paper, lest those words return to haunt them in the middle of a campaign. For the ever-cautious Gore, *Earth in the Balance* was an especially remarkable achievement — an environmental call to arms, a midlife confessional, and a meditation on spiritual poverty in a bloated secular world, written with a hortatory urgency that places it firmly in the tradition of Rachel Carson and Jeremy Rifkin. It remains by far the most revealing self-portrait he has ever offered. At a publication party thrown by Reed Hundt at his home, about forty guests gathered around to hear a few words from the author. "I hope you like it," said an excited Gore, "because that book is *me*."

Earth in the Balance is the essential Gore: thoughtful, earnest, ambitious, crammed with facts, moralizing, hyperbolic, and breathtakingly grandiose. The pages are charged with the evangelistic fervor of a man who believes he can save the world. "We must make the rescue of the environment the central organizing principle for civilization," Gore writes, calling for "an all-out effort to use every policy and program, every law and institution, every treaty and alliance, every tactic and strategy, every plan and course of action — to use, in short, every means to halt the destruction of the environment." Gore casts a host of environmental problems — plundered rain forests, overused pesticides, unrestrained dumping, proliferating greenhouse gases, and a punctured ozone layer — not merely as long-term threats but as manifestations of a coming apocalypse. The world's indifference to these calamities, he argues, recalls the failure to recognize the Nazi threat in the 1930s. "Few could conceive of the Holocaust to follow, but from a distance the pattern of cruelty and destruction now seems clear. . . . Once again, world leaders waffle, hoping the danger will dissipate. Yet today the evidence of an ecological *Kristallnacht* is as clear as the sound of glass shattering in Berlin."

The book is, at its best, a prodigious feat of reporting skill and intellectual virtuosity. It's not every public policy tome that draws on both Joseph Conrad and *Saturday Night Live* to drive home its arguments, and Gore works hard to pump life into a narrative that could have been as dry as the Aral Sea, which he visited. He is a skilled synthesizer and popularizer of others' research and puts it to use in an absorbing short history of climate's impact on civilization, from the disappearance of the Minoans to the Dust Bowl. Gore also has a good reporter's touch for the telling detail and the connectable dots, describing the distance from the ground to the top of the earth's atmosphere, for example, as "no more than an hour's cross-country run," or noting that President Reagan's near-fatal gunshot wound was treated with a blood-pressure medication derived from an Amazonian bush viper.

But there is also an insecurity that lingers in the book's overheated erudition. Gore knows a lot and is intent on making sure everyone knows he's the smartest kid in the class. ("The basic principles behind positive feedback loops are easily understood. We are all familiar with so-called non-linear systems," he wrote in describing interdependency in the earth's ecology.)

He is also fond of metaphors, and the book's dominant one links the plight of the planet with his personal struggles. Gore finds the same patterns of family dysfunction and despair, and the need for spiritual healing, at the root of both:

> I reluctantly concluded that I had to look inside myself and confront some difficult and painful questions about what I am really seeking in my own life, and why. I grew up in a determinedly political family, in which I learned at an early age to be very sensitive — too sensitive, perhaps — to what others were thinking, and to notice carefully — maybe too carefully — the similarities and differences between my way of thinking and that of society around me. Now, in mid-life, as I search through the layers of received knowledge and intuited truth woven into my life, I can't help but notice similar layers of artifice and authenticity running through the civilization of which I am a part. . . . In a way, then, the search for truths about this ungodly crisis and the search for truths about myself have been the same search all along.

He renders a withering judgment on the conventional politics he had practiced and declares that the future of the planet demands a new political courage. "I have become very impatient with my own tendency to put a finger to the political winds and proceed cautiously," he writes.

> The voice of caution whispers persuasively in the ear of every politician, often with good reason. But when caution breeds timidity, a good politician listens to other voices. For me, the environmental crisis is the critical case in point: now, every time I pause to consider whether I have gone too far out on a limb, I look at the new facts that continue to

pour in from around the world and conclude that I have not gone nearly far enough. The integrity of the environment is not just another issue to be used in political games for popularity, votes or attention. And the time has long since come to take more political risks — and endure much more political criticism — by proposing tougher, more effective solutions and fighting hard for their enactment.

There are many culprits in Gore's environmentally threatened world: capitalism, male dominance, a consumer culture that deadens the spiritual side of our nature ("Industrial civilization's great engines of distraction still seduce us with a promise of fulfillment"). But the emotional core of *Earth in the Balance* is a chapter entitled "Dysfunctional Civilization." It is Gore's term paper for his "psychoanalysis by correspondence course," his unified field theory of psychic and environmental turmoil. He argues that the same unquestioned rules and conspiracies of silence that govern addiction, dysfunctional families, and child abuse also perpetuate destruction of the environment. "Like a parent violating the personal boundaries of a vulnerable child," he writes, "we violate the temporal boundaries of our rightful place in the chain of human generations." Gore contends that the dominant unchallenged rule of Western culture's huge extended family — the Cartesian worldview that human beings are separate from the natural world — has facilitated the plunder of the environment. Like Alice Miller's "gifted" children who are unable to challenge abusive or emotionally withholding parents for fear of abandonment, each successive generation of humanity feels dependent on the material comfort and consumer clutter of civilization, "and we dare not think about separating ourselves from such beneficence."

Gore applies the same construct to totalitarian governments and their ability to break the spirit of their citizens. He speaks in a carefully generic way here, but there is little doubt that he is reflecting on new insights into his own childhood:

A developing child in a dysfunctional family searches his parent's face for signals that he is whole and all is right with the world; when he finds no such approval, he begins to feel that something is wrong inside. And because he doubts his worth and authenticity, he begins controlling his inner experience — smothering spontaneity, masking emotion, diverting creativity into robotic routine, distracting an awareness of all he is missing with an unconvincing replica of what he might have been.

The chapter captures something essential to Gore. It takes an enormous self-regard — "the operatic tendency," as Marjorie Williams calls it — to see a big change in one's own life as paving the way for change in the life of the planet. The grandiosity hardwired into his nature demands that whatever he embraces be not only critical but transcendent. It was not enough to rally the public to environmentalism as an urgent and worthy cause: the glass shards of *Kristallnacht* had to be heard crunching underfoot.

Gore's policy prescriptives, which take up the book's final quarter, are just as audaciously global. Normally leery of becoming directly associated with big-spending government programs, he proposes a "Global Marshall Plan" patterned after the American rehabilitation of post–World War II Europe. (That plan cost the United States $100 billion in current-day dollars, Gore writes. The new one would be jointly financed with Japan and the oil-producing nations.) Its overarching objectives would include: stabilizing the world's population through birth control, reduction of infant mortality, and improved education; sharing new technologies with developing countries that will help them grow economically while minimizing environmental damage; simultaneously securing binding commitments from industrial nations to stabilize their production of pollutants like greenhouse gases; and reformulating the economic "rules of the road" to factor environmental welfare into the economic decisions made by nations.

Gore offers specific ideas in each of these broad areas, everything from planting billions of trees to creating a new generation of antitrust laws that would discourage environmentally hazardous vertical integration by corporations (for example, paper companies buying forest land). Gore also advocates "debt for nature swaps": forgiving a country's debt in exchange for emissions reductions. Perhaps most memorably, he calls for a worldwide research effort with the goal of completely eliminating the internal combustion engine within twenty-five years.

On its publication in early 1992, *Earth in the Balance* became a bestseller and was hailed by greens as a modern-day *Silent Spring*. It vaulted Gore to superstardom in the global movement, "an environmental Paul Revere," as the League of Conservation Voters described him. Most reviews ran from respectful to enthusiastic. *Time*'s Lance Morrow called it "a labor of statesmanship, evangelism and scientific exposition," although he noted that Gore "here and there sounds as if his Ancient Mariner had lingered too long in adult-children seminars with John Bradshaw, and humankind might 12-step the earth green again." The book immediately became the right wing's exhibit A in its case against Gore as a liberal, tree-hugging, one-worlder kook. The Cato Institute's Ronald Bailey, writing in the *National Review*, said that Gore "artfully fuses New Age psychobabble with radical environmentalism into the quintessence of political correctness."

But even more moderate voices were disturbed by Gore's alarmism, especially on the future consequences of atmospheric greenhouse gases at the expense of attention to more urgent needs. *The New Republic*'s Gregg Easterbrook, writing about Gore's high-profile role at the 1992 Earth Summit in Rio de Janeiro, where he led the charge against the Bush administration's opposition to an international treaty establishing firm timetables for reductions in greenhouse gas emissions, said there was "something bordering on indecent about the world's heads of state gathering to bestow tens of billions of dollars upon a hypothetical concern like greenhouse warming while not lifting a finger to assist the 3.2 million impoverished Southern [hemisphere] children who die each year of diarrheal diseases communicated through impure water." He said that Gore "seems increasingly to believe that the only correct stance is to press the panic button on every issue."

When inconvenient details surfaced to muddy or undermine the urgency of his global warming message, Gore moved quickly to spin the story back his way. In *Earth in the Balance*, he pays tribute to the oceanographer Roger Revelle for his Harvard lectures about the dangers of the greenhouse effect, crediting the scientist for stirring his early interest in climate change. Revelle, a reader of the book would believe, completely shared Gore's view that global warming is "the most serious threat we have ever faced." But in his 1992 *New Republic* piece, Easterbrook reports that shortly before his death in July 1991 at age eighty-two, Revelle coauthored an article that took a much more tentative line toward the possible long-term effects of climate change. "The scientific base for a greenhouse gas warming is too uncertain to justify drastic action at this time," says the piece in the April 1991 issue of *Cosmos*, a magazine published for the three thousand members of Washington's Cosmos Club. The article was actually written by S. Fred Singer, a former University of Virginia professor and EPA official, with contributions from Revelle and Chauncey Starr, former president of the Electric Power Institute. Entitled "What to Do About Greenhouse Warming: Look Before You Leap," it is far from an anti-global-warming screed. Singer does say that debate over the issue has been characterized by "some facts, lots of uncertainty and just plain lack of knowledge." Among his contentions is that planetary warming has been overestimated by flawed computer models that fail to take into account factors like cloud cover, which could offset rising temperatures. Although Singer and the article's contributors acknowledge that the available evidence points to "a modest warming in the next century," the net impact of the greenhouse effect could be beneficial, they say, in the form of longer growing seasons and fewer frosts. The piece nevertheless endorses public policies to encourage energy efficiency and the increased use of non-fossil-fuel energy sources like nuclear and solar power. Virtually unnoticed when first published, the article became considerably more newsworthy in the summer of 1992. Gore was no longer just an environmentally friendly senator. He was a vice presidential candidate and best-selling author, and his mentor appeared to be distancing himself from the issue he had inspired Gore to embrace.

Shortly after Easterbrook's article appeared in the early summer of 1992, Gore called Justin Lancaster, a research fellow at the Harvard School of Public Health and a former student and colleague of Revelle's. According to Lancaster's deposition in a libel suit later brought by Singer, Gore wanted to know whether Revelle, who had undergone heart bypass surgery toward the end of his life, was "diminished in his mental capacity" during the period when the article was produced. Lancaster said he told Gore that Revelle was "very sharp," but that "he did get tired very easily." Still, Lancaster added in his testimony, "I couldn't tell [Gore] that, you know, that Roger was senile or anything like that."

Gore then asked whether Lancaster thought Revelle had changed his position on global warming. "What did Roger believe?" Gore asked. Lancaster said that Revelle continued to believe it was a "significant threat," and that his views were not consistent with the *Cos-*

mos article. Gore asked Lancaster whether he would be willing, perhaps in collaboration with some of Revelle's colleagues, to write a letter to the editor of *The New Republic* affirming what he had just said. Lancaster agreed and, in a series of phone calls and faxes over the next several weeks, conferred with a top Gore aide, Katie McGinty, on the wording of a response to the Easterbrook piece. That response was eventually published in the magazine's letters column.

Rather than ending there, the matter escalated into a wider academic war. Lancaster wrote to Singer on July 20 asking that Revelle's name be removed from a planned republication of the *Cosmos* piece in a volume of essays on climate change. Commentators were unfairly using the article, he argued, to say that Revelle had reversed himself on global warming. He conceded to Singer that Revelle's "appreciation for the uncertainties [of global warming] may have deepened and broadened, as was true for many of us through the 1980s, but his concern about the seriousness of the threat never diminished." He added that he had learned from Revelle's secretary that Revelle was reluctant at first to be a coauthor on the *Cosmos* piece and that he didn't consent until Singer paid a personal visit to make his appeal.

Singer declined to remove Revelle's name, contending that Revelle had required no such encouragement. Far from it, said Singer, who described Revelle as "more skeptical than I about climate models," adding that he had had a difficult time persuading Revelle to agree to "a more moderate view." Lancaster persisted, however, writing directly to the editor of the planned volume and demanding, unsuccessfully, that the article be withdrawn. A Gore staffer on the Senate Commerce Committee, Anthony Socci, also wrote to the volume's publisher, CRC Press, at the height of the presidential campaign in late October, charging that Singer and to some extent Chauncey Starr "had deliberately set out to discredit Senator Gore . . . having prevailed upon, and unconscionably misused the late Roger Revelle in the process, at a time when Revelle was extremely ill and fragile," a charge Singer denies. Lancaster repeated the same basic allegation in a paper he submitted at the Revelle Memorial Symposium in Cambridge later that year, prompting Singer to sue him for libel. The case was settled the following spring when Lancaster signed a full retraction.

It does appear that Revelle's views on global warming were more nuanced than those of his political protégé. "I agree with your statement that 'Global climate change may well be the most challenging environmental, economic and political issue we have ever faced,'" Revelle wrote to Tim Wirth on July 18, 1988. "However, we must be careful not to arouse too much alarm until the rate and amount of warming becomes clearer. . . . My own feeling is that we had better wait another ten years before making confident predictions." But he also seemed to believe that, despite the unanswered questions, government was not doing enough to address the problem. One of his daughters, Carolyn Revelle Hufbauer, said she remembers her father's disappointment after a 1990 White House ceremony to award him the National Medal of Science, when he had expected to sit next to Chief of Staff John Sununu, an outspoken skeptic about global warming. He relished the prospect of bending Sununu's ear about the Bush administration's inaction, she recalled, but Sununu was a no-show. "I had hoped to tell him what a dim view I take of the administration's environmental policies," Revelle said. Had Revelle lived to see the last decade's worth of evidence, family and friends say, it is likely that he would have supported Gore's push for U.S. participation in an international treaty to limit greenhouse gas emissions.

The Singer-Lancaster fracas has less to do with global warming than with Gore's behavior when his official story was challenged. There is no evidence that Gore directed Lancaster or Socci to try to suppress the *Cosmos* article. But their actions clearly reflect Gore's deep defensiveness about anything that might taint the new green knight's stature conferred on him by *Earth in the Balance.*

◆ 16 ◆

The Dowry

I T WAS nearing midnight on January 11, 1991, and Al Gore was still in his Senate office, still torn about the vote that was just a few hours away. With a book deadline looming, he had scaled back on a lot of routine business, but there was nothing routine about a decision to go to war. A few weeks earlier, on November 29, 1990, the UN Security Council had passed Resolution 678 authorizing President Bush to use whatever means were necessary to expel Saddam Hussein's troops from Kuwait after January 15. Now, with nearly 400,000 troops dug into the Saudi desert, Bush was asking Congress to approve the use of force in the Persian Gulf.

The stakes, and the partisan heat, were enormous. Some experts were predicting that the United States could take tens of thousands of casualties in a ground war with Iraq. Senate Democrats, headed by Majority Leader George Mitchell and Armed Services Committee Chairman Sam Nunn, were pushing hard to delay military action until at least the summer so that economic sanctions might have more time to work. Although Gore tended to oversell the hawkish aspects of his record in 1988, he had never been a "Vietnam Syndrome" Democrat, reflexively opposing any projection of American force. He was also squarely on record against the threat posed by Iraq. In the fall of 1988 he had twice called on the Reagan administration to take a hard line against Saddam for his use of chemical weapons against Iran and his own Kurdish population.

In the Armed Services Committee hearings, he had voiced support for sanctions while holding open the option for military action later. Now, in his darkened office, he wasn't sure. Even if sanctions worked, could they really topple Saddam and compel an Iraqi withdrawal? Who knew? It was possible that whatever hardships sanctions imposed, Saddam might ultimately look even stronger to his people, standing alone against the world community, fighting to make Kuwait part of Iraq. Moreover, waiting until August would necessitate withdrawing nearly half the U.S. forces already in the desert, a move not likely to weaken Iraqi resolve.

Gore's political advisers were alarmed — "apoplectic," as one put it — at the prospect of Gore casting a vote to support Bush on the Gulf War. It risked incalculable damage to his chances for the 1992 Democratic nomination, they argued. Only Leon Fuerth urged that he stand with the administration; though Fuerth's views always carried great weight with Gore, no one was sure which way he would vote when he headed home early that morning.

On the floor later that day, Gore's speech reflected the introspective spirit of the manuscript in progress across the street in the Methodist Building. At times he sounded more like he was sharing with a twelve-step group than speaking to the Senate. "My decision today is the product of an intense, may I say, excruciating, effort to find my way to a place as close to a sense of the ultimate truth in this matter as I am capable of getting," he said. "I have struggled to confront this issue in its bare essence . . . to strike a balance and to take my stand." Gore went on to explain that as tempted as he was to support sanctions, he simply didn't think they would work. "I wish that were so. It may be so. But it does not feel plausible to me. . . . The risks of war are horrendous. The real costs of war are horrendous. Mr. President, what are the costs and risks if the alternative policy does not work? I think they are larger, greater, more costly." He joined 9 other Democrats who broke ranks on a 52–47 vote to authorize the use of force in the Persian Gulf.

It was a gutsy decision, perhaps the one in his career closest to a pure act of conscience. Mitchell, who thought Gore was on board with sanctions, was furious and barely spoke to him for months. Before it was clear how well the operation was going to go, with lighter than expected casualties and a stunningly quick ground war, Gore thought he had foreclosed his political options. "I may just have thrown away whatever future I had with the Democratic Party," he glumly told aide Steve Owens.

Far from wrecking Gore's political rehab, the Gulf War accelerated it. His support for Operation Desert Storm raised his stock as a 1992 presidential prospect, a revival also buoyed by the relative weakness of other big Democratic names. Sam Nunn's opposition to the war had diminished any potential southern base he might have hoped for as a candidate. While Gore cruised to an overwhelming 1990 reelection win (70–30 over Republican William Hawkins of Knoxville), the returns that year revealed the vulnerability of other potential rivals. Bill Bradley came within a free throw of losing to Christine Todd Whitman, squeaking back into office with 51 percent of the vote in New Jersey. New York's Mario Cuomo drew 53 percent. Dick Gephardt pulled 57 percent — solid, but nothing special for a safe seat. Bill Clinton had easily won a fifth gubernatorial term in Arkansas and was gradually wiggling out from under a campaign pledge not to seek the presidency in 1992. But he was also looking over his shoulder. One close friend of Gore's kept fielding calls from Clinton associates trolling for news about Gore's plans, leaving him with the "strong impression" that he would stand down if Gore decided to go.

Publicly, Gore did nothing to discourage the speculation. He insisted that despite George Bush's stratospheric approval rating — 89 percent on April 29, 1991, according to Gallup — he was beatable. He jumped into the debate that spring over economic unfairness in the Reagan years with a proposal that foreshadowed a central Clinton-Gore campaign promise — a middle-class tax cut. He and Tom Downey unveiled the Working Family Tax Relief Act, a bill to cut taxes for 35 million middle-class families by raising taxes on the rich, including an 11 percent surtax on adjusted gross incomes of $250,000 or more. The package went nowhere, but it helped bolster Gore's credentials as an economic champion of the middle class.

Privately, though, Gore was torn. His prospects for the nomination looked at least reasonable, and he really did believe Bush could be beaten. But there was also the question of how many bites at the apple he would get in one career. If he ran in 1992, he risked becoming a two-time loser in presidential politics before he turned forty-five. Then there was his family. Albert was still healing from his car accident, and Tipper had been treated for depression during their son's recovery. She had also been explicit about her desire that he play a more active role in his children's lives. After what happened in 1988, he knew there could be no rationalizing what a candidacy meant personally, no wishful thinking about quality time with his kids. "Take the hardest campaign you've ever done," he told Jay Rockefeller. "Running for the presidency is a hundred times more difficult. It's every hour of every single day." The question remained: Just how hungry was he?

His sluggish performance at several important political events that spring reflected his ambivalence. At the Democratic Leadership Council's annual meeting in Cleveland, it was Clinton who generated the buzz with a tough speech challenging party orthodoxy. He said that too many in the middle class "have not trusted us in national elections to defend our national interest abroad, to put their values in our social policy at home, or to take their tax money and spend it with discipline." Voters needed a "new choice," he said, based on what would become his keystone campaign themes: opportunity, responsibility, and community. Gore, the closing speaker, was considered the biggest disappointment of the conference. He called for Democrats to get over the "Vietnam Syndrome" but, unlike Clinton, backed away from issuing any kind of challenge to the party on domestic policy. He was also panned for his stupefying delivery, the result of his refusal, one former aide said, to practice long enough the night before. Several fund-raisers who attended his June appearance at an IMPAC meeting said his comments were similarly flat.

Only once that spring did Gore connect with an important party audience, at the Louisiana Democratic Party convention, where he gave a heartfelt after-dinner speech thanking Louisianans for their kindness during his son's 1989 surgery at a New Orleans hospital. But the larger impression, friends said, was that the fire was gone. "I think he kind of lost his stomach for it," said Representative Norm Dicks.

Still, Gore couldn't let the idea go. His innate caution told him to hold back, but as the economy, and with it Bush's numbers, began to sag, the race became more attractive. Gore's political brain trust was gung-ho: Peter Knight, Johnny Hayes, Nate Landow, all wanted to see him run. At a staff picnic over the Fourth of July weekend at his Tennessee farm, an aide encountered Gore alone in his kitchen, searching for a soft drink but clearly preoccupied with something else. Gore said he probably needed to make a few remarks to his guests.

"Should I say something about the presidential campaign?" he asked.

"Anything you want to say?" the aide replied.

"Yeah, I can announce I'm going to run," he said jokingly. "I don't know, I don't know. Everybody keeps asking me about it. I'm going to have to do something about this soon."

Back outside a few minutes later, he gathered the staff and their families and thanked them for coming. "I know a lot of you have had on your mind what I'm going to do about running for president," Gore said. Tipper, standing next to him, seemed to freeze for a second, one guest recalled, "like she had no idea what he was going to say." She was braced for another career bombshell, but Gore hung back, saying only that he would decide soon.

In August he took the family to a houseboat on Center Hill Lake near Carthage, where he had water-skied with Donna Armistead as a teenager. The Gore faithful were on full alert. Knight, on a family vacation in Vancouver, kept an ear cocked to the phone in his hotel and was ready to fly home if it rang. It was no silent retreat. Aides were peppered with calls that week as Gore took a last hard look at the electoral and financial calculus. His voice was harried and sometimes testy; conversations began without even a "Hello" or "How are you?" "*Thizzzzal*" ("This is Al"), he would begin. "I just want to know these numbers." He would call back at four. *Click.*

He returned to shore, unshaven and grumpy, with a decision not to run. As word trickled back about the family's floating deliberations, it seemed that Gore was leaning toward it but that Tipper had balked. "He was not happy," said one aide. "It was not a joyous thing. It was hard, hard to give up the political opportunity." Gore said he still believed that a "properly run campaign would have an excellent chance of winning next year." And no, he added, he was not interested in being vice president.

As Al Gore watched the campaign from the sidelines in early 1992, he knew he had let a huge opportunity slip by. Bill Clinton was trailing George Bush in the polls and fighting for his life in New Hampshire after revelations about his relationship with Gennifer Flowers and misleading statements about his draft record. Almost out of nowhere, Ross Perot's angry anti-Washington insurgency was turning the race into a legitimate three-way contest. "I'd like to be president, and I may never have a better chance to run than the one I passed up this time," he told CNN's Larry King on February 3.

Gore insisted that he was comfortable with his decision, but the second thoughts weren't hard for others to discern. He wanted to be the first southern baby boomer through the turnstiles in presidential politics, and it stung to watch Bill Clinton slip in ahead of him. At a dinner in April, Gore talked up Perot's chances with such enthusiasm that it seemed to one of his table companions that he was rooting for him to take votes from Clinton and help Bush slip back into office for a second term, leaving the White House open in 1996.

Gore and Clinton scarcely knew one another before 1992. Their only personal connection was the wary eye each occasionally cast toward the other as a potential rival. They were "two large male dogs put in a fenced area, establishing their territory," as one Tennessee aide to Gore described them. On paper, they seemed to match up evenly enough — forty-something southern Baptists with Ivy League degrees, sons of a new moderate South. Both men called themselves New Democrats and were active in the centrist Democratic Leadership Council (DLC). But the DLC's theology probably ran more heavily in Clinton's blood. He had served as the organization's national chairman, and his state-house roots drew him more naturally to the DLC's devolutionism. Gore knew all the moderate words and music, but he was also a Washington lifer and two-term senator whose DNA retained the imprint of the party's more liberal congressional wing.

Their personal paths to power could not have been more different. Both were family stars, golden boys filled with a sense of inevitability about their future. But where Gore was overwhelmed by a father figure, Clinton grew up searching for one to replace the traveling salesman who died in a car crash three months before he was born. As a teenager in Hot Springs, Arkansas, he had to be both a son and a family protector, stepping between his mother and an abusive, alcoholic stepfather. While Gore's opportunities in life were assured as a scion of the Washington aristocracy, Clinton was the product of an American meritocracy that lifted him from Arkansas to Oxford to Yale Law School.

Under pressure, each has played games with the truth. But where Clinton's lies have been those of self-protection and survival, Gore's have by and large been ones of self-aggrandizement and glorification. Both strove as young men to retain, as Clinton told his ROTC commander, "political viability within the system." Gore joined the army to safeguard his father's political future and hold the door open to his own. Clinton didn't want to go, but he also didn't want to endanger his future by resisting the draft. His circumvention of military service was a sneak preview of all the now-familiar traits: deception, manipulation, a sense of obligation only to himself. He wangled an ROTC deferment from the University of Arkansas just before his July 1969 induction deadline, then broke the commitment and had himself classified 1-A when it became clear that the war was winding down and the impending draft lottery provided a chance for escape. The gamble paid off — his birthday was the 311th date drawn, out of 366, in the first lottery that December.

Even before the political careers of both men began, an important theme of their life scripts had already been written: Clinton had a knack for slipping out of tight spots, whereas Gore did not. Even if Gore had decided, like Clinton, to stave off induction and take his chances in the lottery, it would have done him no good. His number would have been 30, and unless he had pulled a last-minute deferment out of the hat, he would definitely have been drafted.

They shared a passion for the details of policy but approached politics from different places in the heart. For Gore it was a necessary chore, for Clinton an object of love. One enjoyed solitude, the other had a compulsive need for people. They were large men, both over six feet tall, but Clinton's raw physicality filled every room and dominated every encounter. He drew some life-sustaining force from the crowds, reading their moods and adjusting in a split second. One on one, his eyes locked in and always made the other person feel, if only for a stretch of seconds, that he or she was the most important person in the room. Gore often made the other party feel as if *he* were the most important person in the room.

Gore flew to Little Rock in 1987 looking for Clinton's endorsement in the presidential primaries, although his real agenda was simply to keep Clinton from endorsing fellow governor Mike Dukakis. He told Clinton that only southern moderates had any hope of keeping the Democratic coalition together, and that his own success would open the door for Clinton. They were allies, not rivals, he suggested, working toward the same goals. How much of this Gore or Clinton actually believed isn't clear. Gore didn't win Clinton's endorsement, but his appeal seemed to put him in a more prominent spot on Clinton's screen.

That same autumn in Nashville, after a speech to Vanderbilt's Institute for Public Policy, Clinton was up late in his Hermitage Hotel suite, talking politics, as always, with a group put together by a friend from Yale Law School, Nashville attorney Byron Trauger. When Trauger introduced him to Gore's aide Steve Owens, Clinton "locked in" and spent the rest of the evening grilling him on every aspect of Gore's presidential campaign. "He wanted to know everything," Owens recalled. "How Al was holding up, how he was being received." They talked until past 1:30 A.M., driving off everyone else who had been invited. Owens came away with the strong sense that while Clinton may have been a Dukakis guy in 1988, he was measuring the future to see whether it was big enough for him and Gore. In the winter of 1992 mutual friends passed Clinton an early copy of *Earth in the Balance,* which he found enormously impressive, although not enough to give environmental issues a prominent place in his campaign. It did result, a Gore aide said, in "one fairly long discussion about the policy implications of the book" and clearly solidified Gore's place on any serious list of vice presidential possibilities.

Clinton's admiration for Gore was not shared by members of his campaign brain trust. As the spring of 1992 came and the nomination finally appeared secure, lieutenants in the Little Rock war room started putting their favorite names into play for vice presidential consideration. Colin Powell, then still a closet Republican, was at the top of everyone's wish list. If he was available, advisers said, all bets were off. Other choices reflected the conventional formulation for a running mate — someone who brought geographic or ideological balance to the ticket. James Carville and Paul Begala touted an old client, Senator Harris Wofford of Pennsylvania, a Catholic northeasterner with Washington experience dating back to the Kennedy administration. George Stephanopoulos put in bids for New York Governor Mario Cuomo and his ex-boss Dick Gephardt to shore up labor and the party's liberal wing. Only pollster Stan Greenberg made a case for Gore, precisely because of his similarities to Clinton, said one former top aide. He saw Gore as reinforcing all that the campaign was trying, so far unsuccessfully, to establish about Clinton as a new kind of Democrat.

Clinton was listening, but not closely. He put the selection process in the hands of a search committee headed by Los Angeles attorney and Democratic Party eminence Warren Christopher. In April Clinton gave Christopher a list of forty names — both the usual (Gore, Bradley, Nunn, Cuomo, Senator Bob Kerrey of Nebraska) and the unusual (journalist Bill Moyers, Apple computer head John Sculley) suspects. Gore was reluctant when Christopher asked whether he would be interested, but he eventually said yes. He was in the midst of preparing for the Earth Summit in Rio that June and wasn't lusting for the job. But he also felt that, if the party's putative nominee wanted to put his name on a list, then the appropriate answer was yes.

Within a month the other possibility as tantalizing to the Clintonites as Powell — Mario Cuomo — took himself out of the picture. The field had been winnowed quickly to five: Senator Bob Graham of electoral-vote-rich Florida; Wofford, the Carville-Begala favorite; Kerrey, a Vietnam War hero; Representative Lee Hamilton of Indiana, in the mix again in 1992; and Gore.

The choice came at a perilous moment for Clinton; he desperately needed to change the dynamics of the race. Although he had survived Gennifer Flowers and the draft, he was showing serious weakness on the eve of the Democratic National Convention. Greenberg's polling had him in a statistical dead heat with Bush and Perot (32 percent for each of them, 29 for Clinton), but the numbers were also fraught with voter misgivings. Sixty percent of those surveyed rejected the statement that Clinton "makes you feel confident." Sixty-five percent thought he was "too political." Many Democrats and anti-Bush voters were holding back or going with Perot. "The convention must change that. . . . The convention must convey new images," Greenberg wrote in a memo to Clinton.

Shortly before 10:00 on Monday evening, June 30, Gore slipped into a Jeep Cherokee driven by Clinton staffer Mark Gearan for a ride from his Senate office across town to the Washington Hilton, where he was the first of the finalists to have his one-on-one with the nominee-apparent. It was an odd reversal of fortune from their Little Rock meeting, but if that was a source of awkwardness, it didn't remain one for long. By midnight the two were comparing favorite economists, and a conversation scheduled to last for one hour ran for three.

In the days that followed, both men said they came away from their session with a good feeling. Each also took a measure of the other that reflected his own particular needs. Although every presidential nomi-

nee says he wants a running mate who could be president in a heartbeat, aides say the premature death of his father gave Clinton's declaration special resonance. "I could die," he said to one top campaign aide.

But there was another, more fundamental dynamic at work. Gore
was not only presidential material, Clinton told one senior aide, but
Gore reminded him, in both intellect and temperament, of his most
important political partner, his wife. He saw in Gore Hillary's stead-
fastness, the same determination in pursuit of an idea, the same stub-
bornness. And although Clinton never said it explicitly, he must also
have sensed in the dutiful son from Tennessee a capacity for the kind
of loyalty he had received from Hillary, a potential for the same endur-
ance and stoicism, the likelihood that there would never be an unhappy noise.

He continued to meet with the other finalists, but Clinton's body
language suggested that Gore was on a short-list of one. In the final
days before the decision, he reached out to those certain to affirm his
judgment. In early July he called Martin Peretz and asked who he
thought would be the best vice presidential candidate. Peretz, quite
unsurprisingly, said it was no secret that he would like to see Gore at
the top of the ticket, but that he could certainly make an indispensable vice president. "This is a man who will never knife you in the
back," he told Clinton. "This is not a gossiper. This is someone whose
own views about personal honor would guarantee that you would not
have someone who was cooking up trouble against you."

Gore felt even more positive about the prospect of joining Clinton,
who was offering him a genuine partnership, Gore told associates.
"We really connected," he said to a close friend over dinner in early
July. Moreover, he was convinced that Clinton was going to pick
him, a conclusion that his dining companion, a political consultant,
thought was just short of delusional according to all the conventional
calculations of age, region, and ideology. Besides, he asked, why would
Gore even want an office whose occupant inevitably becomes a national joke?

Gore was convinced that he could make a difference in the job, but
it went beyond that. The fact was that he felt increasingly stifled and a
little bit bored in the Senate. His interests and sensibilities were never
really in legislation, and though the vice presidency was no power

center, he might have a better chance of pushing his environmental agenda from the West Wing than as one of a hundred senators. "I'd never heard him say, 'I don't like the Senate anymore, I've lost interest in it, I'm bored, I've got to move on,' but that was certainly my feeling," said Roy Neel.

The vice presidency was also the job his father had sought, and getting on the ticket would be a family victory, a closing-out of unfinished business, and would lift him one step closer to the ultimate prize. Even defeat would not be a calamity — either way, he would automatically be positioned as a major player for 1996 or 2000. As for concerns about the health of his wife and children, Gore decided that time had healed many problems and that a summer-fall sprint to November was a lot less grueling than a slog through the primary calendar.

Another, unspoken line of reasoning hung over dinner that night, his companion thought. Just as Clinton may have seen the chance to acquire another partner of unswerving loyalty, Gore sensed a potential president over whom he might wield unusual influence, even control. Although he respected Clinton's intellect, it was also hard to ignore the man's lack of discipline and resolve. Gore could, in essence, be the steel in Clinton's spine, and he could move some of his agenda in the bargain. "He may have sensed it pretty early," his friend said. "Taken a measure of the guy and said, 'You know, I can say no, he can't. I can pull the trigger, he can't.'"

On the evening of July 8, Bill Clinton sat down in a conference room at the governor's mansion in Little Rock with Hillary, Christopher, and aides Mark Gearan and Bruce Lindsey to finalize the choice. In the last hours there had been a new flutter of sentiment for trying one last time to interest Cuomo, but it was too late to put up someone who hadn't been through the lawyers' background scrub. There was also great fondness for Graham, but all the signs pointed to Gore. Naming another southerner didn't bother Clinton, and it was not totally unprecedented. In his great comeback win against Thomas Dewey in 1948, Missourian Harry Truman had gone with Alben Barkley of Kentucky. This time, in a three-way race, with Perot and Bush competing for conservative whites, the black vote in the South would be critical.

The Gores just happened to be awake when the phone rang at their

Tennessee farm at about 11:30 P.M. "I just think you could be a wonderful president," he told Gore. It was done, and arrangements were made to fly to Little Rock the next morning. Gore didn't call his folks, assuming that they were asleep. But on the other side of the Caney Fork, the lights were still burning. Albert and Pauline were up past 4:00 A.M., watching it all as it broke on CNN.

If there was a pivotal moment in the 1992 campaign, it may have been the scene on the veranda at the governor's mansion the following morning. As the two men and their young families came out, the image resonated with an energy that even Gore's boosters couldn't have predicted. Just like that, it seemed, a generational page had been turned. It wasn't merely Gore's assets that buoyed Clinton — the foreign policy background, the military record, the placid personal life, "the dowry" for this political marriage, as Maureen Dowd and Michael Kelly described it — but his liabilities as well. Gore's formality and rigidity added reassuring increments of maturity to Clinton, anchored him somehow. "If you're inclined to believe that Clinton is a sixties' liberal, you can see it in his face, in his soft features," said one Clinton strategist. As for Gore, "the man just looks like he ought to be a conservative." The next day Clinton proudly compared his choice to George Bush's in New Orleans four years earlier, when he introduced the country to Dan Quayle. "This is my first decision, that was George Bush's first decision. I think if we're evaluated on them, I should be elected president."

No one was happier than the old senator on the farm in Carthage. "I'll take that call!" he said when Gore phoned him after the Little Rock unveiling. Albert Gore offered this capsule review of his son's first outing as a vice presidential candidate: "Hello, honey. It was wonderful. Nothing wooden about it!" The story was playing out as he and Pauline had hoped. Their son was on his way to the White House. "We raised him for it," Albert exulted a few days later.

Not everyone was quite as jubilant. Despite Gore's official line — that his family had healed significantly in the year since his decision to back away from his own race — there were signs that Tipper remained a reluctant warrior. Their Nashville friend John Warnecke, although estranged from Gore, spoke to her periodically, including the week before the vice presidential announcement. He said she was "adamant" that her husband not go on the ticket. "She wanted him home with the kids," Warnecke said. Speaking on the phone with Wren Wirth, the wife of Gore's Senate friend and rival, she sounded more reconciled than gung-ho: "Well," she said, "here we go on our way to try to save the world."

As for Pauline Gore, her earlier qualms about Clinton's character seemed confirmed by the winter's bimbo eruptions. But if it gave her son any hesitation about going to political war with the man from Hope, he didn't let on. Three weeks later, on July 30, Diane Sawyer asked Gore on ABC's *Prime Time Live:* "A friend of mine said to me that one of the things you did have to weigh was would something else come out. Did you ask him about it?"

Gore said, "You're asking do I trust him? I do."

17

Double Date

W IN OR LOSE, 1992 was an opportunity for Al Gore to reintroduce himself to a national audience as a more appealing version of the wooden, self-serious, young know-it-all it saw four years earlier. He intended to use his vice presidential nomination at the Democratic convention in New York to signal that he was a changed man, humbled by the near-death of his son, capable of learning from mistakes, comfortable in his own skin.

This effort to out the "Real Al" had been under way before the accident. After the collapse of his 1988 presidential campaign, friends and supporters began urging him to let the public see more of the private Gore they knew. What evolved was essentially a two-pronged strategy to humanize his image. Publicly, Gore developed a series of gags and one-liners poking fun at himself ("How can you tell Al Gore from a roomful of Secret Service agents? Gore is the stiff one," or "Al Gore is so stiff the racks buy the suits off of him"). Just as Pauline had tried to soften up Albert's image, Tipper did her part, assuring voters that her husband really did know how to relax and enjoy himself. Sometimes she tried a bit too hard, once telling a Nashville reporter that her famously formal husband doubled over in fits of laughter on Sunday evenings watching *America's Funniest Home Videos* with the family. "He will roll on the floor longer than any of us," she insisted.

Behind the scenes, he worked with speech coaches and even a choreographer — "a serious ballet type," he told a Senate colleague in the early 1990s — to help him relax in front of crowds. According to the senator, the dancer encouraged Gore to visualize himself rehearsing in front of an empty theater when he spoke, so that he would not feel as if he were being observed. "Never be performing, don't ever think of yourself as performing," as Gore described the advice to his colleague. "Only think of yourself as rehearsing."

The theme music accompanying his entrance when he made his July 16 acceptance speech to the Democratic National Convention at Madison Square Garden — Paul Simon's "You Can Call Me Al" — underscored the notion of a more informal, accessible Gore. He started his address by bashing George Bush and praising Bill Clinton's gubernatorial record on welfare reform, education, and taxes. He also tried to fashion himself as the Man from Carthage to Clinton's Man from Hope, calling his family's Tennessee home "a place where people do know about it when you're born and care about it when you die."

But Gore was eager to show that he had been chastened and sensitized by his midlife journey. He vowed after 1988 to talk more about things that mattered to him, and he made a description of his son's car accident — much of it adapted directly from *Earth in the Balance* — the speech's emotional center of gravity. "When you've seen your reflection in the empty stare of a boy waiting for his second breath of life, you realize that we were not put here on earth to look out for our needs alone," Gore told the hushed audience. His central point was an inspiring one: we are all part of something larger than ourselves. But what was candid and moving when tucked into a serious four-hundred-page book came across as vaguely exploitative from the plywood podium of a nominating convention. And Gore went one metaphor too far with his son's plight. Just as he linked his own spiritual crisis to the world's environmental decline in *Earth in the Balance,* so did Albert III's brush with death speak to the perilous state of the republic. "And you will see that our democracy is lying there in the gutter," Gore said, "waiting for us to give it a second breath of life."

Gore would make periodic attempts to show a more human side to voters, but his efforts often seemed calculating and overreaching and usually served only to refocus attention on his essential formality. There was also an ambivalence about his efforts to master the requirements of political theater. He appeared to be committed to improving his performance, but it was also as if he found something unseemly about using emotional appeals to convey important political ideas. Gore had always been capable of rousing a crowd at election time, especially when he was on the attack, serving up partisan "red meat." In his two vice presidential campaigns, Real Al, demonstrative, authentic, and funny, popped up from time to time, always prompting a round of stories about the new, more relaxed Gore who had finally come into his own as a campaigner. But Old Al, stiff and monotonic, inevitably returned from hiatus. It was in part a reflection of his father's formality, but also a reaction to what Bob Squier called "this constant, constant assault by people around him to loosen up and share himself with the public."

Gore commands far more control over which Al steps to the microphone than he generally lets on. Two weeks before the 1996 election, New Hampshire Democrat Arnie Arnesen, a former gubernatorial and congressional candidate, was riding with him to a rally at a Londonderry high school gym when she urged him to put more energy into his speeches. "You're not perky enough," she told Gore, whom she had known for several years. Arnesen spoke before Gore and did her best to warm up the audience. For the first few minutes of his speech, he lumbered along as Old Al, before suddenly shifting. "His whole body seemed to change," said Arnesen, who was sitting behind him as he took hold of the crowd, which was roaring by the time he finished. As Gore stepped away from the podium, he looked over his shoulder at Arnesen. "Perky enough?" he asked.

The most important development of the 1992 Democratic convention actually took place in Dallas, the same day that Gore and Clinton delivered their acceptance speeches. Ross Perot withdrew from the race, in part, he said, because the Democratic Party had "revitalized" itself in New York.

As the news broke on television, Clinton reached Gore by phone and teased him. "You were my choice in a three-person race," he said. "But in a two-person race I've got to go with Cuomo." Suddenly the news was all good for the Clintonites. Gore's entrance, Perot's exit, and an adroitly scripted convention all combined to vault the new ticket into more than a twenty-point lead over George Bush. Although Perot would return, and their margin would wax and wane, Clinton and Gore never relinquished the lead they claimed in July.

Before 1992 vice presidential candidates were usually sent on their way after the summer convention, dispatched to fund-raising dinners and backwater media markets with orders to stay on message and out of trouble. But Gore was no usual vice presidential candidate, and his first few hours with Clinton set a tone that remained more or less constant through his two terms in office: he insisted that he be kept close to the action. He and Tipper were originally scheduled to ride along with the Clintons for only the first two days of the weeklong, thousand-mile, postconvention bus tour. But once under way, Gore insisted on sticking around. "He dug his heels in," said one senior Clinton aide. "He wanted the proximity to Clinton." Fortunately, most of the Clinton high command, which discussed the issue on a conference call, agreed. The bus caravan, ginned up by the Clinton campaign manager David Wilhelm to carry some post-nomination momentum into the battleground states of the Northeast and industrial heartland (New Jersey, Pennsylvania, Ohio, Illinois, and Missouri), became something utterly new and fresh: presidential politics as an extended double date.

The guys looked like fugitives from a Dockers ad, kibbitzing at the microphone, tossing a football, and the girls like reunited sorority sisters, bragging on their men, trading stories about kids. As the road show wound through cities and towns long neglected by national campaigns, it tapped some sort of pent-up desire to celebrate what was good and ennobling about politics, producing stunningly large and effusive crowds that waited hours in the heat for the chronically late entourage to appear. When they pulled into Vandalia, Illinois, long after dark, ten thousand people sang "God Bless America" and lit candles. "October crowds in July," exulted Clinton, feeding on the adulation like it was mother's milk. Expertly planned by Hollywood producer Mort Engelberg (who brought the world *Smokey and the Bandit*), the tour was a movable feast for television and still photographers, filled with scenic crossroads and small-town tableaus. And like any summer box-office success, the sequels followed quickly, with subsequent bus jaunts through Texas and Georgia laid on to keep the pairs together.

As pure political message, it was the trifecta. Gore's continued presence at Clinton's side was a tacit reminder of Republicans' embarrassment over Dan Quayle, who was rarely allowed near George Bush once the campaign was on. As the robust, youthful foursome plunged into crowds at "unscheduled" roadside stops, the incumbent's age and isolation were only reinforced. And the palpable warmth between the Gores helped to fuzz over lingering reminders of the rocky marital past at the top of the ticket.

The two nominees continued to complement each other uncannily: Clinton all instinct and impulse, riffing in his speeches, feeling the mood of the crowd, talking himself hoarse. He was terrible in the morning events, layered over by allergies and mental cobwebs, and gained strength as the day went on, hitting his stride after 4:00 P.M. Gore was linear and orderly, out of the gates after seven hours' sleep and a morning run to flag the message of the day with workmanlike efficiency every time. He was eager to show his stuff but also careful to defer to his new commander. "Could I add a brief note to that?" he regularly asked when on stage with Clinton. "Can I say something about that, too?" Once, running over his own time, he apologized to Clinton. "Too long, sorry," he mouthed.

Aides to all four bubbled that the rapport was the real deal, as good inside the bus as it was for the cameras. Roy Neel said Clinton and Gore were "like two guys at their twentieth reunion who didn't really know each other in school but just discovered they had a lot in common. So much so that they decided to take their wives and go away on a road trip." Some of this was genuine, some was spin, some simply a reflection of the staff's relief that mommy and daddy got along — that this historically awkward union, one usually framed by suspicion, resentment, or indifference, was not a rolling disaster.

But the road-show hype also papered over real tensions, as two seasoned political organizations tried to mesh gears at full speed. To many of the Clintonites, Gore was an unwelcome new player in a campaign already balkanized by internal rivalries and competition for the attentions of the boss. Any running mate would have faced the same dynamic, but many Clinton aides, like former Gephardt hand Stephanopoulos, took an especially dim view of Gore — for both his conduct in 1988 and the suspicion that his own simmering White House ambitions would keep him from ever being a completely loyal number two.

Gore's overweening sense of entitlement, generated by the dowry he brought with him and his pedigree as a presidential candidate in his own right, only aggravated matters. He expected to be treated less like the tenant occupying the bottom floor of the ticket than a peer of Clinton's, meaning plenty of joint appearances and lots of face time in the campaign's television spots. That expectation didn't sit well with the campaign scheduling czar and Hillary intimate Susan Thomases, who tried to bounce him from the bus. "He and Susan had a very sharp interchange very early on in the campaign about scheduling," said one former senior Clinton aide. "There were very harsh words back and forth." To ensure that his interests were looked after, Gore dispatched Roy Neel to Clinton headquarters in Little Rock.

Underneath the friction lay an attitude of exceptionalism among the Goreheads, the feeling that their man may have been only the vice presidential nominee but was destined to one day be a better president than Clinton. Later, as Gore labored to distance himself from the serial scandals and misadventures in the Clinton White House, the murmured sentiments grew louder. Pauline Gore, who had long harbored reservations about Clinton's character, made a point of telling *The New Yorker*'s Peter Boyer in 1994: "Bill came up in a *very* provincial atmosphere. And even though he went to Yale, and he went to Oxford, you don't undo or move out of that provincial atmosphere that has influenced you in your early life." Neel, a Gore man who also worked as Clinton's deputy chief of staff, explained that Gore was "less of an instinctive politician than a thoughtful and thorough one. There's a big difference. Clinton's an instinctive politician. Instinctive politicians seduce the public, but they inevitably make monumental mistakes, because they tend to rely only on their instincts. Thoughtful, careful politicians sometimes appear plodding, and they are not so seductive. Masses don't fall in love with them. But they make far fewer mistakes, and they end up being superior at governance." In Neel's estimation, Gore would one day rank with a Harry Truman or Woodrow Wilson.

By the trip's end in St. Louis, Gore was putting his imprint on the campaign's message. As a huge crowd sweltered outside the city library, he was in Clinton's hotel suite making the case for a strong stand against Bush administration policy in the Balkans and calling for military action against Serbian dictator Slobodan Milosevic. Several days later Clinton was criticizing Bush for his failure to get tough with Milosevic. "[Gore] was strongly driven by a very human sense of outrage about what was happening to people in Bosnia," said Anthony Lake, who helped Clinton on foreign policy during the campaign and went on to serve as the administration's first national security adviser. "More than anybody else in the campaign, he was pushing Bosnia as an issue and helped put it on the agenda."

By early fall Stan Greenberg's numbers suggested that Gore was more than just a smart choice that contrasted favorably with Bush's selection of Quayle. In focus groups, voters regularly volunteered Gore as one of the good things about Clinton's candidacy. "Gore's thermometer ratings are consistently higher than Clinton's," Greenberg wrote in a September 22 memo to Clinton. Not only did he strengthen the impression that Clinton represented change, but he was a highly reassuring figure in his own right. "Gore is an escape hatch for those who want to vote against Bush but have doubts about Clinton," said Greenberg. "He allows people to feel good about their change vote (while ignoring or minimizing their questions about Clinton)." He recommended that some ads be produced showing Gore and Clinton together, and that the phrase "Clinton-Gore" be used more prominently in other spots.

As Gore made the transition from senator to running mate, the window of political and psychological insight that had opened for him at midlife seemed to narrow. He had adopted the idioms of therapy and recovery for his rhetoric, as evidenced by his convention speech. But the angry impatience with politics as usual that animated *Earth in the Balance* was muffled. Accepting the vice presidential nomination meant playing by the old rules he claimed to have renounced. "New Age sensibility demands a search for a more honest way to live," Katherine Boo wrote in 1993. "Old Washington sensibility demands the sublimation of that endeavor."

For Gore, that meant accepting that he now answered to a presidential candidate who was largely indifferent to his most deeply felt issue. Clinton admired *Earth in the Balance,* but he and his advisers were nervous about how its mix of eco-spiritualism and big-government prescriptives would be used as a weapon by the Republicans.

Gore didn't run away from what he wrote, but he carefully distanced himself from it as he assumed the traditional duties of the vice presidential candidate, reiterating the carefully scripted lines of the day. To be sure, the Clinton-Gore campaign had an environmental program — increasing automobile fuel efficiency, designating the Arctic National Wildlife Refuge as a wilderness area to stop offshore drilling, lowering carbon dioxide emissions to 1990 levels by 2000. But when Gore spoke about the environment, he used generalities and one-liners about the "false choice" posed by the Bush administration between environmental protection and economic growth. His restraint didn't stop the Bushies from using the superheated prose of *Earth in the Balance* against him. Dan Quayle called him "hysterical" and "bizarre" on the environment. Bush famously ridiculed him as "Ozone Man" and asked, "What kind of people are we dealing with here?"

Gore sent mixed signals in response to the attacks. On one occasion, the politician who claimed to be tired of finger-to-the-wind timidity conceded that he might well have toned down the book if he had known he was going to be on the ticket. "To be honest, I know I would have been more vulnerable to the pressures to be a little more timid . . . [but] I'm glad it's out there, and I'm glad I wrote it."

Most of the time, however, he protested suggestions that he had backed away. "I'm not pulling my punches at all," he said, munching on a soft chocolate chip cookie one afternoon in late September as his bus rolled from Columbus to Albany, Georgia. "I have responsibilities as part of this ticket to talk about a broad range of issues, and I'm doing the best I can with it." Had he ever asked Clinton to endorse the ideas in his book? "The overall goals I outlined in the book are ones that Bill Clinton agrees with," Gore said coolly. "I have not asked him to endorse the specific measures which I recommend as the best ways to reach those goals."

Gore instead threw himself into the "attack dog" role historically filled by vice presidential nominees. In September he delivered a scathing critique of the pre–Gulf War Iraq policy of the Reagan and Bush administrations, charging that loan guarantees and "dual use" technology exports in the 1980s helped Saddam build the war machine that American soldiers had to fight in 1991. The charges were nothing new and grew out of the American "tilt" toward Iraq initiated by Ronald Reagan to prop Saddam up in his war against Iran. But U.S. efforts to bolster the dictator had persisted well after the end of the Iran-Iraq conflict.

Gore drew most of his material from press reports and information developed from an investigation by House Banking Committee Chairman Henry Gonzalez. But he packaged the September 29 address to the Center for National Policy as a major event, delivering a thickly researched term paper of a speech complete with 56 footnotes in the text released to reporters. Gore listed 162 items licensed for sale to Iraq

despite their potential nuclear applications, including powerful super-
computers for missile testing and components for use in the manufac-
ture of Scud missile casings. Moreover, he said, the administration dis-
regarded warnings from various government agencies that Saddam
was continuing to cooperate with terrorists and working to develop
nuclear, chemical, and biological weapons capacity. Bush's record on
Iraq "provides a deeply disturbing look at a blatant disregard for brutal terrorism, a dangerous blindness to the murderous ambitions of a
despot, and what certainly appears to be an ongoing effort to hide the
facts from the American people," Gore said. "Coddling tyrants is a
hallmark of the Bush foreign policy."

One of the most incendiary allegations Gore picked up as part of
what became known as "Iraqgate" was that the Bush administration
helped Saddam buy arms with $1 billion in loan guarantees earmarked
for the purchase of U.S. farm products. He also cited reports that the
White House might have interfered with a Justice Department investigation into billions more in illegal loans made to Iraq by the Atlanta
branch of Italy's Banca Nazionale del Lavoro (BNL). Eventually BNL's
bank manager, Christopher Drogoul, pled guilty to more than sixty
counts of fraud. No hard evidence ever surfaced of a Bush cover-up,
despite multiple Justice Department reviews.

On most occasions, however, Gore stuck with the campaign's basic
economic message: the Bush administration had managed the country for the benefit of the privileged few. "If George Bush went out to
Hollywood and made a movie, he would have to call it *Honey, I
Shrunk the Economy*," began one favorite riff in his basic stump speech.
The president's veto of the Family Medical Leave Act was a familiar
target, starting with a description of the people he had met at Johns
Hopkins during Albert's recovery. Although it was something of a
stretch, comparing his predicament with the sacrifices made by working families to care for a sick child, crowds always responded exuber-
antly. "Some of them weren't as fortunate as I was, in working for people who understood the need for a little time off, and some of them
lost their jobs," he said in a steadily rising voice one September afternoon on the banks of the Delaware River near Bristol, Pennsylvania.
"Some of them had to sell their homes so that they could somehow
come up with the money to be there at a time of family crisis. I know
what this is like, and I know what it feels like. And I'm telling you

there's no way George Bush can look the people of this country straight in the eyes and say he's for family values while he vetoes the family leave bill. That's hypocrisy!"

In his usual windup, Gore went back and forth with the crowd:

"Do you want four more years of trickle-down economics?"

"No!"

"Four more years of read-my-lips?"

"No!"

"Four more years of a phony education president?"

"No!"

"Four more years of a counterfeit commitment to the environment?"

"No!"

"Do you believe it's time for Bush and Quayle to go?"

"Yes!"

Despite his understudy status, Gore seemed to enjoy himself more than he had during any campaign in years. The usual pressures of carrying a campaign were gone, and it drew some of his dormant goofiness to the surface. "I feeeeeeel good!" he sang one day from the front of the plane. When he wasn't channeling James Brown, he would plant his feet on a plastic tray to "aisle surf" from first-class back to the tail as his charter took off. Asked at a September 22 breakfast with Washington reporters when the Clinton-Gore ticket would take a position on the hotly disputed North American Free Trade Agreement (NAFTA), Gore paused for a second and then said solemnly, "I guess this is as good a place to announce it as any." Three dozen journalists leaned forward in their seats for an unexpected side order of news with their eggs. "No," he said, "just kidding." (Clinton and Gore eventually endorsed the pact.)

Gore's parents were having a high time as well, doing their own seven-week bus tour through the South. "All Albert wanted was for someone to say 'go,'" said Pauline. "He was in seventh heaven." The children didn't adjust quite as easily, chafing initially under the new blanket of security. Karenna, who was now nineteen, waived her Secret Service protection when she returned to Harvard in the fall. Albert said she hated the idea "that some Secret Service man has to follow her down the hall to the shower." The other kids, Kristin, Sarah, and Albert III (fifteen, thirteen, and ten, respectively), also bridled, until a crude explosive device was found in a Fort Collins high school gym shortly before Gore was scheduled to speak in late October. "When the children realized that except for the Secret Service their father could have been killed, this drove home" the need for protection, the senator said. "Now they're reconciled to it."

Gore's most uncomfortable moment as a running mate came in the aftermath of his debate with Dan Quayle. The embattled vice president was determined to prove he was not a drag on the Republican ticket, despite the conclusion of Bush's own pollster that there would be a potential net gain of four to six percentage points from dumping him. He went all out to prepare, arming himself with attack lines, put-downs, and a take-no-prisoners attitude. Senator Warren Rudman, the hard-boiled ex-Marine from New Hampshire, role-played Gore in the rehearsals and offered Quayle a surprising scouting report about his competitor from watching him in the Senate — that he rattled easily. "He wasn't a fluid debater," said Rudman. "He wasn't a bad debater, but if you hit him with something he wasn't prepared for, like a lot of people he didn't handle it well. I thought you could fluster him with a few things. I told him [Quayle] I would go after him very hard, very tough, hit him with his book, hit him with some votes that weren't supportable. I thought he didn't handle that type of thing very well." Other advisers, mainly chief of staff Bill Kristol and press secretary David Beckwith, also urged Quayle to take the fight to Gore by forcing him at every chance to become a character witness for Clinton.

The October 13 meeting on the Georgia Tech campus in Atlanta was a shrill and ragged affair (it had "all the intellectual reasoning of the Jack Dempsey–Gene Tunney fight," said *National Journal*), a tiresome ninety minutes of interrupted answers and no-I-didn't-yes-you-did exchanges about abortion, school choice, taxes, and health care. Caught in the crossfire, and lending the proceedings a kind of befuddled dignity, was Perot's running mate, Admiral James Stockdale, the former Vietnam POW and Congressional Medal of Honor winner who offered the most memorable opening statement of any debate: "Who am I? Why am I here?"

Gore set the tone with a rhetorical triple-gainer. He began with a tribute to Stockdale that tacitly reminded the audience of Quayle's wartime stint in the Indiana National Guard. "Those of us who served in Vietnam looked at you as a national hero," he said. Then he freshened up memories of Lloyd Bentsen's show-stopping put-down in his 1988 debate with Quayle ("Senator, you're no Jack Kennedy"). "Mr. Vice President . . . Dan, if I may," said Gore, adding a shade of disrespect, "I'll make you a deal this evening — if you don't try to compare George Bush to Harry Truman [his 1948 comeback against Thomas Dewey had become a source of solace to the Bushies], I won't compare you to Jack Kennedy." Laughter filled the auditorium. Gore finished by reminding viewers that to reelect the aging Bush (who had had health problems) was to place Quayle a heartbeat from the presidency. It was "worth remembering," Gore said, that Truman assumed the job when Franklin Roosevelt died in Georgia, with war in the Pacific still raging. That was "only one of many occasions when fate thrust a vice president into the Oval Office in a time of crisis," he cautioned.

Quayle raised the specter of higher taxes and bigger government under Clinton but cut quickly to his central theme of the evening: "Bill Clinton does not have the strength nor the character to be president of the United States," he said, as applause popped up in the school's Theater for the Arts. "You need to have a president you can trust. Can you really trust Bill Clinton?" He steered every issue back to questions about Clinton's character. "Bill Clinton has trouble telling the truth, and he will have a very difficult time dealing with somebody like President Yeltsin or Chancellor Kohl . . . because truth and integrity are prerequisites to being president of the United States."

Gore, calmer and more poised, generally gave as good as he got and countered one of Quayle's attacks by evoking George Bush's broken "read my lips" pledge of no new taxes. But it was apparent that he was reluctant to defend his running mate's character directly. No less than five times he backed away from Quayle's attacks on Clinton's truthfulness. One typical exchange was a discussion of Clinton's alleged flip-flopping on term limits. Quayle said, "Bill Clinton has trouble telling the truth." Gore asked for a chance to respond, but when he did, he shifted the subject to a previous question about family leave.

Gore was declared the consensus winner in the overnight polling and day-after buzz, but his reticence was noted by the Clintons and their top aides. "There was a real feeling that Gore didn't rise to the occasion," said one senior Clinton adviser. Hillary was especially displeased, the staffer said. For others in the high command, it only added to the suspicion that Gore was out for number one. "He was still a senator, very much focused on himself," said the aide, "with no understanding that he was inextricably linked to Clinton."

Albert and Pauline were waiting on the tarmac when Gore landed in Nashville after 2:00 A.M. on election day. A crowd was chanting, "It's time for them to go," the mantra Gore had been using since his New York acceptance speech. "It's time," said the weary candidate. "Today is the day the Lord hath made. Today is the time for them to go." He was in bed by four and up at nine for breakfast and a forty-five-minute jog across the Caney Fork and onto his father's farm. When he voted that afternoon at Forks River School in Elmwood, a small, elderly woman was sitting in a car outside waiting for him. Alota Thompson, Goat's mother, was weakened by heart trouble and couldn't get out, but Gore went over to visit with the woman who had cared for him on the family farm when he was a boy. "It made her day," said Gordon Thompson. She was dead three weeks later, collapsing in Thompson's living room on Thanksgiving Day.

By the time the Gores were in the air en route to Little Rock in the early evening, the exit polls had confirmed victory. Perot's presence would hold Clinton to 43 percent of the vote, the lowest total for a presidential winner since Woodrow Wilson. But the ticket was a groundbreaker for the Democrats, dashing the GOP's hopes of a permanent "realignment" of the electoral map. Clinton and Gore reclaimed ground in the South and West long lost to the Democrats. One-third of their 370 electoral votes came from states no Democrat had touched since Lyndon Johnson in 1964. Standing on the Old Statehouse porch that night, the first baby boomer ticket exulted in its achievement — and Gore, perhaps trying to make amends for his high-profile omissions in the Quayle debate, said, "I consider this a matter of tremendous honor and pride to work with a man like Bill Clinton. . . . Where I come from, we have a name for that, it's called character."

In the end, however, it was a collapse of faith in George Bush, rather than a great investment of hope in Bill Clinton and Al Gore, that drove the returns. Polls showed that many voters remained skittish, with only a limited confidence in the new president-elect. In a sense, they struck the same pragmatic bargain that Gore had made when he became a running mate. Each threw in with a man whose frailties of character were in plain view but who offered other superseding benefits. For voters, it was the prospect of a new administration to redress the indifference and economic unfairness of the Reagan-Bush era. For Gore, it was a step closer to the prize. Whether he would have his chance depended on the success of the political marriage he had just begun. Gore had tied the knot — in sickness and in health, for better or for worse.

❖ 18 ❖

Veep

SHORTLY after noon on January 20, 1993, Al Gore took the oath of office from Justice Byron White on the steps of the Capitol, using a Bible that had belonged to his sister Nancy. He was running on adrenaline, euphoric and exhausted after staying up until early morning at Blair House to help Clinton with his inaugural address. Usually an early-to-bed sort, he couldn't keep up with the Clintonites accustomed to their night-owl boss. By 4:30 A.M., recalled George Stephanopoulos, the vice president–elect was nodding off in a folding metal chair facing the mock podium, jerking back awake every few seconds before drifting away again.

At a post-inaugural lunch with former Senate colleagues, Gore offered an eloquent toast that captured the hopeful spirit of the day: "May we all not just listen, but truly hear. May we all not just see, but truly understand. And may we all reach deep into our own hearts to summon the will to take action, to keep our commitment to the kind of democracy and the kind of government that never forgets its roots or responsibilities, that remembers it was forged by the courage and vision and ideas of the people it was meant to serve. To our democracy!" The transition to power is the equivalent of spring training for a fledgling administration, a time when even the shakiest team is untouched in the loss column and free to dream. "Everything was hope and promise and energy, boundless energy," said Gore adviser Jack Quinn.

But the new vice president's spirits were tempered by a couple of chilly realities. Despite his rapport with Bill Clinton, he was still entering an office that transformed its occupants into material for late-night monologues. It was a job even he had disparaged as a "dead end" early in the 1992 campaign, before his selection by Clinton. The president had promised him a vastly different kind of partnership, but Gore knew that making good on it meant bucking two centuries of dreary institutional history. Shortly after election day, he commissioned Peter Knight and Reed Hundt to conduct a study of the vice presidency stretching back to the founding of the Republic. Their fifty-page report didn't tell Gore anything he didn't already intuitively know about his new job. But, said Hundt, it was still a sobering exercise "to go back two hundred years and find zero successes."

Gore may have been a heartbeat from the presidency, but he faced competition for Clinton's ear from the cadre of aides who had been with him since the earliest days of the campaign. His relationships with George Stephanopoulos, Harold Ickes, and the others had never been warm, and now he would be working with them more closely than ever. His most formidable rival, of course, was Hillary Rodham Clinton, who made no secret of her intention to become a power center unto herself, reportedly eyeing Gore's West Wing office space. Washington was bubbling with speculation about the his-and-her administration, even a "copresidency."

His post-campaign visibility began to shrink as the swearing-in neared. In joint appearances the "two amigos" theme of the bus trips had given way to a more traditional choreography. Gore receded into Clinton's shadow, standing motionless over his shoulder "like an environmentally correct wooden Native American outside a cigar store," said Bill Kristol.

Gore knew that to survive politically he needed to recast the vice presidency. He resolved to make proximity a priority in relations with Clinton, no small thing when dealing with someone whose position on an issue was often a reflection of his last conversation. "He learned early on the two key ingredients," said former Labor Secretary Robert Reich, an Oxford schoolmate of Clinton's. "If you are physically close to him, whispering in his ear, and are clear and forceful, you have a fairly good chance of, if not persuading, then at least affecting the trajectory of a decision." His goal was to become Clinton's closest and best adviser, to "stay late, show up early," as Hundt paraphrased the approach. Gore camped in a Little Rock hotel as Clinton began assembling the pieces of his administration in late 1992, bird-dogging every meeting.

He also moved to codify his role in the administration. Albert Gore had urged his son, from the beginning of his talks with Clinton about joining the ticket, to obtain "a clear understanding" of his place in the White House. The result was a written agreement, hammered out in November 1992 during a two-hour meeting of Clinton, Gore, and their presumptive chiefs of staff, Mack McLarty and Roy Neel, at the governor's mansion. There was no serious dispute over the substance of the document, Neel said, and its dozen or so points formed the basis of the professional relationship between Bill Clinton and Al Gore. The agreement included a commitment to regular lunch meetings and a guarantee that Gore would be a "principal adviser" on presidential appointments. It also placed two of his most trusted aides, Neel and national security adviser Leon Fuerth, firmly in the decisionmaking loop. Neel received the additional title of "assistant to the president" and a place at the important early-morning meetings of Clinton's senior staff.

Why did two men who were supposed to get along so famously need a formal agreement? Neel insisted that it was not a measure of mistrust but a means of communicating to staff the seriousness with which Clinton took Gore's role. "They both agreed that under Mack and me this was going to be conveyed in one way or the other to the rest of the senior White House staff," he said. "This was the critical thing."

Gore's clout helped secure presidential nominations and appointments for a long list of friends and loyalists. The posts were more than plums for those who had sweated in the vineyards. They combined to form a Gore administration slowly gestating within Bill Clinton's, ready to provide strategic information that might not be as readily available in a hostile West Wing. Reed Hundt landed chairmanship of the Federal Communications Commission; Gore's brother-in-law and family *consigliere* Frank Hunger went to the Justice Department as head of the civil division. Carol Browner, Gore's legislative director in the Senate and later secretary of environmental regulation for the state of Florida, was Clinton's choice for EPA administrator. Kathleen McGinty, another former Senate staffer, headed up the White House Council on Environmental Quality. When diversity concerns (Clinton declared that he wanted a cabinet that "looked like America") and political score-settling cost Tim Wirth the Energy secretary's post, Gore helped create a new environmentally related slot for his friend at State as undersecretary for global affairs.

Peter Knight, installed as deputy director for the presidential transition, helped salt the subcabinet and agency ranks with Goreheads. Thomas Grumbly, staff director of the House Science and Technology Oversight Committee that Gore had chaired, became assistant secretary of energy for environmental management. James Gilliland, a Memphis attorney who cochaired Shelby County's 1992 Clinton-Gore campaign and whose wife, Lucia, had been a Vanderbilt roommate of Nancy Gore's, was named chief counsel at the Agriculture Department.

Later in his first term Gore rewarded Knight by arranging his appointment to the board of Comsat Corporation, the company with exclusive U.S. rights to the INTELSAT system of communications satellites. (The president appoints three of the board's fifteen members.) His former chief of staff and ace fund-raiser had turned to lobbying in the early 1990s and built a sizable portfolio of blue-chip clients, many in the telecommunications industry, based on his association with Gore. A spot on the Comsat board was an important boost to his stature. And Gore didn't forget one of his earliest and most loyal fund-raisers, Johnny Hayes. He arranged Hayes's nomination to a $115,700-a-year seat on the Tennessee Valley Authority board of directors, a post he held until his resignation in 1998 to become national finance chairman for the Gore 2000 campaign.

Yet for all the carefully placed hires, organizational fail-safes, and a friend in the Oval Office, Gore found his first two years as vice president deeply frustrating. He succeeded in bucking the dismal tradition of his office to become the president's closest adviser. Within the boundaries of the administration's limited activism, he wielded significant influence in foreign policy, the environment, and telecommunications. Rarely did Bill Clinton reach a major decision without consulting Gore. "I want to talk to Al" became a common presidential refrain heard by staff members.

But Gore was unable to keep the new administration from making the early string of false starts and misjudgments that left an indelibly negative impression on many voters: cabinet nominees with nanny problems, politically ham-fisted firings in the White House travel office, the unsuccessful attempt to spring gay soldiers from the closet, a White House with a public image all too often embodied by smug, swaggering young boomers like Stephanopoulos. Gore contributed to the disarray and on other occasions was hostage to it, lashed to the mast of a ship that always seemed on the brink of capsizing. He told friends of the "huge chasm" between his office and the presidency, and he skirmished constantly with advisers held over from the campaign, most of whom still regarded him with suspicion and envy for his access to Clinton. His whole initiation experience was, said Reich, "quite traumatic."

How Gore handled both his power and powerlessness reveals a good deal about the kind of president he might be. As his executive style emerged, it carried all the earmarks of his legislative career — keen intellect, fierce competitiveness, self-righteousness, and caution punctuated by bursts of boldness. He was, as one aide put it, "a New Age pragmatist" with no consistent ideological coloring, capable of landing on Clinton's left or right depending on the issue. In the debate over the early economic program, he sided with the "deficit hawks" who favored deep reductions in red ink to win the confidence of the bond market. At the same time he pushed unsuccessfully to raise revenues with a controversial, broad-based energy tax favored by the environmental movement. In 1995 Gore joined strategist Dick Morris in pushing Clinton to offer a balanced budget of his own that could compete with the plan presented by Newt Gingrich and House Republicans. But when Morris later urged Clinton to close a deal with the GOP, Gore insisted that the administration hold out to protect Medicaid, Medicare, and other programs from severe cuts.

His partnership with the president brought other qualities into sharper relief. Where Clinton was famously malleable, constantly assimilating opposing views, appeasing political enemies, and shifting positions, Gore could be immovable on issues he cared about. In the grip of an impassioned plea, his voice rose, he grew red in the face, and he usually went on too long. Many Clintonites were surprised by what one called "a 'damn the torpedoes, full speed ahead' streak" he exhibited from his earliest days on the job, when he urged Clinton, without success, to take an uncompromising line on opening military service to gays and lesbians, even when it was clear there was no prospect of support in Congress or among the Joint Chiefs of Staff. "His instincts were more combative," said Leon Panetta, who moved from OMB director to Clinton's chief of staff in 1994. Although a "damn the torpedoes" attitude can be a useful trait in a president, it also speaks to the arrogant underside of Gore's approach to executive power. Clinton took dispute and debate with aides in stride, but Gore, once dug in, often became defensive and dismissive, flashing the "Gore glare" across the conference table at opponents.

His first major attempt to influence administration policy ended in a stinging failure. Gore believed that Clinton had a limited window of time — no more than a year — to make his toughest choices and boldest moves. The president's senior advisers were deeply divided in the early months, struggling to reconcile campaign promises of new programs and a middle-class tax cut with pressure to win the confidence of the financial markets by cutting the budget deficit. As they prepared to take office, the victors were hit with new projections for the deficit's growth if left unchecked: $360 billion by 1997, and $500 billion by 2000. Gore sided with Panetta, his deputy Alice Rivlin, and Robert Rubin, director of the newly formed National Economic Council, in favoring aggressive deficit cutting, a position Clinton reluctantly embraced.

Although Gore had toned down his environmental rhetoric during the campaign, he saw the economic package as an opportunity to push for the green movement's tax of choice: a broad-based levy based on the use of energy as measured in BTUs (British thermal units). A BTU tax would fall most heavily on coal and other fossil fuels, encouraging industry to use less polluting sources like natural gas. Gore believed that adoption of a BTU tax, which would have raised an estimated $72 billion over five years, could kindle support for similar measures in Europe and Japan, accelerating global environmental renewal. In White House meetings, he stressed the one-time-only opportunity that an incoming administration had to create a new reality, comparing it to Franklin Roosevelt's first days in office during the Depression. "If you're bold," he said, "people will come around."

The BTU tax passed its first legislative hurdle in the House in mid-March but ran aground in the Senate Finance Committee later that spring when Republicans and moderate Democrats from energy-producing states, targets of a heavy lobbying campaign by business groups, balked at the proposal. One problem was that for all of Gore's bullishness on BTU, he had done little to prepare the political ground for such an unconventional proposal. It popped into view so quickly after the inauguration that there was virtually no time for environmental groups to organize a grassroots response to the opposition. Still, he clung tenaciously to the idea, even when Majority Leader George Mitchell told him that its inclusion jeopardized passage of the entire economic plan. Treasury Secretary Lloyd Bentsen, a Texan long friendly to oil and gas interests who had been leery of the proposal from the first, simply announced on *The MacNeil/Lehrer Newshour* that it was dead, to be replaced by a more politically palatable gasoline tax.

What was most revealing about the episode was not Gore's defeat, but his reaction to it. He was crushed, believing that the moment for real reform had passed. "A very searing experience," said one longtime environmental lobbyist who has worked as an informal adviser to the vice president. The setback, he said, seemed to yank Gore back into his campaign-season zone of caution on environmental issues, as if he had been caught straying too far ahead — and to the left — of what the political system would bear. The BTU tax was one of a series of disappointments in 1993–94 for a green movement that had expected big things with Gore positioned near the top. But the demise of the tax was part of a pattern of passivity and timidity on environmental policy. After blasting George Bush for indifference to global warming, Clinton committed the United States to reducing carbon dioxide emissions to 1990 levels by 2000 solely through a program of voluntary compliance. The administration backed away from a campaign promise to mandate tougher fuel economy standards for American cars and instead announced a "clean car initiative" that would require automakers only to develop a prototype for a more energy-efficient vehicle. The White House also backpedaled from its package of proposals to raise fees and royalties for grazing and mining on federally owned land. It took only a pro forma complaint from Senator Max Baucus, an amiable Montana Democrat who is not exactly the most feared man in the Senate, for the White House to withdraw the measures. Even Baucus later admitted that he hadn't expected to prevail.

As BTU succumbed to budget politics, Gore struggled with political problems in the West Wing. His relations with Hillary Clinton, never comfortable, grew increasingly tense as the administration got off to a rocky start. "Hillary was not a big fan of Gore's," said one former senior adviser who remains close to both Clintons. "She thought he overreached, inserted himself and his opinions much too much. The relationship was a very uneasy one, very, very uneasy." The friction reflected more similarities than differences between Clinton's mate and running mate. Both were headstrong, ambitious, personally invested in major administration initiatives (health care and government reinvention), and competing for staff and other White House resources. Each was deadly serious about work and faith (he was a Southern Baptist, Mrs. Clinton a Methodist) and had a closely guarded but discernible goofy streak. Where Gore was capable of breaking into James Brown, Mrs. Clinton was on occasion fond of phrases like "Okee dokey, artichokee."

The weekly lunch was a particular sore point with Mrs. Clinton, who was trying to lighten her chronically overscheduled husband's workload. "Why can't we give him some time by knocking out the lunch?" she asked. But Gore, who had made face time with Clinton a priority, refused to yield. "The president wouldn't knock it out because Gore wouldn't permit him to knock it out," a former Clinton aide said. On some busy days the two didn't sit down in the president's private dining room until 4:30 P.M.

Gore's daily schedule reflected his determination to remain in the loop at every moment. He formed his plans around the president's, intent on not missing any critical meetings in the Oval Office. When he was scheduled to see Clinton, said one former senior presidential adviser, he was "not one to come down and cool his heels in Betty Currie's office waiting for the previous meeting to break up." Although his door was always open to Gore, Clinton didn't feel compelled to include him in every gathering, and the ad hoc style of the early Clinton White House tended to produce more than its share of unscheduled consultations. When Gore learned of one, he usually dropped whatever he was doing. "I mean, I couldn't believe I was seeing the vice president scuttling, scuttling down the hall when he found out there was a meeting he didn't know about," said another former senior aide.

A former midlevel Clinton aide said that a running joke around the chief of staff's office was how quickly the call came from Gore aides trolling for information when they spotted an unfamiliar meeting on the presidential schedule. Gore and his sentinels, she said, approached Oval Office traffic with a Kremlinologist's attention to detail. "There was a huge, huge effort by the vice president's people to try to analyze, What does this mean? What is it? Who's in it? Do we need to be there? The minute you said this was really nothing, they were there." They reflected the wariness of their boss, who suspected the Clinton crowd of trying to undercut him. Even Clinton sensed some of Gore's insecurity. "I really like Al, he's real smart," Clinton told a top political deputy. "But Al's always seeing something where there's nothing."

But even paranoids have enemies, and Clinton didn't fully grasp how many his vice president had in the West Wing. Although Gore had a good rapport with presidential chief of staff Mack McLarty, tensions with Stephanopoulos and others in the old campaign circle were "manifest," in the description of one former presidential aide who was not part of the original Little Rock group. "This was never an especially welcoming, including crowd," he said. "Clinton never understood how off-putting they could be to someone not of the circle." Gore tried to carry off a tactic that the aide called "a classic Machiavellian hugging of his enemies, keeping them close, trying to charm them." But Gore is not by nature a charms-and-hugs politician, and dealings with Stephanopoulos remained especially difficult. Each man had one client — the president — and different ideas of how he was best served. Stephanopoulos regarded Gore as politically tone-deaf, and Gore suspected him for his ties to Gephardt and the liberal congressional wing of the party. "George, I'm going to have to find some scientific procedure to get that Gephardt DNA removed from you," he said after one rocky meeting.

Gore also held Stephanopoulos responsible for the steady drip of blind quotes in the press that frequently depicted Clinton in a negative light, usually as dithering or undisciplined. "He didn't trust George, he thought he was a major leaker," said a former senior administration official who worked for both Gore and Clinton. It exasperated Gore, whose own shop was famous for its lack of chattiness. "These people are killing you," he told Clinton of his loose-lipped staff, according to this official. Gore's dim view of leaking, however, didn't stop him from sitting down with the modern master of fly-on-the-wall journalism, the *Washington Post*'s Bob Woodward, who was working on an inside account of Clinton's first year in office.

When the administration's public image bottomed out in the spring of 1993 after a string of embarrassments, including the firing of the White House travel office director and his attempted replacement with a distant Arkansas cousin of Clinton's, it was Gore who closed the deal to hire David Gergen, former adviser to Nixon, Ford, and Reagan, to smooth relations with the press and the city's opinion-making elite. He even sat at a word processor in a West Wing office and knocked out the press release himself at 6:30 A.M. on the morning the appointment was announced.

Gore's foreign policy background, which had been showcased as a major selling point in 1992, did little to keep the administration from looking disastrously out of its depth. The new president had no intrinsic interest in the subject and had committed nearly all of his energies to fixing the economy and related domestic problems. Management of foreign policy thus fell largely to low-key Secretary of State Warren Christopher, National Security Adviser Anthony Lake, and Gore. But confusion, indecision, poor communication, and bad luck produced a series of setbacks in 1993–94.

A humanitarian mission by the U.S. military to protect food and emergency aid from theft by rival clans in Somalia escalated into a fatal misadventure. On October 3, 1993, a raid to capture the Somali militia leader Farah Aidid ended in a firefight that left eighteen American soldiers dead and more than eighty wounded. Television viewers watched endlessly rerun footage of a dead U.S. helicopter crewman's body being dragged through the streets of Mogadishu. Nine days later, two hundred lightly armed U.S. and Canadian peacekeepers, under UN mandate, steamed into Port-au-Prince on the USS *Harlan County* to prepare for the return of Haiti's first democratically elected president, Jean-Bertrand Aristede, who had been overthrown and exiled in a 1991 military coup. The ship was blocked from landing by a mob brandishing guns and machetes, and after a day of deliberation Clinton ordered it back, again signaling weakness and disarray.

Lake said that despite blistering criticism from Congress and the press, Gore never tried to duck blame or distance himself from these events. "If you're vice president, it's possible to pick and choose, to be there on some issues and take a walk on others that could have a rough edge to them," said Lake. "And he never took a walk."

Gore was inherently quicker than Clinton to favor military force as an option. Even before official CIA reports confirmed Saddam Hussein's involvement in a foiled plot to assassinate former President George Bush with a car bomb on a visit to Kuwait City, Gore had assigned Leon Fuerth to conduct his own inquiry through intelligence sources. Along with the rest of the national security team, Gore urged a tense and tentative Clinton ("Are you *sure* this is the right thing to do?" he asked) to launch a retaliatory cruise missile attack on June 24.

Gore's instincts were the same in the Balkans, where civil war in Bosnia had become Europe's deadliest conflict since World War II. Although direct fighting between Yugoslavia and Croatia had ended in 1993, the Serbian minority seeking independence continued its genocidal onslaught against the Muslim majority. At meeting after meeting, Gore argued passionately for bombardment to force the Serbs to the peace table. Richard Neustadt remembers visiting Gore in the early months and getting clear signals that he and Clinton were not together on the issue. Neustadt left "with the clear impression that [Gore] would have been more forthcoming with force much earlier." But after Christopher was unable to persuade European allies to lift the arms embargo against the Bosnian Muslim and join in air strikes on Serbian positions, even Gore stood down.

His impulses weren't unswervingly hawkish, however, and he brought a willingness to think outside of the box to solve problems. He was the administration's most consistently vocal supporter of former president Jimmy Carter's intervention into diplomatic crises in North Korea and Haiti. Both ended successfully but still proved highly embarrassing to Clinton because of Carter's penchant for televised freelancing. By mid-1994 tensions with North Korea over its nuclear program were bringing relations to the breaking point. For at least two years the country had been using its reactors to produce plutonium that was potentially adaptable to nuclear weapons. Although the North Koreans insisted that they were pursuing peaceful purposes, they had withdrawn from the Nuclear Non-Proliferation Treaty and prevented international inspectors from making detailed measurements. The United States was pushing the United Nations for sanctions, which "Great Leader" Kim Il Sung threatened would lead to the invasion of South Korea.

Carter, who had made a second career as a diplomatic trouble-shooter, had been invited to Pyongyang by Kim a year earlier but declined at Christopher's request. When he was asked again in June 1994, he called Gore, who recommended to Clinton that he be allowed to go. Clinton agreed, but with the strict understanding that Carter was there as a private citizen, not an official envoy. Christopher and others at State regarded the pious Georgian as a loose cannon, and his intervention gave them heartburn. But Gore argued that this was the ideal circumstance for his mediation skills.

Kim told Carter that in exchange for help in getting modern light-water reactors for his country, he would agree to a nuclear freeze, outside inspections, and reentry into the nonproliferation treaty. But immediately after passing word to the White House, Carter infuriated administration officials by going on CNN to announce that an end to the crisis was at hand, automatically narrowing Clinton's options and allowing countries that were not inclined to sanctions to harden their positions. "Nothing should be done to exacerbate the situation now," Carter instructed as Clinton and Gore sat stunned, watching his performance, trying to figure out what to do next. "Can we make lemonade out of this lemon?" Gore asked.

Officials feared that Kim was duping Carter, and over the phone Lake insisted that any deal include more specific assurances that no new plutonium would be produced. Carter's mission was ultimately a success — later that year North Korea signed an agreement halting its nuclear program in exchange for the safer light-water reactors — but not before the president was pasted in the press as "Jimmy Clinton" for leaving the impression that Carter had called the shots in a critical foreign policy episode.

Gore nevertheless pushed again for Carter's involvement, this time in an attempt to dislodge Lieutenant General Raoul Cedras and the military junta that had ruled Haiti since 1991. The United States had one message for Cedras: leave or be forcibly removed. To deliver it, Gore suggested Carter, who knew Cedras and had visited the island numerous times, including as an election monitor in 1990. This time, to keep Carter in check, Clinton dispatched him as head of a three-man delegation, joining Senator Sam Nunn and General Colin Powell. On September 18, 1994, with the 82nd Airborne en route from Fort Bragg and just hours from invading the island, the three men finally coaxed Cedras's resignation. But on his return to Washington, Carter once again couldn't resist sermonizing on CNN. Before briefing Clinton, he gave an early-morning interview praising the notoriously brutal Cedras and announcing that he had made sure the general received proper compensation for the home he had agreed to abandon for his Panamanian exile. The performance enraged Clinton and finally cooled even Gore's enthusiasm for the outspoken ex-president as an envoy.

Clinton's disengagement, combined with Christopher's low-profile approach — and preoccupation with the Middle East — afforded Gore the chance to set up an extensive foreign policy shop of his own, built around four bilateral commissions established with Russia, South Africa, Egypt, and the Ukraine. Although much of the work was nuts-and-bolts — unknotting trade issues and working on technology transfer and economic development — it did yield a few breakthroughs. Gore's diplomacy persuaded Ukrainian officials to return to Russia the remnants of the nuclear missile arsenal in its possession. The Russian commission, cochaired with Prime Minister Viktor Chernomyrdin until his dismissal by President Boris Yeltsin in March 1998, did little to address Russia's rampant economic corruption or to resolve fundamental differences between the two countries on issues like Yeltsin's embrace of Iraq and military equipment sales to Iran. But it was a useful diplomatic back channel for discussions about conflicts in Chechnya and Bosnia, as well as for information on Yeltsin's wobbly health. Although Gore's personal estimate of Chernomyrdin may have been slightly overextended (U.S. intelligence sources accumulated what they considered to be "conclusive evidence of personal corruption," the *New York Times* reported in 1998; when the report landed in Gore's office, the paper said, it was returned with a "barnyard epithet" scrawled across the cover), the connection proved to be valuable again in the spring of 1999. Serving as Yeltsin's envoy, Chernomyrdin would sit at Gore's dining room table to hash out the deal leading to the withdrawal of Serbian troops from Kosovo.

Those who have watched Gore in action with foreign leaders say that while he will never match Clinton for personal charm and handholding skills, he brings a quality of directness that could be an important asset. "I saw foreign leaders who weren't sure where Clinton was at the end of a conversation," said a former top national security official. Gore, he said, is not hesitant to deliver bad news or draw lines.

The flip side, said a former senior State Department official, is that he tends to lecture and browbeat. "I think Gore believes you can shame other people into doing things," he said. "With Gore, it's more 'I know better.' Clinton, for all his 115,000 faults, saying 'I know better' is not one of them."

Gore wanted a major domestic policy initiative to lead and had his eye on welfare reform. But in early 1993 he found himself heading up what seemed like the sort of quintessentially vice presidential chore he had vowed to avoid. "Reinventing government," or REGO, had been part of the campaign message, inspired by political scientist David Osborne's book *Reinventing Government: How the Entrepreneurial Spirit Is Transforming the Public Sector*, which chronicles state and local efforts to make government more efficient and customer-friendly. It was a classic New Democrat idea — fix government, don't demolish it. Still, REGO was sneered at by political advisers as a lemon that might win spirited applause from editorial writers but was likely to alienate powerful Democratic committee chairmen, who were protective of the bureaucratic kingdoms they ruled through the appropriations and oversight process. Nevertheless, REGO, especially the idea of cutting government programs, scored well with the voter "dial groups" set up to monitor Clinton's February address to a joint session of Congress, placing third behind "three strikes and you're out" sentencing programs for repeat offenders and improved job training. It seemed like an opportunity to send the message to anti-Washington Perot voters that Bill Clinton was not the typical government-happy Democrat. The only problem was that no one had any idea what programs should be cut or just how government could be reinvented.

On March 3, 1993, Clinton named Gore to head a six-month examination of the federal government called the National Performance Review (NPR). "We intend to redesign, to reinvent, to reinvigorate the entire national government," Clinton declared. And on the South Lawn on September 7, against a backdrop of two forklifts piled high with government rules and regulations, Gore unveiled his report. It made 384 recommendations for streamlining and energizing the bureaucracy and promised $108 billion in savings and a 12 percent cut in the federal workforce — 252,000 jobs — by 1998.

What happened in the six months between his assignment from Clinton and the ceremony on the South Lawn illuminates a part of Gore's approach to leadership. His reinvention quest ultimately led to some significant reforms, principally in the area of purchasing practices and downsizing of the federal workforce. But what was supposed to be a classic New Democrat initiative took on some Old Democrat features before it was done, with interest groups appeased, political fights avoided, and tough questions deferred.

Gore, always the good Scout, set aside whatever qualms he had about the assignment and made REGO the centerpiece of his domestic agenda. "Reinvention teams" swept into the cabinet agencies, collecting ideas for improving operations. Gore toured the bureaucracy to shake hands, listen to problems, and sell the program to skeptical employees at Tennessee-style town meetings. Despite his initial misgivings, REGO touched the wonkish hot buttons in his makeup. In speeches he enjoyed recounting the vivid stories of red tape and bureaucratic absurdity unearthed by his staff. A favorite was the nine pages of specifications and drawings regulating the kind of ashtrays that could be purchased by the government. To guard against the procurement of defective ashtrays, the General Services Administration outlined a test that involved smashing them with a hammer. "The specimen should break into a small number of irregular shaped pieces not greater in number than 35." Gore brought the ashtray routine to his September 1993 appearance on *The Late Show with David Letterman*, donning a pair of protective goggles as he smashed one. "So let me get this straight," a bewildered Letterman asked. "The taxpayers can help out at home by busting their own ashtrays?"

Gore wanted to send the message that the new administration was clearing out the bureaucratic underbrush and ridding government of pointless regulations. But his broader goal was to transplant to Washington the cutting-edge private-sector management techniques that he admired, emphasizing customer service and continuous improvement. Gore saw that some American companies had become more competitive in the eighties after reinventing themselves, and he challenged federal workers to aspire to the same standard. "If an industry as large and stodgy as the automobile industry can undergo that kind of transformation, then the federal government can as well," he told Energy Department employees at a July 13 meeting.

But Gore's REGO suffered from a muddled and contradictory mission. The initial goal, as he framed it, was a government that both "works better and costs less." Yet these were distinctly different objectives, achieved through means that didn't naturally dovetail. A government that worked better was one in which employees were "empowered," unleashed from mindless rules and regulations that sapped energy and stifled creativity. Gore devoted a considerable PR effort to promoting empowerment, personally handing out "hammer awards" to innovative workers who had smashed through the bureaucratic barriers.

The problem with empowerment was that it was a political nonstarter. Few voters, especially Perot supporters, cared to hear much about "empowering" the federal bureaucrats who represented everything they loathed about Washington. Empowerment was also a slow, evolutionary process that didn't bring immediate or dramatic results. People wanted a government that was less expensive, and they wanted it soon. That meant jobs slashed and offices closed.

But Gore had ignored a critical difference between government and his corporate role models. The companies he admired reinvented themselves through ruthless, remorseless restructuring, achieved by firing tens of thousands of workers, selling off assets, closing factories, and in some cases shipping them abroad. Those workers who were left standing in the leaner, meaner organizations were then "empowered." That kind of painful reckoning was never a part of Gore's vision for REGO. Although government isn't a widget factory, and some of the critical services it provides can never be managed exclusively by the rules of market economics, Gore failed even to entertain the fundamental questions as he launched REGO: What does government do? Could someone else do it better?

One reason those questions weren't asked was that doing so would have required taking on a powerful Democratic Party constituency he would someday need to run for president: the federal employee unions. More than 1.3 million strong, representing 60 percent of the government's civilian, nonpostal workforce, the unions sent Gore an early message that they were not about to be paved over by any reform steamroller. "This is not Texas, and it damn sure ain't Arkansas," said John Sturdivant, president of the 700,000-member American Federation of Government Employees, mentioning two jurisdictions where reinvention was in vogue.

The administration cut a deal with Sturdivant and leaders of the two other major unions, the National Treasury Employees Union and the National Federation of Federal Employees. It created the National Partnership Council, a group of union and government officials, to consider what changes might be made "to make labor management partnership a reality." The deal was essentially a cave to the unions, signaling that the administration would make no serious attempt to change civil service regulations that placed strict controls on how most federal employees were hired, fired, and disciplined.

In other words, personnel cuts were shaped to fit not a long-term reinvention strategy but a short-term political strategy. Virtually all of the reductions were voluntary, created through normal attrition, early retirement, and cash buyouts. Although REGO had promised to make inroads into the government's bloated middle-management ranks, the biggest reductions were actually among low-level clerical and blue-collar workers. In fact, the number of managers crept upward slightly. Keeping hands off labor was "wired in as virtually a precondition to any downsizing," said Donald Kettl, director of the LaFollette Institute for Public Affairs at the University of Wisconsin and a former consultant to REGO. "If they had started out at war with the unions they would have gotten nowhere," he said. But in so doing, Kettl explained, Gore and his reinventors "lost control of who left the government."

As he finished up his six-month review, Gore pushed hard to give REGO a splashy rollout, with two weeks' worth of White House–orchestrated events. He also insisted on announcing up front that his proposals would produce $108 billion in savings when, by budget director Leon Panetta's calculus, the real figure was closer to $30 billion. Stephanopoulos worried that if Gore was wrong, congressional Republicans could demand other cuts to fill the gap, placing protected programs like Medicare, Medicaid, and student loans at risk. Gore lost out on his bid for a big splash. The first lady, already miffed that Clinton's speech kicking off the drive for health care reform had been delayed, put her foot down. But Gore prevailed on claiming the $108 billion in savings.

Many of the changes outlined in the NPR were pushed through administratively, without congressional action, like scrapping the ten-thousand-page *Federal Personnel Manual* and allowing agencies to convert billions in government benefits to electronic payment. But reinventing government also meant reinventing Congress, which had jurisdiction over much of the vast bureaucracy that Gore wanted to tame. Many of the most substantial proposals, like civil service reform, languished on the Hill.

Ironically, Gore managed to fly over perhaps the most egregious example of inefficient, arrogant, and corrupt government — the Internal Revenue Service, which eventually became the subject of hair-raising congressional hearings about strong-arm tactics against taxpayers and its own employees. Kettl, in a 1998 study for the Brookings Institution, asserts that the NPR's failure to detect and reform the massive dysfunction at the IRS, an agency whose problems were manifest to millions of Americans, ranks "as perhaps its most notable failure."

Congress and the administration did find common ground on a significant piece of reinvention legislation. The Federal Acquisition Streamlining Act of 1994 modernized the government's procurement practices, which had been layered over by centralized bureaucracy and outmoded management systems. It introduced private-sector concepts like just-in-time delivery and off-the-shelf purchases to replace the overregulated practices that had stifled competition and raised administrative costs.

Gore cut back his REGO participation after 1993, and the program went through several incarnations as political circumstances changed. In 1995, as Newt Gingrich and the congressional Republicans seized the majority and prepared to force deep cuts in the size and cost of government, the administration used REGO as a vehicle to show that it was also serious about making Washington smaller. This time, Gore challenged federal managers to answer the question he should have asked in 1993: What do they do, and should they be doing it? There were rumblings that the White House might try to compete with the Republicans by proposing to eliminate an entire cabinet agency, such as HUD, Energy, or Transportation. But neither party found a real constituency for it. Much of REGO's focus and direction was lost amid the bitter partisan fighting and government shutdowns caused by battles over the budget.

Gore's efforts add up to a mixed picture. In 1998 the federal payroll was smaller than at any time since 1960 — reduced by more than 330,000 positions (15.4 percent) from 1993. Much of the shrinkage happened at the Defense Department, which is eight times the size of the next largest cabinet agency; REGO accelerated the post–Cold War contraction already well under way. But nearly all other departments were also forced to take significant cuts in personnel. Gore and the NPR claim $112 billion in savings from 1993 through 1999, an assertion that Kettl says is both "unaudited and unauditable," since it is based on ambiguous and hard-to-measure matters like changes in information technology and administrative process.

In the end Gore's REGO probably did save the government some money and certainly helped make it smaller. But it is impossible to argue that it redesigned, reinvented, or reinvigorated Washington as he set out to do. Senior adviser Elaine Kamarck defended the sweeping rhetoric. "If he had set out a bunch of piddly-assed procurement goals, nothing would have happened," she said. Gore, she added, is committed to reinvention for the long term. "He grew up in Washington, and he knows the game. He knows that there are things that if you just wait you can do them."

The biggest lift to Al Gore's stature early in his vice presidency came in the unlikeliest of forums — face to face with Ross Perot on *Larry King Live*. In the fall of 1993 the White House faced heavy opposition from labor and House Democrats to the North American Free Trade Agreement (NAFTA), which dropped most tariff and tax barriers to trade with Mexico and Canada. Clinton and Gore were both dedicated to free trade and argued that the pact would level the economic playing field, opening vast new markets to American goods and creating jobs at home. Republicans charged that the United States was relinquishing its economic "sovereignty" to a cadre of international bureaucrats. The Democratic opposition, led by majority leader Dick Gephardt and his whip, David Bonior, said the accord would accelerate the exodus of high-paying manufacturing jobs across the border. That point was made most vividly by Perot, who predicted that it would produce a "giant sucking sound" made by companies headed for Mexico.

Throughout most of the debate, the administration avoided confronting Perot directly, for fear of offending his supporters. But a slip in his poll numbers that fall led to a change of plan at the White House. Positioning Perot, now a depreciating political asset, as the public face of NAFTA opposition might make it easier for House members with heavy Perot blocs in their district to vote yes. The time had come to take him on, and Jack Quinn thought the vice president should be the point man. Gore's chief of staff (he had replaced Roy Neel, who became Mack McLarty's deputy) had watched his boss for months in NAFTA meetings, displaying total command of the subject, spinning off facts and figures about exports in various parts of the country. Free trade was in Gore's blood, part of a lineage that extended from his father back to Cordell Hull.

Quinn broached the idea in a long conversation with Gore, who circled it cautiously and then agreed. To short-circuit the predictable internal opposition, Gore went directly to Clinton to discuss it. A few days later, on the road in the Midwest, the president let it drop to reporters that the vice president was challenging Perot to a debate.

Gore knew he was taking a considerable risk. Getting manhandled on television by Ross Perot would almost certainly seal the agreement's fate and place him even deeper in the hole with Clintonites who suspected both his loyalty and his political acumen. To prepare he reached back to his journalist's roots and targeted Perot as if he were a crooked Nashville councilman. He asked his staff to assemble everything Perot had ever written or said on the public record and spent two full days studying it in an enormous black briefing book. He watched tapes and staged a mock debate at his Naval Observatory residence featuring Representative Mike Synar, an old friend from the Energy and Commerce Committee, as Perot and Clinton's deputy chief of staff, Mark Gearan, standing in for Larry King. Aides were concerned that he was overpreparing. They stopped the rehearsal when his answer to the first question — "Why are you for NAFTA?" — ran five minutes. Clinton offered his own advice: "Relax, be loose, but don't let the other side get the emotional edge. Make it clear we're on the side of the worker."

Gore realized he needed a human touch to compete with Perot's folksy theatrics, something to yank his argument out from under a mound of eye-glazing factoids. He spotted a magazine photograph of Senator Reed Smoot and Representative Willis Hawley, protectionist coauthors of the 1930 tariff act widely believed to have worsened the Depression, and during the debate presented it to an irritated Perot with the suggestion that he put it on his wall.

Looking for a personal story to tell, he called his boyhood friend Gordon "Goat" Thompson in Elmwood, Tennessee. Thompson, who worked at a Bridgestone/Firestone tire factory near Nashville, remembered Gore as "worried, really worried," about the debate. Gore explained NAFTA and made his case to Thompson for how it would help his industry in the long run by knocking down the 20 percent tax on American tires going to Mexico. Thompson's union, the United Rubber Workers, opposed the agreement, but Gore asked whether he could say on the air that Thompson supported it. He was skeptical at first but consented, more out of loyalty to an old friend than enthusiasm for free trade. Within the first two minutes of the November 9 telecast on CNN, Gore mentioned Thompson. "He's a member of the United Rubber Workers, and he's for this because he's taken the time to look at how it affects his job and his family." Thompson almost immediately regretted his decision. As Gore spoke, his phone began to ring nonstop with reporters' calls. His union leadership was also watching, and the next day at the plant Goat was in hot water.

Debates, with their structured formats and rewards to those who prepare, play to Gore's strengths as a political performer. His plan was to get under Perot's paper-thin skin and goad him into losing his temper, and it worked. He prodded and poked for ninety minutes, pushing Perot to disclose the finances of the anti-NAFTA campaign and confronting him with his record of loony claims, such as having spoken to the person who had "ordered the caskets" for the forty thousand American troops likely to be killed in the Gulf War. He asked Perot about the free trade zone operated by his son at Alliance Airport in Fort Worth, displaying a brochure that promoted the zone as a gateway to business in Mexico. "If it's good enough for him, why isn't it good enough for the rest of the country?" Gore asked. When Perot said the country had been "sold out by foreign lobbyists" working for the passage of NAFTA, Gore reminded him of the lobbyists he had sent to the House Ways and Means Committee in the 1970s to try to secure tax breaks. The attacks left Perot sputtering and stunningly uncivil to a vice president. "Would you even know the truth if you saw it?" he asked Gore at one point.

His strong performance and Perot's meltdown changed the dynamics of the NAFTA debate. In October the public had opposed the agreement by a 33–29 margin. A week after *Larry King*, NAFTA was favored 36–31. Half of those surveyed said they saw at least some of the debate, and of those 43 percent favored the agreement. The pact passed the House 234–200, with a winning coalition split almost evenly between Democrats and Republicans. Clinton's elation with Gore's performance went a long way toward quieting critics in the West Wing. "Everyone knew the stakes for him were high," said Quinn. "It showed he was willing to take risks to advance the president's agenda."

Gore also had to sell NAFTA to a deeply divided environmental community. Opponents feared that the increased industrial activity generated by free trade would deepen Mexico's already staggering pollution problems, especially across the two-thousand-mile border, where the *maquiladoras* — factories owned by or doing work for U.S. companies — have devastated the air, water, and ground. Other activists contended that only by lifting Mexico's economy would environmental quality improve. The three countries signed a separate side agreement establishing environmentally sound "sustainable development" as a goal of NAFTA, but nearly six years later the results are at best mixed. The number of border factories has surged, with corresponding increases in pollution.

Even more alarming to some environmentalists is that the trade agreement Gore championed has given businesses a new way to slide out from under antipollution regulations. One provision in the main text — not the environmental sidebar — has been interpreted to allow companies to sue countries whose laws dilute profits. In 1997, when the Canadian government banned MMT, a gasoline additive, because studies indicated that it could cause nerve damage, the manufacturer, Ethyl Corporation of Richmond, Virginia, successfully sued to lift the prohibition. Some activists charge that the new world of free trade and global economics poses a profound threat to environmental protection. "Gore's vision in *Earth in the Balance* is being destroyed by the rules of the global economic system," said Brent Blackwelder, president of Friends of the Earth.

NAFTA's passage nevertheless helped Gore, and the administration, finally gain some political traction as 1993 wound down. On Thanksgiving Eve a Senate filibuster of the Brady Bill, which required a five-day waiting period and background check for handgun purchasers, collapsed, clearing the way for the president to sign the measure into law. But even during the best of times in the Clinton years, trouble was always brewing. Before year's end, over the advice of political aides, the president and first lady refused to grant the *Washington Post* access to documents about their investment in an Arkansas real estate deal called Whitewater and their relationship with Madison Guaranty, a defunct savings and loan. It was Hillary Clinton, backed by White House lawyers, who steered her husband to the give-them-nothing stance, one more appropriate for corporate litigators than political leaders, and the administration paid an incalculable price for that decision. The stonewalling only fueled congressional and media suspicion about a transaction that, in its worst light, exposed Mrs. Clinton not as a felon, but as a woman who used her husband's political prominence in Arkansas to cash in on cheesy, get-rich-quick deals. It also opened the door for the appointment of an independent counsel, a job ultimately filled by Kenneth Starr, who used his extraordinarily broad legal charter to unearth the extramarital affair that would bring Clinton's presidency to the brink of destruction.

Whitewater and a string of other scandals devoured hours and energy, producing endless strategy meetings and a parade of administration aides testifying before grand juries and congressional committees. It wrecked lives, reputations, and the personal finances (through exorbitant attorneys' fees) of staff members who were often only peripherally involved. Sometimes it seemed that governance was what took place in the intervals between long sieges of damage control.

Gore was unhappy about the constant depletion of time and attention and intervened when he thought he could make a difference. In early 1994 he pushed hard for the ouster of White House counsel Bernard Nussbaum, Hillary Clinton's onetime mentor and chief architect of the Whitewater stonewall strategy. After newspaper stories broke about his improper contacts with Treasury Department officials who were overseeing the Resolution Trust Corporation — the agency investigating the Clintons' Whitewater real estate business partner, James McDougal — Gore told Nussbaum he had to go. "Bernie, your moral compass should always point north, and your compass hasn't always," he told Nussbaum. "I feel compelled to recommend to the president that you resign."

"You can tell the president any fucking thing you want," the hardnosed Nussbaum replied.

Gore was careful about venting his frustrations over Clinton and his scandal-prone lieutenants. But he always left unmistakable signals of his displeasure, communicated with a vocabulary of rolling eyes, arched eyebrows, and deep sighs combined with the occasional ironic aside. It sent a clear message, but one that was difficult for those around him to leak. "Unless you were a perfect mimic, you couldn't pass it on," said a former senior Gore aide.

His caution became even more ironclad after the June 1994 publication of *The Agenda,* Bob Woodward's behind-the-scenes account of how the Clinton White House passed its 1993 economic plan. Based on "deep background" interviews with all the principal players — including Clinton and Gore — it reinforced the image of an undisciplined president presiding over an administration frequently in disarray. Perhaps its most riveting vignette featured Gore administering tough love to a whiny chief executive. The president, according to Woodward, lamenting the difficulties of passing his plan, turned to Gore and asked, "What can I do?"

"You can get with the goddamn program!" said a clearly irritated Gore.

According to a senior administration official, the experience of reading intimate scenes from their political marriage in a best-selling book left both men more circumspect about what they said in meetings at which other staff were present. As the first term progressed, Gore began attending fewer sessions at which he shared the table with a gaggle of aides and reserved his critical advice for one-on-one settings like the weekly lunch.

The Woodward tell-all was the least of their problems as 1994 unfolded. Mrs. Clinton's ambitious health care reform plan, with the goal of universal insurance coverage, was relentlessly attacked by Republicans, big business, and the insurance industry as a vast, big-government boondoggle in the making. A multimillion-dollar television ad campaign, combined with Mrs. Clinton's own imperious and unyielding political style, doomed the program. Gore was publicly supportive but had private misgivings about the complexity of the proposal, which set up regional alliances of doctors, hospitals, and insurers. Reluctant to take on the Clintons, however, he quietly distanced himself from it.

After campaigning in 1992 as enlightened centrists, Clinton and Gore looked like off-the-rack liberals to many voters two years later.

Solid accomplishments like deficit reduction, NAFTA, the Family and Medical Leave Act (which helps employees deal with domestic contingencies like an ill child without placing their jobs at risk), and the Earned Income Tax Credit (to help keep low-wage workers above the poverty line) had been eclipsed by gays in the military, the leviathan health care package, and a steady drip of scandal news. On election day not a single Republican incumbent lost a governorship or a seat in the House or Senate. The GOP took the Senate and captured control of the House for the first time in forty-one years, landing Newt Gingrich two heartbeats from the presidency. The repudiation of Clinton was deeply personal. Network exit polls showed that voters with an unfavorable view of the president chose Republican congressional candidates by an 83–17 margin. His 41 percent approval rating in early December was the lowest since Ronald Reagan had registered the same number in the middle of the 1982 recession. The conventional wisdom had his presidency left for dead.

Tipper Gore said later that she had never seen her husband more discouraged in public life than he was in the aftermath of the 1994 midterm elections. As the year ended, he was staring into the abyss, and the image reflecting back to him was of Walter Mondale, another one-term vice president. He also could not have been comforted by the shot that got big play on the network news one night in early January. As Gingrich prepared to bring down the gavel on the first Republican House in four decades, the president, decked out in rubber boots and camouflage jacket for an Arkansas hunting trip, emerged from the woods proudly displaying his prize: two dead ducks.

◆ 19 ◆

To the Edge and Back

THE BLEAK days following the 1994 election provided an ironic sort of consolation for Al Gore. As Bill Clinton's presidency slipped into near-total eclipse behind Newt Gingrich and the 104th Congress, Gore was getting the best press of his life. Like the backup quarterback on a team whose fans wanted the starter benched, he emerged as a symbol of hope for shellshocked Democrats. His poll numbers were consistently better than Clinton's, and he compiled a stack of stories praising his brains, steady style, and unprecedented influence. "Gore May Be Dull, but to His Party He Shines," read one January 1995 headline on the front page of the *Los Angeles Times*. So marginalized had Clinton become — reduced to protesting at an April press conference that "the Constitution gives me relevance" — that Gore began to emerge as more than a valued vice president, but as a potential replacement at the top of the 1996 ticket. "Disillusioned by Mr. Clinton, Democrats who once doubted Mr. Gore's ability to sizzle in a national campaign now whisper conspiratorially about his presidential prospects," wrote the *New York Times*. The murmurs about Clinton's vulnerability were persistent enough that Gore had to declare for the record that under no circumstances would he accept the 1996 Democratic nomination.

The public spin Gore's handlers offered was also his private position — that his best hope of becoming president was getting Clinton reelected. That meant coming up with a compelling response to Gingrich, who announced his intention to dismantle what he called "the liberal welfare state" and balance the federal budget within seven years. The White House was "wall-to-wall, floor-to-ceiling," as one Clintonite described it, with postmortems and strategy sessions between election day and New Year's 1995. In early December, Elaine Kamarck invited several political scientists, including Richard Neustadt, Gore's old Harvard mentor, to talk with the vice president about what had gone wrong.

Neustadt regarded 1994 as a continuation of the 1992 general election, evidence that the country was still seeking the change Clinton and Gore had promised but not delivered. He likened it to Harry Truman's situation after Republican gains in the 1946 midterm elections. One of the reasons for his great comeback in 1948 — aside from Thomas Dewey and a booming economy — was that he had united the country behind bipartisan issues like foreign policy. His point was that a president who led the country where the opposition was willing to go was a president the opposition might not be able to defeat. Gore agreed that the administration needed to head back to its roots in the political center and seek accommodation with the GOP on issues like trade and government reform. He also thought it might be good politics to displease liberal Democrats on a few issues.

Truman in 1948 had become the inspirational example of choice for presidencies on the ropes. The Bush campaign invoked him as it crashed in 1992. But in Gore's case the more relevant parallel was 1970, the year his father lost his Senate seat. Like his son, Albert Gore had felt the lash of rejection from voters for straying too far to the left. The senator paid for it with his career, and Gore had shaped his own by carefully protecting his left flank, trimming back and minimizing liberal positions at times of maximum political risk. He had done it as a first-time congressional candidate in 1976, in 1988 when he ran for president, and in 1992 as Bill Clinton's running mate. In the winter of 1995, staring down the barrel of a one-term presidency, he was prepared to do it again. He had already begun communing with a shadowy figure from the president's past, one known to aides only as "Charlie," who was plotting the administration's course back to the safe harbor of the center.

The story of Dick Morris and the comeback of 1995–96 is now part of American political lore. He had been at Clinton's side during other career crises, including 1980, when Arkansas voters made him the nation's youngest ex-governor. Morris engineered his return to office two years later, and Clinton never lost another race. In Morris's world, polling was not merely an instrument to help elected officials sell their ideas and govern more effectively — it *was* governance. He once called public opinion research "the ultimate master of the western world." Morris practiced his trade for both Democrats and Republicans, and to other political consultants he was the prince of darkness, without compass or principle. "When Clinton lost the election in 1980, he sold his soul to the Devil," said Democratic pollster Pat Caddell, "and the Devil sent him to Dickie Morris."

Guided by Morris's numbers, the administration picked a series of high-profile fights with the GOP on selected issues, while moving inexorably toward Republican values on matters like tax cuts, anticrime measures, and welfare reform. Morris also oversaw a misleading, and devastatingly effective, television advertising campaign depicting the Republicans as poised to slash Medicare benefits. But the GOP, like the White House, was actually proposing cuts in the annual rate of the program's growth, and the differences between the two plans were minimal.

Gore played a critical role in the Clinton-Morris comeback. For all of his native skills as a politician, Clinton was never comfortable on the attack — a style forced on him as the GOP seized control of the policy agenda. Gore, for all his reputed woodenness, always moved easily into the mode of partisan sniper and did so again to backstop the president in 1995. The linchpin of the Republicans' strategy was the expectation that Clinton, as he had in other situations, would buckle under pressure and sign their seven-year budget into law. But he stood his ground, and at pivotal moments it was Gore who steeled his spine and strengthened his resolve. One former senior Clintonite, who frequently clashed with Gore in the first term, acknowledged him as "the quiet hero" of the 1995–96 budget battle.

If Gore had qualms about embracing Morris, the very embodiment of the focus-group politics he claimed to renounce in *Earth in the Balance,* he never expressed them. "I never saw him blink for a minute on Morris," said one former senior aide who was appalled by the consultant's rise. "He took Morris on faith. This is what the president wanted, this is what Hillary wanted. He was supportive right down the line." With Gore's backing, the Clinton-Morris regime redefined the philosophical mainstream of the Democratic Party, shearing away its last links to the New Deal championed by Gore's father, including welfare benefits as a federal entitlement. The result was a smaller government of limited ambition — "the Small Deal," as *Newsweek's* Peter Goldman described it — "an ad hoc activism that sought to meliorate problems rather than write and staff expensive programs to solve them."

Gore was on board. "We need a change around here, a big change," he told Morris in March 1995, "and I'm hoping and praying that you're the man to bring it."

Gore shared a common cause with Morris — both had been thwarted and shunned by Clinton's circle of aides and consultants. He saw Morris as a strategic ally who could help leverage more control over administration policy and roll back the liberal influence of the campaign crowd headed by Stephanopoulos. Both believed that Clinton had tried too hard to please too many constituencies — Congress, party interest groups, political consultants — and had yet to set a direction and stay with it. When Clinton asked Gore to smooth Morris's integration into a West Wing staff traumatized and divided by his presence, Gore was happy to comply. Morris was, in turn, assiduous in his cultivation of the vice president, meeting with him regularly and enlisting his help in lobbying Clinton to adopt some of his ideas. To further ingratiate himself with Gore, he brought in Bob Squier, the vice president's longtime adviser and ad man, to help with the media campaign against the Republicans.

As Morris emerged from his initial cloak of secrecy, Gore supported his attempts to move the White House toward the center. In a watershed April 1995 speech, Clinton laid out for the first time where and how he would fight Gingrich. He promised to veto measures he considered too extreme, including the Republicans' proposed $200 billion tax cut and a repeal of the administration's ban against assault weapons. At the same time he attempted to preempt the GOP by highlighting his own plans for tax reduction, welfare reform, and government reinvention. Gore ran his pencil through a draft of the Dallas speech, signing off on it, but insisting that Morris's excessive praise for the Republicans be trimmed. "Did you get that shit out?" he asked the speechwriters.

Gore was a major influence in Clinton's decision to offer his own balanced budget to compete with the Republican plan. Morris had been urging the move for weeks, but Gore was opposed through the early spring. He sided with Stephanopoulos, Panetta, and Harold Ickes in contending that the GOP should be left to absorb the daily barrage of Democratic attacks on the harshest features of the proposed cuts. But after House Republicans demonstrated that they could pass a budget resolution (a preliminary measure outlining how the government intends to collect and spend revenues for the next five years), he had a change of heart. Gore argued that the president couldn't credibly attack the Republicans without having a blueprint of his own for balancing the books. He personally called the networks to clear five minutes of prime time on June 13, when Clinton announced that he was prepared to bring the budget into balance over ten years, rather than the Republicans' seven.

Morris later became an ally in perhaps the fiercest inside fight that Gore waged at the White House — convincing Clinton to mobilize against GOP attacks on the environment. Gore ended 1994 in close to total despair over what was to have been his flagship issue. The defeat of the BTU tax, and Clinton's lack of interest in environmental matters, had made it virtually impossible to move any kind of significant agenda. Clinton's inaction was reinforced by several top advisers, including Rahm Emanuel, pollster Stan Greenberg, and Stephanopoulos, who argued that there was little appetite among voters for major new green initiatives. At times the administration's indifference flared into outright contempt. During one meeting before the midterm elections, Chief of Staff Leon Panetta complained about a recent ruling under the Endangered Species Act to protect a mouse called the kangaroo rat. "There is a fucking rat in California who is going to cost us the election," carped Panetta.

At a Christmas party in his Naval Observatory residence, Gore took the top officials of several leading environmental groups aside. He was losing the war, he told them, and needed their help. Gingrich and the House Republicans were preparing to gut twenty-five years' worth of legal protections for the environment. Their agenda included strict new limits on the ability of agencies like the EPA to regulate industry; a so-called takings bill, which would broaden the conditions under which the government was required to compensate landowners when official actions adversely affected their property values; and a moratorium on all new federal regulations through the end of 1995. Realizing that polls had become the revealed truth in the Clinton White House,

Gore issued this challenge to the greens: scour the country for every bit of polling data supporting the position that the environment was still a good issue for Democrats to run on.

The greens complied, and in addition to searching they generated some new numbers of their own, hiring former Gore pollster Mark Mellman to look for weaknesses in the GOP's rhetoric about pollution and regulatory reform. What he found was that while voters were not terribly concerned about the kangaroo rats of the world, they continued to place great value on laws ensuring clean air and water. Mellman also discovered that many voters thought "regulatory reform" meant cutting red tape to facilitate the punishment of industrial polluters — not erasing rules to make the world safer for them. In short, Mellman concluded, Gingrich had badly overreached in his conclusions about what Americans expected from the Republican revolution.

Inside the White House, Gore used polling to support his fight for inclusion of the environment as one of the administration's "lines in the sand" against the Republicans. "He was a bulldog," said one senior administration official, hammering Clinton and others in meeting after meeting. In the "pre-briefs," sessions with aides in which Clinton ran through answers to questions anticipated from the press, Gore policed the president's budget rhetoric to make sure he mentioned the environment at every opportunity. "I remember at least a half-dozen occasions where we'd be rehearsing an answer to a question and Clinton would say, 'Commitment to the elderly, give people the tools they need to compete in the economy,' and Gore would always say, 'And protect the environment!' Clinton would laugh and say, 'And to protect the environment.' It was a standard part of their little routine. Even before Clinton could get the words out of his mouth, Gore would jump in. It had an effect. It made it kind of our corporate litany."

By early spring Clinton was aiming broadsides against the GOP for its war on the environment. He used an Earth Day speech in Havre de Grace, Maryland, to decry reports that lobbyists had met with House Majority Whip Tom DeLay to draft measures easing up on regulatory controls. He promised that he would never sign such provisions into law. "For a quarter-century now, Americans have stood as one to say no to dirty air, toxic food, and poisoned water," said Clinton, having seen the light.

Gore's "greening" of Clinton got a boost from Morris later that spring when the consultant examined the results of a poll he conducted for the Virginia Environmental Endowment, his last private client before coming to the White House full-time. Although traditionally conservative Virginians generally supported less government regulation, the one thousand likely voters Morris queried in May did a "complete turnabout" on environmental issues, said Jerry McCarthy, the endowment's executive director, rejecting looser regulation of hazardous waste and drinking water by three-to-one margins. That got Morris's attention, and green officially became political gold at the White House.

Gore's persistence, and Morris's blessing, made green issues part of the mantra that the administration took into its battle with congressional Republicans — insisting that any budget deal protect Medicare, Medicaid, education programs, and the environment from deep cuts. In negotiations with the GOP, Panetta kept a special list of Gore's "must-haves," which included protection of the Arctic National Wildlife Refuge from oil and gas exploration and preservation of the EPA's enforcement powers.

But Gore's crusade of 1995 was still mostly a defensive action to repel the worst of the Republican aggression. And Clinton's newfound environmentalism, propelled as it was by expedience and not principle, was prone to sudden backsliding. He enraged activists later that summer by signing a supplementary funding bill that contained a rider permitting suspension of environmental laws to salvage diseased or fire-damaged trees in certain national forests. The provision was written so broadly that it was interpreted by a federal judge to permit unrestricted logging in many healthy forests. The blunder earned the White House a thunderous "twenty-one-chainsaw salute" from protesters across the street in Lafayette Park.

Morris helped Gore put the environment on the administration's screen, but he also set in motion events that led to the worst ethical trouble of Gore's career. The issue of money weighed heavily on Clinton and his inner circle throughout 1995–96. Concerned about a challenge in the Democratic primaries, and especially anxious about Colin Powell's as-yet-unannounced plans, the president authorized fund-raiser Terry McAuliffe and political adviser Harold Ickes to be-

gin building a campaign war chest in early 1995 to discourage potential competitors. They amassed more than $9 million by the end of
June, some of which Morris and Squier used to finance the first in a
series of television spots promoting Clinton's record (this one dealt
with the assault weapons ban) and attacking the Republican program.
Later that summer Morris pressed for more television time to pound
the GOP as villains on Medicare. Some aides thought it was madness
to invest so heavily in advertising eighteen months from the election,
especially since they were limited by law to raising $30 million (they
would also receive $15 million in matching funds). But Clinton and
Gore both wanted to press ahead and decided to use the Democratic
National Committee as a fund-raising vehicle to underwrite Morris's
television campaign.

Clinton hated asking for money and made it clear to aides that he
had better things to do than shill for the DNC. He agreed to the usual
chores like appearances at dinners, lunches, and receptions, but he
drew the line at solicitation. "You guys are the fund-raisers," he said.
"I'm not going to make calls to do your job."

Perhaps because he had seen his father, a halfhearted fund-raiser,
badly outspent by Bill Brock in 1970, Gore played the Washington
money game aggressively. Part of his dowry to Clinton in 1992 was the
deep network of financial support he had built over fifteen years in
Washington with the help of Peter Knight, Nate Landow, and Johnny
Hayes. Gore's regular money men included DNC finance chairman
Jess Hay, California real estate entrepreneur Walter Shorenstein, and
Florida banker Howard Glicken, whose two Jaguars bore vanity plates
declaring "Gore 1" and "Gore 2." These men quickly raised more than
$3 million for the presidential campaign.

Gore and his staff were meticulous about the care and feeding of
those who solicited money for him. Fund-raisers who delivered were
lodged in his memory banks forever. When the wife of Alan Kessler, a
Philadelphia attorney who first raised funds for Gore in 1988, had a
baby two years later, Gore called her almost immediately after she got
home from the hospital. In 1989 a friend of Kessler's who had contributed $1,000 to Gore, a young Senate aide named Ken Smukler, com-
plained to Kessler that he had been blown off by Gore at a reception
when he tried to ask about getting a job with the Democratic Senatorial Campaign Committee. When Smukler and Gore were reintro-

duced on the vice president's next visit to Philadelphia, Smukler encountered a more gracious Gore. "You know," said Gore, "I don't really
know what I did, but I'm sorry for it."

Gore wasn't reticent about "eating the spinach," or closing the deal
for a contribution on his own, as he did when he retired his own 1988
debt. He accepted the exercise as part of what it took to win, and it
seemed to tap into his sharp competitive instincts. With his background, he fit easily into the voracious money culture of the 1996 reelection campaign, earning his reputation as "solicitor-in-chief" of the
Democratic fund-raising effort. Four years after the Clinton-Gore
ticket had decried the corrosive influence of money in politics ("On
streets where statesmen once strolled, a never-ending stream of
money now changes hands," they declared in their campaign manifesto *Putting People First*), big-money contributors enjoyed extraordinary access to the White House, down to overnight stays in the Lincoln Bedroom. Gore led the way in ensuring a stream of reelection
cash for Clinton and the Democrats. He was the main event at thirty-
nine fund-raising dinners, lunches, and receptions raising $8.74 mil-
lion. He also hosted twenty-three White House "coffees," to which
major contributors were invited, and joined Clinton at eight others.
Appearing before audiences of well-to-do donors who had just
pledged their cash, Gore often began with an old JFK line: "I am
deeply touched, but not as deeply touched as you."

As an added task, the DNC prepared a lengthy list of potential
donors for Gore to phone. He reached fifty-two, securing nearly
$800,000 in commitments. Gore was gung-ho, to the point where he
apparently felt he didn't have enough to do. Notes by former deputy
chief of staff David Strauss from a 1995 White House strategy meeting
record Gore as saying, "Is it possible to do a reallocation for me to take
more of the events and the calls?"

The phone solicitations would scarcely merit a footnote in political
history were it not for Gore's decision to place the calls from his White
House office, putting him at odds with an 1882 law that barred federal
employees from soliciting or receiving campaign contributions in a
federal building. The Pendleton Act was a relic, a reformist response to
the routine bribery and corruption of the Gilded Age, but it was still
observed by members of Congress, who routinely left their offices to
make fund-raising calls from other locations. There are conflicting ac-

counts of Gore's fidelity to the statute. Peter Knight said that when Gore was on the Hill he always did his phone work from his parents' apartment across the street in the Methodist Building, suggesting that he was aware of his legal obligations. But one Senate aide who requested anonymity said he distinctly recalls Gore soliciting from his office in the early stages of his 1988 presidential campaign. "I remember him calling people in Texas and other places saying, 'I need your help, I need your money,'" he said. In 1995, the year Gore began dialing donors for the Morris television spots, White House counsel Abner Mikva circulated a memo warning that "campaign activities of any kind are prohibited in or from government buildings . . . no fundraising calls or mail may emanate from the White House." Gore's legal status under Pendleton was murky, and after the election he argued that he did nothing wrong. But what was clear was that his usually circumspect instincts had been flattened by the money hunt. As it turned out, his tortured defense and less-than-candid answers about what was at best only a technical violation were what would land him in serious political trouble.

As the budget fight slogged on through the fall toward the end of the year, Gore's toughness seemed to embolden Clinton. On November 1, 1995, with a shutdown of the federal government less than two weeks away unless both sides could agree on a spending plan, Clinton and Gore hosted Gingrich, Senate Majority Leader Bob Dole, Minority Leader Tom Daschle, and House Minority Leader Dick Gephardt at a meeting in the Oval Office. Months of resentment on both sides bubbled to the surface. Gingrich, furious about the Morris-inspired ad campaign that demagogued the Medicare issue, raged at Clinton for running "a chicken-shit operation," and added, "You've been calling me an extremist!" Clinton listened quietly, until Gore broke in. "At least we didn't accuse people of drowning babies," he said, referring to Susan Smith, the South Carolina woman who drove her car into a lake with her two young sons strapped inside and then reported them missing. A year earlier, in one of his dumber cultural commentaries, Gingrich suggested that Democratic policies and the liberal values they promoted were somehow responsible for the horrific crime.

One former senior aide in the room that day said that Gore's head-banging response to Gingrich prompted Clinton to try his own tough talk. After more discussion led to an impasse he said, pointing to his desk, "If you want somebody to sign your budget, you're going to have to elect someone else to sit there because I'm not going to do it. You're going to have to get yourself another president." The year ended in disaster for Gingrich and the Republicans as voters blamed them for the failed negotiations that led to two government shutdowns. Gingrich himself melted down, trapped by the White House, the hard-liners in his caucus, and his own penchant for self-combustion, as when he whined about being snubbed on Air Force One en route back from Yitzhak Rabin's funeral.

Morris and Clinton desperately wanted a balanced budget deal to take into the 1996 political season. But in this case, Gore was not on board. He joined the internal opposition to settlement, a camp that included his old nemeses Stephanopoulos and Ickes. They argued for an agreement that met the priorities they had set in Medicare, Medicaid, education, and the environment and were otherwise loathe to give up budgetary issues Democrats could use as sticks against the GOP in 1996.

It was August 1997 before the two sides signed a plan to balance the budget by 2002. Chastened somewhat by the public relations beating they took for the shutdowns, the Republicans finally agreed to many of the White House's terms. But while the Republicans had lost the war, they won the battle of ideas. They put Clinton and Gore on a forced march to the right, compelling the president, as he did in his 1996 State of the Union speech, to utter words that would once have been apostasy for a Democrat: "The era of big government is over."

Unfolding along with the protracted budget debate was the darkness in Bosnia, where U.S. policy verged on collapse in mid-1995. The televised spectacle of United Nations peacekeepers, taken hostage by the Serbs and chained to telephone poles and bridges as human shields against NATO bombing raids, became a new symbol of American and European fecklessness. In the Senate, Dole pressed for the United States to break with the United Nations and unilaterally lift the arms embargo on the Bosnian Muslims so that they could defend themselves.

Gore feared more disaster if the embargo were lifted. It almost certainly would cause Russia to follow suit to end its embargo and help the Serbs, who would then overrun the Muslims. The British and French would probably pull their troops from the UN peacekeeping force, requiring the United States, under the NATO operations plan, to commit up to twenty thousand troops to cover their retreat. By summer Srebrenica had fallen, producing thousands of new Bosnian Muslim refugees and a fresh wave of ethnic cleansing.

Gore was by no means alone among top administration officials in urging a more aggressive U.S. response. National security adviser Anthony Lake and UN ambassador Madeleine Albright were also deeply frustrated by American impotence. But at a pivotal Oval Office meeting in July, Gore made a memorable emotional appeal for a new policy. He referred to a front-page picture run a few days earlier in the *Washington Post,* showing a young refugee woman, about the same age as his daughter Karenna, who had hung herself from a tree with her belt and floral shawl. "My daughter asked me the other day why we weren't doing anything about it," Gore said. "She's twenty-one years old, and there's a twenty-one-year-old girl hanging from a tree." It was hard to face a question like that, he added, when there were no good answers. One senior official present said that "everyone around the room was very, very quiet," and that no one, including Clinton, responded to Gore directly. But the image he conjured gave momentum to the endgame strategy Lake was preparing to sell to NATO allies. The resulting "carrots and sticks" approach, combining diplomacy with massive bombing to drive all sides to the bargaining table, led to the November 1995 peace settlement reached in Dayton, Ohio, and the deployment of U.S. troops to the Balkans at year's end to enforce its terms.

The high-stakes gambles on Bosnia and the budget, combined with the political near-death experience of the midterm elections, brought Al Gore and Bill Clinton closer together by the end of 1995. It had become a genuine friendship, and the weekly lunches were a place for personal confidences as well as business. Gore spoke to Clinton about his late sister Nancy often enough that Clinton said later that he felt as if he knew her personally. At the heart of the relationship, however, was an interest in policy and each other's political success. They seldom socialized outside the office, either as a twosome or with their wives. And Gore didn't golf, which disqualified him from sharing at least one of Clinton's major off-hour passions. If Clinton wanted to share locker-room banter, there were other male friends in his life, like Vernon Jordan, who filled that role.

Aides to both men detected the competitive tensions of a sibling rivalry. "It was friendly, but kind of like my dick is bigger than your dick," one former senior Clinton aide said. Clinton enjoyed teasing his straitlaced older brother about all the admiring press he received, and about his ambition. For his forty-eighth birthday in 1996, Clinton gave his understudy fake keys to Air Force One and a picture of the duo at a State of the Union address with their faces reversed. But there was also resentment lurking behind the ribbing. Gore was Washington's hometown boy made good, born and raised on Massachusetts Avenue, and a regular on the Georgetown dinner party circuit. He was a reminder to Clinton of his own lack of acceptance by the Washington establishment, "the fucking Washington crowd," he called it.

Like most of the rest of the world, Clinton also poked fun at Gore's wooden bearing. "Hey, I'm Al," he said to aides, standing stiff and motionless just before entering the East Room for an appearance. But he was also usually generous in sharing the spotlight with Gore, often more so than his advisers thought was necessary. "They always said, 'Can't we get a picture of Bill Clinton without Al Gore on his shoulder?'" said one former senior Gore aide. At the elaborate Library of Congress signing ceremony for the Telecommunications Act in February 1996, Clinton paid tribute to Gore and his father by using a pen with which President Dwight Eisenhower had signed the interstate highway system into law. Albert Gore had been Senate cosponsor of the landmark 1956 bill, and four decades later his son helped shepherd a measure that lifted many long-standing competitive barriers for phone, cable, and broadcast companies along the "information superhighway." Gore was visibly moved by Clinton's tribute to his father's legacy.

Each tried, with limited success, to help the other with political and managerial weaknesses. As much as Clinton admired his vice president, he was also a source of bafflement. Clinton told friends that he had never seen anyone come so far in politics with so little appreciation for the deadening effect he sometimes had on audiences. He attempted to sand down the rough edges of Gore's sometimes strident advocacy, encouraging him to be a little easier and more inclusive with those who disagreed with him. Clinton spoke with him, said a senior administration official, "about how to make people feel good about being part of the process, instead of just being right."

For his part, Gore liked to joke that he had helped Clinton become "strategically boring" on occasion, meaning more brief and circumspect in his unscripted comments. He also developed considerable skill at letting the air out of Clinton's anger before he met with reporters. In the pre-briefs before press conferences, Gore used a light touch to relax Clinton, and his often barbed, sarcastic humor was usually on target. In one 1994 prep session, Clinton was advised that he might get a question on the proliferation of sleazy tabloid stories dominating the news, involving figures such as skater Tonya Harding, the Menendez brothers, and Lorena Bobbitt, acquitted by reason of temporary insanity for cutting off her husband's penis. "No matter what you do," Gore deadpanned, "be sure to use the word *penis* as much as possible."

At home the Gores faced their own adjustment to a kind of celebrity they had never experienced. Tipper Gore had an office and small staff at the Old Executive Office Building next to the White House and headed up the mental health segment of the first lady's ill-fated health care task force; her group pressed for a plan that treated emotional disorders on a par with physical problems. But she rationed her time there, spending Mondays and Fridays at home and grabbing whatever opportunities she could to slip briefly out of the official bubble. One summer day in 1993 she impulsively hopped on a motorcycle for a ride around town with a White House staffer, raising her arms from time to time in a "look, Ma, no hands" gesture. When they pulled up to the security checkpoint at the Naval Observatory residence, she pulled her helmet off with a flourish for the surprised guards. One old Tennessee friend remembers encountering her sitting happily in the food court at Reagan National Airport, "completely grubbed out" in jeans, no makeup, and baseball cap planted snugly over her blond hair. Unrecognized by those around her, she was waiting for Karenna's flight to land and clearly savoring the few moments of anonymity.

Her major priority was protecting the privacy of her children, three of them still living at home (Kristin, Sarah, and Albert III; Karenna was away at Harvard) when they moved into the one-hundred-year-old official residence in mid-1993 after several months of renovations. (Later she also took on the care of her aging mother, moving Margaret Carlson Aitcheson into the house.) Tipper Gore liked to say that the vice presidency was more family-friendly than the Senate, with its endless deliberations and unpredictable voting schedule. This is probably an exaggeration, but the Gores did make an effort, aides said, to have family dinners every week. They pulled out Dan Quayle's putting green and had it reseeded for games of badminton, although the vice president was out of action for several months in 1994 after tearing his Achilles' tendon playing basketball. They also set aside nights for movies. Gore's favorite was the IMAX Theater at the Air and Space Museum, where the rest of the family good-naturedly endured repeat screenings of films like *Blue Planet.* "It's a thrill every time," Tipper said with a game smile in a 1996 interview.

Both Gores tried to clear their schedules for the kids' school sports. Sarah was a midfielder on the National Cathedral School soccer squad, Kristin a forward on the field hockey team, and both excelled at lacrosse; Albert played football at St. Albans. Aides say the games were serious family business. "Whenever something was scheduled during one of his kids' games, there was hell to pay," said former chief of staff Jack Quinn.

But the familial cocoon couldn't keep out all unwanted attention. The Gores' three attractive blond daughters became cult celebrities, often juxtaposed, unkindly, with the then-gawky Chelsea Clinton. *Spy* magazine depicted them in a 1993 comic strip as bikini-clad wonk-babes sunning themselves and talking policy ("Duh! Everyone knows that the North American Free Trade Agreement with its new provisions for environmental protection is stoopid fresh," said one) as they eagerly anticipated an evening out at a lecture by Robert Reich ("I hope he uses the overhead projector to illustrate his six-point job retraining plan," said another).

And because they were Gores, the usual adolescent troubles brought unusual, and painful, exposure. In October 1996 Sarah Gore, then sixteen, was cited by Montgomery County police for holding an open container of beer in a car outside a party. Earlier that year, eighth-grader Albert III was suspended from St. Albans for smoking dope during a school dance. School administrators treated it like any other infraction of discipline, with a public announcement — minus the name of the transgressor — in the dining hall. Anonymity didn't keep word from spreading back to dinner tables throughout Washington, and eventually to the press. Gore called leading news organizations around Washington and asked them not to run the story, and all complied.

But when a school official alluded, again without specifics, at a year-end ceremony to the difficulties of the past academic year, the Gores regarded it as an unwarranted public slap at their son. "Tipper felt the school let the family down," said Matt Simchak, Gore's old St. Albans chum who served on the school's board of trustees. "They thought that Albert was especially vulnerable and needed to be protected." Shortly afterward, the Gores cut all ties with the school where they met as teenagers and enrolled Albert in another exclusive private institution, Sidwell Friends, the following fall.

The 1996 election was probably decided in 1995 when Newt Gingrich became the most unpopular politician in America. Bill Clinton and Al Gore campaigned not against Republican nominee Bob Dole but a sinister mutant named "Dolegingrich," who, they said, stood poised to bring the extremism of the Republican revolution to the White House. Meanwhile, Morris's pollster Mark Penn employed a modified version of the Myers-Briggs personality assessment used by employers and management consultants to plumb the psyches of the upscale suburban parents who made up the critical swing vote. An improved economy had pushed other social and cultural concerns to the top of the agenda for many Americans. The research suggested that people worried less about layoffs and more about what their kids watched on television or whether they did drugs. "It's the economy, stupid," had become, "It's values, stupid."

Gore made the entertainment industry one of his principal election-year targets in the values offensive. The new telecommunications bill he championed included a provision Hollywood had fought for years, the so-called V-chip to help parents electronically deflect shows and movies they didn't want their kids to see. The law mandated the V-chip in most new sets and gave the industry one year to devise a "voluntary" ratings system to determine which programs would be blocked. If programmers didn't set up their own system within a year, the government would do it for them. On February 8, the same day Clinton signed the bill, Gore sat down to lunch with a small group of industry heavyweights that included Time Warner's Gerald Levin and Ted Turner, and Jack Valenti, head of the Motion Picture Association of America, Hollywood's lobbying arm in Washington. The gathering was supposed to be a celebration of the groundbreaking new legislation, but Gore also used the occasion to do some arm-twisting. Clinton had invited television and movie executives to a February 29 White House conference on children's programming, and Gore's message to his guests was blunt: the administration held the high ground on this issue. Polls reflected mounting voter anger over the coarsening of popular culture, and the executives were in for a public relations beating if they came back to Washington at the end of the month reluctant to institute a ratings system. "We said, You're going to be in the same room with the president and vice president for two hours," said a senior Gore adviser. "It can be a positive experience or a negative experience." After some shuttle diplomacy by Valenti, the industry was ready to talk about a deal.

Morris again tailored the message to the polls, crafting a series of modestly scaled and carefully targeted initiatives designed to lure the swing vote without arousing fears of more Democratic "big government." "Bitesize works best," he wrote in a March 1996 memo, and every week the little measures were rolled out — addressing domestic violence, tobacco use by minors, student loans and pensions. Sometimes the bites were so small that Clinton and Gore seemed like two city councilmen running for mayor rather than White House incumbents standing for reelection. One offering from the Morris boutique was money for neighborhood crime watch groups to buy cell phones.

There was one enormous campaign-season decision to be made, and it showed the distance Clinton and Gore were willing to travel to guarantee their survival. The welfare reform bill passed by the Republican Congress took a jackhammer to one of the cornerstones of the New Deal: a federal guarantee of aid to poor children. Morris warned Clinton and Gore that a veto — it would be the third such rejection of a Republican welfare reform bill — could imperil reelection. Signing it into law, he said, all but guaranteed victory. The main provisions of the Personal Responsibility and Work Opportunity Act — time limits on benefits and stringent work requirements for recipients — were ideas that Clinton had championed for years. But the bill also ended the sixty-year federal entitlement and replaced it with lump sum block grants to be administered by the states. Republicans had also laced the bill with devastating cuts in funding for food stamps and child nutrition programs and eliminated Supplemental Social Security aid to elderly and disabled legal immigrants. In a blistering floor speech, Senator Daniel Patrick Moynihan, whose views on welfare were once considered conservative, called the measure a travesty: "The premise of this legislation is that the behavior of certain adults can be changed by making the lives of their children as wretched as possible," he said. "This is a fearsome assumption."

Gore was silent during a tense midmorning cabinet room meeting on July 31, where a deeply divided group of senior officials argued their cases for Clinton. Even the "two Bobs," Labor Secretary Reich and Treasury Secretary Rubin, frequently at odds on economic policy, joined Health and Human Services Secretary Donna Shalala, Housing and Urban Development Secretary Henry Cisneros, Panetta, and Stephanopoulos in warning that millions of poor families could be severely harmed by the bill. A new study by the Urban Institute projected that it could push as many as 1.1 million children below the poverty line. Politically, they argued, Clinton could afford another veto. He had already established his centrist bona fides by proposing a balanced budget. With a healthy approval rating and a comfortable lead in the polls, he had enough political capital to weather the criticism.

Proponents, led by domestic policy adviser Bruce Reed, a former Gore speechwriter, and Commerce Secretary Mickey Kantor, warned that Clinton would probably never get another crack at welfare reform, a central 1992 campaign promise. The most noxious aspects of the bill could be amended after the election if the Democrats retook Congress. Summing up their arguments, one senior Gore aide said, "Despite all the crap in this bill, this was his [Clinton's] bill, his vision. He'd basically gotten it." But the original Clinton-Gore welfare bill was actually light-years from the Republican version. It had a tough work requirement (two years and then off the rolls) but included an additional $10 billion for job training and child care. It also preserved the federal entitlement and provided that those who couldn't find work would get federally subsidized jobs.

When the two-hour session broke up, Clinton retreated to the Oval

Office with Gore and Panetta. He was torn between the political up-
side and the potential harm to impoverished children. But Gore urged
that he sign and "tipped the balance," as one administration insider
told the *Wall Street Journal*'s Al Hunt. Although it is impossible to
know with certainty what might have happened had Gore recommended a veto, it clearly would have been more difficult for Clinton to
sign, knowing that his vice president and Treasury secretary, two of his
most valued advisers, disapproved.

(Clinton did ultimately restore some of the worst cuts in the 1997
budget deal with House Republicans. The bill's supporters say it is an
extraordinary success story, and that the dire predictions have so far
been wrong. About 1.6 million families have left the welfare rolls in the
last three years, and state surveys find that up to 70 percent of former
recipients have found work. But critics argue that the numbers have
been leavened by a booming economy. Other studies show that many
of the jobs are short-lived and that many who leave welfare have trouble staying above the poverty line.)

Even with a comfortable lead in the polls, Gore was nervous. He regarded Whitewater as a small-time matter blown grossly out of proportion by the Republican attack machine, but he worried about the
pounding the Clintons were taking, and the possibility of fresh revelations. He also thought that the Clintonites underestimated Dole, a
canny political warrior he had watched up close for years in the Senate. He fretted when Dole's selection for a vice presidential running
mate was Jack Kemp, a considerably more formidable opponent than
others whose names had surfaced before the Republican convention
in San Diego, like Florida Senator Connie Mack. In the days after
Kemp's nomination, Clinton tried to buck up his number two, reassuring him that he could more than hold his own against the loqua-
cious ex-quarterback, as he did in a no-contest October debate.

Gore's 1996 campaign was set up by White House strategists as an
early dress rehearsal for 2000, a chance for him to step squarely into
the role of heir apparent. Clinton spent the first two days of the Democratic convention on a whistle-stop tour of the Midwest, leaving center stage in Chicago all to Gore, and he used it to minister to every important party constituency, from labor to Latinos. Although the vice
presidential nominee traditionally delivers his acceptance speech right
before the presidential candidate, Gore got his own night as the main

event in prime time. His address on Wednesday evening, August 28, would be the most important of his career so far.

From his earliest meetings with Gore to discuss the speech, Bob Squier said it was clear that he wanted to talk about his sister's death. He had rarely spoken of Nancy Gore Hunger in public, although those close to him knew about the grief her memory still triggered. When tobacco policy was discussed at the White House, he could scarcely contain his emotions, to the point where some aides wondered whether his judgment was impaired. "It was more religion than something arrived at in some kind of assemblage of facts," said one former senior administration official. "You knew what was driving it." Clinton, the acknowledged master of political theater, encouraged Gore to talk about her publicly. It would raise an important policy matter in compelling fashion and bring more humanity to his image.

Cigarettes and kids would certainly be one of the issues he addressed in Chicago. The White House was about to announce that the Food and Drug Administration, after eight years of study and debate, would regulate cigarettes and chewing tobacco as drug delivery devices because of nicotine's addictive qualities. The administration's plan called for restricting the access of minors to tobacco products, requiring stores to demand photo identification from young cigarette purchasers, and limiting vending machines to bars and other adults-only locations.

The issue carried such emotional charge with Gore that, according to Squier, no one on his staff dared raise with him an obvious political problem. In memorializing his sister as a victim of cigarette smoking, he exposed himself to questions about his own relationship with the tobacco industry. For seven years after Nancy's death, he continued to take contributions from cigarette manufacturers and grew tobacco on his farm. One aide raised the concern about tobacco farming with chief of staff Ron Klain and communications director Lorraine Voles; he was told that there was no problem because Gore had stopped these activities some time ago. The issue of campaign contributions didn't come up.

Another reason the discussion never took place may have been that Gore seemed to be wavering. He was usually painstaking in his preparation of major speeches, handing out research assignments to aides and lining easels and walls with reams of butcher-block paper that contained outlines, ideas, and fragments of thoughts. But the Nancy question hung in limbo as the convention neared. Early drafts left a section blank except for one notation: "6 minutes."

The passage was still unwritten when Gore arrived in Chicago. Only on the eve of his appearance, during a run-through at a rehearsal podium under the stands at the United Center, did Squier finally prod him into laying down the words, and he said he cried as Gore told the story. Later, in Gore's hotel suite, as Frank Hunger — who supported the tribute to his wife — Tom Downey, and his senior staff looked on in stone silence, Gore repeated it into a tape recorder for speechwriter Dan Pink, who dropped the passage into the text nearly verbatim. Even then, Gore said later, he wasn't sure until shortly before he went on that night that he would use it.

As television cameras cut away to Albert and Pauline, who sat weeping in their VIP seats, Gore told a hushed arena audience about his sister's inability to quit smoking, her diagnosis, and her last minutes drifting in and out of consciousness. "I loved her more than life," he said. "She couldn't speak, but I felt clearly I knew she was forming a question. 'Do you bring me hope?' All I could do was say back to her, with all the gentleness in my heart, 'I love you.' And then I knelt by her bed and held her hand. And in a very short time, her breathing became labored, and then she breathed her last breath. Tomorrow morning another thirteen-year-old will start smoking. I love her, too. And that is why until I draw my last breath, I will pour my heart and soul into protecting children from the dangers of smoking."

Some of the reaction was scathing, even among friends. Taken in tandem with his 1992 account of Albert's car accident, it seemed as if Gore was exploiting his family's pain as an offering to the Oprahization of national conventions, where the values of daytime television — teary confessionals and neatly packaged stories of triumph over adversity — had become commonplace. "Appalled," said one intimate with Tennessee and Washington ties. "You don't talk about your dead sister in a national convention acceptance speech," said a former administration official who had worked with Gore closely on foreign affairs. Andrew Ferguson, writing later in *Time*, called it "the most hair-raising address by a major American politician since Richard Nixon wrapped his long-suffering wife in a 'good Republican cloth coat' and invoked his daughters' dog Checkers." The speech called into question, Ferguson said, the very qualities it was intended to display. "Could anyone who really loved his sister exploit her death so shamelessly?" he asked.

Squier acknowledged that the reception of the speech took the Gore camp by surprise. "All of us were quite startled," he said, including the vice president himself, when morning-after commentary suggested that he had been manipulative and hypocritical. In retrospect, he conceded, he and the rest of Gore's advisers were remiss in not engaging him on the question before he gave the speech. Squier called the group "a circle of people who are blind to some things they shouldn't be blind to."

Fortunately for Gore, much of the convention press corps was wildly distracted the next day by the resignation of Dick Morris, whose toe-sucking liaisons with a hooker at the Jefferson Hotel in Washington had been splashed across the pages of a supermarket tabloid. At a luncheon with reporters, he was asked to reconcile his tribute to Nancy with the years of campaign contributions, the growing allotments, and the folksy speeches currying favor with tobacco farmers. Reflecting the influence of Alice Miller's writing on dysfunctional families, Gore replied that "emotional numbness" prevented him from seeing the issue clearly until years later. "It takes time to fully absorb the most important lessons of life," he said.

Should it have taken seven years after his sister's death? Gore didn't sever his direct ties to tobacco, his growing allotment and campaign donations, until 1991. After watching their sister and daughter die a lingering death from lung cancer, coming to grips with their long and remunerative tobacco tradition was no doubt difficult for the Gores. But a seven-year interval suggests not numbness but laxity and expedience.

Unaccustomed to having his motives challenged and his integrity questioned by a usually friendly press, criticism of the Chicago speech stung Gore. While his position on tobacco hadn't changed immediately after Nancy's death, his current stance had been in place for years before he gave the speech. He lashed out with uncharacteristic public bitterness in a 1997 interview with *The New Yorker*'s Joe Klein. "It was bullshit," he said when asked about the commentary. "People don't change immediately; there's a process of growth. But the press has these two categories — either you're a good guy in a white hat or you're a hypocrite. Human beings are more complex than that."

Moneychangers in the Temple

T HE 1996 convention speech was a watershed for Al Gore. He strode to the podium that evening in the most commanding position of his career, number two in an administration cruising toward reelection and unquestioned front-runner for his party's next presidential nomination. Yet nothing was ever quite the same for him after his "6 minutes" in Chicago. The residue of hypocrisy left by his tribute to Nancy, and the increased scrutiny that came with his status as heir apparent, changed the political environment in which he operated. His speech certainly didn't cause the problems that plagued him over the next two years. But that August evening marked the beginning of a downward arc that left his reputation for probity and prospects for the presidency tarnished.

His fears about new scandal bubbling up to threaten reelection in 1996 turned out to be well founded. This time, however, it was not just the Clintons who would have questions to answer. The first hint of trouble emerged in September, when newspapers began looking at several suspicious six-figure campaign contributions solicited on behalf of the Democratic National Committee by fund-raiser John Huang, a former executive of the Lippo Group, the Indonesian banking and real estate conglomerate owned by the Riady family. The Riadys had always given generously to the Democrats and to Clinton, dating back to his days as Arkansas attorney general. They donated nearly half a million dollars to the party after Clinton's presidential nomination in 1992, the kind of largesse that brought access to the White House. James Riady, scion of the family empire headed by his father Mochtar, visited at least twenty times during Clinton's first term. While administration officials initially described the occasions as social events or courtesy calls, it turned out that the Riadys also had a business agenda, which included urging Clinton to normalize relations with Vietnam and strengthen U.S. economic ties to China. The family was also able to place Huang, an executive in charge of Lippo's U.S. operations, in the Commerce Department as deputy assistant secretary for international economic policy, a post he held for eighteen months.

But it was as a fund-raiser that Huang became a star, working sources in the Asian American community to bring in at least $4 million to the DNC in 1996, part of the torrent of "soft money" that poured into the bank accounts of both parties. Although party funds for specific campaigns, known as "hard money," are strictly limited (only individuals can donate, to a maximum of $20,000 a year), soft money is a wide-open affair. Individuals, corporations, and unions can all contribute unlimited amounts, and they did. The only legal stipulation is that soft money be used for general party expenses like voter education. But as Dick Morris's DNC-financed television ad campaign demonstrated, the distinction between spending for the benefit of the party and for candidates had become virtually nonexistent.

Huang's connections to Lippo raised suspicions about illegal foreign money seeping into the Clinton-Gore campaign. The DNC returned a $250,000 contribution he secured from a South Korean corporation after determining that the money came from the parent company overseas, not the U.S. subsidiary. (Foreign-owned subsidiaries can contribute only if the revenue was generated in the United States.) The party also disallowed a $425,000 donation that Huang obtained from an Indonesian couple with family connections to Mochtar Riady who lived in a modest suburban Virginia townhouse.

Huang's handiwork delivered Gore to the costliest lunch of his career, and one that came to symbolize the money-grubbing ethic of the 1996 campaign. Three weeks before election day, several newspapers reported that Huang had organized a fund-raiser, attended by Gore, at the Hsi Lai Buddhist Temple in suburban Los Angeles on April 29. The event raised $140,000, despite federal laws that prohibit holding partisan political events at institutions with tax-exempt status. The basic circumstances were bad enough for Gore, but what gave the story its truly farcical punch was that some of the temple's monks and nuns, who had taken vows of poverty, admitted to serving as illegal "straw" donors, writing checks for up to $5,000 and receiving immediate reimbursement from temple officials.

Gore's temple appearance was not originally intended as a fundraiser, and he says he was never aware that money changed hands before and after the event. Exactly what he knew may never be completely clear. But like his White House telephone calls to donors, the episode suggests that Gore's zeal for election money in 1996 eroded his judgment, sense of propriety, and usual attention to detail.

His road to the temple began eight years earlier during a reception at Pamela Harriman's Georgetown home. There he met Maria Hsia, a thirty-six-year-old Taiwanese immigrant who had built a lucrative Los Angeles practice as an immigration consultant, helping Taiwan citizens gain U.S. visas. Hsia cultivated a network of political contacts to help her clients, persuading prominent California Democrats like Senator Alan Cranston to write to the Immigration and Naturalization Service (INS) on her behalf. Around the same time she began raising money for them in the Asian American community.

Hsia wanted to be a player in Washington, and so did some of her clients. Among them was Lippo Bank in Los Angeles, a Riady-owned U.S. subsidiary. In 1988 Hsia, Riady, and Huang founded the Pacific Leadership Council (PLC), a lobbying and fund-raising organization that they hoped would someday wield the political clout of the Teamsters or the National Rifle Association (NRA).

Riady had a lengthy lobbying "wish list" that he passed on to Hsia. He wanted to enlist U.S. senators to pressure Taiwan into allowing Asian American banks to open branch offices there, to increase appointments of Asian Americans to top federal positions, and to get assistance for "special, exceptional" immigration cases when they arose. He also sought to encourage more travel by U.S. officials to Indonesia, Hong Kong, and Taiwan, outposts of the Lippo empire. The PLC made plans for just such a trip in early 1989.

Gore was not an influential figure in banking or immigration matters, but he was still one of five senators Hsia invited to travel to Asia at the PLC's expense in January 1989. "I remembered at Mrs. Harriman's house when you mentioned to me that you would like to know the Asian community better and would like to be closer to them," she wrote to Gore on November 22. Hsia's invitation also came with a fairly explicit promise: "If you decide to join this trip, I will persuade all my colleagues in the future to play a leader role in your future presidential race."

The Hsia connection undoubtedly looked attractive to Gore. He was short on cash — having only recently retired a two-million-dollar debt from his 1988 presidential campaign — and up for reelection in 1990. There were also opportunities for Taiwanese investment in Tennessee. The country had recently loosened its laws to permit increased business activity in the United States. Even with a heavy January travel schedule — he was also set to visit the Brazilian rain forests — he made room for the three-day Taiwan segment of the weeklong tour, which also included Indonesia and Hong Kong. Gore became the only senator to sign on for the trip, which was approved by the Senate Ethics Committee as "educational" foreign travel.

Hsia had another client who was an interested party to the trip. Venerable Master Hsing Yun was founder of the Fo Kuang Shan order, a thriving Taiwan Buddhist sect that was expanding beyond the island into a worldwide network of 1.5 million adherents and 130 temples. One of his newest outposts was the Hsi Lai Temple in the Hacienda Heights suburb of Los Angeles. This was no simple pagoda, but a 15-acre, $30 million complex with multiple shrines and meditation halls, classrooms, conference rooms, a nunnery, VIP lodge, auditorium, and museum. The project's grand scale reflected not only Hsing Yun's eagerness to "spread the Dharma," or increase the popularity of Buddhist culture in the United States, but also his aspirations to play a role on the international stage, serving as an adviser to world leaders. Yun helped underwrite travel costs for Gore and the rest of the delegation, which included Huang, Hsia, about a dozen other PLC members, and California officials.

On January 8, 1989, Gore, Peter Knight, and Leon Fuerth flew to Taipei. They dined with local dignitaries, met officials of the American Institute of Taiwan, the informal U.S. diplomatic mission, and hosted a breakfast for fifteen top Taiwanese businessmen to discuss business opportunities in Tennessee. Gore toured the Fo Kuang Shan Temple in Kiaoshing on January 11, where he dined with Hsing Yun. In a 1996 article, the monk said the two had discussed his hopes of winning the presidency. "I said to him, 'You can become president of the U.S.' He was excited upon hearing that and said, 'I will visit you when I become president.'"

The trip inaugurated a relationship between Gore and Hsia that combined fund-raising, policy, and favors. Although never a major player in Gore's financial world, she was a steadfast one. Hsia made good on her promise of assistance, arranging a $250-per-person reception at the Beverly Hills home of a PLC cofounder, Tina Bow, on May 21, 1989, that raised nearly $20,000 for Gore's Senate reelection. She also steered an additional $29,500 his way through the Democratic Senatorial Campaign Committee. In a May 23 letter of thanks, Gore said the 1988 campaign had "left our coffers empty for the upcoming race" and that the money "will allow me to build a strong organization that can repel the inevitable attacks from the Republicans when they field a candidate in the near future." Hsia answered two days later, telling Gore she had great expectations for their partnership. She wanted him "to become one of the senators closest to the Asian Pacific community. But for that to occur, we need time and a special commitment from each other." Part of her commitment was helping to expand Gore's Tennessee fund-raising base by organizing Asian Americans in the state for his Senate campaign and forwarding lists of affluent Chinese American residents to his organization.

As it turned out, Gore hardly needed Hsia's money. The GOP tanks never came rolling over the Tennessee hilltops in 1990, as he had suggested in his letter. He won reelection with 68 percent of the vote, taking every county in the state and not merely outspending but burying his Republican opponent: Gore spent $1.6 million to William Hawkins's $6,500. But he continued to nurture the relationship, supporting her agenda by agreeing to cosponsor a "family unity" amendment to the Immigration Act of 1990 that made it easier for immigrants to bring family members into the country (and benefited Hsia's immigration consulting business). When Gore was researching the religious basis of environmentalism for *Earth in the Balance* in 1991, Hsia answered Knight's request for materials on Buddhism. "He would have been lost without your efforts because the chapter on religion and the environment is integral to his work," an appreciative Knight wrote back on March 6, 1991.

A series of personal and professional setbacks, including a lawsuit from a former business partner, took Hsia out of major fund-raising in the early 1990s. But in 1996 Hsing Yun asked her to deliver a prestigious visitor, either Bill Clinton or Al Gore, to the Hsi Lai Temple. She began by contacting Huang, her old fund-raising associate, who by then had become a DNC vice-chairman for finance. In February she led a temple delegation, including Hsing Yun, to Washington for a Huang-organized fund-raiser featuring Clinton at the Hay Adams Hotel. The temple donated $25,000, gathered, according to Senate investigators, in much the same way as it would be for Gore's visit to the temple in April. Hsia approached the temple's abbess, who approved a check request that was then passed on to the Hsi Lai treasurer. Straw donors were rounded up among the monks, nuns, and devotees, and their payments to the DNC were later reimbursed by the temple.

In the Clinton-Gore White House, money, regardless of where it came from, created access. On Friday afternoon, March 15, Hsia and Huang were able to arrange for Hsing Yun to meet with Gore in his White House office. For Hsia, it was a way to edge the VIP visit that the Venerable Master sought closer to reality. Huang apparently viewed it as a way to stimulate Asian American fund-raising. In a phone conversation with Huang two days prior to the meeting, Gore's deputy chief of staff, David Strauss, jotted on his call log: "John Huang . . . lead to a lot of $ moving support."

Gore was apprehensive about the ten-minute meet-and-greet and spoke with Hsia by phone beforehand seeking assurances that no politics would be discussed. Taiwan was in the midst of its own presidential campaign, which featured an independent Buddhist candidate who had been endorsed by Hsing Yun. Gore didn't want to do anything that could be construed as an endorsement. Hsia assured him there would be nothing more than a photo and an exchange of gifts and pleasantries. At the end of the visit Hsing Yun invited Gore to visit the Hsi Lai Temple. Gore said he would like to and indicated that he planned to travel to California sometime within the next several weeks (nearly always the case in a presidential campaign).

Within a week of the White House meeting, Hsia began campaigning for Gore's appearance at the temple. "Master Hsing Yun . . . could be very helpful for Vice President Gore's reelection," she wrote to Leon Fuerth on March 22. But it was also clear from Hsia's correspondence that the fund-raiser and temple visit were originally planned as two separate events. A day after writing her letter to Fuerth, she wrote directly to Gore: "John Huang has asked me to help with organizing a fund-raising lunch event, with your anticipated presence, on behalf of the local Chinese community. After the lunch, we will attend a rally at

the Hsi Lai temple where you will have the opportunity to meet representatives from the Asian-American community and to visit again
with Master Hsing Yun. The event is tentatively scheduled for April 29."

Sometime after Gore received Hsia's letter, the lunch and the temple
visit were collapsed into one campaign stop. Huang learned that his
location for the lunch, the Harbor Village Restaurant in Monterey
Park, was too far from the temple to accommodate Gore's schedule on
the twenty-ninth, and that one event or the other had to be canceled.
White House officials say that Huang "sandbagged" Gore by combining the two gatherings into one at the temple, even though he had
been warned by DNC officials that there could be no fund-raising
there. The most he could do, officials said they told him, was invite
past and prospective donors, but without any specific solicitation.
Some major contributors canceled when they heard that the lunch
had been moved to the temple. Hsia told associates that Huang
pressed her to make up the shortfall by turning to Hsing Yun, who
came up with the funds from monks, nuns, and temple devotees.

By mid-April Gore's staff had been explicitly informed that the Hsi
Lai Temple was the proposed site for the fund-raiser. An April 11
memo from Huang to Gore's aide Kimberly Tilley referred to the
planned "fundraising lunch" at the temple and asked for guidance so
he could finalize plans. Although Gore's political staff apparently saw
nothing out of place, other White House officials raised red flags.
The National Security Council (NSC), concerned about diplomatic
problems with China, expressed misgivings about Gore's appearance
with the politically active Venerable Master from Taiwan. "I guess my
reaction would be one of great, great caution," NSC staffer Robert
Suettinger said in an e-mail message to Gore national security aide
John Norris on April 19.

April 29 was a typical marathon campaign day for Gore. He left his
Naval Observatory residence at 6:30 A.M. for the cross-country trip on
Air Force Two and didn't return until 5:00 the next morning. The Hsi
Lai lunch was wedged between an address to the National Cable Tele-
vision Association at the Los Angeles Convention Center and a mid-
afternoon flight to San Jose, where he walked a beat with police and
attended an evening fund-raiser at a private home in suburban Los
Altos Hills.

What Gore knew about the Hsi Lai event, and when he knew it, remains unresolved. His former deputy chief of staff, David Strauss, told the Senate Governmental Affairs Committee in 1997 that he was "solely responsible" for telling the vice president that it was a community event. That morning on the plane, however, Gore's press secretary, Peggy Wilhide, and other members of his staff and security detail openly referred to the temple lunch and San Jose reception as "fundraisers" that were closed to the press. The entry in the briefing book he usually consulted shortly before events said that his lunch guests at the temple would be campaign contributors, members of the Democratic Party's Asian Pacific American Leadership Council. Although the entry neither specified that attendance at the luncheon required a donation nor offered an estimated sum that the gathering was expected to raise, it did say that membership in the council required an annual contribution of $2,500 per person or $5,000 per couple.

A high school band played John Philip Sousa tunes as Gore's motorcade pulled up at twelve-thirty, after encountering snarling freeway traffic. Waiting inside the entrance hall to welcome him were Hsia, Huang, California Congressman Bob Matsui, and DNC Chairman Don Fowler. After a brief meeting with Hsing Yun, Gore walked through the temple's courtyard, between a phalanx of monastics, to the Buddha shrine, where he made a flower offering. After a photo session with VIP attendees, he took his place at the head table in the temple's dining hall.

Some details of the visit support Gore's contention that he believed he was attending a goodwill event rather than a fund-raiser. After lunch, with Hsia translating into Chinese, he delivered what staff called his "e pluribus unum" talk, a standard stump speech praising racial and ethnic diversity. There were none of the usual thank-yous he offered to groups of contributors for their financial support. The comments were also in marked contrast to the more typically partisan rhetoric he used at the San Jose fund-raising reception that evening. Other trappings of a fund-raiser were missing as well, like a front registration table and donor cards.

The next day, Huang, disappointed about the amount of money the temple had collected before the lunch ($45,000), told Hsia that he wanted another $55,000. Eleven monastics wrote checks for $5,000 and were reimbursed with temple funds. Huang stopped by to pick up the total take, $100,000, on his way to the airport and back to Washington.

With the footsteps of another scandal growing louder, the Clinton-Gore campaign ended on a sour, uncertain note. Questions about "Indogate," as it was inevitably dubbed, threw the Democrats' poll numbers into a stall. Gore told National Public Radio's Nina Totenberg on October 22 that he understood the Hsi Lai Temple lunch to be a "community outreach" event, and that he learned only after the fact that money had changed hands. But from a man with laserlike attention to detail, the explanation rang hollow. He took few chances down the stretch, avoiding questions about the fund-raiser by bucking them to the DNC. "The correct, savvy, perfectly groomed paragon is haunted and he is unhappy," Mary McGrory of the *Washington Post* wrote on October 29. "Gore's problem is mortification. He is the best-briefed man in Washington. Yet he has insisted that no one told him that when he went into a Buddhist temple in Los Angeles last April there were money-changers present."

The temple wasn't Gore's only headache. The no-holds-barred money hunt in which he so enthusiastically enlisted had landed him in other compromising situations that Republicans were happily promoting. Jorge Cabrera, a businessman and DNC donor ($20,000) who had been convicted of tax evasion and later drug smuggling, was invited to a small fund-raising dinner hosted by Gore. Pictures of the two smiling were now splashed across newspapers and television screens. Adding to his troubles was the precarious political situation in Tennessee. The Clinton-Gore ticket was on the verge of losing — a serious sign of weakness for a candidate who was supposed to have a lock on 2000. The race had been tight all year, and Gore, who had already made thirteen trips there in 1996, added a fourteenth on election eve, an east-west dash through Knoxville, Nashville, Chattanooga, and Memphis.

Clinton and Gore narrowly carried the state the next day, but other news was disappointing. The fund-raising embarrassments had cost Democrats a chance to retake the House. They also deprived the victors of the popular majority they had sought, which had seemed in hand just a few days earlier. (The final numbers were 49.2 for Clinton to Dole's 40.8 and Ross Perot's 8.5.) "God intended for this election to be held October 29, not November 5," said White House political director Doug Sosnik. It sapped some of the celebratory fervor from a historic occasion — the first reelection of a Democratic president since Franklin Roosevelt.

Gore's power position in the West Wing was stronger than ever as his second term began. With Dick Morris gone and George Stephanopoulos and Leon Panetta also moving on, there were fewer significant voices contending for Bill Clinton's ear. To succeed Panetta as chief of staff, Gore supported Erskine Bowles, a genteel, management-minded North Carolina businessman and favorite golf partner of Clinton's (also a former Gore delegate to the 1988 Democratic Convention) who was serving as one of Panetta's deputies. Clinton gave Bowles the job over Harold Ickes, Panetta's other top assistant, and then pushed his loyal 1992 campaign soldier out of the White House altogether when Bowles wanted to name his own staff. Gore, never a fan of the mercurial New Yorker (the feeling was mutual), was happy to show him to the door.

But Gore, a voice for boldness in the early months of the first term, seemed more tentative. Some Clintonites thought he was reluctant to undertake anything that might alienate the Democratic constituencies he would need to compete in 2000. He was also distracted by the campaign finance story, which was growing into a political bonanza for the Republicans. The FBI had been investigating possible attempts by China to buy influence in American politics through illegal campaign contributions, and the GOP suspected Hsia, Huang, and the Riadys of somehow doing Beijing's bidding through activities like money laundering at the Hsi Lai Temple. Senator Fred Thompson, former-Watergate-committee-counsel-turned-character-actor-turned-possible-2000-presidential-contender, was preparing his Governmental Affairs Committee for hearings on fund-raising practices that would keep Gore's misadventures on the front page well into the fall.

Gore continued to insist that he thought the Hsi Lai Temple visit was a community event. But his story began to wobble in January when the first DNC documents emerged suggesting that he might have known it was a fund-raiser. Concerned about containing the damage, Gore's communications director, Lorraine Voles, went to

DNC headquarters to inspect the boxes of files detailing John Huang's fundraising activity that had been made available to reporters. What she saw alarmed her: photocopies of canceled checks to the DNC with annotations that clearly indicated they had been written at the event. This was no "community outreach" meeting. She immediately called Kumiki Gibson, the vice president's counsel. "You've got to come look at this stuff with me," she said.

Voles ordered aides to drop the flat denials that the lunch had been a fund-raiser and to instead characterize it as a "finance-related" event. Gore's answers became more nuanced and contrite. "I did not know it was a fund-raiser," he told *Today*'s Katie Couric on January 14, 1997. "But I knew it was a political event, and I knew that there were finance people who were going to be present." He added that sponsorship of the lunch by the Asian Pacific American Leadership Council, a group of donors that required a contribution for membership, "should have told me, 'This is inappropriate. This is a mistake, don't do this.' And I take responsibility for that. It was a mistake. But I was not told it was a fund-raiser and that's a fact."

For the most part, Gore avoided engaging the campaign finance issue at all, refusing interviews on the subject and staying out of public situations where he would be exposed to impromptu questions from reporters. But on Sunday, March 2, Bob Woodward dropped a voluminous story onto page 1 of the *Washington Post* detailing the 1995–96 White House fund-raising calls for the DNC. It was Woodward who reported that Gore's zeal for campaign money had earned him the nickname "solicitor-in-chief." More disturbing were accusations from unnamed donors that he had been heavy-handed in his pitches for money, almost to the point of coercion. One contributor with major interests in telecommunications and tax policy complained that his call from the vice president contained "elements of a shakedown."

It was the worst hit Gore had ever taken from the press. Even with the Buddhist temple fiasco, his ethical blotter was cleaner than most in Washington, and he was alarmed by the prospect of another fresh stain. He ignored the story through Monday morning, but by early afternoon it was plain that the issue was not going away. As he watched White House reporters pelt presidential press secretary Mike McCurry with questions about the calls, he decided he had to defend himself personally. A press conference was set for 5:00 P.M. Some advisers tried to wave him off, arguing that there were less risky ways to tell his side of the story. Perhaps the years of watching Clinton talk his way out of trouble with Houdini-like virtuosity had persuaded him that he could do the same.

By 3:00 P.M., his office was packed with a who's who of White House scandal spinners and lawyers, including McCurry, Sosnik, Voles, Jack Quinn, Lanny Davis, Paul Begala, Bruce Lindsey, and Cheryl Mills. Speechwriter Dan Pink also sat in, along with Gore's new legal counsel, former Tennessee attorney general Charles Burson. It has never been clear who — if anyone — Gore consulted beforehand about the propriety of the calls, but he was "angry and annoyed," according to one former senior aide, that he had been exposed to legal difficulty. He wanted "more firepower" in his counsel's position and had hired Burson in February 1997 to replace Kumiki Gibson.

Gore paced the floor near the sofas at the front of his office and listened as his assemblage of handlers threw out suggestions. He was calm and focused, even though it was not a setting for sober reflection. "Everybody had an opinion, and it was getting late," recalled Voles. Burson, a soft-spoken Harvard law school graduate who had spent eighteen years in private practice in Memphis before his appointment as attorney general, had drafted a statement for Gore described by one participant as "essentially a legal brief," devoid of any political insight into the risks involved. The law in question, the nineteenth-century Pendleton Act, barred federal workers from soliciting or receiving campaign donations on federal property. But it was not clear whether Pendleton applied to the president or vice president. No court case had ever determined the legality of a situation like Gore's. Thus, Burson concluded, there was "no controlling legal authority" that barred the vice president from making the calls in his office. Voles and Pink went off to rewrite Burson's brief and returned around 4:00 P.M., but Gore didn't care for their version. Yet if there was a consensus piece of advice for Gore from the unwieldy assemblage of handlers, it was to avoid legal jargon. "A number of people warned him not to sound like a lawyer," said one former senior aide. As he left his office for the White House briefing room shortly after five o'clock, his phone rang. It was Clinton, calling to wish him luck.

What followed was a disaster for Gore. Sounding like a criminal defendant taking the Fifth Amendment, he fell back seven times in twenty-four minutes on Burson's legal concoction. "My counsel advises me, let me repeat, that there is no controlling legal authority that says any of these activities violated any law," he said at one point. (When Gore later introduced Burson at a meeting as the man who was responsible for "no controlling legal authority," Burson replied, "I didn't tell you to say it seven times.") Gore also announced that while he had done nothing wrong, he would never do it again. There would be no more fund-raising calls from his office.

By turns ill at ease and defiant, and periodically splaying his hand over his heart as if to signal sincerity, he explained that "on a few occasions" he had made calls to potential Democratic donors using a DNC credit card. Those he asked for money, he said, were neither on federal property nor federal employees. He also denied forcing anyone to contribute. "I never, ever, said or did anything that would have given rise to a feeling like that on the part of someone who was asked to support our campaign. I never did that and I never would do that."

The problem, of course, was not the location of the calls, but the calls themselves. What Gore apparently never stopped to examine, either when he was first recruited to make the solicitations or as he was asked to account for them, was the seemliness of a sitting vice president trolling for cash like a House backbencher. It simply didn't pass the smell test, and Gore's refusal to acknowledge directly the unsavory aspects of the exercise only worsened his political situation.

When he and his aides left the press conference, they were still hopeful that they had taken the energy out of the story. Clinton put his arm around Gore as he left the briefing room. "I watched it, and you did great," he said. "It was the right thing to do." Afterward Gore summoned his entire staff to an odd combination meeting and pep rally in his ornate ceremonial office in the Old Executive Office Building next to the White House. They were waiting as he arrived and greeted him with vigorous applause, as they did Tipper a few minutes later. The mood was not triumphant but more of a combative, "us against them" esprit. Gore began by explaining once again that he had done nothing wrong. He wanted his office to run with the highest integrity, he said. Few things were more important to him than working with honor and integrity. Gore then asked that anyone who knew of unethical activity report it to him. He thanked Voles and press secretary Ginny Terzano for dealing with the press, and Burson for his legal advice, then threw the meeting open for questions.

What followed instead were testimonials to the purity of Gore and his organization. Bill Mason, a veteran of Gore's Senate staff, said it was the most ethical office he had ever seen. Senior policy adviser Elaine Kamarck spoke in the same vein. Gore, with a hint of discomfort, asked again whether anybody had questions. No one did, and the rally broke up.

Gore's initial optimism evaporated when he saw evening news accounts, and he told friends he had made a mess of it. "He realized he had really blown it. He was kicking himself around the block," said one former Senate colleague. "He was very, very upset with himself." The first wave of editorial commentary was scathing. "An unappetizing blend of artificiality, casuistry and condescension," hissed Maureen Dowd of the *New York Times.* His wobbly performance had handed Republicans yet another damaging piece of videotape (along with his visit to the Buddhist temple) to use at election time.

The aftermath was worsened by what appeared to be Gore's attempt to fudge the truth, when he told reporters that the calls took place on only "a few occasions." Shortly after the press conference, administration officials had to add that he called more than fifty people on those few occasions, a number that was revised upward several times in the next few months. (The final tally turned out to be seventy-one calls between November 28, 1995, and May 2, 1996.) The Senate Judiciary Committee asked Attorney General Janet Reno to recommend appointment of an independent counsel to investigate.

Gore's reputation for rectitude made his fall from grace that much steeper. Having sailed through Clinton's scandal-pocked first term without a hair out of place, he was an especially inviting press target. Clinton aide Doug Sosnik said he was convinced that it was part of a hazing ritual for a potential president, to see whether Gore could take a punch. His poll numbers started to erode: the proportion of the public with a favorable opinion of him dropped to just 29 percent, from 49 percent in late January. And March 1997, the worst month of his worst year in politics, was just beginning.

Gore's aides had hoped to change the channel with a long-scheduled trip to China, using it to refocus attention on their man's foreign policy skills. But suspicions by federal investigators that Beijing was trying to buy domestic political influence turned the visit into a far more sensitive diplomatic mission than they had anticipated. In the end it only added to the doubts about whether Gore and his crew were ready for prime time. The trouble began with zigging and zagging explanations about how blunt the vice president had been in warning Chinese Premier Li Peng of the consequences if the allegations turned out to be true. Leon Fuerth, Gore's national security adviser, first said that Gore had assured Li that the campaign finance investigation would not jeopardize the administration's policy of engagement with Beijing. But after reading initial wire service accounts of his meeting with Li, Gore called another press briefing and transformed himself into an unidentified "senior administration official" to insist that he had been tough with the Chinese, promising "very serious" repercussions if investigators found credible evidence.

The trip's most enduring image was a signing ceremony where Gore and Li closed a deal for China to buy five new Boeing jetliners and build 100,000 Buick Century and Regal automobiles in a joint venture with General Motors. Although not widely mentioned at the time, it didn't escape the notice of U.S. environmentalists that the man who once called the accumulated carbon monoxide exhaust from cars "a mortal threat to the security of every nation" was signing a pact to bring 100,000 new vehicles without antipollution devices into the world.

At the ceremony's conclusion five waitresses appeared with glasses of champagne. Li, known as the "butcher of Tiananmen" for his role in the brutal repression of the 1989 protests, raised his glass and smiled. Gore, frozen and stern-faced, images of thirty-second attack ads probably flashing before him, barely moved his. When Li made another attempt, he clinked Gore's glass with such force that some of the champagne spilled to the floor. Gore took a small sip and put his glass down. For the candidate who had denounced George Bush for "coddling dictators," it was a sorry piece of diplomatic theater, reinforcing the message that money trumped just about everything in the Clinton-Gore administration, including human rights.

Back home the media's new prosecutorial tone, calling his integrity and honesty into question, stunned him. His journalistic background had left him with a respect for reporters and what he thought was an insider's understanding of their craft. But the wave of bad press left him brooding and bewildered. "I don't think he's ever going to get used to that part of politics," said Bob Squier. Although Squier could tell he was upset, he never observed the kind of volcanic anger he had seen in other politicians whose public image had suddenly gone south. "His emotions are hard to read," he said. "He's not a Joe Biden, who would be ranting, throwing things against the wall, someone who you would hear through the door. Gore is not a guy you hear through the door."

Although he tried to keep his feelings in check, loyalists took up his defense, suggesting that he had been sucked into Bill Clinton's ethical netherworld through no fault of his own other than a desire to be a loyal vice president. *The New Republic*'s editor-in-chief, Martin Peretz, led the parade, authoring an unsigned "Notebook" item in late March calling his former student "a tempting target for those who believe that everyone had a scabrous underside." In a signed piece the following month, he slammed the press for its "hysteria" over Gore's fundraising and asserted what many Goreheads had believed all along — that their man had more integrity than the president he served. "As for Al Gore, he does not cut corners, ethically or intellectually," Peretz wrote. "Gore is not Clinton." Peretz's editor, however, was not quite a believer. Michael Kelly accused Gore of "glad-handing" Li Peng and quoted an anonymous White House staffer as asking of Clinton and Gore: "Is there *any* moral fiber left in these guys?" Within a few months, Kelly was gone.

Gore's image problems were further complicated by the business dealings of his closest friends and advisers. Although he presented himself to the world as a reformer and a futurist, Gore was also a creature of Washington, and over the years his inner circle had become dominated by lawyers and lobbyists immersed in the city's money-and-influence culture. Proximity to Gore was not the sole reason for their success, but their Gore connection made them especially valuable hired guns for companies with a stake in government policy and decisionmaking. Tom Downey, who lost his House seat in 1992 after writing check overdrafts at the House bank and taking a lobbyist-funded junket, cofounded a firm that would bill $1.8 million in fees from nearly four dozen clients in 1998, including Metropolitan Life Insurance Company and Microsoft Corporation, which was waging a huge antitrust fight with the Justice Department.

Three former Gore chiefs of staff entered the lobbying world in the early nineties to represent corporations with interests in the vice president's policy priorities. After leaving the White House in 1993, Roy Neel became president of the U.S. Telephone Association, the Washington trade association for regional phone companies known as the "Baby Bells." Over his years with Gore, Neel had become an expert on telecommunications issues, and the companies he represents stand to make enormous profits from the information superhighway that Gore has helped to shape, especially through expansion and privatization of the Internet. Jack Quinn was a well-established lawyer-lobbyist for Arnold & Porter before he left to run Gore's vice presidential operation and later serve as White House counsel. When he returned to the firm in 1997, he was barred by federal law from lobbying anyone in the government for five years. But he was well positioned to offer strategic advice to clients and associates at the firm.

Perhaps no one in Gore's world played the influence game harder than his fund-raising point man, Peter Knight, and it was his activities that started to attract the interest of government and congressional investigators. Knight had tried the corporate world briefly after leaving Gore's office in 1989, signing on as general counsel and secretary to the board of the Medicis Pharmaceutical Corporation, but he soon turned to lobbying. In 1991 he joined the law firm of Wunder, Diefenderfer, Cannon & Thelen, where his career took off in 1992 with Gore's vice presidential nomination. After raising money for the Democratic ticket, he became deputy director of personnel for the presidential transition, playing a key role in placing Gore and Clinton loyalists in jobs. When he came back to the firm, his ties to Gore and extensive contacts within the new administration made him the man to see for big corporate clients who needed to do business in Washington. His portfolio bulged with blue-chip companies like Lockheed Martin, the Walt Disney Company, and others in communications, pharmaceuticals, and environmental technology. The Gore connection helped Wunder, Diefenderfer land a four-year, half-million-dollar contract with the Tennessee Valley Authority for "advice and assistance." After running "negative" in the firm's books before mid-1992 — the fees he brought in didn't cover his salary or share of the overhead — Knight billed $2.9 million in 1995.

He worked the velvet intersection of fund-raising and lobbying, where campaign donors become clients and clients become donors. In

1996 Knight's firm helped Fluor, an Irvine, California, engineering firm, win a $5 billion contract from the Department of Energy (DOE) to handle radioactive waste disposal at its Hanford, Washington, facility. Two months before the Hanford contract was signed, on May 3, 1996, Fluor donated $100,000 to the Democratic National Committee.

One Knight client that drew scrutiny from investigators was Molten Metal Technology, a Massachusetts company developing an experimental process to neutralize toxic wastes in a bath of red-hot iron. The firm won a $1.2 million DOE contract in the waning days of the Bush administration and hired Knight in 1993 to help snare more federal dollars. Through the administration's first term, the value of Molten's DOE contracts grew to $33 million, the largesse always tracking closely with well-placed contributions from the company. On March 22, 1994, CEO Bill Haney's charitable foundation donated $50,000 to help fund the Nancy Gore Hunger Chair at the University of Tennessee. Two days later the DOE increased Molten's research funding from $1 million to $10 million. That same day Molten wrote a check to the Democratic Party for $15,000. At the bottom of an April 27 letter to Haney inviting him to a ceremony announcing the Gore chair, the vice president inscribed by hand: "P.S. Thanks Bill! You will never know how much this means to me. You are a great friend."

In 1997 House and Senate hearings, Republicans failed to establish any direct connection between Molten's political contributions and its DOE contracts, or any personal involvement by Gore. But it did provide revealing details about how a Washington operator like Knight worked. His principal contact at the DOE was Assistant Energy Secretary Thomas Grumbly, whom Knight had known since the early eighties, when he was staff director of the House Science and Technology Subcommittee that Gore chaired. House investigators said Knight aggressively courted Grumbly to boost Molten's funding, meeting him over seven dinners and two lunches in addition to business meetings at the DOE. Grumbly and Knight both insisted that politics wasn't involved. "Political contributions played no role in Molten's success story," Knight told the House Commerce Committee's oversight and investigations subcommittee on November 5. He also said he had "never arranged a government contract or grant in consideration for any type of contribution, including charitable contributions." Grumbly, for his part, said he did nothing wrong but acknowledged an error in judgment by meeting with Knight several times outside of his office and creating a perception of favoritism.

Gore tried throughout the spring and summer of 1997 to change the subject, returning to what chief of staff Ron Klain called his "bedrock portfolio" of the environment, high technology, and government reinvention. But his growing vulnerability emboldened potential rivals for the 2000 Democratic presidential nomination. House Minority Leader Dick Gephardt picked up the pace of his travel to important primary states. Senator Paul Wellstone, the outspoken Minnesota liberal, was also organizing. When the Thompson Committee hearings convened that summer — culminating in the appearance of three Buddhist nuns from the Hsi Lai Temple, who clung to their denials that the Gore lunch had been a fund-raiser — morale in the vice president's office bottomed out. To rally his troops, Klain imported former Clinton campaign manager James Carville to deliver a motivational talk. Carville gave the Goreheads the full Ragin' Cajun, urging them to be strong and hold the line against Republicans who were trying to rewrite the results of the 1996 election.

Burson and White House spinners tried to blunt the impact of the Thompson hearings with background briefings and preemptive "document dumps" to get their side of the story to reporters on the scandal beat. Klain held morning conference calls with a war council of outside advisers (including Knight, Neel, Downey, Quinn, Squier, and former press secretary Marla Romash) to discuss where the story was headed. Clinton directed his lieutenants to pitch in and help Gore's relatively inexperienced staff, which had been overwhelmed by the increased scrutiny of the vice president.

But the news got worse. In early September, Woodward reported that more than $120,000 in contributions that Gore solicited over the phone had gone into bank accounts for "hard money" rather than for "soft" funds. The distinction was highly technical but legally crucial for Gore. Unlike soft money, hard money goes directly to finance campaigns and is subject to tighter restrictions. It can be contributed only by individuals, who are limited to annual donations of $20,000. In April, Reno rejected the Senate Judiciary Committee's request for an independent counsel to investigate Gore's phone calls, a decision based in part on her understanding that he had sought only soft money. The law against solicitation on federal property, she said, applied only to the pursuit of hard money.

Woodward's reporting, based on the work of the Thompson Committee, infuriated Reno, whose own investigators managed to miss this salient detail on their first pass through the subject in the spring. She now had no choice. Within twenty-four hours of publication, the Justice Department announced a preliminary review of Gore's case, starting a ninety-day clock ticking toward appointment of an independent counsel. The critical question was, of course, did Gore know he was raising hard money?

For months he had remained convinced that the trouble would blow over. But an independent counsel, with a bottomless budget and broad investigative authority, was a potential career-stopper. Gore had watched Kenneth Starr cut a swath through Bill Clinton's administration and his life. Running for the Democratic nomination with another Starr-like inquisitor poking around in his background — and possibly those of his high-flying lobbyist friends — would be difficult, if not impossible.

Gore had resisted hiring his own lawyer, out of concern that such a move would signal that he had something to hide. But after Justice began its review, it was clear that he needed something more than White House spin to protect his interests, and he turned to former Watergate prosecutor James Neal and Washington attorney George Frampton. Tennessee friends wanted to set up a legal defense fund, but Gore decided to steer clear of more potential fund-raising problems and pay the fees himself. Even with Neal, an old family friend from Nashville, donating $50,000–$70,000 in work, Gore eventually borrowed $100,000 from a Carthage bank to pay his legal bills.

By fall Gore's mood had swung from anger to resignation to hopefulness. "I thought it was much worse in February," he told Voles, so wrung out from scandal duty she found it difficult to even remember February. There were also bouts of Clintonian self-pity as he rounded up the usual suspects to explain his troubles, like the press and Republicans bent on damaging his presidential chances. Convinced he had done nothing wrong, he retained, said one former senior aide, "a real belief that his heart is pure."

Gore's lawyers argued that he didn't know some of the funds he solicited had been diverted to "hard money" accounts. Their assertion was bolstered by the fact that Gore had asked donors for contributions larger than the $20,000 annual limit set by law. One set of evidence weakened Gore's case: a series of four memoranda from Harold Ickes, written between February and July of 1996, explaining that the first $20,000 from each of the donors he solicited would go to hard money accounts. It was impossible, of course, even for Gore, to absorb the volume of paper that flowed through his in box, and much of it went unread. But Heather Marabetti, his executive assistant, told committee investigators that memos from Ickes were the kind that commanded his attention. In an interview with Justice Department investigators on November 12, however, Gore said that he didn't read Ickes's memos because they were usually discussed at meetings, and, further, that he assumed he was soliciting soft money. Moreover, donors interviewed by Gore's attorneys said Gore spoke during the calls about the importance of the DNC media campaign, suggesting that he was operating under the assumption that he was raising soft money.

Gore was traveling on December 2 and had just finished a visit to Woodrow Wilson Middle School in Middletown, Connecticut, when Reno announced her decision to again reject appointment of an independent counsel. The statements of the donors, combined with the absence of "aggravating factors" on Gore's part — coercion, willful attempt to flout the law, or significant misuse of government resources — added up to not much of a case. Aides kept an open phone line to Washington, where the office staff was gathered around the television screen to hear Reno. Gore held back any comment until she was completely finished. "The key was to make sure there were no 'buts,'" said one adviser. There was other good news for Gore that fall. The Thompson Committee had failed to prove its most explosive allegation: that Maria Hsia, John Huang, and other Asian American fundraisers with whom he had done business had been agents of an elaborate Chinese plot to funnel money into the 1996 campaign. But Gore would soon discover that his legal problems were still not behind him.

Just as Gore was evading an independent counsel's investigation, another moment of truth was fast approaching. The scientific consensus on global warming had broadened considerably in the nearly six years since he wrote *Earth in the Balance*. In 1996 the United Nations Intergovernmental Panel on Climate Change (IPCC), comprising 2,500 scientists from more than 150 nations, concluded that there was a "discernible human influence on the global climate" — in other words, greenhouse gases from the burning of fossil fuels were warming the planet. Average annual temperatures on the earth's surface had already increased 1 degree Fahrenheit in the last one hundred years, and the IPCC estimated that the world could be anywhere from 1.8 to 6.3 degrees warmer by 2060.

Disquieting evidence of a fundamental shift continued to accumulate. Spring had started to arrive a week earlier in the Northern Hemisphere. Three of the hottest years in the twentieth century occurred in the 1990s. In early December, 160 nations were scheduled to meet in Kyoto, Japan, to negotiate an international treaty to limit greenhouse gas emissions and control future warming.

Gore had played climatologist-in-chief throughout his vice presidency, trying to focus the public's attention. Perhaps most important, he used his weekly lunches with the president as a global warming seminar. Clinton told a 1995 conference at Georgetown University that he had been "completely persuaded" by the evidence. Yet by the fall of 1997 Gore had miserably little to show for his missionary work. The administration's five-year record on global warming amounted to not much more than rhetorical hot air. As a candidate in 1992, he had denounced George Bush for refusing to commit the United States to a binding target for emissions reductions — a return to 1990 levels by 2000 — at the Earth Summit in Rio and insisting instead on voluntary measures (never met) to reach that goal. But after taking office, Gore discovered that the politics of climate change were far more vexing and intractable than even he had imagined. His emissions-reducing BTU tax failed to make it through Congress in 1993. And with the Republican takeover in 1994, it became all but impossible to impose new restrictions on industries that produced carbon pollution, such as power utilities and automobile manufacturers. Although studies had found that the United States could reduce emissions without huge economic impact or sweeping lifestyle changes for most Americans, organized labor and big business remained deeply wary, pointing to other forecasts of ballooning energy prices, lost jobs, and depressed productivity. It left Clinton and Gore to press business for the same voluntary measures they had declared unacceptable on Bush's watch. Although the rate of increase in U.S. emissions had slowed by 1997, it had come nowhere close to meeting the targets set in Rio, remaining 10 percent above 1990 levels.

None of this sat well with the environmental community, which had grown increasingly exasperated with the administration's record. There had been some genuine accomplishments: deflection of the 1995 Republican regulatory rollbacks; expansion of the national park system; creation of the Grand Escalante–Staircase National Monument in southern Utah, which protects 1.7 million federally owned acres of desert and red rock canyons from future development; and expansion of community "right to know" regulations requiring industries to publicize information about their use of toxic chemicals.

But it was, as one leading environmental lobbyist put it, an agenda of "minimal cost opportunities" that avoided larger and more politically risky issues. Discontent peaked in mid-1997 when Gore dropped out of sight during a contentious White House debate over strict new air quality standards limiting smog and soot in hundreds of cities and towns. EPA Administrator Carol Browner had taken an unyielding stance on the proposals, which were hugely unpopular with business and the big-city mayors Gore was courting for his 2000 presidential run. As complaints about "Al Gore's silent spring" grew louder, eighty-four environmental and health groups wrote to him in late June demanding that he step up to the air quality debate. Gore replied that it was not his role to argue publicly for a specific policy and preempt the president's options before he made a decision. In the end Gore weighed in behind the scenes, "constructively," as one green lobbyist put it, to support Browner and help secure Clinton's approval of the new regulations.

But with each passing year of his vice presidency, Gore's environmental evangelism seemed increasingly to give way to conventional incrementalism. He always vigorously protested any suggestion that he had backed away from what he wrote in *Earth in the Balance,* but his environmentalism seemed increasingly relegated to a separate intellectual account, above and apart from his political life. In the continuous competition between Gore's impulses to boldness and caution, caution had reasserted itself. Daring failures like the BTU tax, for which there was no political support, didn't advance the cause, Gore believed, and might actually hurt it. He would make withdrawals from his environmental account, but only when the political climate seemed safe. Gore continued to admonish and educate, but until the public saw a clear and present danger, in his view there could be no breakthroughs, especially on global warming. "The people haven't given us permission to lead on this issue," he told an Oval Office meeting of environmental leaders to discuss the Kyoto summit.

The proposal the administration took to Kyoto did nothing to hearten green activists. Clinton's plan was even less venturesome than the one that Bush had rejected in 1992: a binding commitment to return emissions to 1990 levels sometime between 2008 and 2012. After that, according to the U.S. plan, a series of market mechanisms would be employed to drive emissions below the 1990 baseline by 2017. They included an international trading system in which pollution permits could be bought and sold, giving companies incentive to cut emissions and sell their rights to another firm for a profit. The United States also insisted that developing countries shoulder some responsibility for limiting greenhouse pollution.

The plan met with broad resistance before deliberations even began. The European Union called on all industrial nations to cut emissions 15 percent below 1990 levels by 2010. A coalition of developing countries, led by China, wanted exemption from any restrictions that might impede their economic growth. The Senate, which would have to ratify any treaty signed by the administration, had already laid down its own marker, resolving on a 95–0 vote that it would accept no agreement that failed to hold developing countries to the same emissions standard as industrialized nations or that produced serious harm to the domestic economy.

As the early December summit approached, Gore faced the increasing likelihood of a huge setback on his flagship issue. Without the United States as a signatory, there could be no meaningful treaty in Kyoto, and the international effort to come to grips with climate change could well collapse. Complicating matters was that the head of the U.S. delegation, Undersecretary of State Tim Wirth, had resigned a few weeks before the start of the talks to take a job with Ted Turner.

After its first week the meeting seemed to be going nowhere as all sides dug into their positions. Gore had planned to remain at home, on the advice of his aides, who feared that presiding over an impasse on his biggest issue would make him look weak and ineffective. But if Kyoto went down the tubes, Gore was sure to take a political hit no matter where he was at the time. He overruled his advisers and flew to Japan on December 6. Barely sleeping on the twenty-hour trip, he conferred by phone with Clinton and the new head of the U.S. team, Commerce Undersecretary Stuart Eizenstat, to reformulate their proposal. It was clear that the United States would have to bring more to the table, and that whatever it signed in Kyoto would never make it through the Senate. The best Gore could hope for was to keep the process alive until American public opinion forced a change in Washington.

In his speech to the delegates, he said that the real challenge was to change the human behaviors that were causing climate change. "To do so requires humility, because the spiritual roots of our crisis are pridefulness and a failure to understand and respect our connections to God's Earth and to each other," he said. But Gore also said that the United States had "listened and learned" in talks with developing nations. "We understand that your first priority is to lift your citizens from the poverty so many endure." He said he was authorizing the American delegation to show "increased negotiating flexibility."

It was a signal that Gore was determined to cut a deal no matter what. He stayed for only sixteen hours, working from a suite in the Old Mayako Hotel where he held back-to-back meetings with all interested parties. But the whirlwind visit changed the dynamics of the conference. All sides gave ground. The United States promised to cut emissions 7 percent below 1990 levels between 2008 and 2012 — a goal that would require cutting the country's greenhouse gas production by one-third from what it might otherwise have been during that period. The Europeans committed to 8 percent, Japan to 6 percent. The final agreement also included the emissions trading plan pushed by Gore and Clinton.

The accord was trashed by Republicans, who predicted that compliance would lead to the loss of 2 million jobs. Critics within the administration called it dead on arrival. "Anybody with a clear-eyed view knows that what we agreed to in Kyoto is impossible," said one senior State Department official. But Gore had kept the process intact and put the signature of the United States on the first legally binding international protocol to fight global warming. Although many environmentalists were disappointed that the pact didn't go further, others recognized that it was probably the best Gore could do given the political circumstances. "It was the most courageous and important thing that Al Gore has ever done," said Greg Wetstone of the Natural Resources Defense Council. "He took the risk of personally going, inserting himself, and ultimately securing an intelligent agreement."

✦ 21 ✦

"One of Our Greatest Presidents"

G ORE's political plan for 1998 was threefold: put the campaign finance scandal behind him, strengthen his ties to important Democratic constituency groups, and, after the November midterm elections, begin a slow emergence from Bill Clinton's shadow. But just when Gore needed to start looking more like his own man, Clinton's affair with Monica Lewinsky kept him confined to the role of dutiful son. Instead of strengthening his identity as inevitable nominee and next president, Gore was reduced to defender and cheerleader, his future tethered more tightly than ever to Clinton's increasingly uncertain fate.

Gore hated what he saw as the investigate-and-destroy culture that flourished in Washington, even though he had made his own contribution in 1992 by hyping Iraqgate as the second coming of Watergate. He considered Independent Counsel Kenneth Starr a Republican partisan, not an impartial prosecutor, a man who saw fit to maintain his $1 million-a-year law practice (including tobacco clients) while pursuing the president of the United States. On January 21, 1998, when newspapers reported that Starr was investigating whether Clinton and Vernon Jordan had encouraged Lewinsky to lie about a sexual relationship with the president, Gore's immediate reaction was much the same as that of other senior White House officials — that Starr was hell-bent on nailing Clinton, if not with Whitewater then by any means necessary.

But like everyone else in the White House, Gore also had no illusions about the president's vulnerabilities. He heard the careful semantic twists in the early denials. ("There is not a sexual relationship," Clinton told Jim Lehrer of PBS on January 21, the *is* clanging like an alarm bell warning about the absence of *was*.) He stood uneasily at Clinton's side several days later, on January 26, as the president angrily wagged his finger at the cameras and announced, "I did not have sexual relations with that woman, Miss Lewinsky. I never told anybody to lie, not a single time — never. These allegations are false."

Gore accepted Clinton's public and private protestations of innocence and leapt immediately to his defense as the Lewinsky story touched off a frenzied atmosphere of rumor and speculation, including even talk about Clinton's resignation. He caucused with moderate Democrats on the Hill and met with small groups of print journalists to signal where he stood. "The president has denied the charges, and I believe him," he said in an interview with five Washington columnists. But Gore later acknowledged his suspicion that he wasn't getting the whole story. "I felt, at the time, that the matter was so painful for him, that he was concealing things that would have given a different impression if he had been totally candid. And so I worried that that was going on," he told ABC's Diane Sawyer in 1999.

More than worried, he was bewildered, and appalled, that Clinton would place his presidency — and his political future — at such risk by having sex with a woman who was roughly the same age as Gore's own oldest daughter Karenna. "It's a kind of conduct, a kind of personal behavior, that is just alien to him," said a close adviser who worked as a senior aide to both Gore and Clinton. "At a personal level this troubled him greatly."

Even a White House that prided itself on trudging through blizzards of subpoenas to do business was stopped dead in its tracks by the Lewinsky scandal. Gore later lamented all the time and opportunity wasted. And although he remained Clinton's closest adviser, he felt a slight sense of displacement from the scandal's weight. The White House bunker began to fill with 1992 veterans returning for the final battle. Mickey Kantor came back from California to coordinate Clinton's legal team. Harry Thomason, James Carville, and other old faces started to become familiar again. Gore's dealings with the campaign faithful had never been easy, and now "the apparatchik crowd," as one former senior Clinton aide described them, was back. "All of a sudden, he is made to feel like an outsider again," said the aide as the investigation unfolded in early 1998. "For someone with his insecurities and anxieties, it's a situation tailor-made for making him crazy."

Gore also knew he walked a perilous line. He didn't want to wade into the middle of a sex scandal whose real dimensions were still unknown. But reporters were watching for the slightest muscle twitch suggesting that he had distanced himself from the president, and he was determined that they would see or hear nothing that could allow them to write that story. Gore took personal loyalty with great seriousness, and taking a walk on Clinton was simply not in his makeup; he was also concerned, however, about the stability and effectiveness of the government. To send a message that he was deserting Clinton in the middle of a crisis would only add to the atmosphere of frenzy and paralysis. He warned his staff to put a lid on any speculation about the future of the administration, and that included even a whisper of the "R" word. Rumors ran wild. Roy Neel took calls from supporters who claimed that the Gores were "gloating about their storybook family image. It was total bullshit."

On January 28, the day after the State of the Union address, Gore traveled with Clinton to the University of Illinois for a speech in the school's cavernous Assembly Hall. When the event was first planned, some Clinton aides were unenthusiastic about the idea of the vice president tagging along. But when the Monica story landed, Gore started looking better than ever as a traveling companion for the embattled president. He intended to leave no doubt about where he stood as he introduced Clinton to the overflow crowd of twenty thousand. He fell into his revival-tent speaking style, with its mix of high-volume growls and verbs contracted to drop the g.

"I'm tellin' you, we're movin' in the right direction. Our air is cleaner! Our water is cleaner! We're cleaning up the toxic waste sites!" Gore raised the volume of his voice even higher: "He is the president of the country! He is also my friend! And I want to ask you now, every single one of you, to join me in supporting him! And standing by his side!" The wattage of Gore's introduction overwhelmed even Clinton. "When he really got going, I wish I had people walking down the aisle passing the plate," he said when he got to the podium.

Reverend Al's stemwinder was just as noteworthy for what it didn't convey. Gore fussed over it, consulting advisers about the tone and wording before scribbling the final version himself on Air Force Two en route to Champaign-Urbana. He would support his friend, but there would be no partisan attacks, no mention of the scandal, and, most significant, no defense of Clinton's character. The young presidential candidate who once quoted Aristotle to affirm that public and private virtue were inseparable was now separating them in defense of his benefactor.

Although Gore's network of friends, advisers, and aides studiously avoided any speculation about Clinton's future, one theme figured prominently in their spin during early 1998: that the coming months posed not a danger but an opportunity. What for years had been considered his liabilities — the stolidity, the woodenness — would be transformed into assets as voters wearied of the Clinton soap opera. "Some of the polling I've seen shows that with the next president, they don't want to go through this anymore," said Lynn Cutler, a Clinton aide who is close to Gore. Clinton's problems, so clearly and painfully personal, would not rub off on Gore, they predicted. As long as the economy remained strong, their man would be just fine.

In the breast pocket of his suitcoat Gore carried a typewritten list of goals for 1998. He displayed it to reporters during interviews, a signal that even in the middle of the Lewinsky mess the business of governing would continue. But Gore enjoyed only limited success on issues in which he was heavily invested, like antitobacco legislation and progress toward ratification of the Kyoto treaty.

The tobacco measure was an attempt to approve the 1997 legal settlement between the industry and a coalition of state attorneys general that required cigarette makers to pay more than $360 billion over twenty-five years in exchange for limits on punitive damages and liability claims. Gore endorsed a tough Democratic version of the bill that denied manufacturers most of the relief they sought from lawsuits, but the White House eventually backed a compromise, authored by Republican Senator John McCain, that would have collected more than $500 billion from the industry over twenty-five years through a $1.10-per-pack price increase. It also set billions more in fines for failure to reach targeted reductions in teen smoking and granted the FDA authority to regulate tobacco. But the bill collapsed along partisan lines in the spring when Republicans branded it a bloated "tax and spend" measure because some of the revenue it raised would have funded a variety of other programs, like after-school child care. Ironically, the bill was also the target of a $40 million advertising campaign crafted by Gore's former media consultant Carter Eskew.

The political climate surrounding the global warming treaty was even more inhospitable. In early March a long-awaited administration study estimated that U.S. compliance with the Kyoto pact would add between $70 and $110 to the average household's annual energy bill over the next fifteen years. That meant a hike in gasoline prices of four to six cents and increases of 3 to 5 percent for electricity, fuel oil, and natural gas. The White House called it a modest economic impact, but many economists were skeptical of the forecast, which was based on several optimistic assumptions, including cooperation from developing countries and the successful introduction of still largely theoretical market devices like emissions trading. Gore and the administration argued that even if the real costs of compliance were higher, the consequences of doing nothing were catastrophic. But congressional Republicans reiterated their resolve to block any attempts by the administration to spend money or introduce new regulations that facilitated U.S. adherence to the Kyoto agreement.

Gore's global warming crusade took its toll on his relationship with business leaders, many of whom regarded him as a green-eyed zealot. "You thought Mozart heard the voice of God?" said Ford CEO Alexander Trotman. "Al Gore hears the voice of God." As the 2000 political season approached, Gore tried to assuage anxiety in the boardroom by softening his rhetoric. While still warning of the dangers posed by climate change, he put a reassuring arm around the shoulders of the auto industry, pledging to "keep an open door and an open mind" to its concerns. "We all recognize the mounting evidence of global warming," he told the Detroit Economic Club on May 8. "We simply must act. But we must act with common sense and realize that most of the solutions will emerge from industry. Private-sector innovations can help us stop global warming — without economic cooling."

As his vice presidency progressed into its second term, the outlines of a possible Gore presidency took clearer form. Two themes, often intertwined, ran through his message: faith in the blessings of science and technology, and vigilance against the darkness that inhabits the human heart. Gore's views on civil rights were formed through the eyes of his father, scorned for his moderate views in 1950s Tennessee and the target of intimidating late-night phone calls and unspeakable mail. The turbulence of that period remained with Gore, and he has used the vice presidency as a pulpit for racial and sexual tolerance. He hosted a series of private dinners for civil rights leaders and scholars at his official residence, and in 1997 he praised lesbian comedienne Ellen DeGeneres for "coming out" in her now-canceled sitcom.

Where Clinton's instincts were to accommodate and placate, Gore drew sharper lines on moral questions and tended to view the world as more starkly divided between good and evil. In a passionate 1998 Martin Luther King Day address at Ebenezer Baptist Church in Atlanta, he argued that racism is not merely a form of ignorance that can be driven back by enlightenment, but an element of the human character that can be controlled but never eradicated. He described the day his father took him to the basement of an old mansion near his home on Fisher Avenue in Carthage to show him the cold metal rings driven into the stone walls to hold slaves. "We have left Egypt," Gore said, "but don't tell me we have arrived in Canaan," he said to Amens and applause. "Don't tell me that our persistent vulnerability to racism has suddenly disappeared and that we now live in a color-blind society." He reflected on how the smallest differences — the color of a street gang bandanna, or the barely visible physical distinctions between the Hutus and the Tutsis — can trigger the most explosive violence. "Einstein taught us that the most powerful destructive force on Earth is found in the smallest container — so small we can't even see it with the naked eye — the atom," Gore said. "Controlling our vulnerability to racism is every bit as crucial to the future of humankind as controlling the power of the atom." Those who claim America has achieved a color-blind society, with no need for legal protections like affirmative action, he said, are wrong. "They use their color blind the way duck hunters use their duck blind," Gore said, as the crowd erupted in cheers. "They hide behind the phrase and hope that we, like the ducks, won't be able to see through it. They're in favor of affirmative action if you can dunk the basketball or sink a three-point shot, but they're not in favor of it if you merely have the potential to be a leader of your community and bring people together, to teach people who are hungry for knowledge, to heal families who need medical care."

Gore also relished his role as chief scientist and technophile, and it is clear that a Gore presidency would reflect his abiding faith in the ability of technology to democratize and humanize. Over opposition from Congress and telephone companies, he championed the "E-rate" program, which requires the industry to subsidize Internet discounts for schools and libraries. When companies started adding small fees to monthly bills to pay for the $1.3 billion in discounts handed out by the FCC (which administers the program) in 1998, critics dubbed it the "Gore tax." A group of telecommunications firms launched a legal challenge, but a federal appeals court upheld the E-rate in July 1999.

He also met regularly with a cyber-cabinet of Silicon Valley executives known as the "Gore-techs" for wide-ranging discussions on technological advances and government policy. Some were skeptical at first, concerned that they were dealing with a dilettante who wanted to effect a cutting-edge pose for political purposes. But Kim Polese, chief executive of an Internet software maker, said her doubts about Gore's sincerity were dispelled after her first meeting with him in 1993. "He asked me about Java," Polese said, referring to the computer programming language, "and whether I thought the incompatibilities in virtual machines between different vendors would work themselves out." A visit scheduled for twenty-five minutes ran two hours.

It often seemed, wrote *Time*, as if Gore viewed the world through his modem and would like everyone else to do so as well. At his office desk in 1997 was a Compaq with a seventeen-inch monitor and integrated tuner usually set on CNN. Off to the side was an erasable white board that sent a copy of his scribblings to a computer file. Staff said he batted out and received as many as one hundred e-mail messages a day, and during meetings with aides he often had one eye on his screen, scanning his mailbox. Gore intended to use e-mail as a way of deemphasizing the importance that subordinates placed on hearing from him, deflecting attention from a more immediate task, but it didn't work that way. His domestic policy adviser Greg Simon rigged his Macintosh to sound a special chime whenever a new message from the veep arrived.

He was seldom more confident or comfortable in his own skin than with an audience of scientists or high-tech researchers. On a 1993 visit to a Silicon Valley firm, he drew laughs when he said the human mind "has a low bit rate, but high resolution." On January 20, 1998, the afternoon after his King commemoration speech, Gore was back in Washington at the National Academy of Sciences, where he shared the stage with Nobel Laureate James Watson and delivered a speech about the

Human Genome Project, which was close to mapping every gene in the human body. He began by expressing amazement at a list of scientific disciplines in which the totality of knowledge was doubling every six to eight months. "It's really incredible," he said. "Some of you take this for granted. Would that it were that way in public service and politics! Sometimes I think there's a process of erosion in . . . my profession that has periodicity of about six to eight months."

Yet as he celebrated the advances of genetic research, he returned again to the habits of the human heart. His National Academy of Sciences speech, entitled "Genes, Jobs, and Justice," warned of the dangers posed by genetic testing, which will soon be able to analyze an individual's predisposition to serious illness. He proposed legislation that would prohibit employers from requesting or requiring genetic information as a condition of hiring. "In the whirlwind of the bio-revolution," Gore said, "we must hold tightly to our deepest and oldest values and make them one with our newest science."

There was also little doubt that a Gore presidency's high-minded rhetoric would be coupled with a chronic political tone-deafness. His 1997 tax returns showed charitable contributions of just $353 on earnings of $197,729. It opened the floodgates for weeks of ridicule about the Gores' stinginess, most of which was unfair. The year before, Tipper Gore had donated $35,530 in book royalties to charity. But for a presidential contender who could expect his finances to be combed through by reporters and potential adversaries, it was politically maladroit.

Other incidents suggested that he and his staff still lacked the instincts for presidential politics. On an April 1998 visit to tornado-damaged Pratt City, Alabama, Gore skipped over predominantly black neighborhoods to tour destruction in white areas. Afterward, instead of talking with victims, he conferred only with local officials. Clinton smoothed over hard feelings with a stopover the following week.

His unscripted encounters with "real" people only reinforced the notion of a man who too often led with his intellect and not his gut. At a Louisiana roundtable discussion of the Family and Medical Leave Act in 1997, a young boy in the audience introduced his mother. "That's your mother?" Gore exclaimed. "She looks like she could be your sister." It was a charming response, and a sentimental "awwwww" rose from the audience. But then he added: "That's a line you hear a lot. In this case, it applies." Gore had stepped on his moment, converting a spontaneous, feel-good exchange into an analytical one. "The brain does more work than the heart," said a former aide who observed the scene.

Gore could lurch from personable and entertaining to soporific within the same appearance. Unlike many politicians, he was conversant with popular culture and often worked references to shows like *Saturday Night Live* into his speeches. He opened his May 1998 commencement address at New York University, which coincided with that evening's broadcast of the final episode of *Seinfeld,* by saluting faculty, students, and staff with the same last names as the show's characters — Kramer at the law school, Costanza at the credit union. The students erupted in laughter when he took Seinfeld's familiar sneering tone and said, "Good-bye . . . Newman!" (the name of a university vice president). The balance of the speech was devoted to his proposed "electronic bill of rights" for the information age, which would restrict online access to private medical records and other personal material. Clearly not the stuff of *Seinfeld* gags, but Gore made it worse by slipping back into his flat, plodding delivery, with the words so painstakingly enunciated that the *Washington Post* reporter Blaine Harden likened his presentation to "the pedantic 'Special English' short wave broadcasts the Voice of America beams to Third World countries."

A weight lifter and marathon runner in excellent shape for his age, he still looked as if he were the Tin Man under the banker's suits — all hinges. When he turned, his whole upper body nearly always turned with him, as if Dorothy missed a few spots with the oil can. The mannequin image inevitably fed itself; minor mishaps that could easily befall any politician stuck to Gore. Appearing on a closed-circuit satellite broadcast from a Los Angeles elementary school in early 1998 to preview the administration's urban initiatives, Gore was caught pantomiming his applause, bringing his hands not quite all the way together. He was concerned that with his lapel mike, clapping might have created a thunderous echo for his audience, another elementary school in Cleveland. But it was another perfect opportunity to discuss Gore's artificial public style.

With the intense scrutiny generated by the Lewinsky crisis and his own plans for 2000, Gore liked to say that his life had become like

The Truman Show, the Jim Carrey movie about a man who discovers that his entire existence is a twenty-four-hour-a-day, seven-day-a-week television series. Locked into the spotlight, he had to find ways to deal with unexpected personal pain. He turned fifty in March 1998, and over that last year he was reminded that time can run out unexpectedly. His Harvard roommate J. G. Landau, the best man at his wedding, died suddenly of a heart attack in 1997, a loss that left him "very, very shaken," said Mike Kapetan. Another Harvard friend, Rick Neustadt, the son of his faculty mentor, drowned in a rafting accident on the Yuba River in California.

His parents' health, especially that of his ninety-year-old father, was becoming an increasing concern. It was painful to watch the decline of the man who had both inspired and bedeviled him. So much so that a former senior aide still in close touch suggested that some of his erratic public performances in 1997 and 1998 may have stemmed in part from the distraction and distress he felt about the situation in Carthage. Pauline Gore was worried as well for her son. The criticism he had taken for his fund-raising phone calls and the visit to the Buddhist temple had been "extremely painful" for her, one family member said. As 2000 approached, she grew more protective of him than ever in her comments, even to relatives. "It's like she's editing herself when she talks," said the family member.

Clinton's legal predicament grew more dangerous on July 28 when Monica Lewinsky's attorneys struck an agreement with the independent counsel's office for immunity from prosecution in exchange for cooperation, which included surrender of a dark blue dress. A few days later DNA analysis of a blood sample provided by Clinton showed that it matched the DNA in a semen stain on the dress. By mid-August, as Clinton prepared for grand jury testimony, the papers were filled with signals from the White House that he was prepared to change his story and admit to some sort of sexual relationship.

Gore knew where the momentum of events could land him, but he discouraged any speculation about impeachment or resignation. Even among friends he was loath to talk about the situation at the White House, or his personal feelings about the crisis Clinton had created. "Silent as a tomb," said Reed Hundt. In periodic meetings of his political brain trust at the Naval Observatory residence (Squier,

Quinn, Neel, Knight, Downey, Penn, Klain, deputy chief of staff Monica Dixon, and ad man Bill Knapp were among the regulars), he was "exquisitely careful not to engage in that kind of conversation," said one participant. But Clinton's predicament hung over the strategic discussions like a weather front. By mid-1998 Gore's hope of establishing his inevitability as the party's nominee was gone, swept away by Lewinsky and his own fund-raising problems. Blood was in the water, and the operating assumption around Gore's dining room table was that he would face a multicandidate field in 2000, possibly including Dick Gephardt, "the two Ks," Senators John Kerry of Massachusetts and Bob Kerrey of Nebraska, Senator Paul Wellstone of Minnesota, and former New Jersey Senator Bill Bradley.

Gore was in Hawaii on Monday, August 17, beginning the second week of a family vacation, when months of suspicion about Clinton's denials ended. By video hookup from the White House Map Room, Clinton testified before Starr's grand jury that he had had "inappropriate intimate contact" with Monica Lewinsky. That night he told a national television audience: "I misled people, including even my wife. I deeply regret that." But as he went on, his message conveyed more anger and resentment than contrition: "This has gone on too long, cost too much, and hurt too many innocent people. Now this matter is between me, the two people I love most, my wife and daughter, and our God. . . . I intend to reclaim my family life for my family. It's nobody's business but ours. Even presidents have private lives. It's time to stop the pursuit of personal destruction and prying into private lives and get on with our national life."

Gore was the target of the predictable "Where's Waldo?" one-liners for placing himself five thousand miles from Washington on the worst day of Bill Clinton's presidency. The vacation — Gore usually takes one in August — had been planned for months. He was on the phone back to Washington nearly a dozen times with aides, and twice with Clinton, before and after the television appearance. He also made sure Knight and Squier were involved, Squier to help prepare Clinton for the cameras and Knight to reassure panicky Democratic donors that the storm would pass. But he withheld public comment in the first hours after Clinton's televised remarks, and the family spokeswoman, Jennifer Devlin, left the impression that he would have been fifty thousand miles away if he could have managed it.

"Did he spend the day on the beach or next to the television?" the *New York Times* reporter B. Drummond Ayres Jr. asked.

"Nothing on that," she said.

"Any comment on the day's Washington events?"

"No comment."

By the time he spoke to reporters at Lihue Airport on the island of Kauai the morning of the nineteenth — nearly thirty-six hours after Clinton's TV appearance — his initial silence had not gone unnoticed among the president's staff. "If he had waited another day or two, I think it would have been a problem," said one senior administration official. This time there was no Reverend Al, growling into the microphone, but a terse, prepared statement that praised Clinton for his "courage" in acknowledging his mistakes before the American people. It then followed the same careful pattern of his previous defenses, affirming his friendship and respect for Clinton's record in office but steering clear of any specific character endorsement. "Now it is time to take what he said to heart and move on to the people's business," Gore said. He took no questions.

It was a reflection of Gore's own brittle political condition that Clinton's confession was not the most distressing piece of political news he received that summer. As it turned out, the more immediate threat to Al Gore's political future was not Bill Clinton, but Al Gore. While he was in Hawaii, the Justice Department confirmed that it had reopened its review of his fund-raising phone calls. Handwritten notations on a newly discovered 1995 memo raised questions about the truthfulness of his claim that he was unaware he had raised hard money. The notes were made by former vice presidential aide David Strauss at a November 21, 1995, White House meeting on fund-raising calls attended by Gore, Clinton, and the president's deputy chief of staff, Harold Ickes. On a memo from four DNC officials, Strauss scribbled "65% soft/35% hard," a notation followed by the definition of soft money: "corporate or anything over $20K from an individual." It suggested that Gore had been told of plans to divert money from the telephone solicitations to hard money accounts. Other jottings from Strauss had no legal significance but were unhelpful politically, reinforcing Gore's image as a gung-ho solicitor in the 1996 campaign: "VP: 'Is it possible to do a reallocation for me to take more of the events and the calls?'" Another said, "VP: 'Count me in on the calls.'"

Within a few days Attorney General Janet Reno began another ninety-day inquiry, to assess whether an independent counsel was necessary. Although there were indications from Justice that such an appointment was still unlikely, announcement of the inquiry came at the worst possible moment, breathing new life into all the unsavory images of 1996 just as Gore was trying to put his 2000 presidential campaign on its feet. It was a particularly ominous development because the stakes were higher than during the last investigation. Most voters had little appetite for protracted legal arguments over where Gore should have been sitting when he picked up the telephone, or the arcane distinctions between hard and soft money. But they knew what a lie was, and the question this time centered on Gore's probity.

The polls had so far been mostly reassuring — Clinton was not yet pulling him to the bottom politically. To the contrary, even after the August 17 confession, most surveys had the president's job approval still floating comfortably in the mid 60s. Nor did Americans hold Gore accountable for Clinton's personal behavior. An August Gallup poll showed that 63 percent considered Gore "honest and trustworthy," while barely one-third felt the same way about Clinton. But that number was at risk if Gore couldn't cut himself free of the fund-raising scandal.

Just as Gore's political fortunes were never the same after his 1996 convention speech, his relationship with Clinton was never the same after August 17. He was angry and bewildered by Clinton's recklessness — it violated the sanctity not only of his marriage but of a six-year political partnership in which Gore had invested everything. Gore continued to defend the president in his travels — he felt that he had no choice. But he picked his spots strategically, deflecting questions for days at a time from members of the national press, then engaging them. In a mid-September visit to politically pivotal New Hampshire, he reaffirmed his friendship with Clinton but made a point in local press interviews of calling his conduct "indefensible." There were also private signs of a new distance between the two men. Their weekly lunches continued, but the vice president who once rushed down the hall when there was an Oval Office meeting he didn't know about became less of a presence.

There were official explanations: his heavy travel schedule for 1998 candidates (in many cases pinch-hitting for the scandal-impaired Clinton), and the legal barriers that kept him out of certain strategy sessions (he was not covered by attorney-client privilege). But there were many meetings he did not have to avoid, and trips he did not have to make, said one senior administration official. He did so, the official said, "to stay out of the muck." Gore had even made himself scarce at the pre-briefs before presidential press conferences, where he had once been a fixture. For the most part, he approached the crisis with a mixture of fatalism and stoicism. "I'm powerless over this situation," he told Jack Quinn, "and I can't try to deal with what I have no control over."

The most desperate moments came in September. As the House moved toward impeachment, key Senate Democrats were ready to bolt, raising the specter of a delegation coming to the Oval Office to tell Clinton his party's support was gone — the same trip Republican elders made a quarter-century earlier to ease Richard Nixon into resignation. "People don't know how close we came to having this thing unravel in September," said one senior administration official, who credits Minority Leader Tom Daschle for keeping members at bay. Starr delivered his impeachment referral to the House, complete with eighteen boxes of supporting documents, and within a day his report was on the Internet, delivering every intimate detail of Clinton's liaisons to millions of Americans, including his daughter at Stanford.

Gore did sit in on a series of emotional meetings that Clinton convened with congressional leaders and cabinet members ("tough, tough meetings," said an aide) to make his apologies personally. Since the 1994 publication of *The Agenda,* Gore had been reluctant to say anything in large meetings that could be described later as criticizing or admonishing Clinton. But in the September cabinet session, as reported by the *Washington Post's* Ceci Connolly, he abandoned his usual discretion. In a tone described by two participants as stern but not harsh, Gore told Clinton he was "disappointed." He urged the cabinet to rally behind the president and concluded with a joltingly blunt warning: "Mr. President, I think most of America has forgiven you, but you've got to get your act together."

Gore ran up thousands of miles in the fall, speaking and raising money for Democratic candidates. With Clinton out of commission, Democrats needed Gore more than ever to rally the party's base. For

Gore, it was a chance to pick up more IOUs for 2000. He stepped into his full partisan warrior mode, bouncing in time to salsa music as he shook hands in the Bronx and ridiculing supporters of the congressional Republicans as the kind of people "who call C-Span at three in the morning, not knowing it's a taped replay." He perfected a Jesse Jacksonian riff that he used at virtually every stop: "We say legislate, they say investigate. We say educate, they say interrogate. We say illuminate, they say instigate. We say unify, they say vilify. We make the tough decisions, they take depositions. We find real solutions, they launch prosecutions. We know our future is nearing, they want to hold more hearings!"

The red-meat rhetoric was a vice presidential tradition at election time, but it also reflected a combination of discipline and denial that was uniquely Gore's. It was as though he believed that if he flew far enough, campaigned hard enough, and shouted loud enough, he could push the chaos in Washington out of his awareness. "I don't let myself feel a downdraft," he said in mid-October. "I just don't let myself feel it."

The White House was euphoric with the election results. Voters seemed to be sending a clear message that Republicans had overreached on the Lewinsky scandal. The party that doesn't hold the White House usually makes solid gains in the midterm election, but the GOP picked up no Senate seats, while the Democrats added five seats in the House, narrowing the Republican majority to 223–212. It was a stunningly poor showing, for which the administration nemesis Newt Gingrich took the blame, resigning not only the speakership but his congressional seat.

Gore got other good news in November when Janet Reno announced, for the second time in a year, that she would not recommend appointment of an independent counsel to investigate his fundraising practices. Although some of her top aides disagreed, Reno concluded that there was no basis for a prosecutable case. She said that Strauss's notes did nothing to prove that Gore lied to investigators when he said he didn't know some of the money he was raising would be diverted to hard money accounts. In interviews with the fifteen people listed as attending the 1995 meeting, only two remembered the subject even coming up. "The range of impressions and vague misunderstandings among all the meeting attendees is striking," Reno wrote on November 24, "and undercuts any reasonable inference that mere attendance at the meeting should have served to communicate to the Vice President an accurate understanding of the facts." Moreover, said Reno, Gore had no motive for lying. At the time of the meeting, the DNC didn't need hard money to fund the television ads but was critically short of soft funds. When Gore was asked to make the calls, he had every reason to assume that the party's specific need was for soft money.

The White House assumed that pressure from public opinion growing out of the election would force House Republicans to stand down on impeachment. It turned out to be a gross misreading of the environment within the GOP caucus, where Majority Whip Tom De-Lay was moving into the vacuum left by Gingrich and galvanizing support for pushing ahead. Impeachment would proceed.

Albert Gore died in Carthage on December 5, three weeks short of his ninety-first birthday, and was buried next to Nancy on a gray, chilly Tuesday afternoon. The old senator never realized his dream of a Gore in the Oval Office, but he had lived a long and full life and took great satisfaction in his son's rise to the job he had once coveted. The passage of time, and a successful second career in business, had helped to ease the bitterness of 1970. There was also a peace that came with vindication — about Nixon, the Vietnam War, civil rights. It all contributed to a late flowering, one family member observed, as his senatorial solemnity gave way to a warmer, more avuncular presence. Albert Gore became a nicer guy.

Time and success had also helped Al Gore make his peace with the powerful patriarch whose shadow he had struggled to escape. He was still his father's son in innumerable ways — pedagogue, technophile, liberal pragmatist — but he had also spent years setting his own course. The old senator's legacy was no longer an obstacle to contend with, but something of which he could be unconditionally proud.

The memorial service in Nashville drew every significant political figure in the state and a fifty-member congressional and cabinet delegation, headed by the Clintons. The seats in front of the flag-draped coffin were packed with old friends and enemies who came to pay last respects, including Dick Gephardt, Lamar Alexander, and Fred Thompson. Although the VIP sections on the main floor of War Memorial Auditorium were packed, the balcony open to the public was at least half empty, a reminder perhaps that time doesn't heal all animosities, and that Albert Gore's liberalism is no more popular in Tennessee today than it was when voters removed him from office three decades ago.

The service was a family enterprise, with each of the Gore children playing unusually public roles. Karenna read from the senator's memoir, *Let the Glory Out,* Kristin recited a poem she had written, and Albert III read from scripture. Near the end the audience heard a scratchy recording of Gore on the fiddle, playing one of his favorite tunes, "Soldier's Joy," as a young congressman at a Washington concert. But the emotional center of the service was Gore's thirty-minute eulogy. He had worked on it for two days straight, rising at four o'clock the Sunday morning after the senator died and writing until late Monday night before the service. It was the best speech he ever gave — funny, generous, and heartbreaking. "He levitated the hall," as one friend put it.

"My father was the greatest man I ever knew in my life," he began. "Most of you know him for his public service, and it could be said of him, in the words of Paul, that this man walked worthy of the vocation wherewith he was called. There were those many, many who loved him, and there were a few who hated him — hated him for the right reason. It is better to be hated for what you are than to be loved for what you are not."

He told the old senator's story with flourish and loving detail, from his hardscrabble youth to his antiwar advocacy, hailing him as a courageous leader and devoted father who not only taught his son how to deliver a newborn calf when its mother was having trouble but instilled in him a sustaining strength. "Children with strong fathers learn trust early on," Gore said, "that their needs will be met, that they're wanted, they have value, they can afford to be secure and confident, they will get the encouragement they need to keep on going through any rough spots they encounter in life."

As Gore lionized his father, he also gently captured the more challenging aspects of his nature, the edgy humor (hooking a dead snake onto a friend's trouser leg) as well as his taskmaster's ethic and love of the limelight. He described the relish with which the senator told and retold the story of his first fiddling interlude at a campaign rally, a tale that invariably ended with the crowd's exuberant response. "My father always chuckled when he delivered his favorite punch line: 'They brought the house down.'" Then there was the young volunteer from the 1992 campaign who returned to Carthage to work on the Gore farm. "The fellow soon left," Gore explained, "and asked me: 'How do you tell a man who is working beside you and is eighty-four years old that you're quitting because it's too hot and the work is too hard?' I had learned the answer to that when I was still young: you don't."

He proudly recounted his father's legislative triumphs, the highway bill, the ABM treaty, his opposition to the poll tax and support for civil rights. Once a man called to complain about the senator's position on desegregation and said of blacks, "'I don't want to eat with them, I don't want to live with them, I don't want my kids to go to school with them,'" Gore said, re-creating a vivid redneck drawl. "'To which my father replied gently: 'Do you want to go to heaven with them?' After a brief pause came the flustered response: 'No, I want to go to hell with you and Estes Kefauver!'"

He died "bravely and well," Gore said, adding how hard it was "to watch the sharpness of a parent fade; hard to watch, in the words of the poet, 'How body from spirit does slowly unwind until we are pure spirit at the end.'" With many in the audience weeping and his own voice quivering slightly, he concluded: "Dad, your life brought the house down."

Clinton didn't speak, but his attendance added an extraordinary resonance to the moment. The president, whose father died before he was born, whose infidelities had set in motion the impeachment proceedings under way in the House Judiciary Committee that very morning, listened as Gore saved some of his most poignant commentary for his parents' marriage. "Of all the lessons he taught me as a father, perhaps the most powerful was the way he loved my mother," he said. "As I grew older, I learned the value of a true, loving partnership that lasts for life."

Saturday, December 19, was filled with split-screen surreality. U.S. air strikes against Iraq, in response to Saddam Hussein's refusal to cooperate with UN weapons inspectors, had entered their third and final day. As the House convened for its last debate before voting on the four articles of impeachment, Speaker-elect Bob Livingston, who had acknowledged that on occasion he had "strayed" from his marriage, stunned members by announcing his resignation after *Hustler*'s Larry Flynt threatened to publish a story about his personal life. Livingston expressed the hope that the president would soon follow his example.

Gore tried to bring some calm to the frenzied atmosphere that week, especially speculation that the air strikes were history-imitating-art in the form of *Wag the Dog,* a popular movie about a president and his aides who fabricate a war to deflect attention from a sex scandal. "Anybody who thinks for one minute that Bill Cohen, a former member of the Senate Republican caucus, or Hugh Shelton, a four-star general of the Green Beret Special Forces branch of the Army, would sit in these meetings and be a part of some politically motivated plan is just crazy," Gore said on Friday. "No serious person can look at the facts and come to that conclusion." Behind the scenes he made calls to solidify the support of moderate House Democrats and enlisted help from former Presidents Jimmy Carter and Gerald Ford, who wrote an op-ed piece for the *New York Times* proposing a plan to expedite a Senate trial and censure Clinton. But time had run out.

Clinton was alone in the Oval Office with his friend the Reverend Tony Campolo as the House began voting. After the first article, alleging perjury before Starr's grand jury, passed along party lines, he went into his adjoining private dining room with aide Doug Sosnik and chief of staff John Podesta to watch the remainder of the voting on television. Gore arrived a few minutes later and sat quietly next to Clinton, at the table where they had shared countless lunches. He tried to minister to his friend, who was filled with anger and grief at what he considered a political hit job by the Republicans. In a quiet voice, he told Clinton he didn't deserve this, and that it wasn't fair. By 2:15 P.M., it was over. The House had passed another of the other three remaining articles, one alleging obstruction of justice. Clinton would stand trial in the Senate.

After the vote, eighty House Democrats piled onto buses and rode to the White House to meet with Clinton and Gore in the East Room. Gore hugged his old enemy Gephardt, congratulating him for his passionate floor speech decrying the partisan tenor of the debate. Surrounded, incongruously, by Christmas trees and other holiday trappings, Gore launched an angry — "fiery," as one aide put it — condemnation of the impeachment process.

He was more statesmanlike when the group gathered on the South Lawn in a public show of support for the president. As Clinton looked on, with reddened eyes and jaw clenched, Gore said: "I do believe this is the saddest day I have seen in our nation's capital. Let me say simply, the president has acknowledged that what he did was wrong, but we must all acknowledge that invoking the solemn power of impeachment in the cause of partisan politics is wrong." Gore added that in refusing to give their members the option of voting for censure, House leaders had kept them from voting their conscience. "What happened as a result does a great disservice to a man I believe will be regarded in the history books as one of our greatest presidents."

Only Gore knows whether he truly believed that. He surely knew that his testimonial would add to the opposition's library of tape, joining the Buddhist temple, his briefing room meltdown, and his toast with Li Peng as grist for future ads, tethering him even more securely to all that the country wishes to forget about the Clinton years. But the vice presidency makes dutiful sons of nearly all who hold it. Al Gore knew what was expected of him, and again, as always, he tried not to disappoint.

Epilogue

Separation Anxiety

G ORE BEGAN what might be the last campaign like all the others, and like all of his father's, at the steps of the Smith County courthouse in Carthage. It was an elaborate production, designed with a mix of imperial flourishes and down-home touches. His stage managers erected a Miss America–style runway and platform, lined with American flags, that jutted from the old red brick building onto Main Street. As the crowd of about five thousand assembled on the warm June morning, fiddlers strolled about giving impromptu mini-concerts, a bit of atmospherics that the candidate himself requested. "Dad would have liked it," he told a former aide.

But the occasion was less a celebratory launch than a scrambling of the jets. Polls showed him lagging badly in contests with the overwhelming Republican favorite, Texas governor George W. Bush. The last man left standing in his own party's field of potential challengers, former New Jersey senator and basketball star Bill Bradley, was still far behind but inching up. Just as troubling were surveys that reflected widespread voter doubt about Gore's ability to lead. Nearly 70 percent saw Bush as a "strong leader," while barely 40 percent viewed the vice president in the same light. Gore had hoped to remain above the fray until fall, running an incumbent-style "Rose Garden" campaign. But Bush's early strength spurred him to move up his formal announcement of candidacy to June 15.

Gore's Bush fixation led him into a badly flawed campaign strategy for much of 1999: to wage what amounted to a general election campaign and let the Democratic nomination take care of itself. Acting as if he were already the party's standard-bearer, he spun off a long list of policy prescriptives before most voters were paying attention. Several top advisers, including ad men Bob Squier and Bill Knapp, urged him to take on Bradley before he gained strength. But Gore was reluctant to do anything that might raise Bradley's profile or splinter the party. He also worried that the further he fell behind Bush, the more Democrats might be inclined to look seriously at an alternative such as Bradley.

This dubious approach was overseen by a political operation that was dangerously adrift. Gore, who tried to make his name as vice president by reforming sluggish, top-heavy government bureaucracies, had concocted one of his own for the 2000 campaign. He placed himself at the center of a managerial scheme that involved members of his family and an unwieldy supporting cast of aides and consultants (Squier, Knapp, pollster Mark Penn, vice presidential chief of staff Ron Klain, and others). Longtime lieutenants like Roy Neel, Peter Knight, and Jack Quinn, all with lucrative law and lobbying practices sweetened by their ties to the Clinton-Gore administration, remained loyal to the cause but were limited in their commitment of time and energy. "There were a lot of lieutenants and no single chief," said Neel. "Not much direction."

About a month before the Carthage kickoff, Gore realized he had to impose some order and asked former California congressman Tony Coehlo to serve as chairman. He had never been particularly close to Coehlo, who raised huge amounts of money for Democratic House members in the 1980s before resigning his seat in 1989 amid allegations that he used political contacts to reap a windfall from junk-bond investments (no charges were ever brought). But Gore needed a manager, not another adviser. While Coehlo tightened up the operation, his autocratic style created almost as many problems as it solved. It led to the eventual exit of the highly regarded Klain, who was unhappy about power draining away from the vice president's office over to campaign headquarters on K Street.

Coehlo also hired former Gore ad man Carter Eskew to run media and message, effectively ousting Squier, whose partnership with Eskew had dissolved years earlier in a bitter business dispute. Eskew's return added another unfortunate footnote to Gore's record on smoking issues, since one of Eskew's recent assignments had been the successful multimillion-dollar ad campaign mounted by cigarette manufacturers in 1998 to kill legislation that would have regulated tobacco. Gore handled his addition to the staff in an especially graceless fashion, never telling Squier about it directly. Squier responded by giving a self-immolating front-page interview to the *New York Times* that reinforced the sense that the wheels were coming off the Gore campaign.

Meanwhile, Gore once again struggled to find a voice as a candidate. All the chronic problems were back on display — the remoteness, the tentativeness, the inability to make an emotional connection with audiences. Friends and supporters attributed the early image problems to "vice presidentitis," the common cold of number twos, who struggle to get taken seriously. They cited the GOP frontrunner's father as a comforting precedent, pointing out that he had trailed Bob Dole in voter estimates of leadership abilities during the early days of the 1988 campaign.

But the numbers suggested a more serious problem — Bill Clinton. Impeachment was receding from public memory with astonishing speed. By autumn 1999, surveys showed that fewer than half the country's voters could remember that the president's Senate trial had ended the previous February. Although Americans had no interest in punishing Clinton — his job approval rating held steady at about 60 percent — the country had wearied of the nonstop White House psychodrama and was eager for the president and the first lady to pass from the scene as soon as their term ended in 2001. "Clinton fatigue" had become a palpable political phenomenon, and Gore was the principal casualty of the public's desire for a fresh start. One spring survey found that 40 percent of those who approved of Gore's work as vice president nevertheless intended to vote for Bush.

Gore's relationship with Clinton, once touted as a history-making executive partnership, was never the same after the Lewinsky scandal. The weekly lunches became less frequent, owing both to Gore's near-constant travel and to his "almost primal bitterness," as *Time* described it, about Clinton's conduct. He was furious over what the president's reckless behavior had done to his competitive position, and his mood didn't improve in May, when Clinton, concerned about the Gore campaign's wobbly start, acknowledged to the *New York Times*'s Richard Berke that he had coached his two-term understudy to loosen up.

The official White House explanation was that Clinton was only trying to help. He had called Berke, administration officials explained, after learning that the paper planned to run a story describing mis-givings about the campaign that he had expressed to others. Clinton emphasized that there had been improvement in recent weeks, but this dramatic effort to extinguish doubts only breathed more life into them. Others attributed more malign motives to the president, cit-ing Clinton's insatiable need for attention and resentment that his two closest political partners, Gore and the first lady — an all-but-announced Senate candidate in New York — had embarked on grand new adventures, leaving him to nurse his depleted presidency through its final days. Whatever his reason, the public meddling left Gore look-ing once again like something less than his own man.

At the same time, several advisers, including his daughter Karenna and (it was later revealed) feminist writer Naomi Wolf, were encour-aging him to make a definitive break from Clinton. That placed them at odds with Mark Penn, who cautioned that Clinton remained ex-tremely popular with Democratic primary voters. (Penn happened also to poll for the president and Mrs. Clinton.) Such vice presidential distancing had been a more tactful process in 1988. George Bush did not call for a "kinder, gentler nation" after Reagan until his acceptance speech in New Orleans. But Gore felt compelled to get a running start.

He bracketed the June 16 announcement in Carthage with his strongest-ever condemnation of Clinton's conduct. "I felt what the president did, especially as a parent, was inexcusable," he told Tennes-see reporters on the eve of his announcement, and he called 1998 "that awful year we went through." The next night, he repeated the message in a primetime interview with Diane Sawyer. Gore mentioned Clinton just twice from the podium in Carthage, praising him for economic renewal at home and peace in Kosovo. But there was no mistaking his message when he promised to make personal morality a central cam-paign theme. "It is *our* lives we have to master if we are going to re-main role models for our children," Gore said, in a breathless, hasty delivery. Peeled to its essentials, the pitch to voters, as the *Wall Street Journal*'s Paul Gigot put it, was that in a Gore administration, "the only blondes they'll read about are his wife and daughters."

But just as the launch of Gore's 1988 campaign had foreshadowed problems with focus and message, so did day one of the 2000 race. It carried twice the usual cargo, proclaiming both the beginning of his presidential race and the dissolution of his political marriage. Given a choice, the press naturally hopped on the break with Clinton, leaving Gore's formal entry into the race as background music. All the talk about separation served only to reinforce the tethered image, and there was also more than the usual aroma of calculation and opportunism about the whole production. Some wondered where all the indignation had been six months earlier, when Gore had stood shoulder to shoulder with Clinton on the South Lawn and said that history would ultimately recognize him as "one of our greatest presidents."

The denunciations left Clinton furious. He recognized that Gore needed to affirm his political selfhood and was reconciled to taking some hits in the process. But no one from the vice president's operation, not even Gore himself, had prepared Clinton for how hard the words would be. Press secretary Joe Lockhart conveyed Clinton's rage with astounding bluntness. "The president and I had the same take," he said. "He was trying to do too much by announcing and trying to separate on the same day."

This remained the central dilemma of Gore's 2000 campaign: how to signal independence yet derive the political benefits of association with Clinton. Separation anxiety sometimes drove him in opposite directions. Later in the summer, he lightened up on personal condemnation and welcomed Clinton's help as a marquee fund-raising attraction. But at other times he didn't seem to know what he wanted. He told a luncheon of *Washington Post* reporters and editors in October that he might not ask the president to campaign for him, much as he had kept his father on the sidelines during his first congressional race, in 1976.

Gore used the summer to unveil a series of detailed policy proposals, which added up to a distinctly more activist — and costly — agenda than Clinton had offered in 1996, a sort of Clinton-plus: providing universal access to preschool education, hiring more teachers, and boosting federal funding for faith-based charities that do drug counseling and job training. He also proposed licensing gun owners, doubling federal spending for cancer research, and paying for one hundred drug agents to close down rural amphetamine labs. As meaty as the issues were, though, the campaign was bloodless and bereft of passion, run by a corporate machine that collected money and churned out endorsements. No party group was unheard from, even the nation's Democratic lieutenant governors, whose pledges of loyalty to Gore were bundled into a triumphant press release. The candidate, meanwhile, remained cocooned inside layers of security and staff, sweeping into and out of events, his personal contact with audiences limited. The organization's burgeoning collection of hired-gun insiders such as Coehlo, Eskew, veteran speechwriter Bob Shrum, and strategist Michael Whouley, few of whom (save Eskew) had any longstanding personal connection to Gore, gave the campaign the look of a mercenary outfit seeking one last big score.

Too often, the worthy proposals were eclipsed by internal problems or silly, avoidable mistakes. On July 23, Gore was canoeing on the Connecticut River in New Hampshire to play up his environmental credentials, and Pacific Gas and Electric released more than a half-billion gallons of water to make sure he didn't run aground — a potentially disastrous piece of symbolism. The campaign insists that it didn't ask for the release, which yielded several days' worth of embarrassing stories. Despite warnings from field operatives about poor morale and sluggish support, the campaign elders insisted that all was well. "They essentially spun themselves into believing their own rosy predictions," said one former adviser.

The rosiness faded with the midyear fund-raising reports. Bush stunned the political world with an unprecedented show of financial muscle, collecting $36.2 million through the first half of 1999. But the more immediate threat to Gore was Bradley. Aided by connections on Wall Street, in professional sports, and in the Silicon Valley venture capital community, he raised $11.5 million, more than enough to mount a credible challenge. Gore collected a healthy sum ($18.5 million), but spent it almost as quickly as it came in. One study showed that he had spent 73 percent more on salaries and overhead than Bradley, underwriting a Rolls-Royce of a campaign bloated by consultants, lavish fund-raising affairs, and studio-quality production values (lighting, for instance) to drive home a presidential image in his public appearances. Between July and September alone, reports showed, the campaign raised $6.5 million and spent $6 million. Adding insult to financial injury for Gore, Bradley had also taken a commanding lead in fund-raising over the Internet.

What money Bradley did spend, he invested wisely. While Gore foundered on the Connecticut and fumbled through his premature general election campaign, young Bradley volunteers spent the summer blanketing New Hampshire. They distributed 100,000 leaflets, knocked on 35,000 doors, and spoke to 10,000 people, in an effort that often doesn't begin until the fall. By early September, Bradley had turned the state from a walk for Gore into a dead heat in most polls.

Bradley's ascent was an overnight success years in the making. Pronouncing politics "broken," he left the Senate in 1996 to teach and collect big fees on the lecture circuit. But there was little doubt among friends and old basketball teammates about where he was aiming himself. As other prospective opponents fell away, Bradley became the sole hope for Democrats estranged from Clinton and ambivalent about Gore. His rumpled, Gary Cooperish lack of polish captured the 1999 zeitgeist in national politics, where "authenticity" had emerged as the attribute of choice. It seemed to signal that if he didn't win, his life would still go on quite nicely, thank you, and it gave Gore's overheated ambition a layer of sweaty desperation. Men of a certain age who had hoop dreams of their own swooned over his basketball legacy, and he was a magnet for independent-leaning Democrats who had once been inspired by Gary Hart and Paul Tsongas.

After months of assuming that the nomination was his by entitlement, Gore finally acknowledged that he was in a fight for his political life. "He looked death in the eye and finally got scared," a friend told *U.S. News & World Report's* Roger Simon. "He saw himself as Dan Quayle waiting in line to fly Southwest Airlines." The last time Gore had stared into the abyss — after the 1994 midterm elections — he had invested his hopes in Dick Morris. Now he turned to his old ally Eskew. Gore said he wanted to reach out emotionally to audiences, talking to them by telling his own life story. Eskew stripped some of the ponderous rhetoric from his stump speech (one early stab at a campaign theme was something called "practical idealism") and replaced it with a more traditional Democratic appeal to "working families." (Probably more by coincidence than design, this was the same phrase Gore had used when he tried to reinvent his troubled 1988 campaign.) Gore overhauled his appearance as well. The man who began his vice presidency best known for *Earth in the Balance* would soon be hearing editorial comments about earth tones — those that replaced the blue of his banker's suits.

Gore gave the retooled presentation its first big tryout at the Democratic National Committee's fall session, on September 25. The gathering in the Washington Hilton ballroom was a testament to how far he had fallen in just a few months. Bradley, who couldn't even get a speaking slot at the committee's March meeting, now held equal billing with the vice president. Gore must have felt as if cold water had been splashed in his face when he heard New Hampshire governor Jeanne Shaheen, whose husband, Bill, chaired his campaign there, say, "We're going to hear from two outstanding candidates. One of them will be president."

Bradley spoke first, owing to an overnight scheduling shuffle that positioned Gore to close the meeting. With reading glasses perched on the tip of his nose, Bradley gave a quietly eloquent speech about life in his hometown of Crystal City, Missouri. Conceding that most party officials had already committed to Gore, he made a broader appeal for Democratic victory in 2000. "I want you to know that whether you're for me or against me, we share that same goal of mutual respect . . . Dick Gephardt may not be for me, but I sure want him to be speaker of the House of Representatives." He ended with the hope that he and Gore could show people "that politics doesn't have to be about negative campaigning."

Gore went for a big entrance to underscore his campaign's new energy, making his way through a crowd of cheering young supporters as the O'Jays' "Love Train" boomed through the sound system. There is little in the way of touch or nuance to Gore's performance style. Taking command of an audience means turning up the volume, and with his career on the line, Gore had it on high. "I want to be your nominee, and I'm going to work my heart out to earn your vote!" he said. Much of the speech was a basic checklist appeal to core Democratic constituencies — women, labor, African Americans, and gays. "I feel passionately about these issues!" he said. But within the first few minutes, he tried something new. Rigged with a wireless mike, he stepped tentatively from behind the lectern and talked about his supposed estrangement from politics as a young man and how his work as a reporter had rekindled his belief in democracy. Whereas Bradley had appealed for civility, Gore test-marketed what would become a prominent line of attack in his primary campaign, taking a veiled shot at Bradley's 1996 exit from the Senate, at the height of the Gingrich era, and urging the crowd "to fight for the right outcome, and not walk away from change, but to stay there digging and fighting."

Gore went to a fund-raiser in suburban Maryland two nights later, hoping to compete with the sports-celebrity glitz of the Bradley campaign by lining up L.A. Lakers star Shaquille O'Neal to appear with Bill Cosby and actress Sonia Braga. (O'Neal was a no-show, but sent his size 22 sneaker.) But the most dramatic change came early the next morning, on Tuesday, September 28. Gore decided to follow through on a decision that the family caucus, especially brother-in-law Frank Hunger, had been urging: to move the campaign to Nashville. Washington had become a quagmire of distractions, filled with discord and leaks and competing agendas. Gore wanted to leave all that, maybe even re-create some of the esprit that had made Clinton's Little Rock operation so successful. He called Coehlo and Eskew when he returned to the Naval Observatory residence after the fund-raiser and met them in the den with Tipper. Gore said he was pulling the operation out of Washington and wanted them both to come; they agreed.

When Gore announced the decision to the press on Wednesday, he tried hard to look like a man who believed he was on the right course. "I welcome the new shape of this campaign," he said of Bradley's surge — a preposterous claim. With an eerily broad smile pasted across his face, he called himself the underdog and invoked Gandhi to make his case for decamping to Nashville. "You must become the change you wish to see in the world," he said. "I want this campaign to become the change we're fighting for." Later that night, on *Larry King Live*, he called the exodus from Washington a "move from K Street to the aisles of Kmart," a spin that seemed both over the top and condescending.

At first the Goreheads indicated that everyone on the campaign staff was welcome to make the move, but that was not the case. In addition to saving money on rent, hitting the road became a graceful way to ease some people out of their jobs. Within two days Gore sacked Mark Penn, who had underestimated the Bradley threat and Clinton fatigue. Gore was mainly tired of Penn's divided attention and replaced him with Harrison Hickman, who has extensive polling experience in the South — the region that could become Gore's lifeboat if Bradley beats him in the early primaries up north.

In mid-October Gore took his revamped road show to Iowa, the state he had walked away from as a presidential candidate twelve years earlier. Given Bradley's strength in New Hampshire, the Iowa precinct caucuses had now become a virtual must-win. The first stop of the day, a pancake breakfast at Central Iowa Community College, in Fort

Dodge, put the "new" Gore on full display. It was in some ways a re-turn to the first hard-fought House race of 1976, a time when he really was an underdog. This was the Gore who stopped at every "meat-and-three" along the road and jogged across a field to greet a lone farmer on his tractor. The podium with the vice presidential seal was replaced by a simple stool, and before he stepped up to the microphone, he spent more than half an hour shaking every hand at the thirty or so ta-bles set up in the school gymnasium. The Secret Service, once con-stantly at his elbow at such events, hung back warily as he posed for everyone with a Polaroid, hoping to get his mug on as many living room mantels in the state as he could before caucus night. That eve-ning, after a sunset rally beside the river in Des Moines, he led a couple of hundred supporters on a march through the streets to the down-town convention center, where the Democratic Party was holding its annual Jefferson-Jackson Day Dinner. The sun caught the golden dome of the state capitol behind them as they strode across the bridge into the city center — a rare moment of joyous energy for a campaign that had been flat on its back for months.

Inside the convention center, three thousand Democrats paid sixty dollars a head for chicken cordon bleu and speeches by Gore and Bradley. Both candidates declined to share the dais, and after a brief, unenthusiastic handshake returned to their tables. Bradley was once again serene, while Gore looked as if he should have tried the decaf be-fore appearing. It's a rare Democratic candidate who is brave enough to invoke Jimmy Carter as a historical model, but Bradley likened the former president to "a clean, rushing mountain stream, washing out the stench that was the Nixon years," leaving the clear implication that the time for another cleansing had come. He compared the race to the Mark McGwire–Sammy Sosa home-run derby of 1998, in which two athletes at the top of their game competed furiously for the record book but still seemed to enjoy the experience and each other. "Why can't American politics be like that?" Bradley asked.

Gore, having none of it, again wandered from behind the lectern to deliver his biographical piece, pointing out that Sosa and McGwire had had to come out of the dugout to compete. He walked to the edge of the stage and looked toward Bradley's table, trying to goad his op-ponent into agreeing to regularly scheduled debates. "Let's have one every week! What about it? Let's have one on agriculture right here in

Iowa! What about it, Bill? If the answer is yes, wave your hand. This year! A debate every week! Seriously! Let's get real about this." The Goreheads had also decided that Bradley's decision to leave the Senate was an issue with some political legs. Popping up from the crowd were signs that said "Stay and Fight" and "AL ways a Democrat," a slam at Bradley's brief flirtation with a third-party presidential run in 1996.

As a rallying cry, "Stay and Fight" was a flimsy conceit at best. Gore did stay when Bradley bailed out, but he didn't always fight. When health care reform died in 1994, he and the administration retreated from the pursuit of universal coverage. During the 1995–96 budget negotiations with House Republicans, Gore fended off the worst of the GOP's assault on environmental policy but in general helped move the Democratic Party closer to core Republican values. Nevertheless, the slogan seemed to give Gore the first real traction he'd had as a candidate. Aides called his October travels the Al-Gore-on-Fire Tour.

Clinton continued to haunt him, however. When Gore shared a stage with Bradley for the first time, at a town meeting at Dartmouth College on October 27, he tried to dispose of the president with the first question he got, even though the questioner never specifically mentioned Clinton. It was a freight train of a query about how he would combat the voter cynicism generated by the campaign finance system, the Republican-dominated Congress, and "the behavior of some members of your administration." Gore first launched into an explanation of why he didn't come out against Clinton more forcefully. He said he shared the audience's anger about the Lewinsky matter, but added, "He's my friend. I took an oath under the Constitution to serve my country through thick and thin. And I interpreted that oath to mean that I should try and provide as much continuity and stability as I possibly could."

By the time the candidates met at Dartmouth, the basic dynamics of the race were in place. Bradley, in his understated way, sought to paint the vice president as a timid incrementalist, committed only to tinkering at the margins of a system that was broken. Gore tried to frame Bradley as fiscally irresponsible, offering programs that would consume the projected budget surplus and throw the nation's finances back into deficit. Their health care reform proposals captured the essential differences between the two. Bradley, arguing that the presidency should be about a few big ideas rather than many little ones, proposed a plan for near-universal insurance coverage. It scrapped Medicaid, the health insurance program for the poor, and replaced it with a sliding scale of subsidies that low-income families could use to buy into the insurance plan used by federal employees. Gore's proposal, less costly, focused on impoverished children but covered only about a third of the nation's 43 million uninsured.

The stylistic divide continued to be just as striking. Gore's hyper-rehearsed hard sell started even before the meeting began. Gore, dubbed "the Eddie Haskell–Energizer Bunny" by *Time*'s Margaret Carlson, took questions from the audience during the prebroadcast sound check and stayed on for more after the event ended, lingering so long that even Tipper said she had to go. Bradley remained relaxed and reflective, continuing to take the high road when he had a chance to swat Gore. When he was asked to comment on fund-raising practices in the 1996 Clinton-Gore campaign, the audience laughed at the size of the piñata being dangled before him. Bradley merely looked at Gore, however, smiled knowingly, and said, "I think there were obviously some irregularities that have been addressed. I'm not going to get into details at this stage of the game." He went on to discuss possible reforms.

Bradley might later have wished that he hadn't let Gore off the hook so easily. In the first weeks of November, the vice president's New Hampshire poll numbers started ticking up. By month's end, he had opened up a twenty-five-point lead nationally. And after a spring and summer of generally adoring press, Bradley started to receive more cold-eyed scrutiny. In early November, the story that he had been meeting quietly for more than sixteen months with Madison Avenue advertising executives to plan his campaign message surfaced. The consultations were a measure of the careful planning Bradley had devoted to his insurgency, and suggested that "authenticity," in the end, might be just another strategy.

After a few weeks, Bradley's idealized vision of a Mark McGwire–Sammy Sosa primary began to give way to the reality that Gore was ready to throw as many knockdown pitches as it took to win. He launched almost daily attacks on Bradley's health plan, picking it apart with the kind of relentlessness, and questionable fairness, that had helped drive Dick Gephardt out of the 1988 presidential race. He jumped on every aspect, including its cost (about $65 billion per year) and Bradley's refusal — in the most hypothetical terms — to rule out a tax increase to pay for it. His criticism rang especially hollow when he later acknowledged that even he couldn't rule out raising taxes as president.

As the pace of the campaign quickened, Gore also took every opportunity to signal that he had moved beyond the Clinton administration and the vice presidency. "I made the internal decision that running for president is a lot more important than being the best vice president I can possibly be," he said. Once again, Al Gore felt he had to remind the world that he was his own man.

But even as the "new" Gore gained ground, chronic problems persisted. His advisers continued to make news as regularly as he did. In early November, reporters learned that Naomi Wolf was collecting $15,000 a month from the financially pressed Gore organization for advice that, according to *Time*, included instruction on how to become a dominant alpha male rather than a subordinate beta. The magazine also reported that Wolf was the one who had urged him to adopt the now legendary earth-tone wardrobe. Wolf, whose most recent book, *Promiscuities*, examined girls' sexual coming of age (and recommended, among other things, that schools teach teenagers a "sexual gradualism" that included mutual masturbation and oral sex as alternatives to intercourse), denied offering any fashion advice and said that the alpha-male business had been mentioned once, in passing. Her duties, she explained, consisted mostly of writing memos about the concerns of women. She had done some of the same things for Dick Morris in 1996, causing only a minor flutter of attention.

Gore's employment of Wolf was not as surprising as it seemed on the surface. His interest in the men's movement and other New Age strains of thought gave him a natural affinity for some of her work. Moreover, he has always looked for advice from strong, smart women, from Pauline to Nancy to Tipper and Elmwood's Edna Armistead. But the story stuck to Gore, both because of his ham-fisted attempts to keep Wolf under wraps (her fee was funneled through campaign subcontractors) and because it reinforced suspicions that he and his campaign were the creation of consultants, coaches, and focus groups.

Late 1999 also marked the return of the compulsion to embellish his résumé. Speaking to a high school audience about his investigation into toxic waste sites as a young congressman in the late 1970s, he said,

"I found a little place in upstate New York called Love Canal." Once again, the straight story would have been almost as laudable as the claim. Gore did in fact hold the first congressional hearings on Love Canal, the neighborhood near Niagara Falls that had been ravaged by leaks from an old underground chemical dump. But the federal government had already declared it a disaster area, as a result of dogged grassroots organizing by residents, not Gore's investigative heroics. He apologized the next day for leaving a "misimpression."

It is a peculiar thing to say about someone who has been elected to public office eight times, but Gore is invariably at his worst as a campaigner, a role that tends to highlight his liabilities and obscure his strengths. His poor tactical sense and his over-rehearsed informality, which suggests phoniness even when there is none, are on constant display, while his assets, such as his keen intellect, deep knowledge of the issues, and engaging personality in smaller settings, are often eclipsed. Old friends who cringe at the new game-show-host wardrobe and the labored congeniality believe that Gore would be a significantly better president than he is a candidate, and wish that he could somehow be appointed to the job.

What kind of president he would be depends largely on the hand that history deals him. A continued economic recovery and perhaps a Democratic Congress could free him to pursue a more activist course than he could for much of the Clinton era. Some of his primary-season proposals point in that direction. Recession or Republican dominance on the Hill would almost certainly dictate the more conventionally cautious course. Yet certain characteristics are bound to emerge under any circumstance. Gore's faith in the transforming and democratizing power of technology would turn the presidency into a bully pulpit for the Internet age. His belief in the immutable evil of racism would keep affirmative action and other civil rights issues at the top of the agenda. In foreign policy, his interventionist view of American power would probably lead to a timelier and more forceful U.S. response when a crisis erupts overseas.

Although Clinton would be gone, Gore would not be completely free of his shadow. As tarnished as Clinton's legacy is, memories of his instinctive charm and political skill would remain as Gore did the job, plodding where Clinton would glide, bringing a tin ear where Clinton would hear the music, lecturing where Clinton would cajole. More at home on line than shaking hands on a rope line, a President Gore would always be a bit of a stranger.

The real test of a leader, though, is his ability to take the citizenry where it is not necessarily willing or able to go on its own. For Gore, that test will be his success in building a domestic and international consensus over the long-term dangers of global warming. He will have to decide, finally, what political risks he is willing to assume in advancing the issue that he says is closest to his core. To do so will require Al Gore's greatest invention — as a leader.

Acknowledgments
Notes
Selected Bibliography
Index

Acknowledgments

I owe more debts of gratitude than I can possibly repay to the many people who helped me to tell this story. This is an unauthorized biography. Neither the vice president nor his wife, Tipper Gore, agreed to interviews. But what was striking about their decision to withhold cooperation was not the doors it closed but the number that remained open. More than 250 people were interviewed for this book, and the overwhelming majority of them agreed to talk on the record. Most who preferred to stay in the background are either still working in the Clinton-Gore administration or have recently left. Those who sat for interviews, often repeatedly, amazed me with their candor, insight, and recall. Some shared not only memories but scrapbooks, correspondence, and other documentation that enriched the narrative. Without them, there would have been no *Inventing Al Gore.*

My colleagues at *Newsweek*'s Washington bureau were a constant source of encouragement and guidance, especially Matt Bai, John Barry, Karen Breslau, Howard Fineman, Michael Isikoff, Dan Klaidman, Wes Kosova, Debra Rosenberg, Bob Samuelson, Steve Tuttle, Greg Vistica, Pat Wingert, and, now at *Time,* Matthew Cooper. They are among the best in the business at what they do. Special thanks are due to former *Newsweek* correspondent Lucille Beachy, whose files on Gore's 1988 presidential campaign were an invaluable resource, rich with behind-the-scenes detail. This book would also have been far more difficult to produce without the generous leave of absence provided by *Newsweek*'s late editor Maynard Parker and by its managing editor, Ann McDaniel.

I was also fortunate — no, blessed — with research assistance from Lucy Shackelford and Paul O'Donnell. Lucy, whose day job is director of information services for *Newsweek*'s Washington bureau, endured nearly three years of often frantic pleas for articles, documents, and archival materials with preternatural cheer and meticulous care. Every long writing project eventually reaches an emotional bottoming out. Mine came in late 1998, when Lucy moved to Chicago with her husband, Eric. When they elected to return a few months later, I was one happy biographer. Paul, an associate editor of the magazine's "Periscope" section, squeezed one reporting gem after another from a series of interviews. Laura Ballman, a former *Newsweek* intern, made an important contribution as well with several interviews of classmates from Gore's days in law and divinity school.

Several current and former members of the Tennessee press corps, who have covered Gore with enterprise and insight from the beginning of his political career, were also enormously helpful. They include Carol Bradley, James Brosnan, Larry Daughtrey, Bruce Dobie, David Lyons, Mike Pigott, and Wayne Whitt.

Once I had a manuscript, friends and colleagues took valuable time to read it carefully and critically. Steve Waldman, Bob Cohn, and Michael Isikoff all offered immensely useful suggestions.

My original editor at Houghton Mifflin, Steve Fraser, helped to shape my early thinking about the project. His successor, Eamon Dolan, handled the editing with a gentle scalpel and abundant patience. Eamon's energy and commitment never flagged, even when completion of the book coincided with both the birth of his first child and the tragic death of his brother. Manuscript editor Cindy Buck soldiered courageously through the chaos of a first-time author's manuscript, imposing order and style. Kris Dahl, my agent at ICM, always took care of business.

It may take a village to raise a child, but it took a family to nurture this book. My in-laws, John and Freida Henneberger, stepped in to help at several critical junctures, at one point even flying in from their home in southern Illinois to avert a babysitting crisis. My brother, Chris, a producer for Reuters television, and my parents, Bill and Patricia Turque, were a nonstop cheering section. Our twins, Connor and Della, had just turned one when I began my research. As their second and third birthdays passed, they started to wonder what their father was doing in his basement office for hours on end, six and seven days a week. "Daddy, do you have to write on Al Gore every day?" Della finally asked. Often I did. But authorship also kept me at home far more than I might have been otherwise, and watching them grow has been my grandest privilege. It is one I share with the truly indispensable force behind this book, my wife, Melinda Henneberger. While contributing her own sparkling writing and reporting on the Monica Lewinsky scandal and the early stages of the 2000 presidential campaign to the pages of the *New York Times,* she took on the role of first reader. Her unsparing but always loving criticism, and her insistence that I say what I really mean, made all the difference. She also served selflessly as de facto single parent during the last difficult months of writing and revisions in the spring and summer of 1999. Her luminous presence lights every page of this book, as it does every day of my life.

Notes

Introduction

ix "new day": Karin Miller, "Gore Opens New Campaign Headquarters in Nashville," Associated Press, October 7, 1999.

x "to lose": Jonathan Alter, "The VP: Nothin' Left to Lose," *Newsweek,* October 11, 1999, 40.

xi "national madness": Peter J. Boyer, "Gore's Dilemma," *The New Yorker,* November 28, 1994, 100.

xii "over profits": Television ad titled "Count On," produced by the Campaign Group, March 22, 1988.

xiii "proceed cautiously": Senator Al Gore, *Earth in the Balance: Ecology and the Human Spirit* (Boston: Houghton Mifflin, 1992; New York: Plume, 1993), 15.
"communication today": Ibid., 170.
"of civilization": Ibid., 269.

xiv "White House": Ceci Connolly, "'Restless' Gore Launches Campaign of 'Values,'" *Washington Post,* June 18, 1999.
"intend to do": Roger Simon, "Gore Lets Loose," *U.S. News & World Report,* October 11, 1999, 24.

Prologue: Nashville, November 3, 1970

1 concession speech: *Nashville Tennessean,* November 4, 1970.
steel executive: Albert Gore, *Let the Glory Out: My South and Its Politics* (New York: Viking, 1972), p. 152.

2 impact on the presidency: Albert Gore Jr., "The Impact of Television on the Conduct of the Presidency, 1947–1969" (B.A. thesis, Harvard College, Department of Government, March 1969).
father delivered: John Seigenthaler, outtake from 1993 interview for videotaped tribute to Albert Gore, on file at the Albert Gore Research Center, Middle Tennessee State University, Murfreesboro.
"love your country": Charles Guggenheim, interview with author, Washington, D.C., September 18, 1997.

Agnew described him: William Chapman, "Agnew Joins Drive to Defeat Senator Gore," *Washington Post,* September 23, 1970.

"first time I met him": *Louisville Courier Journal,* August 6, 1970.

land he owned: Associated Press, September 18, 1970; and Jerry Thompson, interview with author, Nashville, December 11, 1997.

"We Believe In": David Halberstam, "The End of a Populist," *Harper's* (January 1971): 35.

3 eastern third: *Nashville Tennessean,* November 4, 1970. The Associated Press declared Brock the winner just before 9:00 P.M. He had built an 80,000-vote lead in the three eastern congressional districts.

to go quietly: Halberstam, "The End of a Populist."

"shall rise again!": *Nashville Tennessean,* November 4, 1970.

her son in tears: Alex S. Jones, "Al Gore's Double Life," *New York Times Magazine,* October 25, 1992, 40.

"subliminal smut": Halberstam, "The End of a Populist."

1. "Well, Mr. Gore, Here He Is"

4 March 31, 1948: District of Columbia, Department of Human Services, certificate of birth, copy issued June 15, 1987.

"miracle to us": Pauline Gore, outtake from 1993 videotaped interview by Democrats 2000, on file at Albert Gore Research Center (AGRC), Middle Tennessee State University, Murfreesboro.

"On Page 1": *Nashville Tennessean,* April 1, 1948.

"adamant about it": Pauline Gore, interview with Lucille Beachy for *Newsweek* Special Election Team, 1988.

5 cut a deal: Ibid.; see also undated "To Whom It May Concern" note, signed by Pauline Gore, from files of a senior staff member of 1988 campaign.

juniorhood for good: Pauline Gore, 1988 Beachy interview.

"day after day": Pauline Gore, 1993 AGRC interview.

early seventeenth century: Gore, *Let the Glory Out,* 4; and *The Gore Family Newsletter* (July-September 1993): 233. Other Gores moved south and west, to Mississippi and Oklahoma, where Thomas Gore, a blind attorney, was elected to the Senate the year Albert was born. Thomas Gore's daughter, Nina, married the aviator Eugene Vidal, a union that in 1925 produced the literary star of the Gore clan, Gore Vidal. In "The Ruins of Washington" (*New York Review of Books,* April 29, 1982), Vidal claims that the Gores are not Scots-Irish but Anglo-Irish from Donegal. In any event, his ties to the Tennessee Gores are distant at best. He told *Playboy* in December 1987 that, according to Albert Gore, he is a "sixth or seventh cousin."

Christmas 1907: See, for example, Sidney Shalett, "He Licked the Old Man of the Senate," *Saturday Evening Post,* October 11, 1952.

"one another": Albert Gore, *Eye of the Storm: A People's Politics for the Seventies* (New York: Herder and Herder, 1970), 192, 197.

6 build a fire: Ibid.

Bryan's populism: Ibid., 107.

to the House: Albert Gore, interview with Dewey W. Grantham and James B. Gardner, Carthage, Tennessee, March 13, 1976, Southern Oral History Program, University of North Carolina, 4–5.

"there someday": Gore, *Eye of the Storm*, 192.

teaching in Booze and other jobs: Ibid., 194–97.

7 "like the limelight": "Quiet Senate Firebrand," *New York Times*, November 12, 1963.

school superintendent's race: Albert Gore, 1976 Grantham and Gardner interview, 14.

Allen Gore growing uneasy: Ibid., 10.

"full year's work": Gore, *Eye of the Storm*, 199.

Gore succeed him: Ibid., 200; see also *The History of Smith County, Tennessee* (Dallas: Curtis Media, 1987).

on an opponent: Vice President Al Gore, remarks at Service of Celebration and Thanksgiving for the Life of Senator Albert Gore Sr., Nashville, December 8, 1998.

"keep her husband happy": Delores Ballard, "One Proud Mom," *Jackson Sun*, January 17, 1993.

"women were": Pauline Gore, 1988 Beachy interview.

8 Pauline Gore family background: Whit LaFon, interview with author, Jackson, Tennessee, April 17, 1997.

Pauline Gore's first marriage: Commonwealth of Kentucky marriage bond, May 15, 1937, indicates that she was divorced. Two Gore family members, who asked that their names not be used, subsequently confirmed the early marriage.

own course work: Vice President Al Gore, remarks at Vanderbilt Law School distinguished alumni awards dinner, Nashville, March 5, 1999.

family in Arkansas: Pauline Gore, interview with author, Carthage, Tennessee, February 27, 1997.

"old folks' tale": Whit LaFon, 1997 interview.

"anything halfway": Henry Cohen, telephone interview with author, February 17, 1997.

9 "at that age": Hank Hillin, *Al Gore Jr.: His Life and Career* (New York: Birch Lane Press, 1988), 16.

a woman in 1936: Pauline Gore, 1997 interview.

Pauline Gore's sexual harassment allegation: Pamela Hess, "The Perils of Pauline Gore," *George* (October 1998).

"for myself too": Pauline Gore, 1993 AGRC interview.

small farm he owned: Albert Gore, 1993 AGRC interview.

10 more lyrical: Ibid.

rest of campaign: Ibid.

"the crowd": *Washington Star*, August 10, 1958.

housing program: See, for example, George Morris, "The Pride of Possum Hollow," *Collier's*, May 30, 1942.

New York World's Fair: See, for example, *Christian Science Monitor*, November 21, 1941.

the TVA: Albert Gore, 1976 Grantham and Gardner interview, 12.

military prosecutor in France: Associated Press, March 4, 1945; *Washington Star,* November 9, 1952.

ahead of him: Albert Gore, 1976 Grantham and Gardner interview, 5.

11 the campaign: Ibid.

"past tense": Albert Gore to Bernard Baruch, February 27, 1952, House of Representatives Collection, AGRC.

"Vote for Gore": Albert Gore, 1976 Grantham and Gardner interview, 15–16.

Democratic primary: *Washington Star,* November 9, 1952.

"like money": Gore, *Eye of the Storm,* 127.

12 "best I could": Gore, *Let the Glory Out,* 77.

mandating desegregation: Ibid., 104.

Senate floor: Albert Gore, 1976 Grantham and Gardner interview, 49.

"completely ignored": Albert Gore to James R. Falls, September 11, 1954, Senate Collection, AGRC.

its impact: James B. Gardner, "Political Leadership in a Period of Transition: Frank G. Clement, Albert Gore, Estes Kefauver, and Tennessee Politics, 1948–1956" (Ph.D. dissertation, Vanderbilt University, 1978), 684–85.

13 Buford Ellington: Gore, *Let the Glory Out,* 114.

"ultimate solutions": Albert Gore to Lawrence Jones, August 2, 1963, Senate Collection, AGRC.

"of starvation": Albert Gore to Edward Meeman (publisher of the *Memphis Press-Scimitar*), September 16, 1951, Senate Collection, AGRC.

secret appropriations for Oak Ridge: Albert Gore, 1976 Grantham and Gardner interview, 12.

"slow deformity": "Atomic Death Belt Urged for Korea," *New York Times,* April 17, 1951.

14 "type of escalation": Gore, *Eye of the Storm,* 84, 85.

"Harlems and Hamtramyks": Albert Gore to Bernard Baruch, November 10, 1952, House Collection, AGRC.

Democratic Leadership Council: Peter Boyer, "Gore's Dilemma," *The New Yorker,* November 28, 1994.

"in his trade": William S. White, "Gore a Serious Worker," *Washington Star,* June 6, 1956.

"brimstone sermon": Russell Baker, "Gore Also Runs — But for VP," *New York Times Magazine,* April 10, 1960.

"not friendly": George Smathers, interview with author, Washington, D.C., February 18, 1997.

15 "make sure of his vote": Coates Redmon, *Come as You Are* (New York: Harcourt Brace Jovanovich, 1986), 147.

"think he is up to?": *New York Times,* November 12, 1963.

Finance Committee seat: Gore wrote to Johnson on May 2, 1956 (Senate collection, AGRC). "Please permit me to remind you that I am the only Democratic Senator of my class who has not been given a major committee assignment." It didn't help Gore's case that he opposed the oil depletion allowance. Eventually, though, he got his seat.

in early 1961: *New York Herald Tribune,* January 18, 1960.

"into the UN": Wayne Whitt, interview with author, Nashville, January 20, 1998.

16 trade and taxation: For a good discussion of Gore's political situation in the 1950s, see James B. Gardner, "State Politics and National Ambitions: Frank Clement, Albert Gore, Estes Kefauver, and Tennessee Politics, 1948–1956" (paper for the meeting of the American Association for State and Local History, November 5, 1982).

"sense or machinery": Eric Severeid, CBS Radio, November 21, 1958.

Stevenson's choice: *New York Times*, August 15, 1956; *Time*, October 25, 1963.

"changed his features": George Reedy, interviewed by Michael L. Gillette, August 17, 1983, Oral History Collection, Lyndon B. Johnson Presidential Library, Austin, Texas, 7.

Kennedy from winning: Gore, *Let the Glory Out*, 95.

"out of the race": Charles Fontenay, telephone interview with author, April 1, 1998.

17 American capitalism: For a full discussion of Hammer's life and times, see Edward Jay Epstein, *Dossier: The Secret History of Armand Hammer* (New York: Random House, 1996), and Steve Weinberg, *Armand Hammer: The Untold Story* (Boston: Little, Brown, 1989).

investigations of the period: Weinberg, *Armand Hammer*, 106.

hit it off: Bill Allen, interview with author, Lexington, Kentucky, April 14, 1997.

ten head for $10,975: Cecil Wolfson (telephone interview with author, November 4, 1998) said he had no interest in currying favor with Gore and bought the cattle as a gift for his brother and business partner, Louis, who owned a horse farm.

"military establishment": Ibid.

for $751: Rudy Abramson, "Black Angus Clip Clipper for 11 Gs," *Nashville Tennessean*, September 14, 1958.

college education: Jamie Gore, interview with author, Tysons Corner, Virginia, July 22, 1997.

year-end statement: Albert Gore, personal correspondence, AGRC.

after expenses: Albert Gore to Armand Hammer, October 17, 1968, personal correspondence, AGRC.

18 "the good ones": Albert Gore to Armand Hammer, October 28, 1963, personal correspondence, AGRC.

Occidental Petroleum: There were apparently limits to what Gore would do for his friend. Epstein describes Hammer's relationship with Representative James Roosevelt: "What Hammer needed was someone in Congress who would cross the line when necessary, and Roosevelt appeared to be his man"; *Dossier*, 188–90.

Library of Congress: Bill Allen to Armand Hammer, June 4, 1956, personal correspondence, AGRC.

appreciative note: Armand Hammer to Albert Gore, June 1, 1961, Senate Collection, AGRC.

elder Gore's watch: Island Creek's environmental problems are explored in the Tennessee weekly *Williamson Leader* (September 24, 1992). During Gore's ten years as chairman of Island Creek (1973–83), the company was cited by the state of Kentucky for thirty violations. The state's division of water pollution called the firm a "major" polluter.

"tall grass": *Washington Post,* January 18, 1980.

"horse sense": Nancy Fleming, telephone interview with author, May 1, 1998.

society columnist: Betty Beale, telephone interview with author, March 31, 1998. Beale said that Pauline Gore invited her to San Juan one weekend to attend the opening of a Holiday Inn hotel. The chain was based in Memphis.

19 "her husband": Ted Brown, telephone interview with author, November 4, 1998.

"gray in their hair": Gilbert Merritt, telephone interview with author, July 2, 1997.

for the job: Ibid.

"would have held good": Pauline Gore to Nancy Gore, May 31, 1958, AGRC.

"I have really relaxed": Pauline Gore to Katie Louchheim, August 1955, Katie Louchheim Collection, Library of Congress.

20 worm-eaten spruce: *Washington Star,* February 11, 1960.

"he was interested": James Gardner, interview with author, Washington, D.C., February 25, 1997.

"Smile, Relax, Attack": Joe Klein, conversation with author, New York, July 1992.

"my husband": Jerry Futrell, interview with author, Carthage, Tennessee, June 4, 1997.

21 "too closely with him": James Fleming, telephone interview with author, February 2, 1999.

"other behavior?": Pauline Gore, 1997 interview.

"personal truth": *Congressional Record,* October 15, 1991.

2. Never an Unhappy Noise

22 wasn't playing: CNN, *Late Edition with Wolf Blitzer,* March 9, 1999.

"created spellcheck": John Schwartz, "Gore Deserves Internet Credit, Some Say," *Washington Post,* March 21, 1999.

23 "no such contribution": David Maraniss and Ellen Nakashima, "Senator's Son Feels Pull of Political Life," *Washington Post,* December 27, 1999. Gore often told the story of how he'd been sought out by Charles Bartlett, a *Chicago Sun-Times* columnist, who, according to Gore, was helping Humphrey at the convention. Gore said he spent an hour answering Bartlett's questions about the younger generation's antiwar sentiments. But Bartlett said he had no contact with Humphrey then, and that if he spoke to Gore, it was for a story, not a speech. When confronted by the *Post,* Gore backed away from the anecdote, ascribing it to "faulty memory."

for the Internet: Katie Hafner, "No Father of Computing, but Maybe He's an Uncle," *New York Times,* March 18, 1999.

"of a gigabit is": *Washington Post,* February 23, 1993.

magazine profile: Louise Davis, "Pancakes and Protocol," *Nashville Tennessean Magazine,* May 12, 1957, 12.

24 family outings: Jamie Gore, 1997 interview.

periodic stays: Albert and Pauline Gore, interview with author, Carthage, Tennessee, February 27, 1997.

"urban life": Jamie Gore, 1997 interview.

family farm: Albert and Pauline Gore, 1997 interview.

25 Women's Speakers Bureau: Democratic National Committee official biography (press release), 1956.

"up in the air": Isabelle Shelton, "Mrs. Albert Gore Hits Campaign Trail," *Washington Star*, October 1, 1956.

"two weeks at a time": Alex S. Jones, "Al Gore's Double Life," *New York Times Magazine*, October 25, 1992, 40; Pauline Gore, 1997 interview.

kept apartments: *Washington Times*, November 11, 1993.

family friendliness: Mark Gore, interview with author, Washington, D.C., May 20, 1997.

26 Grady Gore from Wilson County: *Gore Family Newsletter* (July-September 1993).

1937 purchase of Fairfax: From chronology provided by the Ritz Carlton through the Washington Historical Society.

the Potomac: *Washington Star*, July 6, 1934.

"ground around it": Grady Gore, undated profile in Smith newspapers, 1952.

Grady Gore support of Dewey: Ibid.

Richard Nixon: *Washington Star*, March 24, 1974.

Samuel Pierce: Michael York, "Top Aide to Pierce Was Go-between with Favor-Seekers in GOP," *Washington Post*, October 27, 1993. In 1953 her mother, Grady's daughter Mary Benton Gore, had married Gordon Dean, Harry Truman's first chairman of the Atomic Energy Commission. He was killed in a 1958 plane crash. Among the major elements of the prosecution's case against Deborah Gore Dean was evidence that she had helped direct HUD contracts to a Miami developer who employed the former attorney general and convicted Watergate figure John Mitchell. Dean's mother was romantically involved with Mitchell at the time of the alleged dealings.

assistant secretary's post: Richard Powelson, "Gore's Aid to Cousin Backfires," *Knoxville News-Sentinel*, July 12, 1989.

as spoiled: Mark Gore, 1997 interview.

27 "Filibuster Party": Betty Beale, "Senators Frolic Outdoors at Gores' Filibuster Party," *Washington Star*, July 22, 1957.

latest gossip: Albert Gore, CNN interview, January 20, 1993.

campaign strategy: Vice President Al Gore, in his remarks at Clifford's memorial service on November 19, 1998, mentioned seeing Clifford at the apartment.

call President Kennedy: Gore, *Let the Glory Out*, 152.

junior membership: Receipts on file at AGRC.

"than we can house": Albert Gore to Ali Heravi, January 10, 1958, AGRC.

Mrs. Lloyd Parker Shippen: Schedule of classes on file at AGRC.

28 "what may happen?": *Knoxville News-Sentinel*, June 4, 1954.

every morning: Mead Miller, telephone interview with Paul O'Donnell, September 18, 1997.

cafeteria line: Jerry Cole, interview with author, Carthage, Tennessee, September 15, 1997.

"I enjoyed it": Albert Gore to Armand Hammer, December 15, 1962, AGRC.

29 "for fifteen minutes": Gordon Thompson, interview with author, Elmwood, Tennessee, October 25, 1997.

"worry anyone": Donna Armistead, interview with author, Hermitage, Tennessee, January 21, 1998.

"an unhappy noise": Katherine Boo, "The Liberation of Albert Gore," *Washington Post Magazine*, November 28, 1993, 11.

"'little politician'": Mike O'Hara, telephone interview with author, January 13, 1998.

"ragging on him": Geoff Kuhn, telephone interview with author, August 8, 1997.

30 "his dad": John Warnecke, telephone interview with author, September 2, 1998.

"own dignity": Michael Kelly, "A Life of Advantage, Enhanced by the Will to Excel," *New York Times*, July 17, 1992.

"political sage": Redmon, *Come as You Are*.

"filling a role": Charles Peters, interview with author, Washington, D.C., May 27, 1997.

31 "anything in the world": Fred Graham, interview with author, Washington, D.C., March 21, 1997.

"for the morning": Nancy Gore to Albert, Pauline, and Al Gore, undated letter, summer 1958, AGRC.

her father: Nancy Fleming, May 1, 1998, interview.

"living room": James Fleming, telephone interview with author, February 2, 1999.

32 wore a white dress: Pauline Gore, remarks in program for the dedication of the Nancy Gore Hunger National Education Program, John F. Kennedy Center for the Performing Arts, December 5, 1995.

"the thirty-two steps": Larry Daughtrey, interview with author, Nashville, June 5, 1997.

33 "I said, 'Uh-uh'": Mark Gore, 1997 interview.

"getting his breakfast": Pauline Gore, 1997 interview.

"damned hillside plow": Ibid. The anecdote first appeared in Peter Boyer, "Gore's Dilemma," *The New Yorker*, November 28, 1994. Mrs. Gore reluctantly confirmed the substance of the story.

"everything in it": Gordon Thompson, 1997 interview.

treed a raccoon: William Thompson, interview with author, Elmwood, Tennessee, September 14, 1997.

34 "he totaled it": Gordon Thompson, 1997 interview.

go steady: Donna Armistead, 1998 interview.

36 Edna Armistead background: Donna Armistead, 1998 interview.

3. Al Gorf

38 "sense of humor": Albert Arnold Gore Jr., St. Albans school transcript.

"interested in pranks": Alfred True, interview with author, Falls Church, Virginia, November 10, 1997.

Bill Bradley: Matthew Simchak, interview with author, Washington, D.C., May 21, 1997.

39 "good relationships": David Ignatius, "The Headmaster Who Had a Firm Grip on Life," *Washington Post*, May 5, 1997.

"for the State": Valerie Strauss, "Collision Course," *Washington Post*, July 9, 1997.

"care of itself": David Bartlett, telephone interview with author, August 4, 1997.

second kind: Matthew Simchak, 1997 interview.

to the turf: 1965 *The Albanian* (St. Albans yearbook), 80.

post Gore coveted: Phil Rosenbaum, telephone interview with author, August 4, 1997.

40 "competent in everything": George Hillow, telephone interview with Paul O'Donnell, September 14, 1997.

"wasn't appreciated": Geoff Kuhn, telephone interview with author, August 5, 1997.

"no close friends": John Siscoe, telephone interview with author, August 4, 1997.

"Al Gorf": 1965 *Albanian*, 35.

41 "wearing no socks": George Hillow, 1997 interview.

"Gore's Disease": Geoff Kuhn, 1997 interview.

smoke cigarettes: Ibid.

from the stress: Jim Gray, interview with author, Washington, D.C., September 18, 1997.

"social mix": John Siscoe, 1997 interview.

"lonely times for him": Donna Armistead, 1998 interview.

every few minutes: Ibid.

his senior year: Ibid.

bed before midnight: Geoff Kuhn, 1997 interview.

42 "talking like this": Ibid.

"it snapped back": Matthew Simchak, 1997 interview.

record in 1964: 1965 *Albanian*, 80–81. "Captain Al Gore worked hard to inspire the team," the yearbook noted.

his senior year: Ibid., 86.

classical music: John Claiborne Davis, *The Ordered Web: Essays in Resurrection* (Washington, D.C., 1986), 167.

"little things": Alfred True, 1997 interview.

"being bold": George Hillow, 1997 interview.

"emotional catharsis": Hillin, *Al Gore Jr.*, 76.

43 U.S. concert: Reed Hundt, interview with author, Washington, D.C., March 27, 1997.

Jackie Wilson: Jerome Powell, interview with author, Bethesda, Maryland, March 24, 1998.

"was into it": Ibid.

"and make out": Mead Miller, telephone interview with Paul O'Donnell, September 18, 1997.

"smitten with Diane": Geoff Kuhn, 1997 interview.

"desire to please": Matthew Simchak, telephone interview with author, May 22, 1998.

44 "big as a house": Geoff Kuhn, 1997 interview.

college years: Denny Scharf, telephone interview with author, August 13, 1998.

strained for a time: Ibid.

a senator's son: John Davis, interview with author, Washington, D.C., September 5, 1997.

Gore's favor: How Gore's SAT scores ranked with those of other incoming Harvard freshmen in 1965 is not known. Both school officials and the Educational Testing Service, which administers the test, insisted that they didn't have those records. In 1966 Harvard told the College Board, publisher of *The College Handbook,* only that "few candidates are admitted with SAT scores below 500."

to thirty-five thousand: George Q. Flynn, *Lewis B. Hershey: Mr. Selective Service* (Chapel Hill: University of North Carolina Press, 1985), 234.

45 "showed up": Reed Hundt, 1997 interview.

University of Alabama-Tuscaloosa: Mead Miller, 1997 interview.

graduation dance: Tipper Gore, *Picture This: A Visual Diary* (New York: Broadway Books, 1996), 5.

"Ti-pi-ta": The song was originally recorded by Horace Heidt and his band, Heidt's Musical Knights, according to the *Washington Post,* December 4, 1986.

"some action": Geoff Kuhn, 1997 interview.

46 "Get off of My Cloud": Gordon Beall, telephone interview with author, July 24, 1997.

"going to marry you": Mead Miller, 1997 interview.

beating her: Bill of complaint, *Margaret Carlson Aitcheson v. John Kenneth Aitcheson,* filed in Circuit Court, Alexandria, Virginia, October 4, 1949.

"everyday life": Filed in Circuit Court, Alexandria, Virginia, January 25, 1950.

hospitalized twice: Carl M. Cannon, "The Unsinkable Tipper Gore," *Baltimore Sun,* June 20, 1994.

other illnesses: Gore, *Picture This,* 18.

47 "animal magnetism": Sandra McElwane, "Her Life, Her Love Story," *Good Housekeeping* (March 1993).

"together ever since": Gore, *Picture This,* 5.

two nights running: Donna Armistead, 1998 interview.

"to the theater": Gordon Beall, 1997 interview.

"up there": Fred Graham, 1997 interview.

48 "feel held with": Lance Laurence, interview with author, Knoxville, Tennessee, September 13, 1997.

4. "Gore, Albert A."

49 "this guy": John Tyson, interview with author, Silver Spring, Maryland, September 30, 1997.

50 "governed the country": Roger Rosenblatt, *Coming Apart: A Memoir of the Harvard Wars of 1969* (New York: Little, Brown, 1997), 91–92.

"going on with Al": Jeff Howard, telephone interview with author, May 12, 1998.

met with Dean Rusk: Gregory Craig, telephone interview with Paul O'Donnell, April 1998. Craig, who later worked at the State Department and became White House special counsel overseeing Clinton's defense in the House impeachment proceedings, was president of the undergraduate council and active in the antiwar movement when Gore was a sophomore.

Memphis State University: Charles Crawford, telephone interview with author, March 6, 1997.

draft a speech: *Washington Times,* August 28, 1996. Gore told the NBC anchor

Tom Brokaw during the 1996 Democratic convention in Chicago that he went to Grant Park in 1968 and witnessed some of the melee but was "more an observer" than a protester. Brokaw responded, "Well, that's like saying you didn't inhale practically." Gore said, "I came here with my family and spent most of my time in the convention hall."

outside of Carthage: Deed of trust, filed April 14, 1969, with the office of the Smith County clerk, Carthage, Tennessee.

51 left-wing dissidents: The 1965–66 *Harvard Crimson Confidential Guide* to courses rhapsodized about "the bearded Peretz," calling him a "showman" and "one of the most articulate and generally enthralling faculty members the Government Department has to offer. Or any department."

Marx and Freud: Peretz said in a 1965 catalog that the themes to be covered included "planning and freedom, reason and irrationality in ideology and institutions, the idea of culture and the role of the elites."

weren't many around: Martin Peretz, interview with author, New York, June 16, 1997.

"alien to his experience": Ibid.

his former student: Peretz's protectiveness led to the 1997 exit of *TNR* editor Michael Kelly, an often scathing critic of Gore and President Clinton for their campaign fund-raising practices and other matters.

cousin Jamie: Jamie Gore, telephone interview with author, August 31, 1998.

52 Memorial Drive: Jeff Howard, 1998 interview.

"always on": John Tyson, 1997 interview; Lillian Ross, "Keeping up with Mr. Jones," *The New Yorker*, April 4, 1994, 57.

"hired gladiator": Rosenblatt, *Coming Apart*, 147.

game incessantly: According to Harvard's Sports News Bureau, Gore played twelve of sixteen games, averaging 2.8 points. His highest scoring game was seven points.

"out of the blue": *Chicago Tribune*, March 11, 1988.

"thing you did": *U.S. News & World Report*, July 20, 1992.

"at the same time": John Tyson, 1997 interview.

the remote Dunster: 1967 Harvard yearbook, 215.

53 "we were there": Vice President Al Gore, Harvard University commencement, June 9, 1994.

"seven of them!": Michael Kapetan, telephone interview with author, February 5, 1998.

"an evening ball": *New York Times*, July 19, 1992.

following year: John Tyson, telephone interview with author, November 12, 1998.

where he worked: Jamie Gore, interview with author, Tysons Corner, Virginia, July 22, 1997.

54 "Please Come to Boston": John Warnecke, telephone interview with author, November 20, 1998.

art cinemas in Boston: Bob Somerby, telephone interview with author, May 21, 1998.

"goes the presidency": Rosenblatt, *Coming Apart*, 91.

Wellesley coffeehouse: Michael Kapetan, 1998 interview.

"in Carthage": Michael Kapetan, 1998 interview.

"curative sciences": Bob Somerby, telephone interview with author, January 30, 1998.

"rest of the story": John Tyson, 1997 interview.

"Man's Place in Nature": Bob Somerby, interview with author, Washington, D.C., November 21, 1997.

55 another academic specialty: Hampton Sides, "Born to Run: The Life and Times of a Thoroughbred Politician," *Memphis* (May 1986): 47.

New York Times: Allan M. Siegal (assistant managing editor at the *New York Times*), telephone interview with author, November 12, 1998, and e-mail on January 3, 2000. According to payroll records, Gore worked at the paper from July 9 to September 9, 1967.

news gathering involved: Jamie Gore, 1998 interview.

kid from Harvard: John Kifner, telephone interview with author, November 19, 1998.

The Fantasticks: Bon Appetit (November 1994).

forty times: *The Crimson Confidential Guide 1967–68*, 49.

56 Cuban Missile Crisis: Allison's research on the Cuban Missile Crisis would result in the highly regarded book *Essence of Decision*.

"a clear thread": Graham Allison, telephone interview with author, August 19, 1998.

"keen and serious": Richard Neustadt, interview with author, Wellfleet, Massachusetts, June 2, 1998.

57 "too far to be stopped": Albert Gore Jr., "The Impact of Television on the Conduct of the Presidency, 1947–1969" (B. A. thesis, Harvard College, Department of Government, March 1969), 39.

network news executives: Ibid., 85–99.

"out of something": Richard Neustadt, 1998 interview.

58 "the primary task": Gore, *Earth in the Balance*, 364.

"father figure": Michael Kapetan, 1998 interview.

"Albert Gore Jr.": Melinda Henneberger, "Author of 'Love Story' Disputes a Gore Story," *New York Times*, December 14, 1997.

"Al's date": Segal told the *Times* that he was "befuddled" by the report, which originally appeared in the December 15, 1997, issue of *Time* magazine. Segal said Gore told him in a phone conversation that he denied telling the reporters he was the model for Barrett, but that he had attributed the statement to a Nashville newspaper reporter who once asked Segal about it. Segal says *Time* omitted that attribution in its account. But neither Gore nor his spokespeople bothered to correct the story until Segal was sought out by the *Times*.

59 trip over himself: Judith and Neil Morgan, *Roger: A Biography of Roger Revelle* (San Diego: Scripps Institution of Oceanography, 1996), 11.

"future of mankind": Ibid., 93.

timber and agriculture: Ibid., 54.

"fundamental way": Gore, *Earth in the Balance*, 6.

age twenty-six: Lawrence M. Baskir and William A. Strauss, *Chance and Circumstance: The Draft, the War, and the Vietnam Generation* (New York: Alfred A. Knopf, 1978).

60 the well-off: According to Baskir and Strauss, only 12 percent of college graduates saw service in Vietnam, compared to 21 percent of high school graduates (*Chance and Circumstance*, 8). African Americans bore a disproportionate burden of the battle in the war's early years. In 1965 they accounted for 24 percent of all army combat deaths, a share that had declined to 9 percent by 1970.

"burning frenzy": Steven Kelman, *Push Come to Shove: The Escalation of Student Protest* (Boston: Houghton Mifflin, 1970), 118. Kelman served in the OMB in the Clinton administration.

draft prospects: Steven Kelman, interview with author, Cambridge, Massachusetts, June 4, 1998.

contemplated suicide: James Fallows, "What Did You Do in the Class War, Daddy?" *Washington Monthly* (October 1975): 5.

returned a card: See, for example, *Boston Globe*, October 17, 1967. In Boston 281 young men burned what they said were their draft cards or turned them over to clergymen at the Arlington Street Church. On Hershey, see George Q. Flynn, *Lewis B. Hershey: Mr. Selective Service* (Chapel Hill: University of North Carolina Press, 1985), 259–60. His directive triggered a huge protest and was eventually overturned in the courts, but the practice persisted.

Oakland Army Induction Center: Flynn, *Lewis B. Hershey*, 259; *Boston Globe*, October 17, 1967.

students on probation: "The War Comes to Harvard," 1968 Harvard yearbook, 62. Most students tried to slip through loopholes rather than challenge the law. Before President Nixon phased out the draft in 1972, about 25,000 young men nationwide had been indicted for violating federal draft regulations. More than 9,000 were convicted, and 3,250 went to prison, although most were paroled within a year. More than 10,000 fled to Canada and other countries. See Baskir and Strauss, *Chance and Circumstance*, 15; and Todd Gitlin, *The Sixties: Years of Hope, Days of Rage* (New York: Bantam, 1987), 291.

61 "brief interlude": Jamie Gore, 1998 interview.

"something real": Jeremy Larner, *Nobody Knows: Reflections on the McCarthy Campaign of 1968* (New York: Macmillan, 1970), 37.

"on the war": Bob Somerby, 1997 interview.

62 "I liked that": Phil Rosenbaum, telephone interview with the author, August 4, 1997.

"U.S. Army": Peter J. Boyer, "Gore's Dilemma," *The New Yorker*, November 28, 1994, 100. Albert Gore made this and other letters from his son available to Boyer. The vice president renounced the views he expressed then, calling them "a college kid's silly language in the midst of a very intense period for the country."

"country's policy": Sides, "Born to Run," 47.

"correct decision": *New York Times*, July 17, 1992.

"against him": Gordon Thompson, 1997 interview.

63 "answer is, why?": *Carthage Courier*, July 31, 1969.

"they had to say": John Tyson, 1997 interview.

"what he did": Pauline Gore, 1997 interview.

"go to Vietnam": David Halberstam, "The End of a Populist," *Harper's* (January 1971).

"for his son": Charles Fontenay, 1998 interview.

64 "lot of concern": Ted Brown, telephone interview with the author, November 4, 1998.

at the notion: See, for example, *Washington Post,* July 10, 1992. According to Albert Gore, Pauline told her son that "her heart was with him. She'd support whatever he wanted to do — including going to Canada with him."

"have much choice": *U.S. News & World Report,* July 20, 1992.

"would convey": Richard Neustadt, 1998 interview.

Clinton-Gore campaign: This individual insists on speaking only under condition of anonymity as a confidential source. Every effort has been made to authenticate the story he tells, but what follows is essentially his account.

66 "some advice": William Westmoreland, telephone interview with author, March 18, 1998. In response to a follow-up letter asking whether he could shed any further light on the matter, he wrote back on May 7, 1998, that he had "no recollection" of conversations with a Gore representative. He offered me no explanation as to why he was contradicting his initial answer to my inquiry. "Young Al has a bright future indeed," Westmoreland wrote, "but I hope he can live up to my expectations." A second letter to the general went unanswered.

reclassified him 1-A: Classification history of Albert A. Gore Jr. provided by Selective Service.

"who will": Albert and Pauline Gore, 1997 interview.

67 "scenario suggested": John Tyson, 1997 interview.

"for diversion": Martin Peretz, 1997 interview.

peaceful and resigned: John Tyson, 1997 interview.

"as myself there": Ellen Nakashima and David Maraniss, "Beginnings, and an Ending," *Washington Post,* December 30, 1999.

5. Men on Horseback

68 through the draft: Andrew J. Glass, "Defense Report/Draftees Shoulder Burden of Fighting and Dying in Vietnam," *National Journal,* August 15, 1970, 1747. Gore's overall service commitment was the standard six years — two on active duty and four on reserve status.

"'Yes, sir'": Knight-Ridder Newspapers, November 30, 1987.

"choice for you": Baskir and Strauss, *Chance and Circumstance,* 51–52, 55.

69 on his behalf: William Westmoreland, 1998 interview.

134 IQ: St. Albans School transcript. The IQ test was taken in September 1964, at the beginning of Gore's senior year.

"choice of assignments": Dess Stokes, telephone interview with author, September 10, 1997.

"newspaper trainee": Department of the Army, form 20, enlisted qualification record for Albert A. Gore, August 13, 1969.

"writes poetry": Ibid.

"spare as a rail": Richard Neustadt, 1998 interview.

70 enraged him: Rosenblatt, *Coming Apart,* 171.

their affairs: Ralph Litzenberger, telephone interview with author, October 15, 1997.

seen and done: Richard Abalos, telephone interview with author, September 23, 1997.

a "kind of parody": Bob Delabar, telephone interview with author, April 29, 1998.

71 horrifically wrong: On March 6, 1998, Thompson and his helicopter door gunner, Lawrence Colburn, were awarded the Soldiers' Medal for saving the lives of at least ten Vietnamese civilians during "the unlawful massacre of noncombatants by American forces at My Lai."

swapped stories: Marty Hendrick, telephone interview with author, October 16, 1997.

"Kennedys doing it": Richard Abalos, 1997 interview.

"perfect four-leaf clover": Bob Delabar, 1998 interview.

72 Private Al Gore: Marty Hendrick, 1997 interview.

"public affairs": Gus Stanisic, telephone interview with author, February 22, 1998.

ten minutes: Bob Delabar, 1998 interview.

with Westmoreland: In a 1999 interview with the *Washington Post,* Gore said Westmoreland asked him why so many young people were against the war. Gore said he told the general that he thought the war was a "huge mistake."

73 "serve in Vietnam": Michael Zibart, interview with author, Nashville, January 21, 1998.

"mysteriously canceled": Sides, "Born to Run," 47.

"November election": *Washington Post,* February 3, 1988.

"Just not true": Melvin Laird, telephone interview with author, August 27, 1997. Timmons wrote on March 19, 1998: "This is the first I've heard of this and find it difficult to believe."

"got involved": William Westmoreland, 1998 interview.

at the Capitol: Mark Gore, 1997 interview.

scaffolding: Michael Kapetan, 1998 interview.

74 for an army private: Marty Hendrick, 1997 interview.

"All You Need Is Love": Gore, *Picture This,* 6.

began to disperse: *Nashville Banner,* October 25, 1984.

"Expando model": Hillin, *Al Gore Jr.,* 75.

"going to win": Richard Abalos, 1997 interview.

vulnerable portfolio: Robert Walters, "Eyes of Tennessee on Texas," *Washington Star,* November 1, 1970.

75 edgy humor: James Doyle, "Tennessee Senator in His Hardest Fight," *Washington Star,* September 28, 1970.

"love your country": Charles Guggenheim, interview with author, Washington, D.C., September 18, 1997.

Washington aristocrat: Ibid.

"the Senator": Vanderbilt Television News Archive; Richard Stout, memo to Edward Kosner and David Alpern, *Newsweek,* August 9, 1970.

76 "telling us about that": Richard Abalos, 1997 interview.

out of touch with Tennesseans: David S. Broder, "Tennessee: Gore Battles Back," *Washington Post,* October 28, 1970.

"do not believe it": *Nashville Tennessean,* July 27, 1969.

"The Frenchier the better": H. R. Haldeman to Harry Dent, September 23, 1970, Nixon Presidential Materials, National Archives.

"homes unsafe": Arlen J. Large, "Gore, Brock, and 'Southern Strategy,'" *Wall Street Journal,* October 20, 1970.

77 white middle class: Brock took a different tone when he ran for the Maryland Republican senatorial nomination in 1994, apologizing to black audiences and calling for more civility and decency in politics. He lost to Ruthann Aron.

"cool and modern": Halberstam, "End of a Populist," 35.

"Operation Townhouse": James R. Polk, "Ex-Nixon Aide Pleads Guilty in GOP Fund Case," *Washington Star,* November 15, 1974. The scheme was administered at the White House's direction by the former Nixon aide Jack Gleason, who fed the funds, sometimes in cash, into crucial contests in Tennessee, Maryland, Florida, and other states. In 1974, as part of the Watergate prosecutions, Gleason and the Nixon adviser Harry Dent pled guilty to misdemeanors for running "Townhouse," named for its headquarters in the basement of a Northwest Washington residence. The prosecutor in the case was Charles Ruff, who went on to serve as White House counsel during impeachment proceedings against Clinton.

Scaife wrote checks totaling $10,000 to the Brock Campaign Committee, Brock for Senate Committee, Citizens for Brock, and TV for Brock, according to letters he wrote to Jack Gleason on July 24 and September 29, 1970, on file in the Nixon Presidential Materials, National Archives.

American POWs: Alex Bontemps, "Antiwar Talk by Senators Aids VC: Brock," *Nashville Tennessean,* September 27, 1970.

flight to Nashville: Shelby Coffey III, "Two Washington Pols Have at Each Other," *Washington Post: Potomac,* September 27, 1970.

fiddle reappeared: R. W. Apple Jr., "Gore Fights for Political Survival in Tennessee Race," *New York Times,* November 1, 1970.

78 hours of sleep: Kathy Sawyer, "Gore Women on the Go," *Nashville Tennessean,* October 25, 1970.

rest of the slack: Ibid.

student coordinator: Ted Brown, 1998 interview.

slightly ahead: Roy Reed, "Tennessee Not Following the Demolish-Gore Script," *New York Times,* October 13, 1970.

since 1965: Stanley Karnow, *Vietnam: A History* (New York: Viking, 1983), 685.

"economic interests": "After the Fox," *Newsweek,* August 17, 1970.

79 Howard Baker: *Nashville Tennessean,* November 4, 1970.

"then I'm not": Kelly Leiter, "Tennessee: Gore Versus the White House," *The Nation,* October 26, 1970.

"his presence": Phil Sullivan, interview with author, Nashville, March 3, 1998.

"as he did": Bill Allen, interview with author, Lexington, Kentucky, April 14, 1997.

losses elsewhere: Richard Harris, "Annals of Politics," *New Yorker,* July 10, 1971.

80 "rise again!": Wayne Whitt, "Dunn, Brock Victorious," *Nashville Tennessean,* November 4, 1970.

encouraged the theme: Among numerous examples, see *Nashville Banner,* December 28, 1978. Albert Gore, asked if the truth had risen, said, "Oh, yes, in my son."

"were stunned": Marty Hendrick, 1997 interview.

to the last: Halberstam, "End of a Populist," 35.

after they lost: Pauline Gore, 1997 interview.

81 "nothing helps": *Washington Star,* December 20, 1970.

"this morning!": *Nashville Banner,* May 13, 1993.

"thirty-two years, Dad": Vice President Al Gore, remarks at Service of Celebration and Thanksgiving for the Life of Senator Albert Gore Sr., Nashville, December 8, 1998.

6. Saving Private Gore

82 just one of the troops: Department of the Army, form 20, record of assignments for Albert A. Gore.

"the fishbones": Alan Leo, telephone interview with author, December 2, 1997.

"look in his eyes": Bob Hinchliffe, interview with author, North Easton, Massachusetts, June 6, 1998.

83 security was good: Alan Leo, 1997 interview.

"more excitement": Ibid.

"I don't remember it": K. B. Cooper, telephone interview with author, January 5, 1998.

"not Gore's decision": Wayne Pelter, telephone interview with author, November 19, 1997.

Gore arrived: Bob Hinchliffe, 1998 interview.

84 in a foxhole: William Smith, telephone interview with author, February 5, 1998.

"our position": Mike O'Hara, telephone interview with author, January 13, 1998.

"crucified him for it": Ibid.

"their forks full": SP-4 Albert Gore, "Assistance Given by 20th Brigade," *Castle Courier,* March 22, 1971.

South Vietnamese troops: Karnow, *Vietnam,* 630; see also Col. Harry G. Summers Jr., *Vietnam War Almanac* (New York: Facts on File Publications, 1985), 223.

85 "lattice-work": SP-5 Albert Gore, "Engineers Build Highways out of Delta Rice Paddies," *Castle Courier,* April 19, 1971.

misleading impression: Associated Press, "Gore Defends Brochure with a Vietnam Photo," *New York Times,* October 26, 1987. "I carried that rifle all over Vietnam and walked like that in every part of the country," Gore told reporters in Casper, Wyoming. "I was not involved in fire fights. I was not in the infantry. I was in areas where combat took place. I did not see combat myself. I was fired upon. The engineers frequently took fire, but we usually had a critical mass of bulldozers and equipment and personnel that made it mostly harassment fire."

he did not: Ellen Nakashima and David Maraniss, "Disillusionment Deepens amid 'Sordid Crusade,'" *Washington Post,* December 31, 1999.

"the U.S. firebase": SP-5 Albert Gore, "Quick Reactions Defeat Sappers," *Castle Courier,* May 3, 1971.

"dogs were barking": SP-5 Albert Gore, "Threatened Overrun of FSB Blue Thwarted by Quick Reactions," *Castle Courier,* April 5, 1971.

"out of there": Sylvester Thompson, telephone interview with author, October 22, 1997.

86 early 1971: Karnow, *Vietnam,* 630–32.

"about it at all": Vice President-elect Al Gore, Vietnam War Memorial Veterans Day ceremony, Washington, D.C., November 11, 1992.

"off-putting": Michael Kapetan, 1998 interview.

"for his sins": Richard Abalos, 1997 interview. Stanisic (1998 interview), for his part, says he doesn't remember the letter.

87 "on my father": Lloyd Armour, interview with author, Nashville, January 20, 1998.

"once or twice": Dennis Hevesi, "Drug Use Emerges as Campaign issue," *New York Times*, November 8, 1987.

"fun in Vietnam": Bob Delabar, 1998 interview.

"unprepared for": Myra MacPherson, "Al Gore and the Window of Certainty," *Washington Post*, February 3, 1988.

88 "much higher": David Lyons, "Gore Learns from Dad's Errors," *Knoxville News-Sentinel*, May 30, 1984.

"very sad": John Warnecke, telephone interview with author, June 16, 1999.

"'going to be fine'": Nancy Warnecke, now Nancy Rhota, declined an interview request.

89 "to the mission": Gore's Department of Army form 20 notes that he was granted an "early out for school."

divinity studies: Tom Ogletree, telephone interview with Paul O'Donnell, May 1998.

"when he left": Tom McGee, telephone interview with author, February 2, 1998.

7. "I Must Become My Own Man"

90 "kind of withdrew": Steve Armistead, *U.S. News & World Report*, July 20, 1992.

"would ever do": Al Gore Jr., interview with Ginny Carroll for *Newsweek*, July 10, 1992.

91 "to be short-lived": Andrew Schlesinger, telephone interview with author, June 18, 1998.

"her advice": Donna Armistead, 1998 interview.

had both taken: Pauline Gore, 1997 interview.

"do both": Quoted in Hillin, *Al Gore Jr.*, 88.

92 money in his pocket: Walter King Robinson, interview with author, Carthage, Tennessee, September 12, 1997.

forced his reinstatement: For discussion of Lawson and the Nashville sit-ins, see Taylor Branch, *Parting the Waters: America in the King Years, 1954–1963* (New York: Simon & Schuster, 1988), 274–80; and James D. Squires, *The Secrets of the Hopewell Box: Stolen Elections, Southern Politics, and a City's Coming of Age* (New York: Times Books, 1996), 169–70.

"counted in life": Jack Forstman, telephone interview with author, January 16, 1998.

"want to do?": Eugene TeSelle, interview with author, Nashville, June 4, 1997.

93 "very Clinton-Gore": Nancy Ammerman, telephone interview with Paul O'Donnell, March 22, 1998.

"public life": Tom Ogletree, 1998 interview.

"taking advantage": Walter Harrelson, telephone interview with author, January 16, 1998.

population growth: Eugene TeSelle, 1997 interview.

"intellectual interest": Edward Farley, telephone interview with Paul O'Donnell, March 22, 1998.

94   "needed to know": Walter Harrelson, 1998 interview.

"cynics are wrong": Vice President Al Gore, Harvard University commencement, June 9, 1994.

95   "all things": Gore, *Earth in the Balance,* 367–68.

Merleau-Ponty: Peter Steinfels, "Beliefs," *New York Times,* May 29, 1999. Steinfels added, "To hear the name 'Merleau-Ponty' trip off the tongue of a major American politician is surely extraordinary. Whether it is a qualification to be president is an entirely different matter."

"are forgiven": Eve Zibart, interview with author, Washington, D.C., August 5, 1997.

96   "of the people": On Truman, see Charles Fontenay, "Frontier to Frontier . . . That's *Tennessean's* Story," *Nashville Tennessean,* April 29, 1962; on the paper's mission, see *Nashville Tennessean,* September 23, 1990.

Gore did in 1956: Gore's connections to the *Tennessean* were more than political: Pauline Gore's brother, Whit LaFon, was married to Evans's secretary.

Montgomery, Alabama, mob: Richard Reeves, *President Kennedy: Profile of Power* (New York: Simon & Schuster, 1993), 128; information on Seigenthaler from John Seigenthaler, oral history interview by Civil Rights Documentation Project, Moorland-Springarn Research Center, Howard University, Washington, D.C.

Nashville politics: Squires, *Hopewell Box,* 189–94.

favorable recommendation: Frank Ritter, interview with author, Nashville, January 22, 1998.

97   "God-given directive": Squires, *Hopewell Box,* 169.

"setting out to do": Phil Sullivan, interview with author, Nashville, March 3, 1998.

"turbulent waters": David Maraniss, "As a Reporter, Gore Found a Reason to Be in Politics," *Washington Post,* January 4, 1998.

"Mrs. O'Leary's cow": Albert Gore Jr., "Hillbilly Day Puts It All Together Again," *Nashville Tennessean,* October 3, 1971.

98   "hell of a story!": Jerry Thompson, 1997 interview.

"as red as red can be": Ibid.

"deadline pressure": Larry Daughtrey, "No Conventional Label Easily Fits Albert Gore Jr.," *Nashville Tennessean,* November 7, 1984.

"hen scratching": Frank Ritter, 1998 interview.

"really pressured": Jerry Thompson, 1997 interview.

99   Joe Friday: Mark Gore, 1997 interview.

"care about people": Gus Stanisic, 1998 interview.

back to Carthage: Alex Wade (owner of 3205 West End Avenue), interview with author, Nashville, June 4, 1997.

hearse and coffin: Michael Zibart, 1998 interview.

100   "change for the better": Frank Sutherland, interview with author, Nashville, March 3, 1998.

101 "himself independently": John Warnecke, telephone interview with author, September 2, 1998.

"graduate student": *Nashville Tennessean,* November 8, 1987.

"loved it": John Warnecke, 1998 interview.

"getting busted": Ibid.

"comments private": Eve Zibart, 1997 interview.

"so inflammatory": Bob Somerby, 1997 interview.

102 "and violence": Stephen Gaskin, interview with author, Summertown, Tennessee, December 12, 1997.

"genre of spirituality": Albert Bates, interview with author, Summertown, Tennessee, April 16, 1997.

"their neighbors": Albert Gore Jr., "Church Group Swaps Views with Commune," *Nashville Tennessean,* March 13, 1972.

"religious life": Ibid.

"'pure state'": Stephen Gaskin, 1997 interview.

103 investigative reporting: E. Thomas Wood, "Al Gore's Other Big Week," *Columbia Journalism Review* (January-February 1993): 36.

1973 dispatch: Albert Gore Jr., "City's Water Financing Headache Nothing New," *Nashville Tennessean,* January 8, 1973.

"get worse": Albert Gore Jr. (reporter for the *Nashville Tennessean*), statement before the Subcommittee on Intergovernmental Relations of the Committee on Government Operations, U.S. Senate, Washington, D.C., May 3, 1973.

August 6, 1973: Vice President Al Gore, comments at the Family Re-Union Conference, Nashville, June 22, 1998.

104 smell them: Gore, *Picture This,* 9.

"two years of age": Tipper Gore, *Raising PG Kids in an X-Rated Society* (New York: Bantam, 1988), 122.

photo editor Jack Corn: Warnecke, 1998 interview.

lab technician: Jack Corn, interview with author, Millersville, Tennessee, March 3, 1998.

next staff opening: Ibid.

"didn't work": Pauline Gore, 1997 interview.

105 "slave wages": *Washington Post,* August 15, 1992.

McDonald refused: For details on the McDonald farm transaction, see Charles R. Babcock, "Gore Getting $20,000 a Year for Mineral Rights on Farm," *Washington Post,* August 15, 1992.

for $80,000: Warranty deed from Occidental Minerals Corporation to Albert Gore, on file in the office of the Smith County clerk.

106 lease payment: Warranty deeds from Albert Gore to Albert Gore Jr. and Mary Elizabeth Gore covering the land and minerals lease sales, on file in the office of the Smith County clerk.

borrowed the rest: Babcock, "Gore Getting $20,000 a Year."

actual mining: Ibid.

for $76,000: Hillin, *Al Gore Jr.,* 100.

congressional salary: Babcock, "Gore Getting $20,000 a Year."

after the story: E. Thomas Wood, "Al Gore, Boy Reporter," *Nashville Scene,* September 17, 1992.

107 "hippie look": Joe Crockett, unpublished portion of interview for Wood, "Al Gore, Boy Reporter."

front-page headline: Albert Gore, "Pouting Metro Junketeers Get a City's Apology," *Nashville Tennessean*, December 2, 1973.

"and took it": Unpublished interview with Metro Council member for Wood, "Al Gore, Boy Reporter."

"for himself": Milton Sitton, telephone interview with author, March 19, 1998.

108 Vanderbilt campus: Wood, "Al Gore, Boy Reporter."

January 19: For an account of the "sting" and other events of January 19, see Albert Gore Jr., "Haddox Indicted for Bribery," *Nashville Tennessean*, February 7, 1974.

Warnecke's house: John Warnecke, 1998 interview.

109 ethics committee: Albert Gore, "Haddox Indicted for Bribery," *Nashville Tennessean*, February 7, 1974.

land it occupied: Albert Gore Jr., "Clariday Owns Stock in Area Council Rezoned," *Nashville Tennessean*, February 6, 1974.

"black community": *Nashville Banner*, February 11, 1974.

"up and coming": Ken Jost, interview with author, Washington, D.C., April 30, 1997.

he was at risk: *Nashville Banner*, June 1, 1974.

110 with transcripts: *Nashville Banner*, May 2, 1974.

his career: Ken Jost, "Haddox Blames *Tennessean*," *Nashville Tennessean*, May 2, 1974.

"this language": *Nashville Banner*, May 4, 1974.

head in his hands: *Washington Post*, January 4, 1998.

"troubled by that": Wayne Whitt, 1998 interview.

111 "role model": Albert Gore Jr., 1992 Carroll interview.

state of Tennessee: Donald Hall, telephone interview with Laura Ballman, May 1998.

"as well as anyone else": Steve Cobb, interview with Laura Ballman, May 1998.

"believed him": Eve Zibart, 1997 interview.

"ahead of schedule": Frank Sutherland, 1998 interview.

at the paper: Lloyd Armour, 1998 interview.

112 "support candidates": Phil Sullivan, 1998 interview.

"Democratic blood": Lloyd Armour, 1998 interview.

"encouraging him": Mark Gore, 1997 interview.

"what I think": Gore, 1992 Carroll interview.

"'You're kidding'": Ibid.

Evins's retirement: "Evins to Retire at Term's End?" *Nashville Banner*, February 23, 1976.

113 "I already have": Larry Daughtrey, 1997 interview.

"a disgrace": Lloyd Armour, 1998 interview.

in Washington: Ken Jost, April 30, 1997, interview.

"'do it right'": James Blumstein, interview with Laura Ballman, May 1998.

"I'll vote for you": Albert Gore, 1997 interview.

"'your candidate'": Pauline Gore, 1997 interview.

114 "they'd get beat": *Larry King Live*, CNN, January 20, 1993.

"no statement on that": Dwight Lewis, "No Shortage of Potential Candidates," *Nashville Tennessean,* March 1, 1976.

threw up: *Nashville Tennessean,* November 7, 1992.

"this basis": Frank Sutherland, "Albert Gore Jr. Starts Drive for Evins's Seat," *Nashville Tennessean,* March 2, 1976.

115 "vote for you": Walter King Robinson, 1997 interview.

8. Carthage Campaigner

116 writing career: Reed Hundt, telephone interview with author, July 1992.

"different direction": *Chicago Tribune,* April 26, 1987.

"a photographer": Jack Corn, 1998 interview.

117 "this race": Ibid.

"a schedule": Richard Harris, "Annals of Politics," *New Yorker,* July 10, 1971.

her husband: Gore, *Picture This,* 4.

"I'll explode": Eve Zibart, 1997 interview.

118 seasoned pol: Gore, *Picture This,* 4.

"my life": Larry Daughtrey, 1997 interview.

119 "like Joe Evins": Bart Gordon, interview with author, Washington, D.C., March 4, 1997.

"abnormal": Alan Carmichel, "Race Hasn't Caught Fire," *Nashville Tennessean,* July 25, 1976. Carmichel wrote: "[Gore] says he is opposed to removing legislation regarding the 'abnormal' practice of homosexuality, but says it is 'senseless' to try and enforce such laws."

cheap handguns: Ibid.

"reposition himself": Lloyd Armour, 1998 interview.

"what I say": Carmichel, "Race Hasn't Caught Fire."

"'simple as that'": Frank Ritter, 1998 interview.

"of firearms": *Nashville Banner,* July 28, 1976.

120 handgun purchases: 1991 *Congressional Quarterly Almanac.*

"right to life": David Lyons, "Gore: Abortion Rights at Issue," *Nashville Banner,* July 28, 1976.

"partial birth" abortions: Douglas Johnson (legislative director, National Right to Life Committee), fax to "interested parties," September 14, 1992.

any circumstance: National Abortion and Reproductive Rights Action League (NARAL), "Vice President Albert Gore on Choice" (February 1999).

"this goal": Representative Albert Gore Jr. to Mrs. James C. Scott, Franklin, Tennessee, August 22, 1984.

"third trimester": Senator Al Gore, interview with Tim Russert, *Meet the Press,* October 6, 1992.

121 at conception: Mark Siljander, telephone interview with author, January 14, 1999.

funded clinics: NARAL, "Gore on Choice."

"Super Tuesday": Michael Kramer, "The New (Low) Levels of the Game," *U.S. News & World Report,* March 7, 1988.

"biological development": NARAL, "Gore on Choice."

covered abortions: Paula Wade and James W. Brosnan, "Gore Backs Funding for Abortion in Health Plan," *Memphis Commercial Appeal,* July 13, 1992.

"right to choose": Gore, *Meet the Press,* October 6, 1992.

122 "always believed that": Albert Gore Jr., interview with David Frost, taped September 21, 1992.

"rule of law": Kate Michelman, telephone interview with author, January 26, 1999.

the *Tennessean:* "In Albert Gore, Jr., 4th District Voters Have Best Choice," *Nashville Banner,* July 6, 1976. "Voters should note Mr. Gore is taking a generally conservative viewpoint," the editorial endorsement said. "He says his personal views are more conservative than those of his father, or the *Tennessean,* whose editorials he helped to write, and we believe him."

123 "business community": Ed Manassah, telephone interview with author, May 5, 1998.

enthusiastic endorsement: *Nashville Tennessean,* July 25, 1976.

the Cumberland Hills: Ken Jost, April 30, 1997, interview.

long shot: Johnny Hayes, interview with author, Nashville, July 29, 1997.

"didn't come in": Walter King Robinson, 1997 interview.

124 out of pocket: 1977 *Congressional Quarterly Almanac.*

his tractor: Noel Clarkson, telephone interview with author, April 16, 1998.

"everywhere at every time": David Lyons, interview with author, Nashville, December 11, 1997.

125 running for mayor: *Nashville Banner,* August 4, 1976.

"eyes open now": David Lyons, 1997 interview.

"like Prince Albert": Ibid.

126 Gore's competitors: Larry Daughtrey and Jim O'Hara, "Gore's Ex-Colleagues Surprised at Pot Use," *Nashville Tennessean,* November 10, 1987.

"he didn't know": Ken Jost, interview with author, Washington, D.C., September 26, 1997.

"'to hurt me?'": David Lyons, 1997 interview.

and reporter: Daughtrey and O'Hara, "Gore's Ex-Colleagues Surprised."

"free ride in '76": David Lyons, 1997 interview.

largest producer: See Epstein, *Dossier,* 215–36. Albert Gore had no direct role in helping Hammer secure the Libyan concession, but he did travel there with Hammer in April 1968 to attend an extravagant dedication ceremony in the desert oil field.

127 "these contracts": Bill Allen, 1997 interview.

$500,000 a year: Epstein, *Dossier,* 303.

"as poor as ever": *Nashville Tennessean,* October 11, 1987.

"the breakfast table": Larry Daughtrey, "Evins's Record Colors Race in Fourth District," *Nashville Tennessean,* May 9, 1976.

went nowhere: David Lyons, "Gore Says Rogers's Charges 'in Error,'" *Nashville Banner,* July 20, 1976.

"to the barns": Frank Sutherland, 1998 interview.

128 friends and supporters: Ken Jost, April 30, 1997, interview.

edged ahead by 100: *Nashville Banner,* August 6, 1976.

watching the news: David Lyons, 1997 interview.

minutes later: Stanley Rogers, interview with author, Manchester, Tennessee, December 10, 1997.

29 percent: 1978 *Almanac of American Politics.*
"the senator": Stanley Rogers, 1997 interview.
"sacred trust": *Nashville Banner,* August 6, 1976.
129 "one step farther": Ibid.

9. Bland Ambition

130 well-wishers: Representative Norm Dicks, interview with author, Washington, D.C., January 29, 1997.
"Sweet vindication": *Washington Post,* January 5, 1977.
"challenge for me": Jack Sirica, "His Father's Record Challenge to Gore," *Nashville Tennessean,* July 16, 1978.
Congressional Research Service: Ken Jost, interview with author, Washington, D.C., April 30, 1997.
"pretty quickly": Roy Neel, interview with Lucille Beachy for *Newsweek* Special Election Team, August 1988.
131 television exposure: Representative Albert Gore Jr., *Congressional Record,* March 19, 1979.
he represented: Roy Neel, interview with author, Washington, D.C., March 20, 1997.
"team he was on": Ken Jost, April 30, 1997, interview.
"of the House": *Nashville Tennessean,* July 16, 1978.
132 domestic affairs: Gore's "liberal quotient," as determined by Americans for Democratic Action (ADA), averaged slightly over 63 percent for his eight years in the House, compared to 53.8 percent for his father in the six years for which ratings are available. No doubt anxious to avoid comparison to his father, Gore recorded his lowest score, 45, during his first year in office. That year he joined with Republicans and southern Democrats to defeat the year's major labor bill, a common-site picketing measure that would have allowed unions with a grievance against a single construction contractor to picket and eventually close down an entire building site, overturning a 1951 Supreme Court ruling that such practices constituted an illegal secondary boycott. His liberal quotient crept up gradually over the next two years, to a high of 74, before sliding back somewhat as his 1984 Senate run approached. His eight-year Senate average was nearly identical to his House number, 65.3, and again slightly higher than his father's, based on incomplete data. The AFL-CIO's Committee on Political Education, organized labor's most influential report card, gave Gore an 80 average in the House and 89.5 in the Senate. Conservative groups scored him with correspondingly low ratings throughout his legislative career. The American Conservative Union, a leading lobbying group, never graded him higher than 29 percent in sixteen years on the Hill and awarded him a zero in 1992. The National Taxpayers Union, the preeminent antitax, antigovernment spending group, usually placed him in the low 20s. Other ratings reflect a middle-of-the-road approach to votes on national security issues. Paul Richter of the *Los Angeles Times* examined Gore's liberal-leaning record in an insightful piece on October 31, 1996.
consumer protection agency: *Nashville Tennessean,* July 16, 1978.

"for synfuels": Eric Black, telephone interview with Paul O'Donnell, July 17, 1997.

MX missile: The American Security Council gave him a 46.6 percent average for his House career, and about the same in the Senate, although annual ratings zigzagged more sharply, depending on which issue was up for a vote. The Council for National Defense, a pro-defense, pro–Ronald Reagan PAC, gave him a zero in 1986.

"finite answers": Katherine Boo, "The Liberation of Al Gore," *Washington Post Magazine*, November 28, 1993, 11.

133 "not terribly controversial": *National Journal*, December 5, 1987.

Earth in the Balance: Gore's LCV scorecard improved in the Senate as his environmentalism evolved. His career rating over eight years was 73 percent.

in 1983: Stephen H. Wildstrom and Peter Hong, "Is Al Gore's Record Really So Green?" *Business Week*, August 24, 1992, 41.

"the debate": Brent Blackwelder, interview with author, Washington, D.C., May 13, 1999. Friends of the Earth endorsed Bill Bradley for the 2000 Democratic presidential nomination.

134 "young man": Michael Kinsley, "TRB: Nice Young Man," *The New Republic*, June 1, 1987, 4.

"through it": Representative Henry Waxman, interview with author, Washington, D.C., April 7, 1997.

"I was trembling": Tom Luken, telephone interview with author, March 13, 1997.

135 "get it back": Les AuCoin, telephone interview with author, February 1, 1999.

in ten: Representative David Bonior, interview with author, Washington, D.C., May 15, 1997.

"between the two": Henry Waxman, 1997 interview.

136 continue uninterrupted: Ken Jost, April 30, 1997, interview.

Freedom of Information Act: *Washington Star*, February 8, 1978.

"from the beginning": Michael Lemov, interview with author, Washington, D.C., March 24, 1998.

"pursue": Phil Sharp, telephone interview with Paul O'Donnell, June 4, 1997.

"this sleepwear?": *CBS Evening News*, May 15, 1977, Vanderbilt Television News Archive.

"spear carrier": Ken Jost, April 30, 1997, interview.

137 birth defects: Kathy Koch, "Cleaning up Chemical Dumps Posing Dilemma for Congress," *Congressional Quarterly*, March 22, 1980, 795.

Gore's staff: Ken Jost, September 26, 1997, interview.

was too important: *Wall Street Journal*, July 30, 1980.

138 chief of staff: Peter Knight, interview with author, Washington, D.C., May 30, 1997.

floor to vote: Ibid.

and Gore: Ibid.

recommended Knight: Ken Jost, April 30, 1997, interview.

139 "the phone": Johnny Hayes, 1997 interview.

"'call today'": Mike Kopp, interview with author, Nashville, June 3, 1997.

took the call: Ken Jost, April 30, 1997, interview.

140 rare free moments: Ibid.

141 "three countries": Eric Black, 1997 interview.

"would be okay": Steve Owens, telephone interview with author, February 3, 1999.

work together: Peter Knight, 1997 interview.

four responded: Helen Dewar, "Gore Seeking to Embody a New Democratic Party," *Washington Post,* November 12, 1987.

142 MIRV . . . missiles: Gore, *Eye of the Storm,* 84.

their backs: Peter Knight, 1997 interview; Sides, "Born to Run," 47.

the panel: Peter Knight, 1997 interview.

turbulent time: For extensive background on the MX and Midgetman debates, see Elizabeth Drew, "A Political Journal," *New Yorker,* June 20, 1983, 39.

143 went to bed: Stan Crock, "Fuerth in Line," *The New Republic,* December 7, 1998, 16.

verification issues: Biographical information on Leon Fuerth from office of Senator Al Gore, October 19, 1992.

"self-discipline": *Washington Post,* June 16, 1998.

144 arms control mentor: Peter Knight, 1997 interview.

of Congress: James Woolsey, telephone interview with author, January 14, 1999.

145 "illusory fear": John Eisendrath, "The Longest Shot: Measuring Al Gore Jr. for the White House," *Washington Monthly* (November 1986): 43.

"their responsibilities": Representative Albert Gore Jr., *Congressional Record,* March 22, 1982, 4830.

well known to Fuerth: See Michael R. Gordon, "The Midgetman Missile — A Counterpoint to the Giant MX, but Will It Work?" *National Journal,* October 1, 1983, 2000. See also John Fialka, "Hot Debate on the Fate of Midgetman Missile Shapes up in Congress," *Wall Street Journal,* March 4, 1986.

146 in dirigibles: For a complete list of MX basing modes, see *Congressional Record,* May 24, 1983, 13540–41.

especially attractive: Drew, "A Political Journal," 39.

had been proposed: Ibid.

147 its findings: See Michael Pertschuk, *Giant Killers* (New York: W. W. Norton, 1986), 181–228.

"force modernization": *President's Commission on Strategic Forces,* April 11, 1983.

"duck to water": James Woolsey, 1999 interview.

"broad and deep": Drew, "A Political Journal," 39.

148 "high-priority basis": Ibid.

"lost fifty votes": Norm Dicks, 1997 interview.

"on the inside": Les AuCoin, 1997 interview.

149 "speaks for itself": Representative Thomas Downey, *Congressional Record,* May 23, 1983, 13372.

"this program?": Representative Albert Gore Jr., *Congressional Record,* May 24, 1983, 13581.

"with the Soviet Union": AuCoin, *Congressional Record,* May 24, 1983, 13583.

a year later: *Los Angeles Times,* January 30, 1992.

150 "smart he was": Jerome Grossman, telephone interview with Paul O'Donnell, February 13, 1998.

10. Strange Blend

151 of Nashville: "Tennessee Democrats Create Two Open Seats," *Congressional Quarterly*, November 7, 1981, 2172.

in the community: James W. Brosnan, "Hunger Vows a Difference at Confirmation," *Memphis Commercial Appeal*, June 17, 1993; "Representative Gore's Sister Dies in Hospital," *Nashville Tennessean*, July 12, 1984.

152 never happened: Nancy Fleming, May 1, 1998, interview.

"unhappy there": Nancy Fleming, March 31, 1998, interview.

alcohol: Ibid.

lung cancer: James Fleming, telephone interview with author, February 8, 1999.

was poor: Ibid.

seem inevitable: Hillin, *Al Gore Jr.*, 116.

153 deepest pockets: Johnny Hayes, 1997 interview.

"PAC community": Brooks Jackson, "Business Money Flocks to Representative Gore," *Wall Street Journal*, February 15, 1984.

entering the race: Ibid.

declined: Martin Tolchin, "Tennessee GOP Fears Losing Baker's Seat to Albert Gore Jr.," *New York Times*, October 17, 1983.

154 for auction: *History of Smith County*, 754.

for a profit: Gore, *Eye of the Storm*, 199.

on his farm: Bonnie Hart, Farm Service Agency, U.S. Department of Agriculture, memo to author, April 14, 1998.

"pasture leasing": Richard Powelson, "Gore Staff Says He Got Income from Tobacco but Didn't Specify It as Such," *Knoxville News-Sentinel*, September 28, 1996.

"'more sense than that'": Phil Ashford, interview with author, Nashville, March 5, 1998.

qualities of nicotine: See Richard Kluger, *Ashes to Ashes: America's Hundred Year Cigarette War* (New York: Alfred A. Knopf, 1996), 542–49.

155 long-term effects: Elizabeth Wehr, "Tough New Cigarette Warning Labels Voted," *Congressional Quarterly*, May 19, 1984, 1203.

would still smoke: Matthew Myers, interview with Michael Pertschuk, December 1984, Michael Pertschuk Collection, Library of Congress.

air quality legislation: Matthew Myers, interview with author, Washington, D.C., October 16, 1997.

156 "tobacco farming": Michael Pertschuk, *Giant Killers* (New York: W. W. Norton, 1986), 69–79.

"a tobacco state": Matthew Myers, 1997 interview.

"to work with": Myers, Pertschuk Collection.

157 "got a deal": Matthew Myers, 1997 interview.

"make it happen": Ibid.

"additional things": Ibid.

"literally quivering": Myers, Pertschuk Collection.

158 "speak, practically": Matthew Myers, 1997 interview.

"screwed them": Rip Forbes, interview with Pertschuk, February 1985, Pertschuk Collection.

"Dingell's killer": Pertschuk, *Giant Killers*, 75.

"makes messes": Mike Kitzmiller, interview with Pertschuk, winter 1985, Pertschuk Collection.

159 birthweight: *Congressional Quarterly*, May 19, 1984, 1203.

"personal courage": Matthew Myers, 1997 interview.

White House meeting: Ceci Connolly and John Mintz, "Unlikely Alliance Enlisted President for Tobacco War," *Washington Post*, March 31, 1998.

160 Vanderbilt Hospital: James Fleming, 1999 interview.

May 30, 1984: Nancy Fleming, March 31, 1998, interview.

"big sisters": Bob Squier, interview with author, Washington, D.C., March 25, 1998.

"loving critic": *Time*, October 19, 1987.

"at another site": Nancy Fleming, May 1, 1998, interview.

with smoking: According to Dr. James Jett, a pulmonary specialist at the Mayo Clinic, adenocarcinoma is the most common type of lung cancer found in non-smokers but is still heavily associated with smoking. About 60 percent of all adenocarcinomas appear in smokers. By comparison, about 90 percent of all squamous-cell carcinoma lung cancers appear in smokers, as do 98 percent of all small-cell lung cancers.

ruled it out: James Fleming, 1999 interview.

161 pro-grower record: Phil Ashford, 1998 interview; Tom Humphrey, "Not All Share in Adoration of Al Gore," *Knoxville News-Sentinel*, September 8, 1996.

"sold it": Marie Cocco, "Gore Behaving as a Southern Gentleman," *Newsday*, February 26, 1988.

tobacco allotments: Bonnie Hart, April 14, 1998, memo. An exact date of sale is not available, but it would have been prior to July 1, 1991, the final date for the sale of burley quotas for the 1991 crop year. Burley allotments are based on poundage, not acreage. In other words, the holder of a burley allotment can plant as many acres as needed to reach a certain poundage quota. When he sold, Al Gore held 1,494 pounds of "basic quota," and Albert Gore held 26,116 pounds.

in 1989: *Knoxville News-Sentinel*, September 28, 1996.

tobacco business: Richard Powelson, "Tobacco Income Left out of Report by Gore," *Knoxville News-Sentinel*, September 8, 1996.

real sentiments: Center for Responsive Politics, July 3, 1996.

U.S. cigarettes: *Knoxville News-Sentinel*, July 7, 1996.

162 $360,000: *Knoxville News-Sentinel*, April 14, 1984.

he declined: Tom Humphrey, "Gore Lands Haymaker, but Ashe Gets in Licks," *Knoxville News-Sentinel*, October 1, 1984.

Walter Mondale: Roger Harris, "Senate Debaters Joke and Joust," *Knoxville News-Sentinel*, October 9, 1984.

but it never washed: "The Senate: Rising Democratic Stars," *Time*, October 22, 1984, 40.

163 same treatment: Carol Bradley, telephone interview with author, February 11, 1999.

"in the U.S. Senate": Carol Bradley, "Gore Seeks Office, Expects Full Debate," *Nashville Banner*, May 30, 1984.

"next six years?": *Time*, August 11, 1952.

164 and independents: Carol Bradley, "Gore Sr. Aided Son's Strategy," *Nashville Banner*, November 8, 1984.

disposing of Ashe: Carol Bradley, 1999 interview.

in twenty-five years: *Congressional Quarterly*, November 10, 1984, 2906.

dust it off: "Al Gore Among New Senators Sworn in Today," *Nashville Banner*, January 3, 1985.

"the beginning": Martin Peretz, 1997 interview.

11. *Lyric Opera*

165 "in the Senate": Peter Knight, 1997 interview.

166 Geneva in 1985: "Arms Control: Negotiations but No Accords," *Congressional Quarterly Almanac* (1985): 175.

in the 1970s: "Fletcher Confirmed by Senate for Second Duty Tour at NASA," *Congressional Quarterly*, May 10, 1986, 1055.

in fifteen years: Robert Pear, "Senator Says NASA Cut 70 Percent of Staff Checking Quality," *New York Times*, May 8, 1986.

hoots than votes: Thomas G. Palmer, "Future Schlock: Government Planning for Tomorrow," *Wall Street Journal*, June 15, 1985.

"smart move": Steve Owens, 1999 interview.

"true nature": Eve Zibart, 1997 interview.

167 if they could: Jennet Conant, "Family First," *Redbook* (March 1994): 81.

"blissful marriages": Gore, *Picture This*, 9.

"'a day, please?'": Reed Hundt, interview with author, Washington, D.C., March 5, 1999.

"deprecating attitude": Ann Grimes, *Running Mates: The Making of a First Lady* (New York: William Morrow, 1990), 98.

168 "the children": Gore, *Picture This*, 10.

"with a magazine": *Purple Rain*, Warner Brothers Records, 1–25510, Warner Brothers Music Corp. Words and music by Prince, copyright © 1984 Controversy Music.

"frightened *me!*": Gore, *Raising PG Kids*.

"same reason": "Ex-official's Wife Tells of Tough Times," *Charleston Daily Mail*, February 28, 1997.

daughter favored: Patrick Goldstein, "Parents Warn: Take the Sex and Shock out of Rock," *Los Angeles Times*, August 25, 1985.

169 none favorably: Millie Waterman (National PTA vice president), testimony before Senate Committee on Commerce, Science, and Transportation, September 19, 1985.

Stanley Gortikov: Gore, *Raising PG Kids*, 12.

"what that means": *Los Angeles Times*, August 25, 1985.

promiscuous sex: Ibid.

"those realities": Stanley Gortikov, telephone interview with author, February 5, 1998.

171 "thoughts or concepts": Stanley Gortikov to Pam Howar, August 13, 1985, attach-

ment to Stanley Gortikov, testimony before Senate Commerce Committee, September 19, 1985.

"illogical conclusions": Frank Zappa, "An Open Letter to the Music Industry," *Cash Box*, August 31, 1985, 3.

Mike Love: Gore, *Raising PG Kids*, 130.

"musical pornography": Marilyn Beck, "Motown Great Blasts Porno on Records, Music Videos," *New Orleans Times-Picayune*, July 22, 1985.

"'across America'": *Rolling Stone*, September 11, 1986.

government censorship: John Danforth, telephone interview with author, March 1, 1999.

172 "unbelievable": Ibid.

"earn a living": Senator Al Gore, opening statement, Senate Commerce Committee, September 19, 1985.

"at stake": Tipper Gore, testimony before the Senate Commerce Committee, September 19, 1985.

country music industry: Senator Al Gore, Senate Commerce Committee hearing, September 19, 1985.

173 "Vaginal Arousal"?: Frank Zappa, testimony before the Senate Commerce Committee, September 19, 1985.

"mind of Mrs. Gore": Dee Snider, testimony before the Senate Commerce Committee, September 19, 1985.

174 "is palpable": Barry Lynn to Senator John Danforth, September 16, 1985.

for one year: Gore, *Raising PG Kids*, 16.

on children: Bob Summer, "An 'R'-Rated Book on Raising 'PG' Kids," *Publishers Weekly*, April 24, 1987, 44.

"for our children": Gore, *Raising PG Kids*, "A Parent's Responsibility" (unnumbered first page).

"commercialize violence": Ibid., 53.

175 "discuss the groups": Ibid., 53.

parental advisory: Ibid., 88.

"campaign donation": Peggy L. Kerr to Albert Gore for President, August 16, 1987.

collect royalties: Bill Holland, "Gore Gets (Mostly) High Marks for His Music-Industry Record," *Billboard*, July 25, 1992.

"unmans him": Hendrik Hertzberg, "Tipper De Doo Dah," *The New Republic*, December 7, 1987.

176 Shirley MacLaine: See Gore, *Raising PG Kids*, 16; Patrick Connolly, "'Esquire' in Love with Tipper Gore," *Nashville Tennessean*, July 14, 1988.

"this situation?": Gore, *Raising PG Kids*, 2.

177 "of the hearing": Henry Schipper, "Gores Polishing Showbiz Apple," *Daily Variety*, November 3, 1987.

lobby for the hearing: Former Senator Hawkins, reached at her home in Winter Park, Florida, wouldn't come to the phone, but her husband Gene conveyed her answers to questions on March 1, 1999. Hollings declined comment.

"reservations about it": Gore, *Raising PG Kids*, 15.

congressional attention: John Danforth, 1999 interview.

with the PMRC board: Smith, *The Power Game,* 121.

"people's views": "Topics of the Times; Dirty Lyrics Worse Than Dirty," *New York Times,* November 11, 1987.

178 "division of opinion": Arlie Schardt, interview with author, Washington, D.C., February 12, 1998.

"for censorship": Gore, *Picture This,* 12.

"Tipper kit": *New York Times,* April 2, 1988.

"liberal-minded people": *Washington Post,* March 29, 1988.

"really unfair": Grimes, *Running Mates,* 106.

already passed: Hilary Rosen (RIAA president), telephone interview with author, March 12, 1999.

179 violent rap lyrics: Steven A. Holmes, "Forgiving Tipper Gore but Not Quayle," *New York Times,* September 6, 1992.

and his wife: Ibid.; Danny Goldberg, "Vote for Clinton or Face the (Scary) Music," *Billboard,* October 17, 1992.

Peter Knight: Bob Woodward, "Gore Was 'Solicitor-in-Chief' in '96 Reelection Campaign," *Washington Post,* March 2, 1997.

accident in 1989: Mimi Hall, "Frightening Experience Now a Tool to Help Others," *USA Today,* May 7, 1999.

180 of the aisle: Dick Deerin, interview with author, Tysons Corner, Virginia, November 12, 1997.

"premature evaluation!": Tipper Gore, interview with author, Washington, D.C., July 1996.

12. *The Warm Puppy Principle*

181 "as a senator": Senator Al Gore, *John McLaughlin: One on One,* July 20, 1986.

for the nomination: Senator Al Gore, interview with Lucille Beachy, *Newsweek* Special Election Team, August 1988.

182 for the presidency: Gail Sheehy, *Character: America's Search for Leadership* (New York: William Morrow, 1988), 189–90.

legislative oversight: John Eisendrath, "The Longest Shot," *Washington Monthly* (November-December 1986): 43.

more than enough: Charles Peters, 1997 interview.

and the presidency: Hillin, *Al Gore Jr.,* 3.

183 "No!": Al Gore, 1988 Beachy interview.

William Jennings Bryan: At thirty-six, Bryan won the Democratic presidential nomination and lost the general election to Republican William McKinley.

Clinton of Arkansas: Mike Kopp, 1997 interview; David Maraniss, *First in His Class: A Biography of Bill Clinton* (New York: Simon & Schuster, 1995), 439. Clinton ultimately passed on a presidential race in 1988; the prospect of disclosures about his personal life loomed large in the decision.

Washington phenomenon: Timothy Noah, "A Washington Tale: Gore Chic," *Newsweek,* February 16, 1987, 20.

184 "was 37": James Reston, "The Media and the Election," *New York Times,* March 15, 1987.

"happening now": Al Gore Jr. to James Reston, undated (c. late 1987 to early 1988), from Reston's papers, Archives Research Center, University of Illinois Library, Urbana.

"the negatives away": Roy Neel, 1988 Beachy interview.

apartment houses: Carl M. Cannon, "This Bull Carries His Own China," *Baltimore Sun*, March 12, 1998.

"Nate's room": Robert Barnes, "Leader Jolts Maryland Democrats," *Washington Post*, June 29, 1989.

in the papers: *Washington Post*, January 26, 1978.

185 an "outsider": Sidney Blumenthal, "The Dawn of the New-Age Democrats," *Washington Post*, May 19, 1987.

"work with you": Nathan Landow, 1998 interview.

from the Capitol: Ibid.

for financial support: Ceci Connolly, "The $55 Million Man: Al Gore's Relentless Hunt for Campaign Dollars," *Washington Magazine*, April 4, 1999.

"fund-raising community": Peter Knight, 1997 interview.

186 the inscrutable: Lucille Beachy, memo to Peter Goldman and Tom Matthews, *Newsweek* Special Election Team, August 1988.

in Gore's direction: Ibid.

"Don't bother me at all": Ibid.

"thinking on it": Mike Pigott, "Gore Not Interested in Presidential Run," *Nashville Banner*, March 24, 1987.

$4 million: Richard L. Berke, "Big Fundraisers Keep Gore Waiting," *New York Times*, November 17, 1987.

187 he dithered: Beachy to Goldman, August 1988.

"do it to me": Gail Sheehy, "The Son Also Rises," *Vanity Fair* (March 1988).

crisp and timely: Al Gore, 1988 Beachy interview.

"following us around?": Tom Matthews and Peter Goldman, *The Quest for the Presidency: The 1988 Campaign* (New York: Simon & Schuster, 1989), 138.

"too soon?": Eve Zibart, 1997 interview.

188 "or the other": Pauline Gore, 1988 Beachy interview.

"his own way": Strobe Talbott, "Trying to Set Himself Apart," *Time*, October 19, 1987.

nice clothes: Robert Sherborne, "Gore Sought Father's Best Advice," *Nashville Tennessean*, April 13, 1987.

"banshee Indian": Ibid.

13. Rolling Alamo

189 "the four top": Senator Al Gore, Senate Caucus Room, April 10, 1987.

190 nondescript red: Arlie Schardt, 1998 interview.

"George Strait": Page Crosland, telephone interview with author, February 3, 1998.

191 had done: Scott Shepard, telephone interview with author, October 22, 1999.

"bought into it": Reed Hundt, 1997 interview.

192 "acquisitive": James Reston, "Private Behavior, Public Responsibility," *New York Times*, December 25, 1987.

"one's life": Al Gore Jr. to James Reston, undated letter (c. late 1987 to early 1988), from Reston papers, Archives Research Center, University of Illinois Library, Urbana.

strip search: Craig R. Whitney to the Honorable Al Gore Jr., May 5, 1987.

"inappropriately personal": Al Gore Jr. to Craig R. Whitney, June 15, 1987.

193 "was unintentional": Associated Press, "Gore Admits a 'Careless' Recount of His Work as a Reporter in 70s," *New York Times*, October 5, 1987.

"all that matters": Richard Nixon to Al Gore Jr., October 7, 1987.

"personal heroes": *Firing Line*, July 1, 1987, Vanderbilt Television News Archive.

194 "of passion": Robert Shogan, *Los Angeles Times*, July 2, 1987.

out of the seven: Beachy to Goldman, August 1988.

"for my country": *Congressional Quarterly*, November 28, 1987.

Democratic mainstream: James Brosnan, "Does 'Liberal' Label Stick to Gore?" *Memphis Commercial Appeal*, October 21, 1990.

Nicaraguan contras: According to the *Congressional Quarterly*, on April 23, 1985, Gore voted against release of $14 million to fund military or paramilitary operations in Nicaragua. Later that year he opposed an amendment to a State Department funding bill that authorized $24 million in humanitarian assistance and converted the $14 million approved in April for nonmilitary use. On March 27, 1986, he voted against a measure that provided $100 million in military and nonmilitary aid to the rebels. That same day he supported a substitute measure sponsored by Senator James Sasser to provide $30 million in exclusively humanitarian assistance. On September 25, 1987, Gore voted for a joint resolution that included $3.5 million in humanitarian aid for the contras.

zero in 1986: *Newsletter of the Council for National Defense*, "Special Report: 1986 Rating of Congress."

under 50 percent: *Congressional Quarterly*, "Directory of Congressional Voting Scores and Interest Group Ratings."

195 a questionnaire: James A. Barnes, "Southern Strategy," *National Journal*, December 5, 1987, 3078.

Jesse Jackson: Ibid.

"new Al Gore": *Congressional Quarterly*, November 28, 1987.

in November: *Nashville Tennessean*, November 8, 1987.

outside Tennessee: Jim O'Hara, "Gore Overruled Campaign Staff on Pot Question," *Nashville Tennessean*, November 9, 1987. Gore declined to name the reporters, saying that he didn't want to subject them to second-guessing.

to raise money: John Warnecke, 1998 interview.

196 "more investigation": Ibid.

"remember it": Peter Knight, telephone interview with author, November 2, 1999.

"reporters that way": John Warnecke, 1998 interview.

state Democratic convention: Fred Martin, 1988 Beachy interview.

197 "being helpful": Dick Deerin, 1997 interview.

"honest about it": Michael Specter and James R. Dickenson, "Politicians Line Up to Admit or Deny Past Marijuana Use," *Washington Post*, November 8, 1987.

198 "his honesty": "Regrets, Praise for Honest Al," *Nashville Tennessean*, November 8, 1987.

"big thing": Larry Daughtrey and Jim O'Hara, "Gore's Ex-colleagues Surprised at Pot Use," *Nashville Tennessean,* November 10, 1987.

remembers: John Warnecke, 1998 interview.

right to privacy: *Nashville Tennessean,* November 10, 1987.

199 "friends to do": John Warnecke, 1998 interview.

"waterlogged sneaker": *Winston-Salem Journal,* August 12, 1985.

near the river: Betsy Kauffman, "Hartford Residents Fear Pigeon River Dioxin," *Knoxville News-Sentinel,* February 14, 1988.

"trashy community": Phil Owens, interview with author, Newport, Tennessee, October 21, 1997.

200 "pure, and clean": *Newport Daily Talk,* December 17, 1986.

"positive and responsible": Al Gore to Jack Ravan, February 9, 1987.

201 "Senator Sanford": Ben Bilus, memo to file, March 19, 1987. The memo was one of plaintiffs' exhibits in a 1990 class-action lawsuit filed against Champion by landowners along the Pigeon. The case ended in a mistrial and an out-of-court settlement.

"on the merits": Terry Sanford, interview with Michael Isikoff, November 10, 1997.

"common sense" solution: Michael Isikoff and Bill Turque, "Gore's Pollution Problem," *Newsweek,* November 24, 1997, 40.

"new negotiations": Al Gore Jr. to Lee DeHihns III (acting EPA Region IV administrator), November 10, 1987.

202 "new ally": "Senator Gore Delivers Reasonable Solution," *Asheville Times,* November 21, 1987.

"scratch yours": Mark Barrett, "Taylor Chastises Clarke for Inaction on Champion," *Asheville Citizen,* January 21, 1988.

generated $110,000: "Gore Endorsements in the South Are Paying Dividends in Campaign Cash," *National Journal,* January 23, 1988, 195.

"ran so well": Mark Barrett, "Bush, Gore Win Convincingly in WNC," *Asheville Citizen,* March 9, 1988.

"industrial civilization": *The Jerry Williams Show,* Fox Television, November 23, 1987.

"passionate": Al Gore Jr., remarks at south Texas presidential candidates' debate, San Antonio, December 15, 1987.

"beside it": Phil Owens, 1997 interview.

sellout: John Stiles, "'Disgusted' with Gore, Supporters of Pigeon River Push for Cleanup," *Knoxville News-Sentinel,* December 29, 1996.

the permit: Rebecca Ferrar, "Gore Spurs New EPA Mediations on Pigeon," *Knoxville News-Sentinel,* February 7, 1997.

paperworkers' union: Tracy Davis, "Canton Mill Is for Sale," *Asheville Citizen-Times,* October 9, 1997; Sandy Wall, "Champion Buyout Approved," *Asheville Citizen-Times,* April 30, 1999.

203 "how she spoke": Arlie Schardt, 1998 interview.

204 a replacement: Ibid.

promote her book: Page Crosland, 1998 interview.

short trips: Dick Deerin, 1997 interview.

"to Lubbock": Larry Daughtrey, "Gore Calm After Plane Takes Spin," *Nashville Tennessean*, December 6, 1987.

had promised: *New York Times*, November 16, 1987.

his family: Brooks Jackson, "Gore Campaign Confirms That Loans Were Made Largely Without Collateral," *Wall Street Journal*, March 25, 1988.

205 "economic fairness": Beachy to Goldman, August 1988.

"over profits": "Count On," ad produced by the Campaign Group, March 22, 1988.

out of the race: "Gore's New Ball Game," *Time*, February 29, 1988, 43.

"perfect kid": Richard Ben Cramer, *What It Takes* (New York: Random House, 1992), 307.

206 "all the time": Larry Daughtrey, 1997 interview.

"Reagan mistake?": Debate at Kennedy Center, Washington, D.C., December 1, 1987.

"bastards": Thomas B. Edsall, "Iowa Winners Face Hurdles in the South," *Washington Post*, February 10, 1988.

207 "be consistent": "Look," ad produced by the Campaign Group, March 1, 1988.

"as president?": "Transformer," ad produced by the Campaign Group, March 1, 1988.

to go around: Matthews and Goldman, *The Quest for the Presidency*, 147.

"be president!": Arlie Schardt, 1998 interview.

208 "rolling Alamo": Matthews and Goldman, *The Quest for the Presidency*, 162.

209 "security of Israel": Roger Simon, *Road Show* (New York: Farrar, Straus & Giroux, 1990), 159.

"than a pulpit": Bernard Weinraub, "Gore Is Asking New Yorkers to Be Kind to an Underdog," *New York Times*, April 8, 1988.

"thing to do": Beachy to Goldman, August 1988.

of his career: Ibid.

"three weeks": Warren Weaver Jr., "Warning from Koch," *New York Times*, April 2, 1998.

210 "campaign was racist": Arlie Schardt, 1998 interview.

"vote for you": Jim Wooten, *ABC World News Tonight*, April 19, 1988, Vanderbilt Television News Archive.

211 "federal penitentiaries?": Al Gore Jr., *New York Daily News* debate, April 12, 1988.

boxes for days: Page Crosland, 1998 interview.

"get a shoeshine": *Nashville Banner*, April 20, 1988.

apologize for Koch: Beachy to Goldman, August 1988.

New York's streets: Bruce Dobie, "'I Learned How to Relax,' Says Gore of Candidacy," *Nashville Banner*, April 22, 1988.

212 after 1:00 A.M.: Beachy to Goldman, August 1988.

14. Into the Ashes

213 with Ed Koch: Edward Walsh and Thomas B. Edsall, "Campaign's Legacy to Gore: Experience and Hard Feelings?" *Washington Post*, April 21, 1988.

"not perfect": *U.S. News & World Report*, July 20, 1992.

"tricky to explain": Eve Zibart, 1997 interview.

214 "listen to": Reed Hundt, 1997 interview.

$40,000 each: Peter Knight, 1997 interview.

"'got it yet?'": Nathan Landow, 1998 interview.

215 Dick Gephardt: Goldman and Matthews, *The Quest for the Presidency,* 171.

"panting after it": Michael Dukakis, interview with author, Boston, June 3, 1998.

his selection: *Nashville Tennessean,* July 13, 1988.

quashed the deal: Dukakis said that he wasn't troubled by Gore's conduct in the campaign, including his charges about the prison furlough program, which he thought were "fair comment, as he did it." As for his choice of Bentsen, Dukakis said, "The road seemed to lead to Bentsen for a lot of conventional reasons," including his ties to Texas, long Washington experience, and "a certain gravitas"; 1998 interview.

"outrage": *Nashville Tennessean,* July 13, 1988.

Jackson's forgiveness: Jim O'Hara and James Pratt, "Strains of Discontent Slow the Music for Gore," *Nashville Tennessean,* July 31, 1988.

216 threatened him: Ibid.

southern coordinator: Ibid.

"his generation": Curtis Wilkie, "Every Which Way but Loose," *Southern Magazine* (December 1988): 27.

"press or not": Gore, *Earth in the Balance,* 9.

217 "small businesses": Senator Al Gore Jr., statement before the Science, Research, and Technology Subcommittee of the House Science, Space, and Technology Committee, June 20, 1989.

four years in the Senate: According to the League of Conservation (LCV) voters, Gore made thirteen "correct" votes out of twenty-two that the LCV considered important environmental issues in 1985–88, giving him a four-year average of 58.5 percent. Chafee voted with the LCV nineteen of twenty-two times during the same period, an 87.5 percent average, and Moynihan voted pro-environment on fifteen of twenty-two occasions, a 70 percent average.

"focused on it": Reed Hundt, 1997 interview.

218 lusty snoring: Tom Lovejoy, telephone interview with Paul O'Donnell, May 1, 1998.

"candy roo": Ibid.

"the Amazon": Gerry Sikorski, telephone interview with Paul O'Donnell, April 15, 1998.

219 vacation to Fiji: David Bartlett, telephone interview with author, August 4, 1997.

ozone layer: Ted Koppel, *Nightline,* February 24, 1994.

220 "hurricane force": Al Gore Jr., "Unbearable Whiteness," *The New Republic,* December 26, 1988.

"sacred agenda": Gore used this phrase in a number of speeches during the late 1980s and early 1990s, including a Senate floor speech on July 19, 1989.

"at this moment": Paul Gorman, interview with author, New York, December 11, 1998.

"relationship with creation": Ibid.

221 had deteriorated: Cambridge Reports, cited in *Christian Science Monitor,* January 2, 1990.

"extremely candid": Gore, *Earth in the Balance,* 10.

222 "of the United States": Tim Wirth, telephone interview with author, July 1992.

"on a couch": Vice President Al Gore Jr., interview with Diane Sawyer, *Prime Time Live,* July 30, 1992.

223 "personal relating": Lance Laurence, interview with author, Knoxville, Tennessee, September 13, 1997.

hand razor: Allen Wheelis, *How People Change* (New York: Harper & Row, 1973), 47–69. The chapter about cutting grass appeared in an earlier Wheelis book, *The Quest for Identity* (New York: W. W. Norton, 1958).

"to live it": Alice Miller, *The Drama of the Gifted Child: The Search for the True Self* (New York: Basic Books, 1994), 36–37; first published in the United States as *Prisoners of Childhood* (New York: Basic Books, 1981). Gore's interest in *The Drama of the Gifted Child* was first reported by Katherine Boo of the *Washington Post* in a remarkable November 28, 1993, Sunday magazine story, "The Liberation of Al Gore."

"becoming numb": Ibid., 135–36.

224 "'have been then?'": Ibid., 30–31, 39.

"up and talk": Lance Laurence, 1997 interview.

"long and hard": *Washington Post,* November 28, 1993.

225 into the roadway: Dennis O'Brien, "Senator Gore's Son, 6, Hit by Car Near Stadium, Condition Serious," *Baltimore Sun,* April 4, 1989.

into his left thigh: Initial news reports said McWilliams was not speeding, but a week after the accident Baltimore police charged him with driving at a speed "greater than reasonable and prudent" and issued a citation for having "failed to exercise proper caution"; *Nashville Tennessean,* April 11, 1989.

"torqued": *Memphis Commercial Appeal,* October 12, 1997.

"'badly hurt'": Pauline Gore, 1997 interview.

his spleen: *Baltimore Sun,* April 6, 1989.

minimum wage: Carol Bradley, "Car Hitting Son 'a Moment of Horror': Gore," *Nashville Tennessean,* April 20, 1989.

226 sleeping bag: *Washington Post,* May 6, 1989.

"supercritical": Gore, *Earth in the Balance,* 363.

"his son": Lorraine Voles, interview with author, Washington, D.C., September 2, 1998.

"on my part": Vice President Al Gore Jr., Harvard University commencement, June 9, 1994.

death and rebirth: Gore, *Earth in the Balance,* 372; Robert Bly, *Iron John* (New York: Vintage, 1992), 84.

rehabilitation: *Washington Post,* November 28, 1993.

227 "meant to us": Gore, *Picture This,* 13.

"in my life": Mimi Hall, "Frightening Experience Now a Tool to Help Others," *USA Today,* May 7, 1999.

professional facilitator: Jackie Calmes, "Low-Profile Consultant Smoothes Gore's Organization," *Wall Street Journal,* April 28, 1998.

15. Gore in the Balance

229 *Earth in the Balance:* "Senator Gore Turns from Politics to the Environment," *Publishers Weekly,* September 27, 1991, 28.

by mid-1991: Ibid.

230 "book is *me*": Reed Hundt, 1997 interview.

"shattering in Berlin": Gore, *Earth in the Balance,* 174, 269, 274.

231 "non-linear systems": Ibid., 50.

"search all along": Ibid., 13.

232 "their enactment": Ibid., 15.

"such beneficence": Ibid., 222, 231, 235–36.

233 "might have been": Ibid., 233.

"operatic tendency": Marjorie Williams, "The Chosen One," *Vanity Fair* (February 1998).

post–World War II Europe: Gore, *Earth in the Balance,* 295–360.

twenty-five years: Ibid., 326.

234 "Paul Revere": Margaret E. Kriz, "Gore — An Environmental Plus or Minus?" *National Journal,* August 8, 1992, 1864.

"green again": Lance Morrow, "A Crisis as Real as Rain," *Time,* May 4, 1992, 76.

"political correctness": Ronald Bailey, "Demagoguery in Green," *National Review,* March 16, 1992, 43.

"every issue": Gregg Easterbrook, "Green Cassandras," *The New Republic,* July 6, 1992, 23.

235 "anything like that": Justin Lancaster, deposition in libel suit filed by S. Fred Singer, April 16, 1993, Superior Court, Middlesex County, Massachusetts.

236 "never diminished": Justin Lancaster to S. Fred Singer, July 20, 1992, defendant's response to production request, document 23, *S. Fred Singer v. Justin Lancaster.*

"moderate view": S. Fred Singer to Justin Lancaster, August 7, 1992.

be withdrawn: Justin Lancaster to Dr. Richard Geyer, August 17, 1992.

"ill and fragile": Anthony Socci to Robert Grant, October 27, 1992, defendant's response to production request, document 53, *S. Fred Singer v. Justin Lancaster.*

237 "environmental policies": Carolyn Revelle Hufbauer, "Global Warming: What My Father Really Said," *Washington Post,* September 13, 1992; telephone interview with author, June 30, 1999.

greenhouse gas emissions: Walter Munk, 1999 interview.

16. The Dowry

239 "more costly": *Congressional Record,* January 12, 1991, 334.

for months: Martin Peretz, 1997 interview.

"the Democratic Party": Steve Owens, 1999 interview.

240 safe seat: "Elections Prompt Gore to Weigh '92 Presidential Bid," *Memphis Commercial Appeal,* November 8, 1990.

presidency in 1992: Maraniss, *First in His Class,* 459–60.

son's recovery: *USA Today,* May 7, 1999.

241 "every single day": Senator Jay Rockefeller, interview with author, Washington, D.C., September 18, 1997.

and community: *Memphis Commercial Appeal,* May 26, 1991.

the night before: Lexington, "Al Gore and the Disappointed Democrats," *The Economist,* May 11, 1991. The speech, said Lexington, was "delivered in a tone that first made you think what a nice voice he has, and then lulled you to sleep."

similarly flat: *National Journal,* June 29, 1991.

New Orleans hospital: *Memphis Commercial Appeal,* May 19, 1991.

"stomach for it": Norm Dicks, 1997 interview.

242 the call came: Peter Knight, 1997 interview.

"winning next year": *Nashville Tennessean,* August 23, 1991.

244 for escape: For a full discussion of Clinton's draft history, see Maraniss, *First in His Class,* 149–205.

have been drafted: Lew Brodsky (director of Public and Congressional Affairs, Selective Service), telephone interview with author, August 4, 1997. Brodsky said the 1970 draft call took the first 195 dates drawn.

same goals: Bob Woodward, *The Agenda* (New York: Simon & Schuster, 1994), 52–53.

245 him and Gore: Steve Owens, 1999 interview.

everyone's wish list: At the end of a long memo to Clinton's vice presidential search team about the attributes of an ideal choice, Paul Begala and Clinton's other political advisers said: "If Colin Powell is interested . . . you can pretty much throw this memo away." It is reprinted in the appendix of Peter Goldman, Thomas M. DeFrank, Mark Miller, Andrew Murr, and Tom Matthews, *The Quest for the Presidency* (College Station: Texas A&M University Press, 1993).

liberal wing: George Stephanopoulos, *All Too Human: A Political Education* (Boston: Little, Brown, 1999), 84, 204.

246 unusual . . . suspects: Goldman et al., *The Quest for the Presidency* (1993), 278.

said yes: Alex Jones, "Al Gore's Double Life," *New York Times Magazine,* October 25, 1992, 40.

and Gore: Goldman et al., *The Quest for the Presidency* (1993), 280.

"new images": Stan Greenberg to Bill Clinton, "Convention Preview," July 12, 1992; reprinted in Goodman et al., *The Quest for the Presidency* (1993).

ran for three: Goodman et al., *The Quest for the Presidency* (1993), 277.

247 "against you": Martin Peretz, 1997 interview.

248 "my feeling": Roy Neel, 1997 interview.

249 broke on CNN: *Nashville Tennessean,* July 10, 1992.

"the dowry": Maureen Dowd and Michael Kelly, "The Company He Keeps," *New York Times Magazine,* January 17, 1993.

"elected president": David Maraniss, "Activist Role Outlined for Gore; Breaking Hill 'Logjam' to Be Vice President's Duty, Clinton Says," *Washington Post,* July 11, 1992.

"wooden about it!": Gail McKnight, "Parents Call Announcement 'a Moment of Great Pride,'" *Nashville Tennessean,* July 10, 1992.

250 "to save the world": Tim Wirth, 1992 interview.

17. Double Date

251 "any of us": *Nashville Banner,* June 18, 1990.

253 as a campaigner: Timothy Noah, "Gentleman Al Gore Shows a Knack for Fisti-cuffs, Taking Combative Stances in Democrats' Corner," *Wall Street Journal,* August 11, 1992. Noah described Gore as "displaying the aggressiveness and passion that were notably lacking when he himself sought the presidency four years ago." See also Edwin Chen, "Gore, Attacking GOP, Emerges as Happy Warrior," *Los Angeles Times,* September 9, 1992: "Having shed much of his stiff image and wooden speaking style, Gore is coming across as a happy warrior as he delivers slashing attacks against the 'Bush-Quayle Administration.'" Four years later Chen and Marc Lacey once again declared Gore not as stiff as expected. "Gore slowly is chipping away at his reputation for stiff formality and penchant for pol-icy arcana," they wrote; see "Gore Is Trying Hard to Craft a Softer Image on the Stump," *Los Angeles Times,* October 25, 1996.

"with the public": Bob Squier, interview with author, Washington, D.C., March 25, 1998.

"go with Cuomo": Goldman et al., *The Quest for the Presidency* (1993), 291.

254 double date: Walter Shapiro, "So Happy Together," *Time,* September 7, 1992.

"in July": Goldman et al., *The Quest for the Presidency* (1993), 484.

255 "Too long, sorry": Cathleen Decker, "Clinton, Gore: Partners in Politics," *Los Angeles Times,* July 22, 1992.

"on a road trip": *Time,* September 7, 1992.

256 "early life": Peter Boyer, "Gore's Dilemma," *New Yorker,* November 28, 1994, 100.

Woodrow Wilson: Roy Neel, telephone interview with author, July 1996.

Slobodan Milosevic: Karen Tumulty, "The Secret Passion of Al Gore," *Time,* May 24, 1999, 44.

"the agenda": Anthony Lake, interview with author, Washington, D.C., December 17, 1998.

257 in other spots: Stan Greenberg to Bill Clinton, September 22, 1992, reprinted in Goldman et al., *The Quest for the Presidency* (1993).

"that endeavor": *Washington Post,* November 28, 1993.

"false choice": "Gore Treads Softly as Environmental Point Man," *Wall Street Journal,* October 16, 1992.

258 "bizarre": *Washington Post,* August 30, 1992.

"I wrote it": *Washington Post,* September 4, 1992.

"those goals": Senator Al Gore, interview with author, on Gore's bus between Columbus and Albany, Georgia, September 23, 1992.

Henry Gonzalez: See Douglas Frantz and Murray Waas, "Secret Effort by Bush in '89 Helped Hussein Build Iraq's War Machine," *Los Angeles Times,* February 23, 1992.

260 "I feeeeeeel good!": Jonathan Feedland, "Al Gore, Goofing Around," *Washington Post,* October 6, 1992.

through the South: *Nashville Banner,* May 13, 1993.

261 "reconciled to it": *Nashville Banner,* January 21, 1993.

dumping him: Fred Steeper, memo to [deleted], July 20, reprinted in Goldman et al., *The Quest for the Presidency* (1993).

"very well": Warren Rudman, interview with author, Washington, D.C., July 23, 1997.

"Gene Tunney fight": *National Journal*, October 24, 1992.

263 "for them to go": Gail McKnight and Duren Cheek, "Gore Declares 'It's Time,'" *Nashville Tennessean*, November 4, 1992.

on Thanksgiving Day: Gordon Thompson, 1997 interview.

"called character": *Nashville Tennessean*, November 4, 1992.

18. Veep

265 sister Nancy: Steven A. Holmes, "For Gores, a Homecoming of Sorts," *New York Times*, January 21, 1993.

drifting away again: Stephanopoulos, *All Too Human*, 115.

"our democracy!": *New York Times*, January 21, 1993.

"boundless energy": Jack Quinn, interview with author, Washington, D.C., May 8, 1998.

266 "zero successes": Reed Hundt, interview with author, Washington, D.C., March 5, 1999.

"cigar store": *New York Times*, January 17, 1993.

"a decision": Robert Reich, interview with author, Cambridge, Mass., June 1, 1998.

"show up early": Reed Hundt, 1999 interview.

267 "clear understanding": James MacGregor Burns and Georgia J. Sorenson, *Dead Center: Clinton-Gore Leadership and the Perils of Moderation* (New York: Scribner's, 1999), 82.

Bill Clinton and Al Gore: Roy Neel, interview with author, Washington, D.C., April 7, 1998.

Clinton's senior staff: This particular practice was actually not new. Richard Moe, Walter Mondale's chief of staff, operated under the same arrangement during the Carter administration. See Jack Nelson, "Despite Jokes, Gore Retains His Influence," *Los Angeles Times*, March 15, 1993.

"the critical thing": Roy Neel, interview with author, Washington, D.C., April 7, 1998.

268 his stature: Michael K. Frisby, "Peter Knight Helps President in Big Way: Bringing in the Funds," *Wall Street Journal*, June 18, 1996.

269 "quite traumatic": Robert Reich, 1998 interview.

"New Age pragmatist": Kenneth T. Walsh, "A Vice President Who Counts," *U.S. News & World Report*, July 19, 1993, 29.

Joint Chiefs of Staff: On the issue of gays in the military, see Stephanopoulos, *All Too Human*, 128. The debate ended in a compromise that has satisfied no one, — the "don't ask, don't tell" policy. Gays and lesbians remain barred from serving openly, but recruiters cannot ask about sexual orientation, and commanders are prohibited from investigating personnel suspected of being gay or lesbian.

"more combative": Leon Panetta, telephone interview with author, November 23, 1998.

270 by 2000: Woodward, *The Agenda*, 82.

reluctantly embraced: At the end of 1993, projections showed a reduction of $180 billion in the 1997 deficit.

"will come around": Woodward, *The Agenda*, 91.

271 gasoline tax: Woodward, *The Agenda*, 221.

expected to prevail: League of Conservation Voters, *Presidential Scorecard* (January 1994).

272 "artichokee": Evan Thomas, Karen Breslau, et al., *Back from the Dead: How Clinton Survived the Republican Revolution* (New York: Atlantic Monthly Press, 1997), 90.

273 "removed from you": Stephanopoulos, *All Too Human*, 204.

274 appointment was announced: Woodward, *The Agenda*, 212.

eighty wounded: For a definitive account, see Rick Atkinson, "The Raid That Went Wrong," *Washington Post*, January 30, 1994.

"took a walk": Anthony Lake, interview with author, Washington, D.C., December 17, 1998.

275 intelligence sources: *U.S. News & World Report*, July 19, 1993.

"right thing to do?": Thomas, Breslau, et al., *Back from the Dead*, 1.

"force much earlier": Richard Neustadt, 1998 interview.

and Haiti: For detailed accounts of the Carter episodes, see Douglas Brinkley, *The Unfinished Presidency: Jimmy Carter's Journey Beyond the White House* (New York: Viking, 1998), 388–436.

276 "this lemon?": Ibid.

"Jimmy Clinton": William Safire, "Jimmy Clinton," *New York Times*, June 27, 1994.

277 in its possession: *The New Yorker*, November 28, 1994.

to Iran: Jacob Heilbrunn, "Just Say Nyet," *The New Republic*, March 22, 1999, 22.

wobbly health: Robert Marshall Wells, "Gore's Serving Loyalty, Ambition," *Congressional Quarterly*, August 17, 1996.

troops from Kosovo: Sandra Sobieraj, "Gore Tries to Polish His Image," Associated Press, June 14, 1999.

278 job training: Morley Winograd and Dudley Buffa, *Taking Control: Politics in the Information Age* (New York: Henry Holt, 1996).

by 1998: Vice President Al Gore, "Report of the National Performance Review," September 7, 1993, iii.

279 the government: Stephen Barr, "Gore Lobs Ashtray at Puffed-up Specifications," *Washington Post*, August 7, 1993.

"than 35": Ibid.

"own ashtrays?": Tom Weir, "You Can Call Me . . . Your Adequacy," Gannett News Service, September 9, 1993.

280 vision for REGO: Two scholars who studied REGO make this point; see John J. DiIulio, *Washington Post*, September 22, 1993; and Donald F. Kettl, "Reinventing Government: A Fifth Year Report Card," Brookings Institution Center for Public Management (September 1998).

"ain't Arkansas": "A Productivity Junkie Takes on Fat City," *Business Week,* July 5, 1993, 76.

281 "partnership a reality": "Report of the National Performance Review," September 7, 1993, 88.

blue-collar workers: Kettl, "Reinventing Government," 19.

upward slightly: Ibid.

"left the government": Donald F. Kettl, telephone interview with author, May 10, 1999.

loans at risk: Stephanopoulos, *All Too Human,* 207.

electronic payment: "National Performance Review Status Report" (September 1994), 4.

282 "notable failure": Kettl, "Reinventing Government," 33.

283 from 1993: Kettl, Ibid., 18.

"unauditable": Ibid.

"you can do them": Elaine Kamarck, 1998 interview.

international bureaucrats: Paul Gigot, "On NAFTA, House GOP Needs Gore's Guts," *Wall Street Journal,* November 12, 1993.

284 parts of the country: Jack Quinn, interview with author, Washington, D.C., November 20, 1997.

to a debate: Ibid.

briefing book: Michael Duffy, "Al's Secret Debating Tricks," *Time,* November 22, 1993, 41.

Larry King: Fred Barnes, "More Gore," *The New Republic,* December 6, 1993, 14.

"the worker": Burns and Sorenson, *Dead Center,* 189.

285 "really worried": Gordon Thompson, 1997 interview.

in hot water: Ibid.

favored the agreement: Gerald F. Seib, "Voters' Tide Turns Toward Support of NAFTA, as Debater Gore Helps the Pact, and Vice Versa," *Wall Street Journal,* November 17, 1993.

286 "the president's agenda": Jack Quinn, 1997 interview.

at best mixed: See Richard Chacon, "Pollution Flows at U.S.-Mexico Border; NAFTA Brings Industry but Little Cleanup," *Boston Globe,* September 27, 1998; Karen Brandon, "A Vision Unfulfilled; NAFTA at 5," *Chicago Tribune,* November 29, 1998; Susan Ferriss, "Oversight Groups Coexist Uneasily with NAFTA," *Atlanta Journal and Constitution,* August 2, 1998.

"economic system": Brent Blackwelder, 1999 interview.

287 for that decision: Stephanopoulos, *All Too Human,* 226–27.

"thing you want": Bob Woodward, *Shadow: Five Presidents and the Legacy of Watergate* (New York: Simon & Schuster, 199), 245.

288 "goddamn program!": Woodward, *The Agenda,* 281.

himself from it: Ann Devroy and Stephen Barr, "Gore Bucks Tradition in Vice President's Role," *Washington Post,* February 18, 1995.

289 midterm elections: Tipper Gore, 1996 interview.

19. To the Edge and Back

290 unprecedented influence: A December 1994 NBC-*Wall Street Journal* poll showed Gore's positive rating at 44 percent to Clinton's 41. His disapproval rating of 28 percent was eleven points lower than Clinton's.

"He Shines": Paul Richter, "Gore May Be Dull, but to His Party He Shines," *Los Angeles Times,* January 17, 1995.

"relevance": President Bill Clinton, White House news conference, April 18, 1995.

"presidential prospects": Elaine Sciolino and Todd S. Purdum, "Gore Is No Typical Vice President in the Shadows," *New York Times,* February 19, 1995.

Democratic nomination: Ibid.

291 gone wrong: Winograd and Buffa, *Taking Control,* 59; and Richard Neustadt, telephone interview with author, July 7, 1999.

a few issues: Bob Cohn, Bill Turque, and Karen Breslau, "Merge Right, with Caution," *Newsweek,* November 28, 1994, 26.

292 "western world": Stephanopoulos, *All Too Human,* 385.

"to Dickie Morris": Thomas, Breslau, et al., *Back from the Dead,* 11.

were minimal: Elizabeth Drew, *Showdown: The Struggle Between the Gingrich Congress and the Clinton White House* (New York: Simon & Schuster, 1996), 323.

293 "programs to solve them": Thomas, Breslau, et al., *Back from the Dead,* 213.

"to bring it": Dick Morris, *Behind the Oval Office* (New York: Random House, 1997), 116.

against the Republicans: Ibid., 141.

the speechwriters: Bob Woodward, *The Choice* (New York: Simon & Schuster, 1996), 139.

294 balancing the books: Drew, *Showdown,* 217–18.

"cost us the election": Bill Turque and Thomas Rosenstiel, "Turning Clinton Green," *Newsweek,* July 15, 1996, 26.

295 to run on: Ibid.

regulatory reform: Mellman had polled for Gore in his 1984 Senate and 1988 presidential campaigns.

Republican revolution: Ibid.

"poisoned water": Ann Devroy, "Clinton Issues Broadside on Environment," *Washington Post,* April 22, 1995.

296 three-to-one margins: Jerry McCarthy, telephone interview with author, June 1996. See also John H. Cushman Jr., "Environment Gets a Push from Clinton," *New York Times,* July 5, 1995.

"must-haves": Leon Panetta, 1998 interview.

healthy forests: *New York Times,* December 5, 1995.

297 potential competitors: Woodward, *The Choice,* 103–5.

television campaign: Ibid., 235–36.

"your job": Bob Woodward, "Gore Was 'Solicitor-in-Chief' in '96 Reelection Campaign," *Washington Post,* March 2, 1997.

presidential campaign: Michael K. Frisby, *Wall Street Journal,* June 18, 1996.

"Gore 2": Phil Kuntz and Jill Abramson, "A Fund-raiser for Gore Retools His Career with an Aura of Clout," *Wall Street Journal,* April 29, 1997.

from the hospital: Hilary Stout, "Gore Lays Strong Groundwork for the Future, Loyally Campaigning, Fighting GOP on Budget," *Wall Street Journal*, January 8, 1996.

298 "sorry for it": Ken Smukler, telephone interview with author, March 18, 1997.
eight others: *Washington Post*, March 2, 1997.
commitments: Senate Governmental Affairs Committee, final report on campaign fund-raising, March 1998.

299 "from the White House": Paul Starobin, "Gored by an Old Law," *National Journal*, March 8, 1997, 471.
reported them missing: Bill Turque, Evan Thomas, and Bob Cohn, "Missing the Moment: What's Really at Stake," *Newsweek*, November 17, 1995, 26.
horrific crime: Thomas B. Rosenstiel and Edith Stanley, "For Gingrich, It's 'Mr. Speaker!,'" *Los Angeles Times*, November 9, 1994. Gingrich said: "How a mother can kill her two children, 14 months and 3 years, in hopes that her boyfriend would like her, is just a sign of how sick the system is, and I think people want to change. The only way you can change is to vote Republican."

300 "another president": *Newsweek*, November 17, 1995.
Rabin's funeral: Ibid.
were lifted: Woodward, *The Choice*, 256.

301 knew her personally: *Washington Post*, March 31, 1998.

302 faces reversed: J. F. O. McAllister, "A Veep Who Leaves Prints," *Time*, September 2, 1996, 37.
"Washington crowd": Woodward, *The Choice*, 102.

303 "as much as possible": Bill Turque, "What Mr. Smooth Is Teaching Mr. Stiff," *Newsweek*, September 2, 1996, 26.
official bubble: "Home for the Holidays with the Gores," *USA Today*, December 13, 1993.
surprised guards: Matthew Cooper, memo to Evan Thomas, *Newsweek*, January 16, 1997.

304 playing basketball: *USA Today*, December 13, 1993.
"every time": Tipper Gore, 1996 interview.
at St. Albans: *Washington Post*, November 22, 1994.
"hell to pay": Jack Quinn, 1998 interview.
"re-training plan": "Tipper Gore's Diary," *Spy* (November 1993).
outside a party: Martin Weil, "Gore's Daughter Cited for Alcohol Possession," *Washington Post*, October 1, 1996.

305 in the dining hall: Matthew Simchak, telephone interview with author, May 3, 1999.
all complied: The *Weekly Standard* mentioned Albert's incident, without using his name, in its March 25, 1996, edition.
"to be protected": Matthew Simchak, 1999 interview.
"Dolegingrich": Thomas, Breslau, et al., *Back from the Dead*, 3.
swing vote: Mark Penn and Doug Schoen, "Neuro-Personality Poll," memo excerpted in ibid., 231–36.

306 loans and pensions: Morris's agenda for March 20, 1996, White House strategy meeting, reprinted in Thomas, Breslau, et al., *Back from the Dead*, 244–45.

307 "fearsome assumption": Jonathan Alter, Bill Turque, and John McCormick, "Washington Washes Its Hands," *Newsweek*, August 12, 1996, 42.

308 "tipped the balance": Albert R. Hunt, "Albert Gore Warms up for 2000," *Wall Street Journal*, September 12, 1996.

found work: Christina Duff, "Why a Welfare 'Success Story' May Go Back on the Dole," *Wall Street Journal*, June 15, 1999.

poverty line: See Peter Edelman, "Clinton's Cosmetic Poverty Tour," *New York Times*, July 8, 1999.

fresh revelations: Woodward, *The Choice*, 418–19.

October debate: Matthew Cooper, memo to Evan Thomas, *Newsweek*, January 16, 1997.

309 sister's death: Bob Squier, interview with author, Washington, D.C., March 25, 1998.

adults-only locations: The tobacco industry challenged the FDA's rulemaking authority, and in August 1998 a federal appeals court sided with cigarette makers. The Justice Department appealed to the Supreme Court, which agreed in April 1999 to hear the case.

political problem: Bob Squier, 1998 interview.

310 "6 minutes": *Washington Post*, March 31, 1998.

told the story: Bob Squier, 1998 interview.

311 "so shamelessly?": Andrew Ferguson, "His Struggle to Get Real," *Time*, September 22, 1997.

"be blind to": Bob Squier, 1998 interview.

"lessons of life": David S. Broder and Dan Balz, "Gore Had to Cross 'Numbness' Barrier on Tobacco Issue," *Washington Post*, August 30, 1996.

"more complex than that": Joe Klein, "Learning to Run," *The New Yorker*, December 8, 1997, 53.

20. Moneychangers in the Temple

312 Riady family: Glenn R. Simpson, "Gore Is Linked to John Huang on 1989 Trip," *Wall Street Journal*, December 13, 1996.

313 ties to China: David E. Sanger, "President Admits He and Indonesian Had Policy Talks," *New York Times*, November 16, 1996.

for eighteen months: Ruth Marcus and Ira Chinoy, "A Fund-raising Mistake; DNC Held Event in Buddhist Temple," *Washington Post*, October 17, 1996.

both parties: Ibid.

U.S. subsidiary: Ibid.

Virginia townhouse: *Wall Street Journal*, December 13, 1996.

tax-exempt status: *Washington Post*, October 17, 1996.

314 temple officials: Phil Kuntz, "Instant Karma: Cash Gets to Democrats Via Buddhist Temple," *Wall Street Journal*, October 17, 1996.

Georgetown home: U.S. Senate Committee on Governmental Affairs, special investigation into campaign finance practices (hereafter "Governmental Affairs Committee investigation"), final report (March 1998), 15.

Asian American community: Governmental Affairs Committee investigation, deposition of Howard Hom (August 27, 1997), 15–18.

National Rifle Association (NRA): Ibid., 24.

Lippo empire: James Sterngold, "Political Tangle of Taiwan Immigrant," *New York Times*, June 9, 1997.

315 foreign travel: Senators Howell Heflin and Warren B. Rudman to Senator Al Gore Jr., February 10, 1989.

130 temples: Kevin Sullivan, "Monk at Issue Is an Icon in Taiwan," *Washington Post*, October 25, 1996.

and museum: John Aloysius Farrell, "Gore Avoided Money Pitch in Disputed Temple Visit," *Boston Globe*, September 4, 1997.

world leaders: John Mintz, "Fund-raisers Pressured Temple After Gore Visit; 12 Donors Were Reimbursed," *Washington Post*, June 13, 1997. Hsing Yun later told Senate investigators that he had no interest in American politics. See William C. Rempel, "Temple Leader Denies Political Purpose to Donations," *Washington Post*, August 17, 1997.

"'become president'": Quoted from *Universal Gates Monthly* (May 1996), translated from Chinese by Becky Chan for the Governmental Affairs Committee.

316 Senate reelection: William C. Rempel, Alan C. Miller, and Henry Weinstein, "Buddhist Temple Repaid Some DNC Donations," *Los Angeles Times*, May 23, 1997.

Democratic Senatorial Campaign Committee: Governmental Affairs Committee investigation, final report, 20.

his organization: Ibid., final report, 17; and Hom deposition, 78–81.

consulting business: Ibid., 26.

317 chairman for finance: William C. Rempel and Alan C. Miller, "Temple's Political Giving Hidden in '93, Records Say," *Los Angeles Times*, October 12, 1997.

by the temple: Ibid.

"moving support": David Strauss, testimony before the Governmental Affairs Committee, September 5, 1997.

would be discussed: Governmental Affairs Committee investigation, final report, 46.

318 "sandbagged": Christopher Drew and Don Van Atta Jr., "Early Warnings on Gore's Temple Visit," *New York Times*, June 12, 1997. See also Rempel, Miller, and Weinstein, "Buddhist Temple Repaid Some DNC Donations." Senate investigators, however, dispute the suggestion that there was a last-minute switch and say that the restaurant's management declared in a sworn statement that no one contacted them about holding a fund-raising lunch there on April 29, 1996. Governmental Affairs Committee investigation, final report, 76.

to the temple: *Los Angeles Times*, May 23, 1997.

"great caution": Robert Suettinger to John Norris, April 19, 1996, reprinted in Governmental Affairs Committee investigation, final report, 75.

319 "solely responsible": David Strauss, testimony before the Governmental Affairs Committee, September 5, 1997.

closed to the press: *Boston Globe*, September 4, 1997. The *Globe* reporter John Aloysius Farrell attended the temple event on an off-the-record basis but was released from the agreement by Gore's staff.

per couple: Ibid.

dining hall: Governmental Affairs Committee investigation, final report, 53.

donor cards: *Los Angeles Times,* November 2, 1996.

another $55,000: Governmental Affairs Committee investigation, final report, 56.

320 to the DNC: Charles Babington, "Gore Turns Deaf Ear to Fund-raiser Queries," *Washington Post,* November 1, 1996.

"money-changers present": Mary McGrory, "Off the Straight and Narrow," *Washington Post,* October 29, 1996.

television screens: Elizabeth Drew, *Whatever It Takes: The Real Struggle for Political Power in America* (New York: Viking, 1997), 197–98.

and Memphis: Charles Babington, "Gore Woos Home-State Voters, Many of Whom Waltzed off in '94," *Washington Post,* November 5, 1996.

321 "not November 5": Drew, *Whatever It Takes,* 239.

more tentative: See Joe Klein, "The End of a Conversation," *New Yorker,* May 12, 1997.

322 "stuff with me": Lorraine Voles, telephone interview with author, August 11, 1999.

himself personally: *Washington Post,* March 2, 1997.

323 replace Kumiki Gibson: Gibson, now in private practice in Washington, did not respond to an interview request. In 1999, Gore named Burson his new chief of staff.

"getting late": Lorraine Voles, interview with author, Washington, D.C., September 2, 1998.

324 "right thing to do": Alexis Simendinger, "Gore's Team Gears Up," *National Journal,* May 31, 1997, 1094.

325 "condescension": Maureen Dowd, *New York Times,* March 5, 1997.

few months: John F. Harris, "Gore: Fund-raising Calls Broke No Law; Further Solicitations from Office Are Ruled Out," *Washington Post,* March 4, 1997.

May 2, 1996: James W. Brosnan, "Gore's White House Calls Raised at Least $625,000 for Democrats," *Memphis Commercial Appeal,* August 27, 1997.

take a punch: Howard Kurtz, *Spin Cycle: Inside the Clinton Propaganda Machine* (New York: Free Press, 1998), 261.

late January: Richard L. Berke, "Gore's Stumble Entices Rivals for 2000 Race," *New York Times,* March 11, 1997. The poll was taken by CBS News.

326 into the world: "The Great Green Hope," *Sierra* (July-August 1997).

glass down: John F. Harris, "Funds Probe Won't Mar U.S.-China Ties, Gore Says," *Washington Post,* March 26, 1997.

327 "through the door": Bob Squier, 1998 interview.

"scabrous underside": "Notebook," *The New Republic,* March 24, 1997, 10.

"Gore is not Clinton": Martin Peretz, "Cambridge Diarist: Easy Call," *The New Republic,* March 31, 1997, 42.

"these guys?": Michael Kelly, "TRB from Washington," *The New Republic,* April 14, 1997, 6.

Microsoft Corporation: Burt Solomon and W. John Moore, "Hometown Boy," *National Journal,* June 26, 1999, 1872.

328 "Baby Bells": Ibid. Also see Susan B. Glasser and John Mintz, "The Insiders Behind Gore," *Washington Post,* June 14, 1999.

environmental technology: Bob Woodward, "Lobbyist's Lucrative Ties to Gore," *Washington Post,* October 17, 1997.

in 1995: Michael Weisskopf and Viveca Novak, "Al's Cash Machine," *Time,* September 22, 1997, 36.

329 Democratic National Committee: Ken Silverstein and Jeffery St. Clair, "The Giant Sucking Sound," *In These Times,* April 28, 1997.

the company: *Time,* September 22, 1997. Also see Edward Walsh, "Lobbying Role of Ex-Gore Aide Examined," *Washington Post,* November 6, 1997.

"great friend": Letter first obtained by Michael Weisskopf of *Time* for October 16, 1997, story on *CNN/Time All Politics* Web site.

meetings at DOE: *Knoxville News-Sentinel,* November 16, 1997.

"charitable contributions": Statement of Peter S. Knight, House Committee on Commerce, Subcommittee on Oversight and Investigations, November 5, 1997.

330 of favoritism: Bill Sammon, "Ex-Official Calls Meeting Donors a 'Mistake,'" *Washington Times,* November 6, 1997.

"bedrock portfolio": Jill Lawrence, "Gore Is Going Back to the Basics," *USA Today,* June 2, 1997.

1996 election: Lorraine Voles, 1998 interview.

scrutiny of the vice president: Daniel Klaidman and Karen Breslau, "The Trouble with Al," *Newsweek,* September 22, 1997, 39.

331 in the spring: Ibid.

legal bills: James W. Brosnan, "Gore Takes Out $100,000 Loan to Pay His Legal Expenses," *Washington Times,* May 13, 1998.

hard money accounts: Governmental Affairs Committee investigation, final report, 12.

remember February: Lorraine Voles, 1998 interview.

332 commanded his attention: Ibid., 13.

at meetings: Ibid., 23.

333 by 2060: Sharon Begley, "How to Beat the Heat, *Newsweek,* December 8, 1997, 34.

the 1990s: Michael D. Lemonick, "Courting Disaster," *Time,* November 3, 1997, 65.

1990 levels: Margaret Kriz, "After Argentina," *National Journal,* December 5, 1998, 2848.

334 air quality debate: "Environmental Groups Say Gore Has Not Measured Up to the Job," *New York Times,* June 22, 1997.

new regulations: James Gerstenzang and Marla Cone, "Clinton Gives OK to Tougher Rules to Clean Up the Air," *Los Angeles Times,* June 26, 1997.

hurt it: In an August 1998 meeting with environmentalists, as reported by *Time's* Jay Branegan April 26, 1999, Gore said: "Losing on impractical proposals that are completely out of tune with what is achievable does not necessarily advance your cause at all, and in fact could set it back by convincing politicians that the issue is too risky to revisit."

335 greenhouse pollution: President Clinton, address to National Geographic Society, Washington, D.C., October 22, 1997.

domestic economy: Senate Resolution 98, passed July 25, 1997.

December 6: Richard L. Berke, "Gore Walks a Political Tightrope at Environmental Talks in Kyoto," *New York Times,* December 9, 1997.

336 "negotiating flexibility": Vice President Gore, remarks at the United Nations Committee on Climate Change, Conference of Parties, Kyoto, Japan, December 8, 1997.

"intelligent agreement": Greg Wetstone, interview with author, Washington, D.C., December 17, 1998.

21. *"One of Our Greatest Presidents"*

337 United States: Woodward, *The Choice,* 419.

338 the Hill: Thomas Edsall and Helen Dewar, "Gore Leads Effort to Build Support for the President," *Washington Post,* January 27, 1998.

Washington columnists: David M. Shribman, "Gore Defends His President, Emphatically: 'I Believe Him,'" *Boston Globe,* January 23, 1998.

339 "total bullshit": Roy Neel, 1998 interview.

embattled president: Richard L. Berke, "The Gore Guide to the Future," *New York Times Magazine,* February 22, 1998, 30.

to the podium: Roger Simon, "U. of I. Provides Clinton with Temporary Respite," *Chicago Tribune,* January 29, 1999.

Champaign-Urbana: Berke, "The Gore Guide to the Future."

340 "through this anymore": Ibid.

would continue: Susan Page, "Loyal Gore Steadfast in His Support," *USA Today,* January 26, 1998.

liability claims: *USA Today,* June 18, 1998.

from lawsuits: Jeffrey Taylor, "Gore Supports Democrats' Tough Antismoking Bill," *Wall Street Journal,* February 12, 1998.

child care: Wendy Koch and Bill Nichols, "Legislation's Defeat Has Effects Beyond Tobacco," *USA Today,* June 18, 1998.

341 natural gas: Joby Warrick, "White House Predicts Low Cost for Pact on Warming," *Washington Post,* March 4, 1998.

Kyoto agreement: John Fialka, "Global Warming Debate Gets No Consensus in Industry," *Wall Street Journal,* April 16, 1998.

"voice of God": Lee Walczak and Richard S. Dunham, "'President Gore' Doesn't Sound So Bad to Business," *Business Week,* February 9, 1998.

"economic cooling": John Harris, "Gore Seeks to Reassure Business He's No Enemy," *Washington Post,* May 9, 1998.

343 "Gore tax": John Schwartz, "FCC to Expand 'E-Rate' Funding," *Washington Post,* May 26, 1999. See also Karen Tumulty and John F. Dickerson, "Gore's Costly High-Wire Act," *Time,* May 25, 1998, 52.

two hours: John Simons, "How a Vice President Fills a Cyber-Cabinet: With Gore-Techs," *Wall Street Journal,* March 13, 1998. See also Elizabeth Shogren, "Silicon Valley Group Provides Brain Trust for Vice President," *Los Angeles Times,* August 25, 1997.

do so as well: *Time,* May 25, 1998.

veep arrived: *Washington Post,* November 29, 1997.

344 $197,729: Associated Press, April 14, 1998.

following week: Susan Page, "Clinton Soothes Alabama's Pain," *USA Today,* April 16, 1998.

345 "Third World countries": Blaine Harden, "Yadda Yucks for Gore," *Washington Post,* May 15, 1998.

public style: David S. Broder, "The Gore that Meets the Eye," *Washington Post,* February 4, 1998.

346 "very shaken": Michael Kapetan, 1998 interview.

in California: *Los Angeles Times,* July 7, 1995.

sexual relationship: Richard L. Berke, Neil A. Lewis, James Bennet, and David E. Sanger, "Clinton Weighs Admitting He Had Sexual Contacts," *New York Times,* August 14, 1998.

"a tomb": Reed Hundt, 1999 interview.

347 storm would pass: Susan Page, "Gore Will Support President 'Through Thick and Thin,'" *USA Today,* August 19, 1998.

348 "No comment": B. Drummond Ayres Jr., "Gore an Ocean Away from the Hearing in Washington," *New York Times,* August 18, 1998.

"people's business": *USA Today,* August 19, 1998.

phone calls: Phil Kuntz, "Agency Reopens Probe into Gore Fund-raising," *Wall Street Journal,* August 18, 1998.

"'the calls'": Michael Grunwald, "Fund-raising Memo Leads to New Probe of Gore Role," *Washington Post,* August 21, 1998.

349 about Clinton: The poll was conducted August 21–23 for both CNN and *USA Today.*

no choice: Thomas M. De Frank, "The Veep Remains True Blue to Boss," *New York Daily News,* September 11, 1998.

"indefensible": *Washington Post,* September 18, 1998.

350 "control over": Woodward, *Shadow,* 456.

351 "feel it": Ceci Connolly, "Gore Tests Wings Above Scandal's Turbulent Air," *Washington Post,* October 14, 1998.

352 "are not": Vice President Al Gore, remarks at Service of Celebration and Thanksgiving for the Life of Senator Albert Gore Sr., Nashville, December 8, 1998.

355 "that conclusion": Michael Janofsky, "A Spirited Defense of Clinton Thrusts Gore into the Spotlight," *New York Times,* December 18, 1998.

wasn't fair: See Elizabeth Shogren and James Gerstenzang, "After a Disastrous Day, Clinton Expresses Resolve," *Los Angeles Times,* December 20, 1998.

356 jaw clenched: Caryn James, "One Screen Could Not Capture It All," *New York Times,* December 29, 1998.

"greatest presidents": Federal News Service, remarks after meeting with congressional Democrats, South Lawn of the White House, December 19, 1998.

Epilogue: Separation Anxiety

357 same light: David S. Broder and Richard Morin, "For Gore, Support Is Conditional," *Washington Post,* March 16, 1999.

358 time and energy: Knight and Neel both indicated that they would take leaves from their positions and go to work full time for the campaign in early 2000.

"Not much direction": Roy Neel, telephone interview with author, September 23, 1999.

ever brought: Richard L. Berke, "Gore Adds Former Whip To Campaign," *New York Times,* May 11, 1999. See also Marianne Lavelle and Kenneth T. Walsh, "Al Gore's Risky Asset," *U.S. News & World Report,* December 13, 1999, 31.

359 Gore campaign: Melinda Henneberger, "At the Helm of Gore's Campaign, 2 Old Friends Who Don't Speak," *New York Times,* July 9, 1999.

previous February: Pew Research Center, September 1999 report.

for Bush: *Washington Post,* March 16, 1999.

"primal bitterness": Michael Duffy and Karen Tumulty, "Gore's Secret Guru," *Time,* November 8, 1999, 34.

360 "our children": Announcement speech, Carthage, Tennessee, June 16, 1999.

"and daughters": Paul Gigot, "Gore's Theme: Boredom Is an Aphrodisiac," *Wall Street Journal,* June 18, 1999.

361 "same day": John M. Broder and Don Van Atta, "Aides Say Clinton Is Angered as Gore Tries to Break Away," *New York Times,* June 26, 1999.

in 1976: Ceci Connolly, "Gore May Forgo Help From Clinton," *Washington Post,* October 16, 1999.

362 $6 million: Jeanne Cummings, "Mission Control: Gore, the Executive, Shakes Up Marketing of Gore, the Candidate," *Wall Street Journal,* November 12, 1999.

363 "Southwest Airlines": Roger Simon, "Gore Heads for the Hills," *U.S. News & World Report,* October 11, 1999, 22.

364 "be president": Bill Turque, "Reinventing Gore," *Newsweek,* October 4, 1999, 44.

"negative campaigning": Bill Bradley, Democratic National Committee, fall session, Washington, D.C., September 25, 1999.

"these issues": Al Gore, ibid.

"and fighting": Ibid.

365 they agreed: *Wall Street Journal,* November 12, 1999.

"fighting for": Al Gore, press conference at Washington, D.C., campaign headquarters, September 29, 1999.

Clinton fatigue: John F. Harris and Dan Balz, "Gore Campaign Drops Pollster Penn," *Washington Post,* October 2, 1999.

366 "Nixon years": Bill Bradley, Jefferson-Jackson Day Dinner, Des Moines, Iowa, October 9, 1999.

"like that": Bradley, Ibid.

367 "about this": Al Gore, Ibid.

"possibly could": Susan Page and Jill Lawrence, "Bradley, Gore Spar Gently," *USA Today,* October 28, 1999.

368 Energizer Bunny: Eric Boehlert, "Gore's Premature Obituary," *Salon,* November 12, 1999.

campaign message surfaced: Richard L. Berke, "To Polish His Image, Bradley Has Worked with Madison Avenue for 16 months," *New York Times,* November 9, 1999.

369 "possibly be": Michael Kranish, "Gore Hits Road with New Look, Message," *Boston Globe,* November 28, 1999.

369 wardrobe: *Time*, November 8, 1999, 34.

of women: Melinda Henneberger, "Naomi Wolf, Feminist Consultant to Gore, Clarifies Her Campaign Role," *New York Times*, November 5, 1999.

370 "Love Canal": Ceci Connolly, "Gore Paints Himself as No Beltway Baby," *Washington Post*, December 1, 1999.

"misimpression": Hadley Pawlak, "Gore Explains Latest Exaggeration," *Associated Press*, December 1, 1999.

Acknowledgments

375 agreed to interviews: Gore's aides told me that he decided to withhold cooperation because he was angry that I had interviewed his parents, former Senator Albert Gore and his wife, Pauline, without his permission. Whether this is true or not is difficult to say. My letters to the vice president, both before and after visiting with the Gores, went unanswered.

Selected Bibliography

Baskir, Lawrence M., and William A. Strauss. *Chance and Circumstance: The Draft, the War, and the Vietnam Generation*. New York: Knopf, 1978.

Blumay, Carl, with Henry Edwards. *The Dark Side of Power: The Real Armand Hammer*. New York: Simon and Schuster, 1992.

Bly, Robert. *Iron John: A Book About Men*. New York: Random House, 1990.

Boggs, Lindy. *Washington Through a Purple Veil*. New York: Harcourt Brace, 1994.

Brinkley, Douglas. *The Unfinished Presidency: Jimmy Carter's Journey Beyond the White House*. New York: Viking, 1998.

Cramer, Richard Ben. *What It Takes: The Way to the White House*. New York: Random House, 1992.

Davis, John Claiborne. *The Ordered Web: Essays in Resurrection*. Washington, D.C., 1986.

Davis, Lanny. *Truth to Tell: Notes from My White House Education*. New York: Free Press, 1999.

Drew, Elizabeth. *The Corruption of American Politics: What Went Wrong and Why*. Secaucus, N.J.: Birch Lane, 1999.

———. *Showdown: The Struggle Between the Gingrich Congress and the Clinton White House*. New York: Simon and Schuster, 1996.

———. *Whatever It Takes: The Real Struggle for Political Power in America*. New York: Viking, 1997.

Epstein, Edward Jay. *Dossier: The Secret History of Armand Hammer*. New York: Random House, 1993.

Flynn, George Q. *Lewis B. Hershey: Mr. Selective Service*. Chapel Hill: University of North Carolina Press, 1985.

Fontenay, Charles. *Estes Kefauver: A Biography*. Knoxville: University of Tennessee Press, 1980.

Gitlin, Todd. *The Sixties: Years of Hope*. New York: Bantam, 1987.

Goldman, Peter, Tom Matthews, and the Newsweek Special Election Team. *The Quest for the Presidency 1988*. New York: Simon and Schuster/Touchstone, 1989.

Goldman, Peter, Thomas M. DeFrank, Mark Miller, Andrew Murr, and Tom Matthews. *The Quest for the Presidency 1992*. College Station: Texas A & M University Press, 1994.

Gore, Al. *Earth in the Balance: Ecology and the Human Spirit*. Boston: Houghton Mifflin, 1992.

Gore, Albert. *Eye of the Storm: A People's Politics for the Seventies.* New York: Herder and Herder, 1972.

——. *Let the Glory Out: My South and Its Politics.* New York: Viking, 1972.

Gore, Tipper. *Picture This: A Visual Diary.* New York: Broadway Books, 1998.

——. *Raising PG Kids in an X-Rated Society.* Nashville, Tenn.: Abingdon, 1987.

Graham, Katharine. *Personal History.* New York: Knopf, 1997.

Grimes, Ann. *Running Mates: The Making of a First Lady.* New York: Morrow, 1990.

Hillin, Hank. *Al Gore Jr.: His Life and Career.* New York: Birch Lane, 1992.

Karnow, Stanley. *Vietnam: A History.* New York: Viking, 1983.

Kelman, Steven. *Push Comes to Shove: The Escalation of Student Protest.* Boston: Houghton Mifflin, 1970.

Key, V. O., Jr. *Southern Politics in State and Nation.* New York: Knopf, 1949.

Kluger, Richard. *Ashes to Ashes: America's Hundred-Year Cigarette War.* New York: Knopf, 1996.

Kurtz, Howard. *Spin Cycle: Inside the Clinton Propaganda Machine.* New York: Free Press, 1998.

Lewis, John, with Michael D'Orso. *Walking with the Wind: A Memoir of the Movement.* New York: Simon and Schuster, 1998.

MacPherson, Myra. *Long Time Passing: Vietnam and the Haunted Generation.* Garden City, N.Y.: Doubleday, 1984.

Maraniss, David. *First in His Class.* New York: Simon and Schuster, 1995.

Miller, Alice. *The Drama of the Gifted Child: The Search for the True Self.* Rev. ed. New York: HarperCollins, 1994.

Morgan, Judith, and Neil Morgan. *Roger: A Biography of Roger Revelle.* La Jolla, Calif.: Scripps Institution of Oceanography, 1996.

Morris, Dick. *Behind the Oval Office: Winning the Presidency in the Nineties.* New York: Random House, 1997.

Pertschuk, Michael. *Giant Killers.* New York: Norton, 1986.

Redmon, Coates. *Come as You Are: The Peace Corps Story.* New York: Harcourt Brace Jovanovich, 1986.

Reeves, Richard. *President Kennedy: Profile of Power.* New York: Touchstone, 1994.

Rosenblatt, Roger. *Coming Apart: A Memoir of the Harvard Wars of 1969.* New York: Little, Brown, 1997.

Sheehy, Gail. *Character: America's Search for Leadership.* New York: Morrow, 1988.

Simon, Roger. *Road Show: In America Anyone Can Become President. It's One of the Risks We Take.* New York: Farrar, Straus, and Giroux, 1990.

——. *Show Time: The American Political Circus and the Race for the White House.* New York: Times Books, 1998.

Squires, James D. *The Secrets of the Hopewell Box: Stolen Elections, Southern Politics, and a City's Coming of Age.* New York: Times Books, 1996.

Stephanopoulos, George. *All Too Human: A Political Education.* New York: Little, Brown, 1999.

Thomas, Evan, Karen Breslau, Debra Rosenberg, Leslie Kaufman, and Andrew Murr. *Back from the Dead: How Clinton Survived the Republican Revolution.* New York: Atlantic Monthly, 1997.

Vidal, Gore. *Palimpsest.* New York: Penguin, 1996.

Weinberg, Steve. *Armand Hammer: The Untold Story.* Boston: Little, Brown.

Wheelis, Allen. *How People Change.* New York: Harper & Row, 1973.

Winograd, Morley, and Dudley Buffa. *Taking Control: Politics in the Information Age.* New York: Holt, 1996.

Woodward, Bob. *The Agenda: Inside the Clinton White House.* New York: Simon and Schuster, 1993.

——. *The Choice.* New York: Simon and Schuster, 1996.

——. *Shadow: Five Presidents and the Legacy of Watergate.* New York: Simon and Schuster, 1999.

Index